CW00925857

THE ASTROLOGICAL
HISTORY
OF THE WORLD

THE ASTROLOGICAL
HISTORY
OF THE WORLD

MARJORIE ORR

vega

Acknowledgement

Many thanks to the redoubtable Lois Rodden for her meticulous birth data sourcing, in her books and on www.astrodatabank.com. For countries charts, Nick Campion's *The Book of World Horoscopes* (Cinnabar Books) was an invaluable resource. Neil F. Michelsen's *Table of Planetary Phenomena* (ACS Publications) was also of immense help in tracking major conjunctions back to the year zero. And Janus software (www.astrologyware.com), whose ephemeris provided start and finish dates.

Any mistakes are my responsibility. I would be grateful for any errata. Contact me via email through: www.astroinformation.com

© Vega 2002
Text © Marjorie Orr 2002

All rights reserved. No part of this book may be reproduced, stored in a retrieval system or transmitted in any form or by any means, electronic, mechanical, photocopying, recording or otherwise, without the prior permission in writing of the copyright owners.

ISBN 1-84333-015-6

A catalogue record for this book is available
from the British Library.

First published in 2002 by
Vega
64 Brewery Road
London
N7 9NT

A member of **Chrysalis** Books plc

Visit our website at www.chrysalisbooks.co.uk

Printed and bound in Great Britain by
Butler & Tanner Ltd. Frome and London

CONTENTS

INTRODUCTION

Astrology provides a language, a language that gives expression to the influences affecting different moments in time. In these moments are born:

- **People**, stamped with the spirit of the time. World personalities—leaders, emperors, kings, queens, dictators, politicians, artists, religious figures—and ordinary people carry the theme of the astrological influences that exist around the time of their birth. This determines their temperaments and the broad patterns of their life.

- **Historical events**. Great works of art, wars, natural disasters, revolutions, discoveries, inventions, peace treaties, alliances, federations all occur within a time frame, which also carries an astrological marker. When the same star conjunctions and patterns recur—often hundreds of years apart—similar kinds of events again take place. It is almost as if there are cosmic rays which stimulate revolutionary rage or, more beneficently, an artistic renaissance or a religious revival.

- **Countries**. These are also born in specific moments, and the identity of the nation, its racial characteristics, the talents of its people, and the pattern of future events are reflected in the astrology of the moment. Major events in a country's history can be plotted through the ongoing 'transits'—planetary movements—affecting the birth chart.

The movements and aspects of the outer planets from Jupiter onwards in their endless cycling around one another are connected to major world events, defining generations and offering a new perspective on history. Astrology tracks the ongoing movements and effects of these wide-sweeping influences, the constant churning of human life, the rise and fall of dynasties, empires and cultures, and the destruction and creation of countries.

Astrology also freeze-frames moments in time, building a chart for an exact minute in an exact place which pinpoints the planetary positions and their relationship to the horizon with mathematical precision. The astrological chart of that highly specific moment and the event's position on the surface of the Earth tell you exactly where the Sun, Moon and the eight planets of the solar system (excluding Earth)—Mercury, Venus, Mars, Jupiter, Saturn, Uranus, Neptune and

Pluto—were in relation to each other and to that geographical location at that precise moment. No one knows why this should be significant but it is, and an awareness of this significance has existed for many centuries. The interpretations of astrology and star positions have been handed down to us over the past 5000 years, and we still use a good deal of what was working astrology in Greek times.

The underpinnings of astrology are still an ongoing puzzle. The 'why', however, does not interfere remotely with the 'how'. We used the compass for 300 years before anyone came to understand why it worked. Modern mainstream science in its arrogance assumes that what cannot be explained does not exist. This book says: look at the evidence.

Astrology is hugely complex, working with an almost infinite number of variable cycles which are constantly shifting in relation to one another. We cannot yet grasp the full extent of its capacity to inform us about an even more complex world of outer events and human behaviour. It almost certainly would not give us the whole answer, even if we understood it better. But it is a partially opened door which does allow us to peer through a crack into an underlying reality, so vast, so awesome, so multifaceted and multidimensional that is is likely to remain for ever unknowable.

A working astrologer for 20 years, resolutely uninterested in *why* astrology worked, and focused totally on where and when it could be of most benefit, even I have been riveted in researching and writing this book. All astrologers, surviving in a world that treats them with fairly unconcealed contempt, struggle with doubt and uncertainty about their craft. My faith has been more strongly confirmed than even I expected. I *know* astrology works—in its own slightly peculiar fashion, admittedly, astonishingly accurate at times and maddeningly vague at others—but I share most rational people's anxiety about something that falls within no accepted framework of explanation. Astrology doesn't make sense. It shouldn't work—and yet it does.

I was utterly thrilled to find that Giotto painted the Padua frescoes in 1305 on a Uranus (enlightening) and Neptune (spiritual/artistic) conjunction. These two planets come together only rarely. Blissfully, next time around in 1482, they witnessed Botticelli and Perugino painting the frescoes in the Sistine Chapel. Michelangelo, who later went on to paint the Sistine Chapel ceiling, was born at the start of that particular conjunction. Skip ahead two conjunctions to 1820 and William Blake was illustrating *The Book of Job*; back to the conjunction of 799 and *The Book of Kells*, the great first illustrated book of the Gospels, was being produced.

Uranus (scientific) and Neptune (visionary) can also produce breakthroughs in the field of knowledge. The French mathematician Pierre de Fermat formulated his Theory of Probability in 1654 during a Uranus–Neptune conjunction. Fermat's Theorem, the last great mathematical puzzle, was solved during the recent conjunction of these two planets in 1993. Wat Tyler's Peasants' Revolt in England in 1381 happened when Saturn came together with Neptune, stimulating hope for a better society. Subsequent conjunctions of these two planets saw Friedrich Engels publish his book *The Condition of the Working Classes in England* in 1845, then saw the Russian Revolution in 1917, the Tiananmen Square Students' Revolt in 1989 and the British Poll Tax Riots in 1990.

Even I shivered at the eerie synchronicity of a specific eclipse cycle, repeating approximately every 18.5 years, which fell one day after the death of Diana, Princess of Wales, in September 1997. Its previous occurrence in 1979 was within days of Earl Mountbatten being killed in a bomb explosion. Running back through the same cycle to 1961, it covered the period of Diana's birth and the death of Dag Hammarskjöld, UN Secretary-General. Further back still the same eclipse cycle marked the assassination of the King and Crown Prince of Portugal in 1907.

I had not expected to find the complex link between Jupiter–Saturn conjunctions (usually thought expansive, optimistic, and the trigger for a new era) and death. John Lennon was born under one in 1940, made his debut on the next in 1960, and was assassinated on the next in 1980. J. F. Kennedy came to heady power on one such conjunction, and Princess Diana sailed into her fairy-tale marriage on another. Like Icarus of Greek myth, whose wax wings melted when he dared to fly too near the Sun, all these bright beginnings came to sad ends, illustrating how Jupiter's high hopes were brought low by depressive Saturn's bleak realism. Even the bright star under which Jesus Christ was born is thought to have been a Jupiter–Saturn conjunction.

The exciting new field of astrocartography, developed single-handed by the late Jim Lewis, has opened a whole new vista of possibilities. Plotting the individual birth chart, or even the country or organization's, onto the world map throws up startling nuggets of information. Margaret Thatcher has one of her four Mars (aggression) lines straight through the Falklands. George W. Bush has one of his Mars lines through Afghanistan. J. F. Kennedy was killed on his Pluto (power and destruction) midheaven line through Dallas. Jackie Onassis, who married Greek shipping magnate Aristotle Onassis, has one of her four Venus (love or indulgence) lines through Greece. Princess Diana, who was said to be about to marry Dodi al-Fayed before her life was tragically cut short, had one of her Venus lines through Egypt.

These are astonishing examples, but one should not expect astrology to have all the answers. There is no all-encompassing system that can grasp the mysteries of the universe. We need to accept astrology for what it is—an utterly fascinating peek through a crack into a world we do not understand, the world we live in.

HOW ASTROLOGY WORKS | 1

For more than 5000 years, going back to the Sumerians of Mesopotamia who brought literacy to mankind, the stars are known to have been studied as divine oracles. As language and consciousness developed, astrology on a parallel track became more codified.

The old mythological names remain, creating an aura of mysticism and magic, but the underlying reality of astrology is mathematical. Astronomically aligned standing stones, painstakingly constructed to point to eclipses on an obscure 18.5-year cycle, are a monument to early man's extraordinary ability to calculate. At every stage in astrology's development—Pythagorean Greece, the Arab civilization that followed, the Mayans, even up to the 16th-century Scottish logarithm inventor John Napier, an alchemist, astrologer and scientist—it was mathematicians who were the driving force.

Modern astrology uses horoscopes as devised by the Greeks, who were the first to use a circular birth chart, taking the pattern of planets in the solar system at the moment of birth, setting them down on paper within the map-grid reference of the zodiacal belt, named after 12 of the 88 constellations. They added another artificial element by dividing the 360-degree birth chart circle into 12 houses, starting with the sign on the horizon at the moment of birth (the 'ascendant', see page 15). Thus in a birth chart there are almost 2500 different variables from which interpretations may be drawn: the planets, the signs and the 12 houses.

For reasons that are not remotely clear, the positions of the planets at the moment of birth provide a great deal of highly detailed information about temperament, talents and family background. The interpretations we use today are essentially as they were 2500 years ago, amplified by the insights of the great astrologers since then, and with deeper psychological insights acquired in the 20th century. Astrological understanding and accuracy were given even wider significance with the relatively recent discovery of the outer planets, Uranus (1781), Neptune (1846) and Pluto (1930).

The sign in which the Sun sits at the moment of birth (the birth sign) is seen astrologically as describing key elements of character, the core of an individual's identity, so even the mere fact of a birth sign—Aries, Taurus and so on—gives a wealth of detail about characteristics and behaviour. Even sceptics admit to being surprised at the clusters of certain similar signs working together in one office or profession. Fashion designers are often Cancerians; explorers, scientists, and music and movie adepts are often Pisces; pop singers Gemini; journalists Virgo or

9

Gemini; bestselling novelists Aries or Virgo; singers and naturalists Taurus; sex experts and computer buffs Aquarius; army officers tend to be Leo or Scorpio. There is scientific evidence, too, that the time of year an individual was born does make a difference. Geniuses and the psychologically unbalanced are more likely to be born in February; criminals in the winter; high-fliers in the spring.

Most observations are based on the simplified 12-sign astrology that media columns use, predicting general trends from the constant cycling of the planets in relation to that particular sign. In-depth astrology, though, uses the time, date and place of birth to calculate the view a baby would get (if it could see) of the solar system planets including what was on the horizon at the exact moment it was born. The accurate time is crucial, but the latitude and longitude of birth also fix the horizon line. Babies born at exactly the same moment but in different global locations will see a different view of the universe.

People often ask what difference a premature or induced birth will have on the birth chart. Intriguingly, respected French statistician Michel Gauquelin found that non-induced babies had similar charts to their parents, with the same positions for certain planets: perhaps this is nature's mysterious way of creating closer bonds—it is almost as if the baby chooses to be born at a particular time. Where there is a caesarean birth, Pluto is often on the horizon, describing an adult personality that is overly defensive, as if the birth and every subsequent first meeting is threatening. Recent research on the adverse effects of invasive births back up astrology's findings: drug-induced births often occur with dreamy, spaced-out Neptune on the ascendant. Pregnancy trauma can also show in the chart.

There is something entirely mysterious about the birth chart. It tells of family background that was in place before the baby was conceived, even back to grandparents. The chart does not reflect just a date-stamped personality, entirely the product of the moment of birth. It reflects a highly complex mix of factors, all of which contribute facets to personality and pattern of the future life. For instance, an Aries will react differently than a Scorpio to the same family dynamic. A mid-sixties child be will explosively different in temperament to a late-fifties child. The chart gives layer upon layer of dimension. Some features are utterly specific to the kind of birth, the parents' make-up at that time, the 'random' chance of being born mid-afternoon with a ninth-house Sun (indicating a person who travels, philosophizes, writes) or born earlier with a fifth-house Sun (indicating a dramatic, fun-loving person); these features ripple out to the wider effects of the broad influences of the time and culture, all interconnecting in the mystery of the individual human being.

In all of this there is one difficulty, however: that of freewill. To be passively fatalistic is clearly not helpful; yet to argue that we all have totally free choices is arrogant and delusional. We are bound by our temperament—reflected in our Sun sign and elsewhere—with its strengths and limitations, by our family patterns (Sun and Moon aspects) and by our era-specific patterns (outer planets). Within those parameters, some—though not all—do have a limited degree of choice. In the words of psychoanalyst Carl Jung, 'Freewill is the ability to choose that which of necessity we must do.' Deeper self-understanding, which astrology and other therapeutic disciplines can give, broadens the range of our freewill. Again, Jung says that what we are unconscious of meets us from outside as if it were fate. For the lucky, there is a balance between fate and freewill, but no one is born, or lives, in complete control of their destiny.

Astrology will not predict death, though it can warn of danger. Fascinatingly, and quite unfathomably, charts appear to carry on after death. When Sigmund Freud's reputation took a severe dent in the early 1980s, his birth chart registered the stress, even though he had been dead for 40 years. When the play and film *Amadeus* appeared, Mozart's birth chart reflected career success as if he was still alive.

Prediction is even harder to explain. Why should plotting present planetary positions in relation to a birth chart, which records a moment in time long past, mean anything at all? Yet it does. Bill Clinton's jolting, jarring career crisis and loss of control occurred as the Uranus–Neptune conjunction in Aquarius from 1996 onwards opposed his natal grouping of Saturn, Sun and Pluto in Leo. Saturn's movements clearly marked Mrs Thatcher's rise to power, crossing above her descendant as she first became a cabinet minister, and reaching the peak of her chart at the midheaven when she was elected prime minister.

Ultimately, I am reduced to saying that one part of the explanation for astrology must be geophysical or astrophysical. We know that the Moon's resonance shifts vast quantities of water twice daily in tidal flows; that the full Moon makes people more disturbed and makes them bleed more in operations. Likewise, eclipses have a proven effect on the flow of mistletoe sap and on the behaviour of monkeys. Chemical reactions, too, can vary according to cosmic influences, including sun spots.

But if these influences have a specific effect on an individual depending on the time, date and place of their birth years before, then the search for an explanation—way beyond our present understanding—has to point to a universe that, as Einstein believed, is essentially mathematical in nature: 'All things are numbers,' he said. David Bohm, the London physicist, concluded more explicitly, 'Our brains mathematically construct objective reality by interpreting frequencies that are ultimately projects from another dimension, a deeper order of existence that is beyond space and time.'

The mythological and supernatural gloss of astrological language may seem more exciting than anything as prosaic as numbers, but mystical mathematics may yet prove to be the ultimate answer—as John Addey put it, 'All organic life dances to the tune of certain frequencies.'

POWER PATRONS

Political astrology has a long and illustrious history. Its 'power patrons' include Tiberius, the Roman emperor, who used to throw astrologers who displeased him onto the rocks from his clifftop palace in Capri. The enlightened administrator Emperor Hadrian (see *Saturn–Uranus*, page 42 and *Neptune–Pluto*, page 25), the builder of the great wall in northern Britain that bears his name, as well as Emperor Titian, who destroyed the Temple at Jerusalem (see *Uranus–Pluto*, page 32) and his brother Domitian, were all accomplished astrologers. Charlemagne (see *Uranus–Neptune*, page 28), the vastly powerful ninth-century ruler and early Renaissance man, who promoted architecture, education and the arts and was versed in the culture and knowledge of the Middle East, had as his astrologer Alcuin of York, who had studied initially at the monastery in Iona in Scotland.

Astrology was taught in the ecclesiastical colleges right up to the 14th century. Most kings, popes and Holy Roman Emperors had their astrological advisers. A 12th-century Archbishop of Canterbury even issued an edict warning of the dangers of an impending eclipse, suggesting that the population stay indoors for three days. Queen Elizabeth I's personal astrologer was John Dee, one of the greatest of the Renaissance scholars, being a noted geographer, navigator, mathematician, astronomer and intriguingly—with the cypher code he developed—the first secret-service spy. The renowned early astronomers Tycho Brahe, Johannes Kepler and Galileo Galilei worked as court astrologers in Scandinavia and on the Continent for separate monarchs. In the 16th century, John Napier—a Scot and the father of modern mathematics and inventor of logarithms—was an alchemist and astrologer like his father before him; one family member's horoscope is carved on the wall of their castle. The Italian artist Caravaggio painted an astrological fresco for one of his patrons, Cardinal del Monte, a Vatican intimate, who was an alchemist. The 16th-century Catholic Church was still a firm supporter of astrology, with Pope Paul III (1534–49) using astrology to schedule his audiences, much as Reagan did five centuries later.

During the English Civil War in the mid-1640s, the last of the great court astrologers, William Lilly, gave advice through intermediaries to both Oliver Cromwell and his opponent Charles I. Lilly, like others who have mixed astrology with politics, found it a dangerous game to play. He was imprisoned several times for treason. He was even arrested for predicting the Fire of London in 1666, 18 years before it happened. When it did happen, the authorities thought he must have had a hand in setting it. Robert Boyle, the 17th-century Irish physician who discovered the circulation of blood, accepted the principles of astrological treatment.

It is said by some historians (and denied by others) that in 1774 North America had its constitution set by astrologers, since the founding fathers Jefferson and Franklin were both Freemasons: masons always kept up a healthy interest in the subject. In more modern times Teddy Roosevelt used to keep a copy of his birth chart on the office wall in the White House to remind him of his tendency to lose his temper. Joseph Kennedy, father of President J. F. Kennedy, visited astrologers in London when in Britain as US ambassador.

In the 20th century, no Western world leader—with the exception of Boris Yeltsin—has used astrology to the same degree as US president Ronald Reagan. Yeltsin's tumultuous few years in power have been clearly detailed on his birth chart. When Reagan's ex-chief-of-staff Donald Regan's book came out in 1988, saying that 'the president's schedule and therefore his life and the most important business of the American nation was largely under the control of the First Lady's astrologer', a publicity storm ensured. Yet the astrologer Joan Quigley had indeed been instrumental in timing the president's speeches and travel arrangements and was privy to discussions that led to a warmer relationship with Mikhail Gorbachev and the defusing of the Cold War. Even Donald Regan's accolade that 'I think the nation owes Ms Quigley a vote of gratitude' was lost in a welter of derision.

Indira Gandhi, the Indian premier, certainly used astrologers, among other advisers, and the question was always murmured as to whether she had known in advance of her impending assassination. General Lon Nol, the leader of Cambodia when it became the Khmer Republic, was known to take astrological advice on all matters.

Hitler is widely though mistakenly thought to have depended on astrologers for advice. In fact he banned all occult practice in 1938, and during the war sent most astrologers to the concentration camps—including Karl Ernst Krafft, who had probably saved his life in 1939. Employed on a small retainer as an intelligence adviser, Krafft had predicted that Hitler would be in danger from an explosion between 7 and 10 November. On 8 November Hitler and his party left unexpectedly early from a social function. A bomb went off minutes later, killing seven people. Krafft died in a camp in 1945, having been imprisoned since 1941.

Despite his scepticism, Hitler knew his rise to power had been foretold by Elsbeth Ebertin, Germany's foremost astrologer in 1923. Not knowing whose chart she was analyzing, she wrote of a 'man of action ... destined to play a Führer-like role in future battles. He will expose himself to personal danger by excessively incautious action and could very likely trigger off an incontrollable crisis'.

Himmler, who was a great advocate of astrology, kept two charts in his research file which he and Hitler perused in the dying days of the war. One was of the Führer, drawn up in 1933, and the other was a horoscope of the Republic drawn up in 1918. Both predicted the outbreak of war in 1939, victories until 1941, then a series of defeats with the worst disasters in 1945. Peace was predicted for August of that year, but with an ambiguous hint at German victory: 'After the peace there would be a difficult time for Germany for three years; but from 1948 she would rise to greatness again.'

Carl Jung, the Swiss psychoanalyst, reckoned that understanding a birth chart give him as much information about a patient as two years' analysis would. French wine-growers now use Rudolph Steiner's astrological calendar as a part of their horticultural plan. Nearly 50 per cent of Wall Street brokers are thought to consult astrological charts in their business.

2 | ASTROLOGICAL MEANINGS, CORE CORRESPONDENCES

The raw data of astrology are the Sun, the Moon and the eight planets in the solar system (Mercury, Venus, Mars, Jupiter, Saturn, Uranus, Neptune and Pluto), and the 12 signs (Aries, Taurus, Gemini, Cancer, Leo, Virgo, Libra, Scorpio, Sagittarius, Capricorn, Aquarius and Pisces). The signs are named after 12 of the 88 constellations in the heavens which fall roughly in a circular arc, but are not by any means exact matches.

Constellations vary enormously in size, breadth and distance from the solar system. The zodiacal belt of the 12 astrological signs is an artificially constructed map-grid reference, of exact 30-degree slivers of the 360-degree circle of the Earth. The only astronomically exact point of the zodiac belt is Zero Point Aries, a line through the centre of the Earth, which coincides with the start of the sign Aries. As the Earth is tilting slowly backwards on its axis, this point is also moving backwards through the heavenly constellations, giving rise to the great 2000-year epochs (see page 18).

The planets and signs have meanings attached to them, many originating before Greek times but evolving as our understanding has deepened and as additional outer planets, such as Pluto and Uranus, have been discovered.

THE INNER PLANETS

Sun: The core identity. Our work drive or direction in life. The psychological inheritance from the father.
Moon: Our emotions, home, mother, body, and the past. What nurtures and comforts.
Mercury: Communication, writing, speaking. the rational mind. Short-distance travel. Restless, alert, analytical.
Venus: Love, luxury and light-hearted enjoyment. Diplomacy.
Mars: Energy. The libido—sex. Anger, confrontation, competitive drive. Sporting ability.

THE OUTER PLANETS

Jupiter: Lucky, expansive, confident and easy, lazy, over-hopeful. Tolerant and broadminded though can be self-righteous.

Saturn: Limiting, restricting, self-disciplined, depressive. Hard-working, creates structure and order. Traditional. The giver of laws and rules. The Grim Reaper.

Uranus: Insight, invention, breakthrough. Rebellious, a pioneer, scientific, against the natural order.

Neptune: Kind, dreamy, vague and uncertain. Spiritual and creative. Platonic love. Great sacrifice.

Pluto: Power, control, destruction and rebirth. Transformation and regeneration. Great wealth, or greed, possessiveness, and great endurance. Secretive and jealous.

OTHER IMPORTANT POINTS

Moon's North Node: Not a planet but a point where the ecliptic of the Moon's circling of the Earth crosses the Earth's path round the Sun. The challenge in life where the unknown is faced, and thus vital to psychological development. Often ties public figures into the collective. The point of destiny.

Midheaven: Career, reputation, direction and ambitions in life.

Ascendant: The horizon at birth. First impressions. The image, often hiding a different reality. The face that is shown to the outside world.

Descendant: Opposite the horizon at birth. How the individual relates to others; what kind of partner is sought.

ASPECTS

Aspects are the mathematical relationships between planets e.g. 90 degrees ('square'), 180 degrees ('opposition'), 120 degrees ('trine'), 60 degrees ('sextile'), 0 degrees, thus in the same place ('conjunction'). Aspects come either from two transiting planets moving at the same time in the heavens, giving the 'mood of the moment', or they can be calculated from present planetary positions in relation to a birth chart, which is the freeze-frame of the moment when that person or country was born.

◆**Aspects are of three basic varieties: conjunction, hard and soft.**◆

Conjunctions. Two or more planets together (within a few degrees) in the same sign. The meaning depends on the planets involved. The Sun and Venus together are sugary sweet and lazy. Uranus and Pluto together are explosively rebellious. If more than two outer planets are together—which is extremely rare—momentous turning points in history occur.

Hard aspects. The square (90 degrees) and opposition (180 degrees), which both mean that the energies of the planets are at cross purposes, or pulling against one another.

Soft aspects. The trine (120 degrees) and sextile (60 degrees) are a smoother flowing together of the energy of the planets, though even they can be troublesome if outer planets, like Pluto or Neptune, are involved.

OUTER PLANET CONJUNCTIONS

Jupiter–Saturn: Occurs every 20 years. Idealism meets materialism. Expansive, the birth of new hope, though over-confidence brings crashing disappointment.

Saturn–Neptune: Occurs three times a century. Turning dreams (Neptune) into reality (Saturn), associated with the fight for workers' rights, though can be paranoid or disorienting as Neptune undermines established structures and the sense of reality.

Saturn–Uranus: Occurs approximately every 46 years. Uranus rules change and Saturn rules the status quo, so can produce jarring though ultimately beneficial changes, incorporating the best of the old with the best of the new. Often has economic repercussions.

Saturn–Pluto: Occurs three times a century. Heavy, dark energy, associated with war and the suffering or misery of the masses. Always requires endurance. Success or survival only through great effort.

Uranus–Neptune: Occurs approximately every 170 years. Inspired artistic or spiritual influence, though highly strung. Natural disasters seem to happen frequently on square or opposition.

Uranus–Pluto: Occurs every 110 or 150 years. Explosively disruptive, rebellious. Sweeping, sudden changes to the settled power structures, though often ending in chaos. A dark time.

Neptune–Pluto: Occurred only four times in past 2000 years. Mystical, inventive, scandal-prone.

ELEMENTS AND TRIPLICITIES

The 12 signs are divided into four groups of elements: fire, air, water and earth. The signs in each of these groups are then divided into 'triplicities'. These are three categories that describe their characteristics, which are termed either cardinal, fixed or mutable.

Fire: Aries, Leo, Sagittarius. Energetic movers and shakers. Imaginative, intuitive and not practical. Colourful.

Air: Gemini, Libra, Aquarius. Thinkers and communicators. Emotionally detached.

Water: Cancer, Scorpio, Pisces. Emotional, tuned into subtle undercurrents. Touchy, self-protective.

Earth: Taurus, Virgo, Capricorn. Practical, sensible, realistic.

Cardinal: Aries, Cancer, Libra, Capricorn. Have initiative, go-getters, good at starting new projects but not good at finishing, restless.

Fixed: Taurus, Leo, Scorpio, Aquarius. Solid, unbudgeable, stubborn, have endurance. Not good starters.

Mutable: Gemini, Virgo, Sagittarius, Pisces. Adaptable, restless, bend to circumstances rather than influencing them.

THE SIGNS

The starting point of each Sun sign varies a day or two each year, so the dates given below are an average and may not be accurate. For exact dates in any given year, check with a professional astrologer, or on the Internet.

Aries *(21 March–20 April)* The Ram. Ruled by Mars. Likes to win. The adventurer, competitive, aggressive, short attention span. Courageous, daring, self-centred. Entrepreneurial, with a strong imagination. Outspoken.

Taurus *(21 April–20 May)* The Bull. Ruled by Venus. Likes power and money. Earthy, practical, steady, enduring. Materialistic, possessive, greedy. Stubborn, jealous, sensuous, controlling. Artistic through the body, often musical or singing.

Gemini *(21 May–21 June)* The Twins. Ruled by Mercury. Likes to talk. Communicative, nervy, versatile, inventive, curious, moody. Split.

Cancer *(22 June–23 July)* The Crab. Ruled by the Moon. Likes to feel part of the tribe. Home, family-oriented. Security-conscious, patriotic, attached to the past. Highly emotional and self-protective. Easily hurt, but essentially giving. Creative, ambitious.

Leo *(24 July–23 August)* The Lion. Ruled by the Sun. Likes to look regal, wealthy and influential. Enjoys love, money, children and entertainment. Proud, vain, self-aware. Theatrical, dramatic, flamboyant. Self-centred, slightly pompous. Stubborn.

Virgo *(24 August–23 September)* The Goddess of the Harvest/The Virgin. Ruled by Mercury. Likes to be of service. Practical, hard-working, health-oriented. Fastidious, perfectionist, attentive to detail. Worrying, analytical, discriminating.

Libra *(24 September–22 October)* The Scales of Justice. Ruled by Venus. Likes balance and harmony. Socially conscious, fair-minded, keen on agreements and partnerships. Communicative. Wise though indecisive. Diplomatic, elegant, tasteful.

Scorpio *(23 October–22 November)* The Scorpion. Ruled by Mars and Pluto. Likes to be in control. Emotional, secretive, investigative, jealous, possessive, power-hungry. Good with money, resourceful. Sexual.

Sagittarius *(23 November–22 December)* The Archer/Centaur. Ruled by Jupiter. Likes to roam free. Communicative, a philosopher though sometimes self-righteous and narrow-minded. Outspoken, cheerful, optimistic. Interested in human behaviour and social structures, foreign countries and travel.

Capricorn *(23 December–20 January)* The Mountain-climbing Goat. Ruled by Saturn. Likes to achieve. Hard-working, practical, ambitious, goal-oriented. Materialistic, conventional, rule bound. Unemotional though has a sensual side. Controlled, orderly, snobbish.

Aquarius *(21 January–18 February)* The Water Carrier. Ruled by Saturn and Uranus. Likes to invent and to impart knowledge. Communicative, detached, rebellious, pioneering, stubborn. A maverick, eccentric but essentially tolerant of differences. Keen on progress, anti-tradition. Likes computers, astrology.

Pisces *(19 February–20 March)* The Two Fishes. Ruled by Neptune and Jupiter. Likes to dream, be creative or spiritual. Emotional, sensitive, dislikes confrontation. Kind, compassionate, self-sacrificing. Intuitive, musical, visionary.

INTO THE AGE OF AQUARIUS:
THE GREAT EPOCHS EXPLAINED

Astrology's perspective on the universe takes into account the fact that our view of the constellations shifts as the Earth tilts backwards infinitesimally slowly in the heavens. Every 2000 years approximately, the line drawn through the centre of the Earth moves into a different sign. Hence we are moving into the much vaunted Age of Aquarius, one of the great epochs, and out of the Age of Pisces which started around the time of the birth of Christ. Each of these epochs coincides with a different stage of development of mankind.

The Age of Leo: 10,000–8000 BC
Leo, symbolized by the lion, ruled by the Sun, is courageous, artistic, family-centred, giving out warmth. This is the age of the hunter-gatherer, and the dawn of agriculture, with the cultivation of wild cereals. Animals are not yet domesticated so wild flocks are rounded up to provide sustenance and for breeding. It is also the end of the last Ice Age. Rock paintings record early man's need to create a lasting record of his presence.

The Age of Cancer: 8000–6000 BC
Cancer, symbolized by the crab, ruled by the Moon, is home, family and tribe-oriented, worshipping the Great Mother and the Moon as the fertility providers. This is the age when communities started to gather into protected settlements, with defensive protection against wild animals. In Jericho the people lived in huts made of sun-dried mud, which became a widespread method of construction in the Middle East.

The Age of Gemini: 6000–4000 BC
Gemini, symbolized by the twins, ruled by Mercury, is the communication planet, restless, versatile, wandering. This is the age of the development of written or drawn communication, starting with cuneiform, pictographs and hieroglyphs. Initially devised for trade and barter, and derived from an earlier token system, writing was increasingly used for administration.

The Age of Taurus: 4000–2000 BC
Taurus, symbolized by the bull, sign of the farmer, coincided with the start of settled agricultural communities, as the nomads formed together in groups to cultivate the land. Taurus is associated with culture, comfort and security. Its Venusian aspects are seen most clearly in the Egyptian civilization, which by 3500BC was flourishing in cities along the fertile Nile Delta. The great bull sarcophaguses of ancient Egypt are testament to the reverence in which this animal was held.

The Age of Aries: 2000 BC–AD 0
Aries, the warrior sign, symbolized by the ram, associated with iron, coincides in the great epochs with the development of metal, which replaced stone and wooden implements and was used for agriculture, household utensils and weapons. The first European states were settled under the flourishing Minoan culture, then the

Greek. Aries' entrepreneurial talents were put to good use: trading increased dramatically. Sporting prowess became the greatest achievement in Greek culture, reflecting Aries' competitive streak. Bronze technology gave way to iron, with an increase in military activity, which saw the construction of Europe's massive defensive fortresses.

The age of Pisces: AD 0–2000

An age of artistic and religious inspiration, with the great messiahs—Christ, Mohammed and Buddha—carrying the vision of mankind. Pisces is creative, spiritual, concerned with individual sacrifice for the greater good. Suffering for mankind is one of its traits, witnessed in the Christ myth. The early Jesus cults had the fish as their secret symbol, and the Christian New Testament story concerns itself with fishermen and feeding the multitude. Buddhism is the passive facet of Pisces, caring, opposed to killing, living a good life and aspiring to nirvana, a blissful state removed from earthly suffering. Pisces is connected to realms beyond, so revelations from God come directly to the prophets like Mohammed, who bring those revelations to the people. Pisces' darker side is orgiastic, devouring, savage, impersonal, inhumane.

The age of Aquarius: 2000–4000

A high-tech, computer crazy age; the information revolution and genetic engineering are but two of the wild scientific developments that would have been unthinkable even 100 years ago. These are just the beginning, though, a pointer to what lies ahead. Aquarius is the sign of knowledge, scientific breakthroughs and discoveries. Man takes on god-like powers, manipulating the environment and our species. What he does runs against biology, so the old gender-specific categories and cultures will no longer hold. Test-tube babies, frozen sperm and eggs, clones, spare-part transplants, a world that George Orwell and Aldous Huxley uncannily foresaw, all this is now unstoppable. Aquarius is detached emotionally, friend rather than family oriented, so the breakdown of the old domestic structures—already in evidence—is part of the picture. Essentially tolerant, and humanitarian, Aquarius appreciates individual differences of culture, custom and creed, so some have spoken of a golden age coming. But Aquarius can be uncompromising in its demand for complete freedom without interference. The old social glue no longer works. What the Prometheus myth, often associated with Aquarius, tells us, however, is that playing with the power of the universe carries with it dangers. There will be a physical price to pay for an over emphasis on the intellect and scientific supremacy. The emotions and the body, split off from natural roots, may rebel.

3 | THE PAST 2000 YEARS
History in the making

The cauldron of history is constantly bubbling: empires and dynasties rise and fall, dark ages are followed by Renaissance cultural peaks, national boundaries shift. It is difficult to grasp a sense of order and meaning in such diverse events.

Astrology can help us to see a pattern in all of this, tracking complex cycles which constantly revolve in relation to one another as planets, moving at different speeds, come together in the heavens, separate and eventually realign, sometimes hundreds of years later, but not always in the same zodiacal sign. Jupiter takes 12 years to make a complete orbit, Saturn 29 years, Uranus 84, Neptune approximately 170 and Pluto 250 years. The conjunctions of two or more of these planets appear to coincide with major historical markers—civilization shifts, invasions and peace treaties—highlighting certain social issues, fostering repression or coinciding with periods of scientific progress or artistic achievement. Certain countries appear to resonate more to one set of planets joining together than to another. Uranus–Neptune conjunctions appear to trigger significant events in English history, for example; Saturn–Uranus conjunctions seem to affect Dutch, Italian and Scandinavian history. Uranus–Pluto homes in on the Jewish story, and recurs through the rebellious history of Scotland.

The merging of the energies of these different planets appears to give rise to repeating effects that mirror the chemical mix in both positive and negative capacities. Saturn, for example, is practical. When mixed with creative, spiritual, visionary Neptune, it will bring this energy to bear in an attempt to ground Neptune's dreams and produce tangible results, and can thus push for a better society. Conversely, Neptune can undermine Saturn's grip on reality and rationality and lead to paranoid worries.

INFLUENCES AND ASPECTS

The following lists describe the energies of the individual planets, as well as the combined influence they exert when in conjunction with each other.

Planets
Jupiter: expansiveness, idealism
Saturn: structure, authority, rationality, tradition, death
Uranus: enlightenment, revolution, science

Neptune: creativeness, spirituality, intuitiveness, lack of realism
Pluto: power, control, wealth, sex, death/rebirth

Conjunctions

Jupiter–Saturn: expansiveness, a heralding of new beginnings, a new messiah, overly high expectations leading to disappointment; the influence lasts 12–18 months

Saturn–Uranus: gives structure to new changes, swings between old and new, dictatorial; the influence lasts two to three years

Saturn–Neptune: gives structure to dreams (religious, social or creative), or undermines old structures and rational thinking and so heightens worry; the influence lasts two to three years

Saturn–Pluto: indicates authoritarian power structures, brutal action, a lack of humanity, a struggle to survive; the influence lasts two to three years

Uranus–Pluto: revolutionary, often violent, explosively disrupting existing power structures, often with catastrophic results; the influence last five to six years

Uranus–Neptune: highly strung, indicative of religious inspiration, artistic enlightenment and scientific breakthroughs; the influence lasts seven to eight years

Neptune–Pluto: signals megalomania, with fey, mystical, artistic, sexually inspired, scandal-prone characteristics; the influence can last 20 years

Saturn comes together with Neptune three times a century, and has a fascinating track record in connection with workers' rights and women's power. Queen Elizabeth I (in 1558), Elizabeth II (in 1953), and Benazir Bhutto (in 1989) all came to power under a Saturn–Neptune conjunction (see *Saturn–Neptune*, page 37). In England, Wat Tyler's Peasants' Revolt of 1381 was followed in later centuries by similar uprisings under the same star alignment, including the Russian Revolution in 1917 and the rise of the Solidarity movement in Poland in the 1980s.

Uranus and Neptune have come together only 10 times in the past 2000 years, and their conjunction coincides with 'golden ages' of social progress, medical breakthroughs, the birth of new religions or heresies and, most notably, inspired spiritual art. As we saw in the introduction, Giotto painted the Padua frescoes on one such conjunction in 1305; next time around in 1482 Botticelli and Perugino painted the Sistine Chapel; and in 1820 William Blake illustrated *The Book of Job*.

The slow-moving Neptune and slower Pluto come together only four times in 2000 years (see *Neptune–Pluto*, page 25). Erotic art flourishes under this fey, mystical, scandal-prone influence. It was a marker on the birth charts of Adolf Hitler, Mao Tse Tung, Joseph Stalin—all born in the late 19th century and the three most brutal power figures of the 20th century—and that of Attila the Hun (born *c*. AD 406), and it was also in place during the infamous Tamerlane's campaign of terror in Central Asia in the late 14th century.

Uranus and Pluto meet in the same sign seven times in 1000 years. We experienced their revolutionary violence in the mid-1960s with the Vietnam War, the Arab-Israeli Six Day War, and other rebellions, both social and political. The previous occurrence in 1850 produced a plethora of European revolts and rebellions. This conjunction also appears to promote mathematical knowledge.

Faster-moving Saturn and Uranus come together three times a century, coinciding with empires collapsing and countries forming, with mass migrations of people, humane social laws and good literature, and—oddly enough—with seemingly more assassinations than usual.

Saturn–Pluto, another three-times-a-century occurrence, seen most recently in 1982 with the Falklands War, the Israeli invasion of Lebanon and the Sabra-Chatila refugee-camp massacres, is a starkly tough influence, connected with war, widespread misery, and times of religious repression.

Less frequent are the triple or even quadruple conjunctions of the outer planets, which produce a toxic melting pot of conflicting energies. The next two pages look at these awesome heavenly congregations. A mind-boggling quadruple conjunction of Jupiter, Saturn, Neptune and Pluto held sway over AD 412, to be followed 30 years later by a shattering Uranus–Saturn–Pluto conjunction. At that time there was a huge civilization shift as the Roman Empire declined, Britain was invaded by the Picts, Scots and Anglo-Saxons, and the Dark Ages began. We have lived through two triple conjunctions this century, with the Jupiter–Saturn–Uranus alignment in Taurus in 1941 as Hitler's rise to power peaked. Even stronger in effect, Saturn, Uranus and Neptune were close in Capricorn in 1988 to 1989 as the Iron Curtain disintegrated and the face of history changed dramatically.

MULTIPLE CONJUNCTIONS

The heavenly congregation of any three of the four outer planets (Saturn, Uranus, Neptune and Pluto) moving through the same sign together has only happened 10 times in the past 2000 years. These conjunctions clearly have a major, though often confusing, astrological effect, which can cover specific events over a decade or more. But they more essentially point to major civilization shifts, whose effects ripple out for decades and sometimes centuries to come. Being faster-moving, Jupiter comes into contact with other planets and conjunctions more often, so triple conjunctions involving Jupiter tend to have a lesser effect.

The fifth century
412: Saturn–Neptune–Pluto–Jupiter in Taurus ◆ 440–44: Uranus–Pluto–Saturn in Gemini and Cancer
The Dark Ages ◆ The Fall of Rome ◆ Attila the Hun ◆ The Jin Dynasty

These multiple conjunctions coincide with the start of the Dark Ages, which begin with a bleak century of confusion and mass migration, reeling from the double impact of a quadruple conjunction followed rapidly by a triple. We see the fall of the Roman Empire, the Barbarians taking over the European continent, and the Romans leaving Britain; this latter event leads to a revival of Celtic culture but also allows Picts, Scots and Anglo-Saxons to invade and settle in large numbers, forcing many Britons to flee to Brittany. Attila the Hun, the legendary megalomaniac ruler immortalized in Wagnerian operas and nicknamed the Scourge of God, is born in about 406 under the early Neptune–Pluto conjunction (also the astrological stamp for Hitler, Mao Tse Tung and Stalin). Having murdered his brother, he devastates the countries between the Black Sea and the

Mediterranean between 434 and 453, until he himself dies, perhaps murdered by his bride on the night of his wedding, resulting in the disintegration of his empire. Elsewhere, Slavs raid and settle in the Balkans, and in China the oppressive Jin Dynasty falls in 420, giving way to 150 years of confusion.

The sixth century
582: Saturn–Uranus–Pluto in Pisces square Neptune
The birth of Mohammed ◆ Buddhism in the East ◆ The birth of Tibet

Uranus–Pluto is essentially revolutionary, but falling in spiritual Pisces with a visionary Neptune square the main thrust is towards establishing new religious beliefs. Thus are sown the seeds of the Islamic Era, with Mohammed's birth in 570; his life peaks at the next triple conjunction in 622 when he establishes himself as a spiritual and political leader. Buddhism is now the dominant religion in China, Japan and Korea. The mountainous kingdom of Tibet comes into being, along with several small Thai kingdoms. The Sui Dynasty reunites China.

The seventh century
623–625: Saturn–Uranus–Neptune in Virgo
The founding of Islam ◆ The rise and fall of empires and dynasties

A more benign triple conjunction, its principle thrust is towards establishing new spiritual and social changes and cultural values. Mohammed makes the flight from Mecca to Medina in 622, declaring himself the leader of Islam. This is the beginning of the Islamic calendar. The Persian Sassanids, who have controlled much of the Middle East, fall with the destruction in 624 of the birthplace of Zoroaster, the centre of their faith; this is the effective start of the mediaeval Greek Byzantine Empire. China is united under the Tang Dynasty, heralding a new era of greatness. Tibet enters a golden age under Srong-Tsan with Lhasa as its capital. The Merovingian Dynasty in Europe declines, with power passing to the founders of the Carolingian Dynasty. India is lapsing into the Dark Ages.

The 10th century
912: Saturn–Neptune–Pluto in Gemini ◆ 944: Uranus–Saturn–Pluto in Cancer
The rise and fall of dynasties and empires ◆ Monastic reform

Another century like the fifth, with a double dose of major alignments, it sees more major shifts. In China and Germany, dynasties that rose under the previous triple conjunction in 623 now fade. The Tang Dynasty collapses with the Chinese Empire fragmenting in the Period of the Five Dynasties. In 912, the death of Louis the Child, last Carolingian ruler of Germany, makes way for the Saxon kings, a decisive break with the past. Vikings settle in Normandy. The beginning of monastic reform is marked by the building of Cluny Abbey.

The 14th century
1306: Jupiter–Saturn–Uranus–Neptune in Scorpio
The Renaissance ◆ The Ottoman Empire ◆ Militant Christianity ◆ Plagues

23

The first quadruple conjunction in 900 years, with spiritual Neptune, inspired Uranus and practical Saturn together with expansive Jupiter, it holds the seeds of positive change. This is the start of the European Renaissance, an astonishing outpouring of artistic talent and inspiration starting with the works of Dante and Giotto and extending onwards through two centuries of intellectual and cultural magnificence.

Specifically the conjunction also coincides with the expulsion of the Crusaders from the Holy Land. The order of soldier-monks, the Templars, is brutally dissolved, sending much esoteric knowledge underground. The conjunction also sees the founding, between 1299 and 1311, of the powerful Ottoman Empire, which succeeds the Seljuk Empire; it will last for 600 years, until 1923. Temur, the Great Khan, dies; Mongol rule in China declines into civil war. The Mongol Empire converts to Islam.

Gunpowder is first manufactured in the West. The great plagues are about to descend on Europe: this less beneficial side of Saturn–Neptune is a marker for the St Vitus Dance outbreak of 1021, the Spanish 'flu outbreak of 1918 which killed 20 million, and the AIDS epidemic that started in the late 1980s. The seeds of the Reformation of the Church are being sown. This conjunction is the nearest thing to the one we experienced at the end of the 1980s, although it falls in a different sign.

The 18th century
1713–14: Saturn–Uranus–Pluto in Virgo
The Age of Enlightenment ◆ The Hanoverian dynasty ◆ North America ◆ Invasions and revolutions in the East

The War of Spanish Succession ends with the Peace of Utrecht between France, Britain, Holland, Portugal and Prussia, which effectively establishes for the first time a European balance of power. Western Europe now begins a period of economic growth. This triggers the Age of Enlightenment, with scientific inquiry breaking down the old beliefs; academies and observatories proliferate and there are new movements in art, architecture and music, while philosophical thinkers such as Voltaire argue for a more humane social order. George I becomes the first Hanoverian king of Britain, now (since 1707) united with Scotland, effectively keeping Catholics off the throne. The Scottish Jacobite Rebellion is defeated. The Mughal Empire disintegrates. Mongols invade Tibet and destroy the Chinese Army. Britain goes to war with France over the North American territories. There are revolutions in Russia. The slave trade begins. Large-scale German and Scots-Irish immigration to North America starts.

The 19th century
1848, 1850–52: Saturn–Uranus–Pluto in Aries and Taurus
The birth of communism ◆ The rise of Germany ◆ Revolutions

Known as the 'year of revolutions', 1848 is already suffering from the Uranus–Pluto effect as revolts spring up all over Europe. Joined by rigid, austere Saturn two years later in 1850, a major culture and power shift is inevitable. The *coup d'état* of Louis Napoleon launches the Second French Empire. The unification of modern Germany effectively begins after 1848, and its rise as an aggressive world power gets under way. Karl Marx and Friedrich Engels publish their *Communist Manifesto* in 1848, sowing the seeds of the notion of workers' control of industry. The Crimean War begins in 1854, and is lost by Russia, which starts a process of liberating the serfs, a step along the way to the revolution of 1917. The internal Taiping Rebellion in China against official corruption and high taxation costs 20 million lives. In North America, Texas and California become states of the union.

The 20th century
1988–91: Saturn–Uranus–Neptune in Capricorn
The collapse of communism ◆ The end of the Cold War ◆ The end of apartheid ◆ The European Union

The Communist regimes of Eastern Europe, whose ideological base was set by Marx and Engels in the previous triple conjunction, fall. The Iron Curtain is lifted; the Cold War ends; the USSR starts to break up; and the Balkans disintegrate into violent chaos. As in the previous two triple conjunctions, there is another attempt to alter the face of Europe as the EEC becomes the European Union, with the Maastricht Treaty aiming for closer political and economic union. Apartheid crumbles in South Africa.

MAJOR CONJUNCTIONS

Neptune–Pluto
400–420 in Taurus and Gemini ◆ 892–919 in Taurus and Gemini ◆ 1383–1411 in Taurus and Gemini ◆ 1876–1902 in Taurus and Gemini

Pluto and Neptune, the slowest of the outer planets, come together only rarely— four times in 2000 years. In the previous epoch, the Age of Pisces, their meeting occurred, oddly, always in the same signs. Their direct influence covers 20 to 25 years: Neptune, marginally faster than Pluto, edges closer as they both move through the heavens.

Pluto's domain in astrological terms is the deeper, darker realm of wealth, sex, death and rebirth, power and control. It has a scorpionic intensity, a need to plumb the depths to find the heights of transcendence. Mythologically associated with Pluto (also known as Hades), god of the underworld, a power figure of great wealth who abducts Persephone (the maiden Kore), he is primitive but also transformational. The myth of Pluto/Hades and Persephone/Proserpine is symbolically connected to that of the Egyptian god Osiris and his journey into the after-life—the motivating force behind the Pharoahs' desire to build pyramids and ornate death chambers to see them safely into the next world. The myth also has echoes in the Sumerian legend of the descent of the goddess Inanna, who is stripped of earthly and material glory and humiliated in order to be reborn with more wisdom. Even Persephone's rape becomes an initiation into the darker side of life and sexuality, leading her from innocence as the protected mother's child to taste the fruits of passion, which in biting from the pomegranate she refuses to give up. Sexuality and power are the two abiding motifs of Pluto.

Neptune astrologically is seen as a spiritual, creative, compassionate influence, touched by the suffering of the world, and frequently leading to a belief in sacrifice. It is an otherworldly energy, often rejecting the flesh or material values for the sake of a greater dream, on many occasions a religious vision.

Mythologically connected to Neptune, god of the sea, it has a dissolving, undermining quality. The rational mind with its Saturnine make-up gives way to Neptune's subtly corrosive influence, causing paranoid worry and a loosening grip on reality. The mists on the surface of the constantly shifting ocean, the deceptive sea depths, the engulfing currents, the mesmerizing wonder and great beauty of the world below the watery surface are all part of the Neptunian realm; the intangible, the unseen, the barely visible, are all the focus of this Piscean will-o'-the-wisp energy. Neptune swims in fantasies, visions, dreams and hallucinations. It is often associated with the world of films, photography and music, and thus with great ethereal beauty. The image takes on a lustre that is not contaminated by the gritty imperfections of reality. Sacrifice in the name of love—a pure, holy agape, rather than erotic love, a love that is not tainted—is Neptune's dream.

There is, however, a cruel streak in Neptune's dismissal of the real world and the body. In Greek mythology, after the god Neptune has lost the ground war to Athena, the wise warrior-goddess, he takes revenge by raping Medusa, who in her victimhood becomes a ferociously ugly outcast. When the hero Perseus beheads the Medusa, he goes on to rescue the maiden Andromeda from the clutches of a sea-monster, another face of Neptune, who has chained the beauty to a rock. Revenge and inhuman cruelty often sit side by side with extreme compassion, great creativity and strong religious yearnings in this complex energy. Financial and other scandals always have a whiff of Neptune about them, with its quality of deceptiveness and its persuasive sleights of hand. Confidence tricks come under Neptune's banner, with its inability to set boundaries or to distinguish between thine and mine, and its tendency to lie and distort.

Neptune and Pluto together create a fey, mystical mix of energies, both wonderful and terrifying at the same time. Historically the combination is connected with the rise of great powers with epically brutal leaders; with art, especially erotic literature; with scientific advances in such intangibles as electricity, radio and telephone; with religious events; and with scandals.

The rise and fall of great powers
These two planets together in the same sign coincide with the rise of great powers, often led by brutal dictators, and a consequent dissolving of previous empires, starting with the fall of the Roman Empire and Britain's decline into the Dark Ages in the fifth century. Attila the Hun (born *c.* 406), who devastated the Eastern Mediterranean in a campaign of terror in the fifth century, and Joseph Stalin (born 1879), the revolutionary Marxist whose brutal purges led to the death of some 20 million Russian peasants by execution or famine in the 1920s and 1930s, were born 1400 years apart but both under the sway of a Neptune–Pluto conjunction in Taurus. Adolf Hitler (born 1889) and Mao Tse Tung (born 1893), the other two major destructive power figures of the 20th century, were born with Neptune close to Pluto in Gemini. When the 14th-century conjunction was at its peak, Tamerlane the Great was terrorizing the Middle East. More recently, in the final 20 years of

last century, the Englishman Cecil Rhodes was forcefully attempting to create a British colonial African super-state from south to north. In a chilling pointer to the Holocaust of the next century, the British invented concentration camps during the Boer War. In North America, the Native American Indians were finally driven into total submission, and America was established as an imperial power, having won the Spanish-American War. Germany, now reunified, was rising steadily under Bismarck to become a super-power.

Neptune in its visionary aspect, mixing with Pluto's power drive, creates a delusional though often devastatingly effective megalomania. Both planets in their negative roles are chillingly inhumane. Neptune puts the dream above reality, writes off human sacrifice as a necessary cost to gain the end. Pluto as the arch controller reduces individual humans to objects, pawns on the chessboard; the puppetmaster reigns supreme.

Artistic works

When Pluto's sexual obsession comes together with Neptune's creative artistry, great erotic works result. The greatest erotic work of literature, the *Kamasutra*, was written under the sway of a Neptune–Pluto conjunction. Nine hundred years later Chaucer produced his bawdy *Canterbury Tales*, on cue, over a period of 17 years during the peak of the conjunction's influence. Next time around Sir Richard Burton, the African explorer and sexual connoisseur of native pleasures, translated *The Thousand and One Nights*, or the *Arabian Nights*. When he died in 1900, his wife burnt many of his writings, because she considered them to be scandalous.

Elsewhere a different balance is maintained as Neptune's beautiful visions hold Pluto's primitive *id* under control. The Japanese Renaissance flourished in the 10th century with poetry, painting and literature, much as another bountiful outpouring of literature, art and drama came about from 1880 onwards, with Gauguin and Cézanne in painting; a wealth of plays by Chekhov, Ibsen, Oscar Wilde and George Bernard Shaw; and music from Debussy, Elgar, Puccini, Tchaikovsky, Rimsky-Korsakov, Borodin, Verdi, Sibelius, Dvorak and Wagner. Neptune's sure touch with the arts also embraced film, with the first movie showing in Paris in 1895.

Scandals

Scandals are also part of the Neptune–Pluto story, with three epic examples in the 19th century. In 1892 the Panama Canal scandal broke in France, with ensuing trials for corruption and financial mismanagement. In 1894, Jewish Alfred Dreyfus was unjustly accused of treason, on the basis of forged evidence produced at his trial, and imprisoned for life on Devil's Island. Due to the efforts of campaigners such as Emile Zola, the Dreyfus Affair became a *cause célèbre* and he was eventually freed, although it took years to clear his name. In 1895, Oscar Wilde, at the height of his dramatic reputation with hit plays like *An Ideal Husband* and *The Importance of Being Earnest*, sued the Marquess of Queensberry, the father of his lover Lord Alfred Douglas, for calling him a homosexual. He lost and was subsequently tried for homosexuality and imprisoned. He died in exile in France in 1900.

Religion and science

Neptune–Pluto also presides over the high and low points of religion. St Augustine's *Confessions* appeared with St Jerome's Vulgate Latin translation of the Bible under one such conjunction in AD 400; Alfred the Great's translations of great religious works appeared 500 years later under the next conjunction. The Roman Catholic Papacy was divisively damaged 500 years on, and by the next conjunction Nietzsche, in 1886, was talking of God being dead and Marx was writing religion off as 'the opiate of the masses'. Neptune raised the vision, then dissolved it. The rise of science provoked a papal encyclical condemning the new metaphysics in 1879, but the inexorable progress of the new scientific and social thinking was unstoppable. Karl Marx's Communist three-volume magnum opus *Das Kapital* (1867–95), and Sigmund Freud's *Interpretation of Dreams* (1900), as well as T. H. Huxley's coining of the term 'agnostic' in 1869, began a religious erosion that plunged the 20th century into a welter of disbelief.

As might be expected, the type of scientific inquiry provoked by Neptune–Pluto verges on the intangible, starting at its earliest with alchemy in AD 400 and Zosymus describing experiments that were a mix of basic chemistry and mysticism. In AD 900 the great Arabian prince, astrologer and astronomer Al-Battani was at his peak. By the late nineteenth century the telephone was invented, electricity and radio waves were mastered, X-Rays were in use, airships were launched, and sound and picture recording was about to revolutionize leisure activities.

Uranus–Neptune

99–119 in Gemini and Cancer ✦ 274–87 in Cancer and Leo ✦ 442–60 in Cancer, Leo and Virgo ✦ 616–28 in Leo and Virgo ✦ 790–802 in Virgo and Libra ✦ 958–69 in Virgo and Libra ✦ 1132–43 in Libra/Scorpio ✦ 1299–1311 in Libra and Scorpio ✦ 1473–85 in Scorpio and Sagittarius ✦ 1647–59 in Sagittarius and Capricorn ✦ 1815–27 in Sagittarius and Capricorn ✦ 1988–2000 in Capricorn and Aquarius

Uranus brings an enlightening, illuminating, electrifying energy to whatever it touches. It works with blinding flashes of mental inspiration, and is associated with science, mathematics, high-speed computer energy, television and astrology. The planet of sudden change, it shines light on the past, encouraging an archaeological interest in ancient history, and paradoxically thrives on the leading edge of exciting new developments for the future. Uranus is a rebel, a pioneer, an experimenter, the one who is willing to walk away from the consensus, who refuses to compromise. Uranus with its devastating honesty is well represented by the small boy in the Hans Andersen story who says 'But the Emperor has no clothes on', and tells the truth even if it means risking social exclusion. Uranus dislikes the status quo and insists on freedom from rigid authoritarian structures and societies.

Essentially a humanitarian influence, Uranus promotes a tolerance of all races, creeds and cultures, and prefers a wide network of cooperation, variety in diversity, rather than evangelizing for a one-belief world. But in its drive for total independence of thought and speech, its constant need to overturn the past, to destructure stability, it can lead to social chaos and anarchy, and can be disruptive to family or tribal bonds.

In mythology Uranus is connected to Prometheus, the god who brought fire to mankind, paving the way for the invention of metal tools for use in agriculture and industry. He is a bringer of knowledge, a mental energy which fosters a developing scientific consciousness. For giving away divine secrets, however, Prometheus was punished by his fellow gods and condemned to be chained in eternity to a rock, having his liver torn out by an eagle during the day only to have it regenerate by night. The body and the instincts are often a weak spot where Uranus is concerned. The bite-back effect of man's over-development of the intellect, his tampering with life through genetic engineering, releasing atomic power and meddling with the Earth's environment is increasingly obvious. Everything comes at a price.

Uranus is also a mythological sky god, castrated by his son Saturn (*Kronos*, or time, in Greek) at the instigation of Gaia, the great earth mother, who was angry with Uranus for banishing her children. In certain legends, his genitals, cast into the sea, were transformed into Aphrodite, the goddess of love. Uranus as an astrological energy is thought to be anti-biological, not rooted in sexual instincts or family ties. It can lead to perversity, lack of emotional connectedness and an overly intellectual approach to sex.

Uranus combined with creative, spiritual Neptune is a highly strung influence, inspirational in art, science and social thinking, with high ideals and soaring vision. What the combination can lack is common sense, which is both its strength and its weakness. With no Earth grounding and thus no limits, it can rise to magnificent achievements; or it can foster irrational fanatical thinking, so extreme that it misleads. The oppositions and square aspects seem to cause more problems in this regard. They also appear to be disaster-prone, as the earthquake cycle of 1906 to 1910 would seem to show.

Art

The meeting of enlightening Uranus with spiritually and artistically visionary Neptune has coincided with the production of the greatest religious art of our history. This has humble beginnings in AD 100 when the Christians began to bury their dead in catacombs outside Rome: the frescoes decorating the walls were the first Christian art. Three conjunctions later *The Book of Kells*, the great illuminated Gospels, was produced at Iona Monastery in Scotland. During the next conjunction the first Gothic-style church was built. The Abbey Church of St Denis was to set a trend for the glorious Renaissance cathedrals that spread across Europe to Chartres, Lausanne and Angers. At the same time Byzantine craftsmen were working on St Sophia Cathedral in Kiev. But the beauty of the synchronicity was best captured in Giotto's painting of the Padua frescoes in 1305, in an artistically fertile time that also produced Dante Alighieri's *Vita Nuova,* which told of his love for Beatrice. Then blissfully, next conjunction around in 1480, Botticelli and Perugino were painting frescoes in the Sistine Chapel. Around this time Botticelli also painted his *Birth of Venus*, showing Aphrodite rising from the foam, as she was reputed to have done after Uranus's genitals were thrown into the sea. Michelangelo, arguably the greatest of the religious painters, was born just at the start of this conjunction. On the next conjunction, St Peter's in Rome was finished by Bernini in 1656, and in 1820, William Blake was painting his illustrations for *The Book of Job*. In 1988, Martin Scorsese's film *The Last Temptation of Christ* was a sad attempt to emulate the great religious art of the past, a reflection of the godless 20th century.

Social progress

Liberal reform and advanced social thinking reflect the connection between forward-looking, tolerant Uranus and Neptune's ideals and pity for the suffering. In the earliest conjunction of the past two millennia in the years following AD 99, the Roman Emperor Trajan's administration was exemplary, and agriculture was encouraged. Five-per-cent state mortgages were given for buying farm land, along with family allowances, and the poor children in Rome, as well as their parents, were given the corn dole. Hadrian took over in 117, further improving government administration and establishing a liberal regime. Around 616 Chinese Emperor T'ai T'sung codified the law, introduced the examination system, reissued the Chinese classics, and increased his country's trade and prosperity. In 790 the Emperor Charlemagne founded an academy at his capital, Aix-la-Chapelle, to which leading scholars of his age, such as Alcuin of Iona, were invited. He promoted education, architecture, bookbinding and the arts, created stable administration and good laws, and encouraged agriculture, industry and commerce. He appointed a chief justice and judges, and assemblies of nobles and bishops to consider and approve his ethics and to report on state affairs. The Classical Heian Period, the golden age of Japan, started around 794 with Kyoto founded as the City of Peace. The Khmers of Cambodia begin their rise to prosperity at the same time, leading to the building of the great Hindu temples.

Empires and golden ages

Uranus–Neptune conjunctions coincide frequently with the high points of civilizations, when social and artistic ideals flourish. Rome was at its height under Trajan and Hadrian at the start of the second century, with the rebuilt Pantheon a fitting symbol for the glory that was the Roman Empire. China was united in a new era of greatness in 618 in the Tang Dynasty. Tibet moved into its golden age then as well. Next conjunction on, Charlemagne, the greatest of the early European rulers, wielded enlightened power over a vast kingdom. The Ottoman Empire, set to last for six centuries, got under way in 1300 on the triple conjunction of Uranus, Neptune and Saturn. The European Renaissance flourished for 200 glorious years from this point as well. Nearer our time the European framework began to stabilize during these conjunctions, with the end of the Thirty Years' War in 1648 guaranteeing the independence of the Netherlands, the German states and the Swiss cantons. In 1815 the Congress of Vienna set the political future of Europe. Then in 1991 the Maastricht Treaty brought closer economic and political union in Europe.

Both Uranus and Neptune in different ways have a capacity for undermining or dismantling settled structures. The fragmentation of the USSR in 1988 mirrors the collapse of political unity in Russia under a previous conjunction in 1139, when the separatism of the various provinces disintegrated the Russian federation that was in place. Russia was also freed from Mongol rule in 1480. Independence being a Uranian concept, the liberation of parts of South America by Simon Bolivar in the 1820s, and the Ottoman loss of the Balkans by the early 20th century, fit the theme.

South Africa's history has been triggered by Uranus and Neptune: Cape Town was founded by Dutch settlers in 1652; the Cape was further settled by substantial numbers of British next time round in 1820; and South Africa met another significant historical marker under the last conjunction in 1990 with a Law Commission paper calling for the abolition of apartheid; this led to the first multiracial elections in 1994 and to Nelson Mandela becoming president, all under the sway of these two planets. Swiss history is also keyed into these influences, with initial independence in 1474 further ratified in 1648.

The British monarchy
The story of the British Isles and its monarchy coincides with key episodes during Uranus–Neptune conjunctions, starting with the collapse into the Dark Ages in 450 as the Romans left and the Saxon invasion overwhelmed the country. Richard III of England, the legendary hunchback of Shakespeare's play, had his two nephews murdered in 1483 to protect his power base, though it did not survive long: Henry VII founded the Tudor Dynasty later that year. On the next conjunction Charles I was beheaded, and Britain became a commonwealth for the first time, with Oliver Cromwell as Lord Protector. The British monarchy was again rocked to its foundations in the late 1980s with a plethora of royal scandals. Queen Elizabeth II's *annus horribilis* was in 1992, another Uranus–Neptune hit: three of her children's marriages ended in separation or divorce, her Windsor Castle home was badly damaged in a fire, and she paid income tax for the first time in her reign. Back in 1139 a previous English civil war had been fought over the succession, and in 1307 with Robert the Bruce crowned King of Scotland, the English invasion north of the border was repelled.

Religion
Uranus forces change, which represents a break with the past, and can be a rebel. Neptune is spiritual, mystical and visionary. Not unexpectedly, these conjunctions are associated with the acceptance of new beliefs and conversions of individuals or nations to a different religion. Most obviously the birth of Islam occurred on the Uranus–Neptune–Saturn triple conjunction in the years after 610 when Mohammed experienced his first vision in which the archangel Gabriel told him he was the messenger of Allah. By 630 he had taken Mecca and established the new faith. Under the next conjunction (791) Buddhism became the state religion of Tibet. Subsequent conjunctions saw Scandinavia Christianized (965); the conversion of the Mongol Empire to Islam (1295); substantial numbers of Chinese converts to Christianity (1306); and the first Dalai Lama of Tibet enthroned (1473). Closer to our time, the Mormon Church was founded after Joe Smith had his vision in 1825; only two years before, John Darby split away from the Church of England to found the Plymouth Brethren closed sect.

Heresy is part of the rebellious Uranus story, but so is fanatical repression: Mani, founder of the Manichean faith, was executed under this conjunction in 276; and the Spanish Inquisition was set up in 1478. During the most recent conjunction, fervent beliefs leading to fanaticism were clear in the Iranian Ayatollah Khomeini's *fatwa* (death threat) against Salman Rushdie, author of *The Satanic Verses*, in 1989. In 1993 and 1994 two extremist cults hit the headlines: the David Koresh fundamentalist cult at Waco in Texas was besieged by the FBI, and deaths ensued; and in Switzerland and Canada there were multiple suicides and murders among Solar Temple cult members who believed they would be reincarnated on Sirius.

Science

Neither Uranus nor Neptune have a reputation for practicality, but both are inspired. Uranus is an original thinker, good with numbers, prone to sudden flashes of intuition. Archimedes, the Greek mathematician, was at his peak during the conjunction of 232 BC, and hit on his major inspirational principle of fluid displacement when immersed in his bath; *'Eureka!'* ('I have found it!'), he famously shouted, running down the street, a truly Uranus–Neptune experience.

Neptune is a dreamer, an explorer of unseen realms, and more instrumental in scientific discovery than is generally thought. Neptune is watery but often associated with infinities of outer space, or science that deals with the unthinkable. Under its influence, the intangibles of electromagnetism were discovered and electricity identified in 1821; and physicist Stephen Hawking's even more fantastic flight into the fundamental secrets of the universe was published in *A Brief History of Time* in 1988. Leonardo da Vinci, hugely prolific in art and invention, designed a parachute in 1480. Pierre de Fermat, the French mathematician whose correspondence with Blaise Pascal established the Probability Theory in 1654 under the Uranus–Neptune conjunction, had just prior to this set the most famous mathematical puzzle of them all—Fermat's Last Theorem. For 350 tantalizing years it lay unsolved until the recent conjunction in 1993, when English mathematician Andrew Wiles finally solved it.

An intriguing parallel also occurs in obstetric medicine with Soranus, a physician from Ephesus, publishing a key work under the conjunction of AD 100, describing methods of contraception and recommending abortion where the safety of the mother was at risk. Nine conjunctions later, in the late 1980s, surgeons operated on a foetus that was removed from the mother's womb and which they later returned to it; then in 1990 a foetus was operated on within the mother's womb.

Uranus–Pluto

70–77 in Aquarius ✦ 182–88 in Gemini ✦ 321–35 in Aquarius and Pisces ✦ 573 –86 in Aquarius and Pisces ✦ 685–98 in Gemini and Cancer ✦ 831–37 in Pisces; 942–50 in Cancer ✦ 1083–96 in Pisces and Aries ✦ 1195–1207 in Cancer and Leo; 1340–48 in Aries ✦ 1453–59 in Leo ✦ 1592–99 in Aries ✦ 1704–17 in Leo and Virgo ✦ 1843–57 in Aries and Taurus ✦ 1962–69 in Virgo

The meeting of Uranus, the sky god, and Pluto, god of the underworld, is a potent combination of disparate energies. The Uranian tendency to disrupt, to set free, to undermine the status quo, to rattle prison bars, and to aim for creative chaos rather than stability is one half of the equation. The other is Pluto, determined to keep control at all costs, to repress, suppress, and maintain power in the hands of the autocrats and dictators. Uranus is an energy of electrifying light, while Pluto's realm is one of darkness. Uranus explodes into life with sudden shocking movements, is honest to a fault, tears down the veils of hypocrisy, shines light on hidden places, insists on full disclosure, and demands that the past be consigned to the dustbin. Pluto, on the other hand, battens down the hatches, thrives on secrecy and subterfuge, wields fear as a weapon against any attempt to undermine its control, and hangs on with grim determination to what has been.

Uranus, the firework, mating with Pluto, the scorpion, understandably creates a build-up of tension which can detonate into revolutions, rebellions, even earthquakes, or can bring established political structures crashing down. Pluto's darkness, hatred and connection to the shadow energies is often projected onto society's scapegoats. The Jewish story, and Black African-American history from slavery to Martin Luther King's civil-rights movement, have strong connections with these conjunctions. The inherent tolerance and humanitarian ideals of Uranus cause a toxic chemical brew when mixed with Pluto's need to annihilate separate identity as a threat to the power base.

Essentially a destabilizing influence, the end result of Uranus–Pluto conjunctions is not always constructive, progressive, or helpful in laying new foundations that will stand the test of time. In the great universal war between stability and creativity, there needs to be a balance. Uranian creativity needs a degree of chaos to flourish, but too much anarchy leads to demolition, not to lasting achievement; Pluto often leads to its own downfall because of its inability to adapt. The transitions of change are impossible to negotiate if total control is demanded at every stage.

Africa and African-Americans
The independence of modern Africa, key events in South Africa, and the African-American civil-rights movement are all interlinked in the Uranus–Pluto conjunction in Virgo running through the mid-1960s. The effects are seen early with heavy fighting in the Congo in 1964; then, over the next four years, came independence from colonial rule for 12 African states, with a unilateral declaration of independence by the white government of Southern Rhodesia in 1965. Major figures in the struggle to ensure black civil rights were assassinated or suppressed, with Nelson Mandela sentenced to life imprisonment in South Africa in 1964 on the day of a solar eclipse; Malcolm X was assassinated in 1965, and Martin Luther King and Senator Robert Kennedy were both assassinated in 1968 (as John Kennedy had been back in 1963). Also in 1963 Martin Luther King delivered his famous 'I have a dream' speech to a peaceful demonstration of 200,000 African-Americans, asking for equal treatment, in the midst of violent protests over desegregation of schools and buses in the United States; major race riots followed the deaths of Malcolm X and King. In 1966, Hendrik Verwoerd, prime minister of a South Africa tightly controlled by apartheid, was stabbed to death.

Under the previous conjunction in the 1840s and 1850s Natal, in eastern South Africa, had become a British colony, and another Anglo-African War broke out, after which the Orange Free State came into existence. In the United States in 1852, Harriet Beecher Stowe published *Uncle Tom's Cabin*. In 1854 there was the so-called 'War for Bleeding Kansas' between free states and pro-slavery elements, as the Missouri Compromise of 1820, which had allowed slavery to remain legal in certain states, was overturned; not all slaves were deemed free, however, until Abraham Lincoln's declaration of 1862, when the

Jupiter–Saturn conjunction was in Virgo (see *Jupiter–Saturn*, page 51).

Go back one more conjunction to 1713, and Britain was taking over the slave trade to South America; go even further back to the one in 1592, and British participation in transatlantic slavery began.

In one of its manifestations, Uranus–Pluto is about the struggle between the forces of total oppression and the will for freedom. Pluto's need to project its hatred and contempt outwards, its need to control that which is different and therefore deemed inferior, is a devastating energy when confronted—as the assassination of virtually all high-profile black civil-rights campaigners makes clear.

Revolutions and rebellions

Uranus–Pluto conjunctions never occur without major outbreaks of violence, revolution and rebellion. Often they are battles against oppression, an explosive attempt to escape from excessive control, though given the unstable nature of the mix, the results are far from predictable. Much of Africa became peacefully independent during the last conjunction in the mid-1960s, but the USSR tightened its grip on control, invading Czechoslovakia when liberal reforms threatened to gain ground in 1968. The Cold War between the United States—self-styled freedom fighters—and the USSR threatened to overheat into a third World War with the Cuban Missile Crisis in 1962, when President Kennedy was on a collision course with the Russians over missile bases in Cuba. America, having scored decisively, then sailed unwisely into the humiliating Vietnam War, a five-year losing battle against Communist forces. The Six Day War in 1967 between Israel and the surrounding Arab states resulted in the Jews occupying the Old City of Jerusalem for the first time since AD 135 (see *Uranus–Pluto: Religion*, page 35). Bitter fighting also broke out between the Greeks and Turks over Cyprus in 1964, resulting in partition. Then the military coup in Greece in 1967 put the colonels in power. Violent clashes flared in Paris between students, striking workers and the police, although the Gaullist government went on to win a sweeping victory. In the same year street demonstrations in Londonderry were an early warning of the Irish troubles to come.

Back in the mid-1850s, the Uranus–Pluto conjunction then (see *Multiple Conjunctions*, page 24), strengthened by the presence of Saturn, saw a plethora of revolts, rebellions and revolutions in Europe. So severe was the situation in 1848 that it became known as the 'year of revolutions', with outbreaks of violence in Sicily, Paris, Venice, Berlin, Milan, Parma, Hungary and Czechoslovakia. Rome declared itself a republic, and the drive to reunify Germany became clear; Louis Napoleon staged a *coup d'état* to found the Second French Empire; and the United States declared war on Mexico. The British were fighting the Sikhs in India and the Kaffir War in South Africa. In China, the internal Taiping Rebellion of 1855, in protest against corruption and high taxation, cost 20 million lives before it was suppressed. The seeds of the workers' revolution were sown with the publication of Karl Marx and Friedrich Engels's *Communist Manifesto*.

Going back another conjunction to the years after 1704, there was a revolution in Russia and there were major wars in Europe, including the long-running, decisive War of the Spanish Succession (1701–14), which was to push back

Spanish imperialism for good. In Britain, Scotland—against great resistance—was drawn into a union with England in 1707; the Old Pretender James Francis Stuart, father to Bonnie Prince Charlie, failed in his attempt to land in Scotland and claim the throne the following year. The Hanoverian monarchy of Britain, which still sits on the throne today, began in 1714. The British were also at war with the French over the North American territories.

On the previous Uranus–Pluto conjunction around 1595, France was at war with Spain and Spain with England. The Spanish Armada—the attempted invasion of England—famously failed. English control of Ireland was threatened in O'Neill's Revolt.

The First Crusade of Christian Europe against the Muslim Middle East began on a Uranus–Pluto conjunction in 1095, with Jerusalem being taken in 1099. The Third and Fourth Crusades were launched on the next conjunction between 1190 and 1204.

Greek history is also keyed into Uranus–Pluto. The Greek Empire was partitioned in 1204, and civil war started in 1341. The Greek Byzantine Empire effectively ended in 1453 with the fall of Constantinople to the Ottomans, having been founded on the Saturn–Uranus–Neptune conjunction of 623 (see *Multiple Conjunctions*, page 23).

Key dates in Britain's internal civil disputes that have entered the national mythology fall under the sway of these violent Uranus–Pluto influences. They include the Saxon invasion of 450, the Danish settlements of 835, the Scottish wars of 1342 and 1715, the Irish revolts of 1593 and 1968, the first War of the Roses for succession to the English throne in 1455, and the founding of the Hanoverian Dynasty in 1714.

Britain's colonial ambitions have also been affected, for good or ill. The Hundred Years' War between France and England started on the Uranus–Pluto conjunction of 1338 and finished on the next one in 1453, with England being driven off the Continent. The attack by the Spanish Armada, intending to invade English soil, failed in 1597. Between 1843 and 1857 Britain was at war with the Sikhs (1845), the Chinese (1856), in South Africa (1850), and in the Crimea against the Russians (1854), with the infamous Battle of Balaclava and the Charge of the Light Brigade. The final conjunction of the 20th century, in the mid-1960s, saw Britain giving up not only the African colonies but also Malta, Barbados and Jamaica, effectively relinquishing her imperial power.

Religion
Certain key dates in Jewish history, and indeed the history of Jerusalem, fall under Uranus–Pluto conjunctions, starting with the Jewish revolt against the Romans in AD 70. The Romans then sacked Jerusalem, destroying the Temple, the ancient centre of Jewish religious life and traditionally the site of Jacob's dream of angels ascending a ladder to heaven. This was the beginning of the Jewish diaspora, or dispersal; the oral laws of Moses were added to the Pentateuch to form the Torah which would bind future Jews together. The winning of the Six Day War by the Israelis under the latest conjunction in 1967 saw the Jews occupy the old city of Jerusalem for the first time since they had been expelled.

In AD 70, the Romans also destroyed the Qu'mran Essene Jewish community.

They left behind the Dead Sea Scrolls, Hebrew and Aramaic texts that were not rediscovered until the Saturn–Pluto conjunction of 1947.

Under another Uranus–Pluto conjunction, the Dome of the Rock in Jerusalem, the great mosque, was built on the Temple Mount in 691 by the Umayyad Caliph to commemorate the Muslim tradition that Mohammed ascended to Paradise from this spot, making it the third most holy place of Islam after Mecca and Medina. Jerusalem was also occupied by the First Crusade in 1099.

There were also two major Jewish massacres under Uranus–Pluto, one sparked by religious differences, the other by anti-semitism. The first took place in the Rhineland in 1095 when Pope Urban II called for a crusade to free the holy places in Jerusalem; the second in 1348 in the wake of the 25 million deaths from the 'Black Death' plague in Europe, for which Jews were blamed.

The most significant event in the establishment of Christian doctrine, the great Church Council of Nicaea, was summoned by the Roman Empero, Constantine in 325 under this influence, in an attempt to maintain unity. It suppressed the Arian heresy which denied the divinity of Christ.

The first of the European military Crusades to recover the holy places of Palestine from Muslim occupation were launched five Uranus–Pluto conjunctions later in 1095. Although Jerusalem was initially taken in 1099, the Crusades failed in their purpose, the West benefited greatly from the culture, mathematical knowledge, esoteric beliefs and trade that were gained from the East. The Fourth Crusade, too, was undertaken on one of these conjunctions in 1204.

The persecution of the Cathars also started under this brutal pairing of planets in 1205. Originally from Bulgaria but settling in Southern France and Italy, the Cathars were a heretical Gnostic sect who were sceptical of much of the Bible, believing that Christ was an angel and that the material world was irredeemably evil but that man's soul was good. Ultimately they were wiped out a century later by the Inquisition.

Natural disasters

Clearly famines, earthquakes and other natural disasters are an ongoing occurrence around the globe, but the disruptive effects of Uranus and Pluto do find their place here. Significant natural disasters have descended without warning under their influence, with the 1960s being marked by a series of devastating earthquakes. During that decade the worst recorded earthquake in Africa killed 12,000 in Agadir, Morocco, and there was a volcanic eruption in Tristan da Cunha. Further earthquakes occurred in Skopje, Chile, Turkey and Iran, killing 12,000 in 1968. In 1966 the Aberfan mine slag-heap disaster killed 116 schoolchildren, and Florence was flooded, ruining art treasures.

Under a previous Uranus–Pluto conjunction, Tokyo was almost destroyed by an earthquake in 1703. Further back in AD 79, the separating Uranus–Pluto conjunction of AD 76 was in a complex relationship to Saturn, Neptune and the Leo New Moon when Vesuvius erupted, engulfing Pompeii and Herculaneum and leaving the inhabitants entombed in lava.

The Black Death of 1348, which killed 25 million in Europe and devastated Asia, occurred around a conjunction then, as did the Plague in London in 1592 which killed 15,000. Around the same period (1594–97) the last great

European famine was caused by harvest failures and high grain prices. This scenario was repeated in Ireland with the Potato Famine in 1846.

Mathematics

In 1202, during the Uranus–Pluto conjunction, the Italian mathematician and indefatigable traveller Leonardo Fibonacci of Pisa had a 'bolt-from-the-blue' inspiration which resulted in what became known as the Fibonacci sequence. This is a sequence of numbers in which each number is the sum of the preceding two— 1, 2, 3, 5, 8, 13, 21, 34, 55, 89, 144 and so on. Recently it has been discovered that this number sequence has startling parallels in the plant kingdom. Most daisies, for instance, have 34, 55 or 89 petals, asters 21, marigolds 13. The biological world appears to be based on a mathematical molecular code which is written into its DNA. What Fibonacci discovered, during this detonating planetary influence hundreds of years before genetics could prove the significance of his discovery, was that there are universal laws of the physical world that have a proven mathematical basis. Thirty-two years earlier when Fibonacci was born, in 1170, there was an exact Uranus–Pluto square; when Uranus moved to cross Pluto in 1202, illuminating the darkness of creation represented by that planet, Fibonacci's genius produced the astonishing answer to one of the mysteries of the universe. In that year he also wrote the earliest Latin account of Arabic (Hindu) mathematics, a decimal system involving the then relatively advanced concept of zero. According to the historians of the period, Indian mathematicians had developed this system in 575, also under a Uranus–Pluto conjunction. Even more astonishing, the history books also point to the year 325 (yet another conjunction) as a key date for the development of Mayan arithmetics, also based on a duodecimal system and also involving the concept of zero. The Mayans were obsessed with the significance of time and its calculation, and were superlative astronomers and astrologers.

Saturn–Neptune

Saturn represents authority, structure, rational thinking, conventional values, material wealth, rules, regulations and discipline. Saturn forces us to face reality, to put order into chaos, to show the finite within the infinite. Associated with Kronos, the god of time (known as Saturn to the Romans), it marks the passage through life and points to the inevitability of death. In mediaeval astrology, depression, melancholy, old age and inflexibility were all attributed to his influence. But Saturn's practical application and sheer meticulous hard work does leave tangible achievements and enduring monuments behind. At one end of the Saturnine spectrum, there is the benefit of law, order and prosperity through self-discipline; at the other stands the Grim Reaper—Death.

The decay and disintegration of time are represented in Kronos's castration of his father Uranus, the inexorable fading of fertility and virility, which moves down onto the next generation of maturing adults. But there is also a destructive envy rooted in Saturn, symbolized by Goya's bloody portrait of the god eating his children to prevent them overtaking him. This is the authority figure who refuses to face his own mortality, represented by the children.

Saturn and Neptune are opposing energies. Saturn cuts down to size, discriminates, criticizes, delays, creates obstacles, and forces a process of refining by

37

tiny stages into solid substance. It has a quality of earth, metal, bone, unbendingness. Neptune, on the other hand, is creative, spiritual, constantly drifting in fantasies, visions and inspirations, and dislikes the gritty edge of reality. When in good balance, Saturn can give shape to Neptune's dreams and make them come true; Neptune's ideals of a better society, with help for the underdog and the suffering, can be made real, and its creativity and spirituality can move towards genuine fulfilment in long-lasting achievements. Self-sacrifice for a greater good is a key element.

Saturn–Neptune conjunctions, which occur three times a century and exert influence for a span of two to three years, are connected with significant events in the fight for a better society in giving workers humane rights and women more power. But Saturn can also exert an authoritarian veto. Religious repression by the State is also part of the Saturn–Neptune story.

Neptune, with its dissolving action, can also insidiously undermine Saturnine structures. Associated at one extreme with paranoia, when rational thinking functions are overwhelmed with psychotic hallucinations, it also points to physical illness when the body's structure starts to disintegrate, and on a wider scale when empires and dynasties crumble and collapse.

Women's rights

Saturn–Neptune has not been traditionally thought of as a feminist influence, but focal points where women came to the fore are clearly marked by this conjunction. Both Queen Elizabeth I and Queen Elizabeth II came to the throne to exert tremendous feminine influence over matters of state on Saturn–Neptune conjunctions—in 1558 in Taurus, and 1953 in Libra. Both of them were enduring monarchs in typical Saturnine fashion, Elizabeth I ruling for 45 years, the present Queen still in place after 50 years. Both Queen Elizabeth II and Queen Victoria, who reigned for 63 years in the 19th century, have Saturn–Neptune squares in their birth charts, a key indicator of self-sacrifice for the sake of duty; and all this in spite of Protestant reformer John Knox's trumpet blast, on Elizabeth I's accession, against the 'monstrous regiment of women'. Knox thundered that promoting 'any woman to bear rule, superiority, dominion or empire above any realm, nation or city' was 'repugnant to nature, contumely to God ... a subversion of good order, of all equity and justice'.

Benazir Bhutto became the first woman prime minister of Pakistan on the conjunction in Capricorn in 1988, though it proved a short-lived triumph. Around the same time, Margaret Thatcher, the first British woman prime minister, handed in her staff of power and resigned.

In Britain the power and emancipation of women was marked in two stages: the Married Women's Property Act of 1882, under the conjunction in Taurus, gave wives for the first time ever the right of separate ownership. Then on the next conjunction in 1917–18 in Leo, Maud Royden became assistant preacher at City Temple in London, thereby becoming the first Englishwoman to have a permanent pulpit in London; factory workers shortened their hair to bobs to allow them to work more efficiently; and women over the age of 30 were given the right to vote. In 1988, on the Saturn–Neptune conjunction in Capricorn, the first woman bishop was appointed in the United States by the Anglican Church, although the Pope during the same period spoke out against women priests.

In art and literature, there are key points of interest in works about or by women. Jane Austen's first novel *Sense and Sensibility* emerged in 1811 under the conjunction in Sagittarius. Next conjunction around, in Aquarius and Pisces in 1847, Charlotte Brontë's *Jane Eyre* and Emily Brontë's *Wuthering Heights* met with public acclaim.

In the previous century, on the conjunction in Virgo in 1773, Oliver Goldsmith's play *She Stoops to Conquer* and Laclos' *Les Liaisons Dangereuses* looked archly at women's behaviour. In 1665 under Saturn–Neptune in Aquarius, Molière produced *The Misanthrope* and *The Dumb Lady*. In similar vein during the last conjunction in 1989 in Capricorn the sculptor Anish Kapoor picked up the mood of the moment with his *Mother as Void* work; and Pedro Almodovar, the Spanish film-maker, produced his cult movie *Women on the Edge of a Nervous Breakdown*.

The repression of women, especially the persecution of witches, also has its place in the Saturn–Neptune panoply. This emerges from the masculine Saturnine fear of the mysterious, less rational feminine in Neptune. It is also the rational mind's paranoid fear of superstition and the supernatural. In 1486 the infamous *Malleus Maleficarum* (the 'Hammer of the Witches'), which encouraged the zeal of witch-hunters, was published under the conjunction in Sagittarius. In 1736, under Saturn–Neptune in Gemini, the English statutes against witchcraft were repealed, and in 1952 during Saturn–Neptune in Libra the Witchcraft Act was finally repealed. During the same period (1953) Arthur Miller's renowned play, *The Crucible*, about the persecution of the Salem witches, reached the stage.

Workers' rights
Workers' rights and the fight for a fairer society are a key aspect of the Saturn–Neptune conjunction, when Neptune's compassion for the victim meets Saturn's ability to organize in a constructive way. If the balance is wrong, however, then Saturn's authoritarian need to exert order and maintain the status quo can completely crush the Neptunian dream.

The English Peasants' Revolt during the Saturn–Neptune conjunction in Aries in 1381, demanding an end to serfdom and greater freedom of labour, was suppressed and its leader, Wat Tyler, beheaded. Two conjunctions later, in Virgo, Irish rebel Jack Cade leading the Kent and Essex peasants' revolt, was also killed. Another two conjunctions further on, in Pisces in 1524, there were extensive peasants' revolts in Germany.

By 1845 with Saturn–Neptune in tolerant Aquarius, Friedrich Engels, fellow founding father of Communism along with Karl Marx, was writing *The Condition of the Working Class in England*. Still under the same influence, the Irish potato-crop failure of the following year drew attention to the plight of the starving and the suffering. By the next conjunction in Taurus in 1881, British prime minister William Gladstone had passed the Irish Land Act to prevent excessively high rents, although the outrages of 1882, when 10,500 Irish farming families were evicted, (see *Multiple Conjunctions*), gave every indication that Saturnine rigidity and greed still held sway. In the United States, the American Federation of Labor was founded in Pittsburgh in 1881.

One conjunction on, in 1917 in Leo, striking Russian workers rose up, and were joined by soldiers to overthrow the last feudal tsardom. Meanwhile in Britain the Labour Party adopted Sydney Webb's *Common Ownership of the Means of Production* in keeping with the spirit of the times. During the same period, the emancipation of women also gained ground as a silver lining to the devastating cloud of the First World War: increasing numbers of women worked in factories and on the land in jobs previously held by men who had been killed or were fighting on the Continent.

During the last Saturn–Neptune conjunction of the 20th century, in Capricorn in 1989, Solidarity, the Polish workers' party, came to power in democratic elections. The fall of the Communist regimes in Eastern Europe freed workers to control their own lives and government. There was also mass rehabilitation of Russian citizens who were victims of Stalin's brutal purges, Stalin himself having succumbed on the Saturn–Neptune conjunction of 1953. Also in 1989, the Tiananmen Square demonstration in China, staged by students and workers, was brutally suppressed, resulting in 2000 deaths. In Britain just a year later there were the violent Poll Tax Riots, the first serious mass revolt against the government in decades.

The history of the slave trade resonates with Saturn–Neptune as well as with Uranus–Pluto (see *Africa and African-Americans*, page 33). In 1415, during the conjunction in Cancer, the Portuguese took their first African possession. In 1702, with Saturn–Neptune in Aries, the Asiento Company was founded to transport African slaves to Spanish America; it was taken over by the British in 1713 under a Uranus–Pluto conjunction. In 1808, with Saturn–Neptune in Sagittarius, the United States prohibited the import of slaves from Africa. Finally, in 1989, apartheid was abolished in South Africa under the Capricorn conjunction.

Religion

Neptune is the spiritual influence while Saturn represents the State, the status quo, authority versus individual freedom, and acts of repression are marked by these conjunctions. In the recent Saturn–Neptune conjunction in Capricorn in 1989, the Ayatollah Khomeini declared a *fatwa*, or death threat, against author Salman Rushdie for blasphemy. Such acts have happened under Saturn–Neptune in all religions throughout time. Starting in AD 89 in Gemini, astrologers and philosophers were expelled from Rome. In 302 in Virgo, Christian churches were destroyed by the four rulers of the Roman Empire, books were burnt and congregations dissolved. In 624, on the triple conjunction in Virgo (see *Multiple Conjunctions*, page 23) the birthplace of Zoroaster was destroyed. In 841 in Capricorn, the Tibetan king tried to suppress Buddhism. In 843 the Greek Church returned to Orthodoxy (a highly Saturnine energy) after the Iconoclast Controversy. In a classic State-versus-Church dispute in England in 1164, in Sagittarius, the Archbishop of Canterbury, Thomas à Becket, defied Henry II, refusing to allow his clergy to be punished in secular courts, for which he was condemned to exile. On the next conjunction in 1200 in Pisces, imperial authority in Italy was given to the Pope, merging Church and State. In 1380 in Aries John Wycliffe's translation of the Bible had him expelled from Oxford. On the next Saturn–Neptune conjunction in 1416 in Cancer, the Kashmiri king destroyed Hindu temples and forced conversion to Islam. At the same time the Council of Constantinople ended the Great Schism of the Papacy.

The struggles of the early Reformation and establishment of the Protestant Church were also marked in 1522 by Saturn–Neptune in Pisces, when Martin Luther, the German religious reformer, was imprisoned after his attack on the Church of Rome. In 1559 in Taurus, John Knox, the Scottish Protestant reformer and protégé of John Calvin, returned to Scotland to campaign against the Church of Rome. In 1594 in Leo, the Calvinist Protestant Huguenots were granted freedom of worship in France.

In 1628 in Scorpio the Pope canonized Ignatius Loyola, founder of the Jesuits; the order was dissolved in 1773 under Saturn–Neptune in Virgo.

In its positive aspect, Saturn creates structure and solidity, so religious building is not uncommon under its influence. The great cathedral of Notre Dame in Paris was planned and begun in 1163 under Saturn–Neptune in Sagittarius; in 1344 in Aquarius, building began on Prague Cathedral. Back in 698 in Aquarius, the Monastery of St Peter's in Salzburg had been founded. In 1450 (in Virgo) the new St Peter's in Rome was financed (another highly Saturnine realm). In 1703 in Aries, the foundations of St Petersburg were laid, and in 1847, in Aquarius and Pisces, the Mormons founded Salt Lake City.

Health and medicine

The dual face of Saturn–Neptune in providing practical care for the suffering and in the insidious undermining of the body's health both find a place in world history.

An epidemic of St Vitus Dance (chorea) broke out in Europe in 1021 when Saturn and Neptune were together in Aquarius; the disease causes involuntary jerky movements and leads to brain deterioration, and was so called because victims prayed to St Vitus, the patron saint of dance. The plague that devastated Europe and Asia during the 1340s was marked by the Saturn–Neptune conjunction in Aquarius of 1344, and the Uranus–Pluto conjunction at the same time (see *Uranus–Pluto*, page 36, and *Multiple Conjunctions*, page 24). The outbreak of bubonic plague in London in 1665 and the Great Fire of London a year later both took place when Saturn and Neptune were together in Capricorn. In 1846 in Aquarius, widespread famine in Ireland followed the failure of the potato crop. During the 1917 and 1918 conjunction in Leo, there were massive casualties in the First World War, especially at Passchendaele, and the Spanish 'flu epidemic of 1918 killed 20 million in Europe, the United States and India. By the conjunction of the late 1980s in Capricorn, the AIDS virus was running amok, causing countless deaths in Africa, Europe and the United States.

Medical advances are also highlighted under Saturn–Neptune, with the physicians' meeting place in Rome, the Schola Medicorum, being set up in AD 17 in Sagittarius; in 1739 in Cancer, the London Foundling Hospital was established; and by 1881 in Taurus, Louis Pasteur had discovered the anthrax vaccine.

Astronomy

Neptune's yearning for outer space is backed by Saturn's practical application in several key astronomical events. It also oversees several notable scientific events in the intangible Neptune realms of magnetism and chemistry.

The National Observatory in Paris was founded during the Saturn–Neptune conjunction in Capricorn in 1667. During the same period, Isaac Newton, physicist, mathematician and alchemist, measured the Moon's orbit. On the next conjunction in 1704, Newton, discoverer of the principle of gravity and inventor of the reflecting telescope, published his *Optics*. Further back, in 877 in Pisces, the great Arabian prince, astrologer and astronomer Al-Battani began his astronomical observations.

41

In more recent times in 1953 in Libra, astronomers discovered a new scale of space outside the solar system; and in 1989 in Capricorn, physicist Stephen Hawking published his *A Brief History of Time*, looking at the dawn of creation.

Collapsing empires

Although certain empires and dynasties were founded under Saturn–Neptune—notably both Queens Elizabeth being crowned (1558, 1953), and King Henry VII founding the Tudor Dynasty in England in 1485, in Sagittarius—the principal theme is of dissolution and disintegration. Neptune undermines the Saturnine status quo. The Boston Tea Party in 1773, with Saturn–Neptune in Virgo, was the beginning of the end for British colonial rule in North America. American radicals, objecting to punishing taxation and high-handed authoritarian measures, dumped imported tea cargoes, which the British were trying to offload from surplus Indian stocks, into Boston harbour. This led to the War of Independence two years later, when America finally freed itself from imperial shackles. The conjunction of 1773 fell on the Virgo eclipse of that year (as did the one preceding the Pearl Harbor bombing of 1941), emphasizing its effect.

In similar vein the Saturn–Neptune conjunction of 1881 in Taurus saw the British defeated in the Boer War, leading to the independence of the Transvaal. Further back, in the fifth century (see *Multiple Conjunctions*, page 22), the crumbling Roman Empire abandoned final claims to the British Isles under the 411 conjunction, again in Taurus; but by the next one, in Leo in 446, Britain was being over-run by Picts, Scots and Saxons, and the Dark Ages were beginning. India also lapsed into the Dark Ages in 625 in Virgo (see *Multiple Conjunctions*, page 23). Even earlier a chaotic period began for the Roman Empire in 233 (Saturn–Neptune in Aries), with 37 emperors in 35 years; in 411 in Taurus Rome was sacked by the Visigoths; and in 553 in Aries Italy was ruined after the Gothic War.

Russian history also keys into Saturn–Neptune, as it does to Uranus–Neptune (see page 30), and Uranus–Pluto (see page 34). The last tsar, Nicholas II, abdicated in 1917 under Saturn–Neptune in Leo and was executed along with his family, ending the Romanov dynasty. In 1989 in Capricorn (see *Multiple Conjunctions*, page 25), the USSR started to fragment.

The legendary King Macbeth of Scotland, immortalized in Shakespeare's play, was defeated at Dunsinane in 1057 under Saturn–Neptune in Taurus, when the wood appeared to move towards the castle as foretold by the witches—a fitting symbol for the paranoia and superstition engendered by the negative aspects of this pairing.

Saturn–Uranus

Occurring approximately every 45 years, this conjunction spans three years or so in influence. Saturn—practical, conservative, upholder of the prevailing tradition, respecter of the past—meets Uranus the liberator, pioneer, innovator, torchbearer for the future, symbolizer of sudden change and creative thought and catalyst for sweeping away outworn structures to make way for new possibilities. In positive vein, this conjunction preserves the best of the old and merges it with the best of the new, but it can be a jolting, jarring transition all the same. Sudden states of tension give way to a release of tension as Saturn's rigidity is forced to give way under Uranus's explosive need to be free. The mood is prone to swing between optimism and pessimism.

This can also be a catastrophe-prone combination, since both planets will, in their negative aspects, lay waste rather than give way. Saturn, the envious patriarch, will destroy rather than hand over power. Uranus will reduce order to anarchy rather than compromise. In their own way both can be highly dictatorial. Saturn the Grim Reaper is often pictured with a curved scythe in hand. Uranus is the thunderbolt, light-giving but earth-shaking.

In cooperation they can promote a golden age of enlightened justice and constructive scientific advance. Uranus, the sky god, was the bringer of civilization and the initiator of culture; Saturn brings prosperity and material wealth through regulated work and good agriculture. But the balance is tricky to get right.

In classical mythology, Saturn the son castrates Uranus his father, throwing his genitals into the sea and cutting off his virility for ever. But he who lives by the sword dies by the sword: as Saturn destroys the generation before him, so will he in the fullness of time and old age be brought low himself. There is an inevitability around Saturn–Uranus conjunctions, more so even than the other cycles, an inevitability that what is raised up high will be brought low, and vice versa. In the words of the *I Ching*, the great Chinese book of wisdom, 'It is the law of heaven to make fullness empty and to make full what is modest.'

In the myth, the castration of Uranus results in the Furies being let loose to devastate the land; paradoxically it also results in Venus-Aphrodite, the goddess of love, arising out of the ocean, perhaps hinting at the dual nature of Saturn–Uranus, which encompasses both terror and great beauty.

The pace is never steady around these conjunctions since Saturn, as Kronos representing time, moves steadily, refusing to be hurried, while computer-speed Uranus demands instant results and firecracker activity.

Social reform
Liberal administration is one of the keynotes of this conjunction, a felicitous merging of Saturn's need for disciplined order and Uranus's fair-minded, humanitarian tolerance. Under an early Saturn–Uranus conjunction in Libra in AD 127, the Roman Emperor Hadrian codified the laws of Athens. Although ruthless and tyrannical, he was an able administrator, intellectual and cultured. He encouraged the arts and architecture, built the Pantheon, founded the Athenaeum, and brought the Roman Empire to its greatest point.

On the next conjunction in 173 in Aries, Marcus Aurelius, the adoptive grandson of Hadrian, wrote his *Meditations*. Forced by circumstance to become a fighting emperor, he was by temperament a philosopher, founding chairs of philosophy in Athens for the four disciplines, Stoic, Platonic, Peripatetic and Epicurean. After his death he was remembered as the ideal emperor. The pendulum swing of Saturn–Uranus, from repressive to enlightened, can be seen transforming the Saracens in 763 in Taurus from military conquerors into liberal administrators when they founded Baghdad.

The *Magna Carta*, the 'Great Charter', of 1215 on the Saturn–Uranus conjunction in Libra, was also a hint of the impetus of this conjunction for progressive change. In 1215 at Runnymede, King John of England sealed this statement of civil rights which laid out the liberties for different classes of citizens, after his disastrous foreign policy and oppressive misuse of sovereign power had caused his barons to rebel. The charter limited the power of the monarch, defined the duties of the population, and confirmed the freedom of the Church. In 1351, with Saturn–Uranus in Taurus, the Statute of Labourers was also laid down in England to regulate wages in the wake of the devastation of the Black Death.

The ideal of the Saturn–Uranus dream of a golden age is beautifully portrayed by the French political philosopher and educationalist Jean-Jacques Rousseau, in *A Treatise on the Social Contract*, which laid out the common good as the basis for social justice. It was written in 1762 under the conjunction in Aries and his slogan, 'Liberty, Equality, Fraternity', became the banner cry of the French Revolution and later progressive movements (alhough as events turned out, the initial inspired idea, once sown, is always harder to root than philosopher-thinkers imagine). In recent times the Saturn–Uranus conjunction in Capricorn in the late 1980s (see *Multiple Conjunctions*, page 25) also contributed to the sudden sweeping away of repressive regimes and an upsurge in democratic ideals; the transitions to a new stability are still ongoing, and have not been smooth.

André Barbault, the French astrologer, points to Saturn–Uranus's significant effect in recent times in the field of economic activity, especially investment in heavy industry. It was most notable in the 'Black Monday' stock market crash of 1987 when Saturn–Uranus was in Sagittarius; worldwide recession followed as the conjunction moved into Capricorn.

The arts
The contribution of Saturn–Uranus to civilization and culture in its 'golden age' aspect is evident in several legendary works of literature, many with sexual or romantic themes. These reflect perhaps the mythical Venus arising from the foam after the clash for supremacy between Saturn and Uranus.

The high point of the Grail legends and Arthurian romances come to a climax in Wolfram von Eschenbach's *Parzival*, written in 1212 under Saturn–Uranus in Virgo, and immortalized in Wagner's opera in the 19th century. In 1850, during the conjunction in Aries, Richard Wagner staged *Lohengrin*, the second of his Ring Cycle operas, based on the Grail legends—of which the story of Parsifal formed the final part.

Another haunting legend of tragic lovers that was to last the course of time and be carried into 20th-century culture by a Wagnerian opera was that of Tristan and Iseult, or Isolde, produced in its earliest forms by the Anglo-Norman poet and troubadour Thomas of Brittany during the Saturn–Uranus conjunction of 1170 in Pisces. In the legend, Tristan dies separated from his beloved Iseult. During the same period Chrétien de Troyes was writing *Le Chevalier au Lion* about the Arthurian legends and the knights of the Round Table.

The melancholy of Saturn, which dooms love to grief, is echoed in later works of art such as Verdi's *La Traviata* (completed in 1853, with Saturn–Uranus in Taurus), in which the heroine Violetta dies having given up her lover for the sake of his family's reputation; hypocrisy is a highly Saturnine quality. Again in Puccini's opera *La Bohème* (1896, with Saturn–Uranus in Scorpio), the abandoned lover Mimi dies of consumption. In the same year Rostand's *Cyrano de Bergerac*, the story of a great unrequited love, was published, as was Thomas Hardy's tragic novel *Jude the Obscure*, dealing with the suffering of love. These enduring truths about the human condition continue to hold our interest as different art forms continually reworking the same themes.

In the fertile 14th century at the start of the Renaissance, when the Saturn–Uranus conjunction appeared three times along with other major planetary influences (see *Multiple Conjunctions*, page 23), there are cultural treasures galore, some of them keyed into this pairing. In 1305 and 1306 in Scorpio, Jean de Meung's 18,000-line addition to the poem *Roman de la Rose* appeared (the earlier part was written *c*. 1240 by Guillaume de Lorris), and Giotto painted his frescoes in the Arena Chapel in Padua. In 1351 in Taurus, Boccaccio's *Decameron* appeared, and Petrarch was writing his *Rime sparse*, a long collection of lyrical writing and love poems. During the final conjunction in 1398 in Sagittarius, in opposition to the Neptune–Pluto conjunction (see *Neptune–Pluto*, page 27), Chaucer was putting the finishing touches to his bawdy epic *The Canterbury Tales*.

Comic sexuality with an underlying serious theme was seen again two centuries later in *Pantagruel*, the most famous work by François Rabelais, the French monk, doctor and writer, produced in 1532 with Saturn–Uranus in Cancer. Rabelais' irreverent mockery and coarse comic satire won him great acclaim and heavy criticism. Here, Saturn's goat-like sexuality, frequently represented by the god Pan, comes to the fore.

Perhaps because of its presence in the air sign Aquarius, a more refined aspect of Saturn–Uranus in 1580 produced Edmund Spenser's *The Shepheard's Calendar*, which heralded the age of Elizabethan poetry, and St John of the Cross's epic poem about spiritual loss, which has become a 20th-century byword for depression, *The Dark Night of the Soul*.

Religion
Religion is not a key concept for either planet, except in Saturn's need to impose a moral order according to the prevailing hierarchy of the day, and Uranus's determination to be free to think as it pleases (though it tends to believe more in humanity than in divinity).

There are significant events at the beginning of the Reformation in England in 1532, with Saturn–Uranus in Cancer, and the breakaway from the mainstream Roman Catholic Church. In 1533 Henry VIII, the Rabelaisian English monarch with a taste for serial wives, was excommunicated, marking the final severance of England from Rome. In the same year Martin Luther, the Protestant reformer, translated the Bible. The Jesuit Order, a fittingly military and educational body, was formed in France. Their rigorous organization and argumentative subtlety (both highly Saturnine qualities) were legendary. Their founder Ignatius Loyola was canonized, and paradoxically the Order dissolved under Saturn–Neptune conjunctions.

The Jewish diaspora and persecution are connected to Uranus–Pluto (see page 35), but two major destructive episodes in the Jewish story do occur under Saturn–Uranus conjunctions. One took place in 1306 when Philip IV expelled Jews from France during Saturn–Uranus in Scorpio (along with Neptune–Jupiter, see *Multiple Conjunctions*, page 23). More significantly and catastrophically this century, when Saturn–Uranus occurred in Taurus (Hitler's sign) in 1942, the Nazis met to discuss the 'final solution to the Jewish question', the genocide of the European Jews. Six death camps were set up: Auschwitz, Bergen-Belsen, Madjanek, Chelmo, Sobibor and Treblinka; in the USSR, half a million Jews were killed by the Germans. The call for a Jewish national home, made under Saturn–Uranus in Scorpio in 1896, was not fulfilled until the Saturn–Pluto conjunction of 1947–48.

Nothing can adequately describe the Holocaust, but the Neptune–Pluto conjunction in Hitler's chart (as with Stalin, Mao Tse Tung and Attila the Hun, see *Neptune–Pluto*, page 26) was obviously a key factor in the delusional megalomania that had such destructively inhumane consequences. But the 1942 Saturn–Uranus conjunction may be a hint of the misuse to which Uranus's scientific knowledge can be put when in the hands of repressive Saturn, which in its highly negative aspects is connected both to death and to Satan.

Empires, countries and rulers

In the constant ebb and flow of history, with empires, dynasties and even countries continually shifting, rising to glory then crumbling into dust, establishing a pattern is not simple. What is clear about Saturn–Uranus conjunctions, in their appearances every 45 years, is that they do coincide with the founding of several enduring countries or federations, such as Scandinavia, Poland, Italy and the Dutch republic. With Saturn's propensity to organize and build long-lasting structures, and Uranus's to innovate, perhaps this is not surprising. The subsequent histories of these countries are littered with key events on later Saturn–Uranus conjunctions.

The kingdom of Italy was established in 492, during the Saturn–Uranus conjunction in Aquarius when Theodoric, King of the Ostrogoths, took over the West Balkans and Sicily after the assassination of the German king, Odoacer, the previous ruler, and his son. During the next conjunction, in Leo in 535, Justinian set out to recover Italy from the Goths. He captured Sicily and Naples, restoring Roman power.

Other key events followed with these planetary pairings. Louis II, King of Italy, was crowned emperor by the Pope in 901, with Saturn–Uranus in Capricorn. Two conjunctions later, in Capricorn, in 992, Venice became independent. In 1805, in Libra, Napoleon Bonaparte, Emperor of France, was crowned King of Italy. By defeating Russo-Austrian forces, he forced Austria to give up its land in Italy. By 1861, on the Saturn–Uranus square, north and south Italy had come together again in a single kingdom. On the next full conjunction in Scorpio in 1896, Italian troops were defeated in the Ethiopian War, causing the government to fall. In 1943, when the Saturn–Uranus conjunction had moved out of Taurus into Gemini, Mussolini surrendered and Italy withdrew from the Second World War.

Denmark, Norway and Sweden all have trigger points in these conjunctions. The early concept of a Scandinavian union was established in 1397 under Saturn–Uranus in Sagittarius when the Swedish, Norwegian and Danish Crowns united under the Danish Crown. Norway itself had unified 500 years earlier in AD 900, during the Saturn–Uranus conjunction in Capricorn, with Harold Fairhair as monarch. In 1034 in Cancer, the death of Cnut (Canute), King of England,

Denmark and Norway, was significant: the Anglo-Scandinavian Empire disintegrated after that. Five centuries later, the death of King Frederick of Denmark in 1533, under Saturn–Uranus in Cancer, led to civil war. In 1625 in Leo, Denmark entered the Thirty Years' War. In 1715 in Virgo, Prussia, Saxony, Hanover, Poland and Denmark formed an alliance; war was declared on Sweden, and Norway was attacked. The date generally used for the foundation of modern Denmark is when the liberal constitution was set in 1849, under Saturn–Uranus in Aries. Olof Palme, the prime minister of Sweden, was assassinated in 1986 as Saturn moved into Sagittarius, approaching the conjunction with Uranus.

Further south, the Dutch republic was founded with the Union of Utrecht in 1579 on a Saturn–Uranus conjunction.

France's evolution into a unified state was a gradual process from the fifth century onwards, but in 1214, on the Saturn–Uranus conjunction in Libra, one of the most important battles of European history—at Bouvine—established France as the chief kingdom of Europe. The French beat the English allies and Germans, shifting the European power balance. Although the defining moment of France's modern history, the revolution of 1792, did not fall on a Saturn–Uranus conjunction, the seeds were sown in Jean-Jacques Rousseau's *The Social Contract*, with its slogan of 'Liberty, Equality, Fraternity', published under the conjunction of 1761.

France's most celebrated rulers took up power or position on these planetary pairings. In 1715 in Virgo, the five-year-old Louis XV (*le Bien-aimé*, or 'well-loved') assumed the throne in France on the death of his great-grandfather. He was a popular monarch but a poor administrator, and is remembered as much for his 'reigning' mistress Madame de Pompadour as for his good works. In post-revolutionary France, Napoleon Bonaparte named himself hereditary emperor in 1804 on the Saturn–Uranus conjunction in Libra, extending his territorial powers from France to Italy, from the Pyrenees to the Dalmatian Coast. At a domestic level, he improved secondary education and restored the Church. On the next conjunction in 1852, after a *coup d'état*, his nephew Louis Napoleon became emperor of France. He was a humane ruler in the style of Saturn–Uranus, regulating the price of bread, encouraging public works to improve the lives of the working classes, remodelling Paris, and organizing international exhibitions.

Two of Russia's legendary rulers also came to power on these conjunctions: Ivan IV (the Terrible) in 1533, and in 1762 Catherine the Great; she became empress when Peter III was assassinated after only six months on the throne. Key dates in the 20th century include the Battle of Stalingrad in 1942, under Saturn–Uranus in Gemini, in which the Germans were forced to surrender to the Red Army; and the conjunctions in the late 1980s in Sagittarius and Capricorn, when the USSR fragmented.

Saturn–Pluto

Tremendous resistance to adversity and a formidable defensiveness come to the fore when these two tough, essentially masculine energies come together. Their appearance in tandem is usually an invitation to a walk on the dark side of life. Saturn, rigidly disciplined, status-driven, melancholy and authoritarian, has no reason to mellow when combined with Pluto's power-hungry need for control. If anything, both planets become more entrenched when their energies are merged. Achievements of substance can occur, but only through slow, patient hard labour and usually a good deal of suffering, too. Stamina counts when they are around; some sacrifice is always demanded.

Liz Greene, the Jungian analyst and astrologer, talks of the obsessiveness, intense frustration and self-destructive quality of Saturn–Pluto contacts—purification through ordeal by fire. At the macrocosmic level of world events, they often coincide with wars, massacres and assassinations, as in 1982 with the Falklands War, in 1947 with the bloody partition of India and Pakistan, and in 1914 with the First World War.

At a mythological level, both planets have a connection with death. Saturn as the Grim Reaper points to the inevitability of disintegration through time, or of the cutting short of a lifespan through misfortune. Pluto, ruler of the underworld, oversees the passage to the next life, through the vale of darkness to rebirth in another realm. Saturn forces his father to face his own mortality by castrating him, but then refuses to face his own, preferring to eat his children rather than hand over the staff of authority when old age comes along. Saturn's great strength in stability and structure is also a weakness when faced with transitions or situations demanding flexibility and compromise. Pluto in a slightly different way is also incapable of giving way gracefully. A world view based solely on power sees only the victorious or the oppressed. There can be no quarter given when compromise is seen as a sign of weakness, a lowering of defences as potentially life-threatening.

Astrologically, Saturn–Pluto also represents the magician, giving the ability to wield occult power at a practical level for good or ill. They do have positive uses in their awesome strength and their ability to withstand extreme pressure and put up with mass misery and suffering. But they do have to be seen as a pairing where good emerges only after times of great endurance. 'The night is darkest just before the dawn' is a saying that could be used to describe their energy. In Egyptian mythology, Nut, the great goddess, opens her legs every morning to allow the Sun to be born and swallows it again every night. Saturn–Pluto resists letting the light in to begin a new day and allowing the cycle of waxing Sun and waning Moon to continue on its endless wheel.

Arts
Saturn–Pluto creativity always walks on the dark side. During the 1947 Saturn–Pluto conjunction in Leo, notable emerging literature included *The Plague* by the pessimistic existentialist writer Albert Camus; *The Diary of Anne Frank* by a young Jewish girl killed during the Holocaust (written during the Saturn–Uranus conjunction of 1942–43); and Tennessee William's dark sexual tragedy *A Streetcar Named Desire*. In the following conjunction in Libra in 1982, Chilean novelist Isabel Allende's riveting but shocking *The House of the Spirits* came out alongside two major works about the Holocaust, Thomas Keneally's *Schindler's Ark* and Primo Levi's *If Not Now, When?* Thomas Mann's novel *Death in Venice* (later made into a film by Luchino Visconti), about an older man's fascination with a young boy in the midst of a deadly epidemic, coincided with the 1913–14 Saturn–Pluto conjunction in Cancer. In 1883 in Taurus, Friedrich Nietzsche's *Thus Spake Zarathustra* emerged as his sanity crumbled. In 1818 in Pisces, Mary

Shelley's *Frankenstein* created a terrifying monster. One conjunction further back in 1787, Wolfgang Amadeus Mozart was writing his masterpiece *Don Giovanni*. This opera combines rampant sexuality with a stark examination of death and the forces beyond the grave; Mozart wrote it when the Saturn–Pluto conjunction was in Aquarius, his own sign perhaps reflecting the composer's fear of his overwhelming father, who died that year. The opera finishes with the reckless Giovanni being pulled inexorably towards death as a result of his failure to accept responsibility. Mozart himself died four years later, aged just 35.

Religion

Freedom of choice is not a Saturn–Pluto concept, so heresies, or beliefs that do not fall in line with the established order, come under pressure during these conjunctions. In 1616 during the conjunction in Taurus, the Italian astronomer and mathematician Galileo was threatened with torture by the Inquisition unless he agreed not to teach the Copernican system, which put the Sun at the centre of the solar system. He recanted to protect himself in 1633, but the sentence passed on him was, staggeringly, formally retracted by the Pope only in 1992 (during the Saturn–Pluto square).

In 1517 in Capricorn, Martin Luther, Protestant reformer and famously outspoken critic of the Church, nailed his thesis denouncing the sale of indulgences to the door of the Wittenberg Palace church, for which he was excommunicated. But his determination was such that by the time of the next conjunction in Aquarius and Pisces in 1551, his Lutheran followers were assured of their freedom to practise their religion.

Assassinations

In the history of the past 2000 years, there is no shortage of assassinations and violent mayhem, but the Saturn–Pluto effect does appear to coincide with particularly epic acts of murder or execution. Most famously in the 20th century, the assassination, on the conjunction in Gemini in 1914, of the Archduke Franz Ferdinand of Austria-Hungary and his wife by Serb students in Sarajevo, triggered the devastating First World War. The beheading of the English king Charles I after the English Civil War took place during the Saturn–Pluto conjunction in Gemini in 1649. The trial of Mary Queen of Scots in 1586, with Saturn–Pluto in Aries, led to her execution a year later. Two other English monarchs met untimely ends during Saturn–Pluto pairings: King Edmund of England was murdered by an outlaw in 944, with the conjunction in Cancer; and King Edward the Martyr was murdered in 978, with Saturn–Pluto in Virgo, probably by servants of his stepbrother, Ethelred II, who succeeded him.

Russian history also resonates to these bleak moments, not surprisingly perhaps since the beginning of the Vanangian Empire of the Ros (the Swedish name for seamen, hence 'Russia') occurred as Saturn and Pluto came together in Aries in 849, when Vikings took Kiev. In 1016 in Sagittarius, St Vladimir I, Great Prince of Russia, died; on taking the throne his son murdered his brothers. During the conjunction in Aries in 1584 that sent Mary Queen of Scots to the scaffold, Ivan the Terrible of Russia killed his son in a fit of rage, and then died himself. In 1881 in Taurus, the tsar was assassinated; his autocratic son Alexander III took over, reversed his father's liberal reforms and adopted repressive policies, persecuting Jews.

49

The Roman Empire is also littered with murderous moments during these tough conjunctions. In AD 10 in Libra, Augustus lost three Roman legions, massacred by the German leader Arminius. In AD 79, on the next conjunction in Aquarius, Vesuvius erupted, burying Pompeii and Herculaneum in molten lava. Two years later in AD 81, under the same influences, Emperor Titus died, succeeded by his brother Domitian, suspected of hastening his end. In 113, with Saturn–Pluto in Aries, Emperor Trajan mounted a campaign of spectacular conquest, reaching the Persian Gulf. In 175, in Gemini, Cassius suppressed a rebellion and declared himself emperor, only to be killed by one of his centurions. In 243 in Virgo, Gordian III was murdered, while campaigning in Persia, by his army commander, who became the first Arab emperor. In 280, in Sagittarius, Emperor Probius was killed by mutinous soldiers, rebelling against his severe discipline.

Nineteenth century to 2001
Events of the three Saturn–Pluto conjunctions in each century are a chilling reflection of their destructive, unyielding, repressive energy. Good can emerge, but only after times of endurance, and usually great suffering. Most recently in 1982, when the conjunction was in Libra, the Falklands War between Britain and Argentina (see Margaret Thatcher in *Astrocartography*) flared up. Israel also invaded the Lebanon; and the Sabra/Chatila refugee-camp massacres aroused international anger and condemnation. At the same time, Solidarity, the Polish workers' organization, demonstrated against martial law, only to have the Soviet authorities tighten their repression.

In 1946–48, with Saturn–Pluto in Leo, the messy partition of India and Pakistan led to massacres and killings; six million people were forced to move state. With the start of the Cold War, the Iron Curtain descended between Russia and Western Europe, a fitting symbol of Saturn–Pluto's utter determination to build defensive barriers. Japanese and German war-crime tribunals were ongoing, bringing to public awareness the extent of the atrocities of the Second World War.

Back in 1914, the conjunction in late Gemini then Cancer began with the assassination, as we have seen, of Archduke Franz Ferdinand, leading to the appalling destruction of the First World War. One conjunction earlier in 1882, Saturn–Pluto in Taurus saw the outrages in rural Ireland when 10,500 families were brutally evicted. Tsar Alexander III was at the same time exerting an iron rule in Russia, forcing Orthodox beliefs on the population, and persecuting dissidents.

Saturn–Pluto's repressive tendencies were also on display in 1819 in Pisces, when freedom of the press was abolished in Germany and universities placed under State supervision in an attempt to check revolutionary and liberal movements. The Peterloo Massacre took place in England at the same time: the militia charged a crowd in Manchester for listening to speeches on parliamentary reform and the repeal of the Corn Laws.

During the recent Saturn in Gemini opposition to Pluto in Sagittarius, the suicide plane attacks on the World Trade Center in New York and the Pentagon on 11 September, 2001 killed 7000 people, triggering America's war on terrorism.

Jupiter–Saturn

Jupiter—expansive, idealistic, high-minded, a soaring energy—is usually described by astrologers in glowingly positive terms. It brightens, keeps optimism high, boosts confidence, smooths rough edges and produces pots of gold at the end of the rainbow. The downside is a tendency to impracticality, or paradoxically to narrow-mindedness when its lofty philosophy moves into self-righteousness. Mythologically connected to Zeus, the supreme deity (who fathered myriad children—many of them illegitimate, to the intense aggravation of his wife, Hera), it is an energy that brings Olympian aspirations. The thunderbolt and the eagle were Zeus's symbols, although Jupiter as ruler of Sagittarius is also connected with Chiron, the centaur, the wise but wounded healer, philosopher, teacher, who helps others but cannot cure himself.

The Jupiter–Saturn mix is an interface of opposites. Idealism versus materialism; high-flying boundless ambition versus melancholy awareness of the inevitable limitations of life; the urge for immortality versus the Grim Reaper at the core of the human condition. The birth of a new messiah for the culture, or an upsurge of optimism, are usually seen as the outcome of Jupiter–Saturn conjunctions, which occur every 20 years and whose influence spans about 12 months. Saturn's ability to give structure and apply self-discipline has the capacity to ground Jupiter's soaring vision, but the balance is difficult to strike. Disappointment can follow the heady new beginnings, as Jupiter's tendency to attempt too much too soon crash-lands. The combination of energies is symbolized by the myth of Icarus, who ignored his father's advice and flew too close to the Sun, which melted his wax wings and caused him to plummet to Earth and die.

Jupiter–Saturn can, then, tell a cautionary tale about the dangers of inflated ambition. This has uncanny resonances in the assassinations or untimely deaths of American presidents and other major figures, such as Princess Diana and John Lennon, and even Queen Victoria's consort Prince Albert, who were raised to mythical status only to be cut short in their prime.

Cultural icons

The Zeitgeist, or spirit of the age, is often carried by personalities whose lives seem marked out in some special way by destiny. Messiahs in their own sphere, they bear the hopes of their era, often reflected in these conjunctions. The most influential pop group of all time, the Beatles, was centred on John Lennon, a Liverpudlian Catholic born in 1940 with Jupiter–Saturn in Taurus; Lennon became the unlikely hero of a generation, with his wit and his songs of peace and protest. The Beatles' debut occurred on the 1960 conjunction in Capricorn, and Lennon's shocking death on the conjunction in Libra in 1980. He was a legend, who died at the age of 40, and whose life was seemingly fated by these paradoxical conjunctions to rise high only to short-circuit.

Similarly, Diana, Princess of Wales was born in 1961 on a waning Jupiter–Saturn conjunction in Capricorn and Aquarius, and was married in 1980 during the exact Jupiter–Saturn conjunction—fittingly in the relationship sign of Libra—in a fairy-tale wedding watched by 700 million TV viewers around the globe. Tragically, high hopes disintegrated through the unhappy and increasingly scandal-prone years that followed, ending in her sudden death in a Paris car crash in 1997 (see *Astrocartography*, page 245 and *Eclipses*, page 248).

The attempted assassination of Pope John Paul II also occurred in 1981 on the Libra conjunction. Queen Victoria's much-loved consort Prince Albert died at the early age of 42 from either typhoid or cancer, sending his widow into seclusion for years. Victoria herself died during the Jupiter–Saturn conjunction in Capricorn in 1901, after a long and successful reign.

American presidents

Jupiter–Saturn has a special relevance to the United States and American history. One of the key dates after the Declaration of 1776, when hostilities with the British came to an end and American independence was formally recognized in 1783, fell during the Saturn–Jupiter conjunction in Capricorn.

More tragically, every American president in the past 200 years who has been inaugurated on a Jupiter–Saturn conjunction has either been assassinated or survived an assassination attempt or else has died while in office; only two, Thomas Jefferson and James Monroe, are exceptions to this rule.

J. F. Kennedy, elected in the hope of a new 'Camelot' in 1960, with Jupiter–Saturn in Capricorn, was dramatically shot in 1963 in Dallas. Ronald Reagan, elected on a ticket to reduce taxes, deregulate the economy and strengthen defences, was a Hollywood-style president, bringing flamboyant promises after Jimmy Carter's lacklustre term of office. Reagan, inaugurated under Jupiter–Saturn in Libra, survived serious injuries sustained in an assassination attempt in 1981.

Franklin D. Roosevelt, the reforming president, was voted in for an unprecedented four terms, the second of which, in 1940, fell during Jupiter–Saturn in Taurus. He created a mood of hope with his uplifting 'fireside chat' style of radio broadcast. He died in office three months after his fourth inauguration in 1945, aged 63.

Warren Harding, elected in 1920 with Jupiter–Saturn in Taurus, an unremarkable compromise candidate, represented a desire for normality after the unsettled years of the First World War. His sudden, early death at the age of 58 in 1923 was attributed to the shock of learning of the imminent exposure of corruption in his Cabinet, on a scale unprecedented in White House history.

William McKinley, voted to a second term of office in 1900 under Jupiter–Saturn in Capricorn, was an expansionist president who added to America's colonial empire and aggressively boosted trade on a global scale. He survived less than a year of his second term, being shot by an anarchist on 19 September and dying eight days later; he was 58 years old.

James Garfield, elected with Jupiter–Saturn in Taurus in 1880, upset his party by insisting on the freedom to make political appointments as he chose, and was shot by a deranged admirer of his critics in the July of his inauguration year, dying two months later from the wounds, aged 50. He was succeeded by Chester Arthur, whose health suffered badly under the strain of office.

Most famously of all Abraham Lincoln, elected for his first term of office on the Jupiter–Saturn conjunction of 1860 in Virgo, promoted national unity and declared an end to slavery. He survived through the years of the Civil War to his second term, but was shot by an actor in April 1865, months after his second inaguration; he was 56.

Elected in 1841 in the run-up to the conjunction in Capricorn, William Henry Harrison campaigned on his military reputation as a log-cabin frontiersman and victor over the Native Americans. He caught pneumonia at his inauguration and died a month later.

Intriguingly Thomas Jefferson, born in 1763 and one of only two presidents to survive a Jupiter–Saturn election, has the conjunction in his birth chart in Leo and Virgo. Roosevelt, who was born in 1882 and who survived through to his fourth term, also has a Saturn–Jupiter conjunction in Taurus in his chart.

George W. Bush, elected on the Jupiter–Saturn conjunction of 2000, faced a dangerous presidency, with the terrorist attacks of 11 September, 2001, setting off a global war against terrorism.

4 THE PAST 100 YEARS

Decade by decade, year by year

The past 100 years, like those before, saw a constant interplay of complex, repeating planetary cycles, similar to—but never exactly the same as—what had occurred before. These planetary positions, conjunctions and aspects coincided with major historical events and with the birth of individuals, all carrying the stamp of their time. This chapter looks decade by decade, and year by year, at what happened during a period that is familiar to us—either as a result of direct experience or through family stories. In each decade we shall look in-depth at the birth charts of three notable personalities, moulded by the mood of the moment of their birth, their family dynamics, and the fated chance of their time of conception.

The 20th century opened on the dying embers of a mystical and enlightening, yet delusional and undermining Neptune–Pluto conjunction, which had held sway over the final two decades of the previous century. As the decline of Christianity was signalled, so was the imminent startling rush of new scientific discoveries, and the way was paved for humankind to achieve the ability to play god, manipulating the powers of the universe and of life itself in the arenas of nuclear physics and medicine. Film, television, sound recordings, the stuff of mass culture were developed; the seeds of the global information revolution were sown. The great dictators of the 20th century were also born under this conjunction—Hitler, Stalin and Mao Tse Tung. The birth of this century held great promise and heralded great dangers in the misuse of power—political, scientific and cultural.

Through the sweep of the 10 decades, with the outer planets constantly interplaying, this century saw two triple conjunctions, always an indicator of times of massive change, upheaval and opportunity. Saturn, Uranus and Neptune came together in the late 1980s, an astronomical alignment not seen since 1306 (in Scorpio), when the European Renaissance started and the Ottoman Empire was founded; and before then in AD 625 (in Virgo), when Islam was born. This recent triple conjunction fell in Capricorn, the sign associated with business enterprise and political institutions. The end of the Cold War, the fall of the Berlin Wall, the disintegration of the USSR, the escalating Balkans crisis, closer European Union and a global economic recession were the immediate results, but the long-term consequences in either a cultural or spiritual revival have yet to be seen. The outcome of the AIDS epidemic, which is killing the youth in Africa at a catastrophic rate, has also yet to be seen in historical perspective.

The triple conjunction of Jupiter, Saturn and Uranus in 1940, a more frequent occurrence, falling this time in power-hungry Taurus, coincided with Hitler's early success in the Second World War in his drive to establish German superiority over Europe and Russia. Jupiter together with Saturn (occurring every 20 years) usually produces a messianic figure, who topples dramatically. Saturn together with Uranus produces jolting changes, with intransigent and dictatorial attitudes.

The First World War started on a brutal Saturn–Pluto conjunction, a not unusual occurrence happening three times a century; on this occasion it was in Cancer, a sign associated with home-based and feminist values. The break-up of traditional values and the family can be traced to this period, which in the West also irrevocably established women's equality with men.

The other notable period was the 1960s, coinciding with the tumultuous, revolutionary violence of the Uranus–Pluto conjunction, seen only once a century. This one in Virgo accompanied the Vietnam War, the African-American civil rights battles in the United States, Mao's Red Revolution in China, and escalating violence in the Middle East between Israel and her neighbours.

More frequent outer conjunctions and planets in square and opposition also have powerful effects. The unsettling Uranus–Neptune opposition of the first decade paralleled a run of earthquakes and natural disasters. The troubled Uranus–Pluto square across the beginning of the 1930s coincided with the Great Depression and the rise of the Third Reich. The highly creative Saturn–Neptune opposition of 1935 and 1936 saw an outpouring of artistic talent. The tough Saturn–Pluto conjunction in Leo from 1946 to 1948 saw the troubled births of Israel, and India and Pakistan, as well as the disclosure to an appalled world of the extent of Nazi and Japanese atrocities in the Second World War. The early 1950s were marked by the humanitarian, reforming Saturn–Neptune conjunction squaring revolutionary Uranus, which saw the birth of the flower-power, hippie generation.

We finished the century with the inspired though ungrounded conjunction of Uranus and Neptune in scientifically minded, communicative Aquarius. The computer Internet revolution was breaking down global boundaries at a frightening rate. Genetic engineering was enabling us to tamper with food production as well as clone farm animals and humans, with unknown long-term results.

If the past is any guide, the major civilization shifts that started in the triple conjunction of the late 1980s will last until the next triple conjunction, falling well into the 22nd century.

PLANETARY POSITIONS FROM 1900

In the sweep of the 20th century, the five outer planets move as usual at varying speeds in relation to the Earth, passing through the signs of the zodiac belt. Pluto, the outermost, wends its way inexorably and slowly through half the signs, starting in Gemini in 1900, and finishing in Sagittarius in 2000. Neptune is only marginally speedier, while Uranus, staying around seven years in each sign, completes the entire cycle every 84 years. Saturn takes two and a half to three years per sign, completing one cycle every 29 years. Jupiter stays approximately a year in each sign. Because the planets go retrograde every few months, their entry into new signs can be a tentative crossing backwards and forwards over the cusp, the crossover between one sign and the next. In Pluto's case this can mean one or two years hovering between different signs. The complex relationship of these five planets in the different signs and in their varying cycles to each other—in conjunction (together), in square (90 degrees) and in opposition (180 degrees)—coincide with events in the world that have a startling resonance with the meanings of the planets and signs, and striking similarities to previous occurrences of those aspects.

Of the five outer planets, the three slower-moving ones—Uranus, Neptune and Pluto—are the key indicators of the great collective shifts and set the general pattern, so their placings are given below.

Uranus in Sagittarius: until December 1904
Uranus in Capricorn: December 1904 to February 1912
Uranus in Aquarius: February 1912 to April 1919
Uranus in Pisces: April 1919 to April 1927
Uranus in Aries: April 1927 to June 1934
Uranus in Taurus: June 1934 to August 1941
Uranus in Gemini: August 1941 to August 1948
Uranus in Cancer: August 1948 to August 1955
Uranus in Leo: August 1955 to November 1961
Uranus in Virgo: November 1961 to September 1968
Uranus in Libra: September 1968 to November 1974
Uranus in Scorpio: November 1974 to February 1981
Uranus in Sagittarius: February 1981 to February 1988
Uranus in Capricorn: February 1988 to April 1995
Uranus in Aquarius: April 1995 to February 2008

Neptune in Gemini: until May 1902
Neptune in Cancer: May 1902 to September 1914
Neptune in Leo: September 1914 to September 1928
Neptune in Virgo: September 1928 to October 1942
Neptune in Libra: October 1942 to December 1955
Neptune in Scorpio: December 1955 to January 1970
Neptune in Sagittarius: January 1970 to January 1984
Neptune in Capricorn: January 1984 to January 1998
Neptune in Aquarius: January 1998 to April 2011

Pluto in Gemini: until September 1912
Pluto in Cancer: September 1912 to August 1938
Pluto in Leo: August 1938 to October 1956
Pluto in Virgo: October 1956 to October 1971
Pluto in Libra: October 1971 to November 1983
Pluto in Scorpio: November 1983 to January 1995
Pluto in Sagittarius: January 1995 to November 2008

1900-1909

The rare occurrence of the mystical, creative, scandal-prone Neptune–Pluto conjunction in Gemini straddles the opening of the decade, having been in place for the previous 10 years. In addition, Uranus across the zodiac in Sagittarius in aspect to Pluto until 1904 adds to the complexity, bringing a turmoil of influences and events. Revolutionary, rebellious Uranus in opposition to power-hungry Pluto, around only once every 100 years or so, gives rise to social disruption and fanatical tendencies, and jolts new inventions and ideas into existence. Saturn across the heavens from Neptune coincides with great artistic achievements, Dionysian madness and general anxiety.

The Uranus–Neptune opposition picks up from 1904 running until 1912, giving rise at its exact aspect between 1906 and 1910 to a plethora of natural disasters, especially earthquakes and fatal, man-made accidents. Uranus in Capricorn is the signifier of changes in business and political structures. Neptune in Cancer throws up sentimental religious beliefs, and an idealistic emotional attachment to family values. The opposition produces a conflict of interests with irrational beliefs leading to polarized arguments.

1900

The year 1900 sees the continuation from 1899 of complex, stressful, high-pressure influences, with the five outer planets grouped in opposing pairs across the zodiac. Neptune and Pluto travelling slowly together for only the fourth time in two millennia—on every occasion in Gemini—coincides with new mystical and artistic ideas, scientific inventions, scandals, and fundamental changes in social attitudes. The revolutionary, disruptive Uranus–Pluto opposition recurs for the first time since the French Revolution in 1792. Saturn in opposition to Neptune, a three-times-a-century polarity of materialism versus spirituality and compassion, focuses—not always positively—on the plight of the disadvantaged.

Confused, frightened, exhilarated, bubbling with inspired but, frankly, mad ideas, this is a melting pot on the brink of a new century. Artists and great thinkers are born; key figures die. Entrepreneurial, optimistic Jupiter in Sagittarius lifts the edge off the bleak harshness of 1899. Fanaticism and extreme political ideas are in vogue.

Events
An intense total solar eclipse close to power-hungry Pluto falls on 28 May, 10 days after the relief of Mafeking in the Second Boer War, started in 1899. The lunar eclipse following on 13 June coincides exactly with the Boxer Uprising in China. One week later the German ambassador in Beijing is assassinated, at the beginning of the siege of the foreign legations by the Chinese nationalist Boxers. Around the November eclipse, British chief-of-staff Lord Kitchener orders the internment in concentration camps of women and children in South Africa, and extends the 'scorched earth' policy destroying Boer farms. Russia occupies Manchuria.

Science and technology
Magnetic tape is invented. The Zeppelin airship's first trial flight takes place. Eastman Kodak launch the Box Brownie camera for one dollar. The Paris 'Metro' underground opens.

Culture
Sigmund Freud publishes *The Interpretation of Dreams*. Claude Monet paints his *Water Lilies*. Auguste Rodin has a major Paris exhibition. Joseph Conrad publishes *Lord Jim*, Anton Chekhov *Uncle Vanya* and L. Frank Baum *The Wonderful Wizard of Oz*. Edward Elgar's *The Dream of Gerontius* and *Finlandia* by Jean Sibelius are written. Charles Rennie Mackintosh designs Glasgow School of Art.

Births
Politician Adlai Stevenson; Earl Mountbatten; film-maker Luis Buñuel; composers Kurt Weill and Aaron Copland; psychoanalyst Erich Fromm; writer Thomas Wolfe; actress/singer Marlene Dietrich; HM Queen Elizabeth, the Queen Mother.

Personalities born in 1900
Contradictory, complex, richly dimensioned and with rather see-saw tendencies, personalities born in 1900 have a gambler's luck and optimism, with successful Jupiter beside inventive Uranus. Controlling Pluto opposing Jupiter provides the will to override social niceties to get their own way. Saturn–Neptune does indicate a paranoid streak but also lends depth to artistic creativity. Personalities born in this year are deeply compassionate, but only sporadically, sometimes in rather self-absorbed ways. Uranus opposing Pluto designates those who are innovators and revolutionaries, able to cope in times of major change and upheaval—which they sometimes provoke; they can also be extremists. Neptune–Pluto hints at a fey streak, a need to space out into dreams, fantasies or mystical beliefs. They may have difficulty keeping a sense of perspective and mental balance. Those born with Saturn in Capricorn between 22 January and 18 July, and again after 19 October, are more practical and well-adapted to emotional or social hardship from childhood.

1901
Explosive Uranus in the middle of its six-year opposition to powerful Pluto continues to see upheavals and revolution, but overall the high-stress influences are gradually easing off after two difficult years. Idealistic Neptune eases into Cancer for 15 years, subtly altering and undermining family relationships and domestic values. Economic pressures and the growth of a more materialistic culture signposted by austere Saturn in Capricorn reward self-reliance at the cost of emotional nurturing. Jupiter also in Capricorn increases the wealth of the rich, preserves the status quo, emphasizes tradition over innovation. The 20-yearly conjunction of these two planets creates sudden expansion and contraction, success after disappointment. In mediaeval astrology it was often connected to a change of rulership. The birth of all the great religious figures—Moses, Buddha, Jesus and Mohammed—is connected to Jupiter–Saturn conjunctions.

As the year progresses, the existing mood of high-level nervous tension recedes with only intermittent disruptions. More common sense, along with capitalism, prevails with the earthy Capricorn planets, Jupiter and Saturn, although Neptune and Pluto together in Gemini continue to support innovative ideas, creative talent and rather mystical thinking. The contradictory swing between opposites fosters both compassion and selfish greed. The Jupiter–Saturn conjunction requires patience and the overcoming of disappointments to establish security.

Events

The Commonwealth of Australia is born. Queen Victoria dies three days after Jupiter joins Saturn in Capricorn, which is also the sign of the British chart (see *The Birth of Nations*, page 239). President McKinley is shot and dies eight days later; his assassin is executed. US military rule is ended in Cuba. In Russia students and workers riot, and martial law is introduced. The management of concentration camps in South Africa by the British is denounced in Parliament. The Boxer Rising formally ends in China. Oil is discovered in Texas. The mass production of cars begins in Detroit. The Pacific Railway Company is founded in the USA. The first petrol-engined motor-bicycle appears in Britain. Instant coffee is invented, and production begins of Gillette safety razors. The first Nobel Prizes are awarded. The modern Pentecostal movement, which encourages the practice of speaking in tongues, is born.

Culture

Woodrow Wilson, later US president, publishes *History of the American People*; Edward Elgar completes his *Pomp and Circumstance* marches. Picasso's 'Blue Period' starts. Edvard Munch paints *Girls on the Bridge*, and Paul Gauguin *The Gold in their Bodies*. Rudyard Kipling's *Kim* appears. Playwright August Strindberg writes *The Dance of Death*, Anton Chekhov writes *The Three Sisters*. Ragtime is popular in the USA but is denounced and banned by the American Federation of Musicians.

Births

English novelist Rosamond Lehmann; Hirohito, emperor of Japan; Achmed Sukarno, President of Indonesia; singer Louis Armstrong; French novelist André Malraux; George Horace Gallup, inventor of Gallup Polls; film-maker Walt Disney; anthropologist Margaret Mead.

Personalities born in 1901

Fey revolutionaries, with a potent mix of Uranus, Neptune and Pluto, personalities born in 1901 are interested in what lies beyond surface realities. They are destined to live through times of social and political upheaval. Programmed for unstable conditions, they do not settle well into security or boring routines, and may hold extreme political and social views. Jupiter aspecting Saturn and Neptune adds creative talents, a depth of spirituality and charitable impulse. Those born with Jupiter (after 19 January) and Saturn in Capricorn, are practical, businesslike, and determined to turn their ideals into solid results, and are better adapted than others at keeping their paranoid anxieties under control. Those born with Neptune in Cancer between 20 July and 26 December have high-minded—and probably unrealistic—expectations of an ideal home and family life, and are psychic, sentimental and religious in an emotional way.

Walt Disney

Born 5 December 1901, 12.35 am Central Standard Time, Chicago, Illinois.
Chart: Sun, Uranus in Sagittarius ◆ Mars, Saturn, Jupiter, Venus in Capricorn ◆ Mercury, Moon's North Node in Scorpio ◆ Moon in Libra ◆ Ascendant in Virgo ◆ Neptune in Cancer ◆ Pluto in Gemini

59

With creative Neptune in equally creative Cancer at his midheaven, Walt Disney was astrologically prepared to be a ruler of the film business. A highly successful animator and cartoon-maker, he was destined to make a career out of his dreams. The creator of Mickey Mouse, Donald Duck and Pluto entertained cinema-goers, young and old, for over 40 years, and his legacy is considerable. A clutch of planets—Mars, Saturn, Jupiter and Venus—in earthy, materialistic Capricorn gave substance to his fantasies, which might otherwise have stayed drifting around in his head. A Sagittarian like Steven Spielberg, he was flamboyant in his ambitions, but idealistic too. Wanting to stamp his mark on society, he became 'the king of family entertainment'. With inventive, technical Uranus close to his Sun, he was designed to be an innovator and a pioneer. The placing of both planets suggests a sharp mind, a ready tongue, an eye for detail and a determination to maintain standards. A fair-minded, rather clean Libra Moon, and a fastidious Virgo ascendant, hints at his need to keep everything rather sweetly sanitized.

A difficult start to life with a Mars–Saturn conjunction in the chart area of his upbringing, squaring the Moon and opposing Neptune, suggests that, like Spielberg and others, he channelled his unhappiness into re-creating an adult fantasy-land full of childish delight. His *Snow White and the Seven Dwarfs*, *Fantasia* and *Bambi* not only entertained generations of children, they fulfilled a strong need within himself for a safe, colourful, happy-ever-after place, in contrast with his early experience. The rather cruel Mars–Saturn aspect was perhaps also what drew him to volunteer as a Red Cross ambulance driver as a 16-year-old, in the last days of the First World War.

The reasons for his early bankruptcy lay in his basic character traits and the pressures of the time. The placing of the Scorpio Moon's North Node in his chart area of personal finances suggests a disinclination to take personal responsibility for money, and the over-optimistic Mars–Jupiter conjunction in Capricorn, opposing Nepturne at his birth, gave him a temperamental urge to expand too fast. When his financial collapse came in the early 1920s, the over-expansive Saturn–Jupiter conjunction in Libra was conjunct to his Moon, and squaring Neptune, Mars and Jupiter in his chart.

He was born under a Jupiter–Saturn conjunction, and, as in the case of others who carry this stamp (see *Princess Diana* in 1961, page 163), seems, for good or ill, to have been strongly affected by the 20-year recurrence of these planets together. However, his early failure resulted in him going off to Hollywood and finding professional success. The first silent Mickey Mouse cartoon, which virtually spawned an entire industry, came when disciplined Saturn crossed his Sun, grounding his visions. He moved quickly into sound, voicing Mickey's high-pitched squeak himself. His career moved in an upward spiral for the next 21 years, culminating in a peak in the years after the war. His sudden death in December 1966 came as the heavyweight, highly stressful Uranus–Pluto conjunction crossed his Virgo ascendant.

1902

The violent effects of the explosive Uranus–Pluto opposition, which adversely affected 1899 to 1901, are mitigated by the more tolerant Jupiter in Aquarius. Less fanatical postures are adopted, extremism is fading. Saturn is midway through its three-year stay in materialistic, workmanlike Capricorn, creating business structures and disciplined procedures with fewer distractions from unrealistic Neptune, now trailing out of orb in the opposition in Cancer. The mood is quieter than for several years, with keen anticipation of peaceful times to come. Fanatical disturbances because of Uranus–Pluto still occur but less frequently as agreements are reached.

There is a growing, albeit temporary, sense that racial, social and religious differences matter less, resulting from Jupiter's year-long stay in Aquarius. Humanitarian ideals are stressed. Jupiter in easy aspect to Uranus brings moments of joy and a release of tension. Jupiter in better aspect to Pluto brings increased confidence, the capacity to resolve troublesome situations without imposing rigid dictatorial control.

Events

The Boer War ends. The Triple Alliance between Germany, Austria and Italy is renewed. King Edward VII and Queen Alexandra of Great Britain are crowned. Coal miners strike in Pennsylvania over demands for higher wages. The Aswan Dam in Egypt is officially opened. In China, an imperial decree abolishes the traditional binding of women's feet. The Pepsi Cola soft-drink brand is founded. Pierre and Marie Curie isolate radium salt. Hormones are discovered. Teddy bears become popular after US President Theodore Roosevelt refuses to shoot a bear cub.

Culture

William James, US psychologist and philosopher, publishes *Varieties of Religious Experience*, while his brother Henry James publishes *The Wings of a Dove*. Rudyard Kipling's *Just So Stories* appear, as do Joseph Conrad's *Heart of Darkness*, Arthur Conan Doyle's *The Hound of the Baskervilles* and André Gide's *The Immoralist*. Paul Cézanne paints *La Dame en Bleu*, Paul Gauguin *Horsemen on the Beach*, Claude Monet *Waterloo Bridge* and Picasso *Woman with a Scarf*. Auguste Rodin sculpts *Romeo and Juliet*. Claude Debussy composes *Pelleas and Melisande* and Edward Elgar 'Land of Hope and Glory'; Gustav Mahler's Symphony No. 5, Sergei Rachmaninov's Piano Concerto No. 2 and Jean Sibelius's Symphony No. 2 also appear. Italian tenor Enrico Caruso makes his first recording, and Scott Joplin's *The Entertainer* is first performed.

Births

Art historian Nikolaus Pevsner; pilot Charles Lindbergh; architect and designer Arne Jacobsen; writer John Steinbeck; composers William Walton and Richard Rodgers; scientific philosopher Karl Popper; poet Stevie Smith; Ayatollah Ruhollah Khomeini.

Personalities born in 1902

Less complex and luckier individuals than those born in the two preceding years, personalities born in 1902 are still revolutionaries at heart. They have strong opinions, inquiring minds and a determination both to provoke and to thrive in times of great change. Those born after 6 February with Jupiter in Aquarius are highly tolerant of differences of class, creed and religions. They mix well and are idealistic about the common aims of humanity. Usually with hard lessons of an austere childhood behind them, they are keen to build up material security, and work exceptionally hard to that end, often sacrificing emotional indulgence. They have little time for frivolity. Those born after 22 May with Neptune in Cancer are sentimental about religion, home and family values, and are rather psychic, though not always realistic.

1903

The heavy influences of 1899–1901 are increasingly scattering and make for a less eventful year, with the Uranus–Pluto opposition the only remaining indicator of disturbance. Jupiter and Neptune are in emotional water signs. Saturn leaves austere, materialistic Capricorn for scientific Aquarius. Pluto in Gemini continues to promote innovative ideas that will stand the test of time. Uranus unsettles old structures and kick-starts, not always peacefully or successfully, new beginnings. It usually coincides with social and political upheavals, and usually as a result of fanatical disagreements. Neptune in Cancer and Jupiter in Pisces bring a sentimental tone and charitable impulses, along with lethargy, confusion and a lack of concentration.

Events

Congo atrocities are revealed. The King and Queen of Serbia are murdered. The grievances of the US coal miners are settled. The United States acquires the Panama Canal. Detroit becomes the motor capital of the world. The first speed limit for cars in Britain is introduced, and the first legal-aid scheme for prisoners. Severe famine affects Russia. Emmeline Pankhurst launches her campaign for female suffrage in Britain. Women's Trade Union League starts in the United States. Orville and Wilbur Wright make the first successful flight of an aeroplane powered by a petrol engine. Electrocardiography is invented. The world's first unbreakable shellac disc is produced. Oscar Hammerstein builds Drury Lane Theatre in New York.

Culture

Helen Keller's *The Story of My Life* is published, as are Henry James's *The Ambassadors* and Jack London's *The Call of the Wild*. George Bernard Shaw writes *Man and Superman*. Philosopher G. E. Moore publishes his *Principia Ethica*. Antonio Gaudi begins work on the upper transept of Sagrada Familia church in Barcelona. Edvard Grieg writes *Moods*, Arnold Schoenberg *Pelleas and Melisande* and Erik Satie *Trois Morceaux*.

Births

Sculptress Barbara Hepworth; child-behaviour expert Dr Benjamin Spock; actor and singer Bing Crosby; writers George Orwell and Evelyn Waugh; British politician Alec Douglas-Home; art historian Kenneth Clark; artists Graham Sutherland, Marc Rothko and John Piper.

Personalities born in 1903

Still the generation stemming from 1899 of the Uranus–Pluto opposition, some individuals born in 1903 display the temperamental streak found in the revolutionary fanatic or stubborn extremist. With Jupiter in tolerant Aquarius until

21 February, however, and then in compassionate Pisces thereafter, all aspecting sentimental Neptune in Cancer, they are also of a kindly disposition, keen to promote good works. Quietly in control, they are lucky, open to new ideas and opportunities. Those born after 21 January with Saturn in Aquarius have inquiring, scientific minds.

Dr Benjamin Spock

Born 2 May 1903, 2 am Eastern Standard Time, New Haven, Connecticut.
Chart: Sun, Mercury in Taurus ♦ Moon, Neptune in Cancer; Venus, Pluto in Gemini ♦ Mars in Virgo ♦ Uranus in Sagittarius ♦ Saturn, ascendant in Aquarius ♦ Jupiter in Pisces ♦ Moon's North Node in Libra

Bing Crosby

Born 2 May 1903, 4 pm Pacific Standard Time, Tacoma, Washington.
Chart: Sun, Mercury in Taurus ♦ Moon, Neptune in Cancer ♦ Venus, Pluto in Gemini ♦ Mars in Virgo ♦ Uranus in Sagittarius ♦ Saturn in Aquarius ♦ Jupiter in Pisces ♦ Moon's North Node in Libra ♦ Ascendant in Aries

Born on the same day, these two considerable figures in 20th-century American life—one a doctor, the other a singer/actor—had an influence that affected people worldwide. Born at slightly different times on different sides of the American continent, these Taureans had the same core energies but focused towards different objectives. Both had a formidable 'grand square' of planets in their chart, a complex mix of squares and oppositions in the mutable signs of Sagittarius, Gemini, Pisces and Virgo, signifying great restlessness, high nervous tension, and a tendency to spread interests over too wide a range. A superficial charm suggested by the Venus–Pluto conjunction, which is sugary-sweet but manipulative in aim, obscured the power drive of the ruthless Mars–Pluto square. Bing Crosby's amiably laid-back, rather mild-mannered screen persona was, after his death, exposed as something of a sham, when stories emerged of gratuitous cruelty towards his children. Pluto preeminently wants to remain in control, and Crosby left his very considerable fortune bound up in trust funds which his children could not touch until they were 65; his youngest son shot himself when he could no longer support his family.

Benjamin Spock, perhaps more wisely, chose to direct his energies through dynamic Mars in health-oriented Virgo into spreading child-care notions through his bestsellers. The Mars–Jupiter opposition squaring onto Pluto which is found in both charts is a dynamically confident, arrogant aspect, making for foolhardy actions and a self-righteous evangelical zeal for promoting one's own cause. Like Venus–Pluto, it tends to be friendly in appearance but self-serving in intention.

Taurus, the birth sign of these two figures, is a highly physical sign, often connected to the voice or music, with an impressive array of talent to its credit— Ella Fitzgerald, Burt Bacharach, Irving Berlin, Fred Astaire, Oscar Hammerstein, for example. Its focus on the body also fosters medical talents: Florence Nightingale and Sigmund Freud share the sign with Benjamin Spock.

In these two personalities the Taurus Sun clearly anchors their rather manic drive for success, giving weight to Pluto's determination to accumulate either great influence or great wealth or both. Bing Crosby accumulated a fortune from radio, records, films and TV, reckoned to be in excess of $300 million. With Saturn in Aquarius squaring the Sun, both men felt failures, a notion instilled by their over-disciplinarian, disapproving fathers. Spock picked up the scientific, inquiring inclination of this placing. Crosby, however, did not use his scientific leaning, but allowed the energy to manifest in its emotionally cold, domineering, rule-setting agenda.

The Uranus–Pluto opposition is quite revolutionary in its aim, producing personalities who either bring new ideas to birth, unsettle the status quo or personally live through times of great turmoil. Spock, the pioneer, stands beside Crosby, the deceptively light popular singer and dysfunctional family man.

1904

Tense, innovative Uranus moving into businesslike Capricorn starts a 10-year opposition to intuitive, unrealistic Neptune. An uneasy see-saw of energies, it splits social attitudes, favours eccentric, deceptive arguments. Sensible Saturn in inquiring Aquarius moves into trine with Pluto, an indicator of tough struggles in the intellectual arena, but here it provides a useful counterbalance.

Peculiar ideas flourish, with overtones of rather maudlin sentimentality and misplaced psychic beliefs. People are forced to choose sides in social and political matters, and usually do so in a highly strung, reactionary fashion. There is a neurotic mood, with escapist tendencies into sex or alcohol, or delusionary day-dreams of happiness. The profound Saturn–Pluto contact adds a sombre but responsible tone, demands endurance, but very slowly forces through major changes.

Events

War breaks out between Russia and Japan, a two-year conflict in which Japan inflicts substantial damage. Two days before September's total solar eclipse falling in Virgo, squared by Pluto in Gemini, the British expedition in Lhasa forces a treaty on Tibet, demanding UK consent to any concession of territory to a foreign power. The Russian fleet fires on British trawlers in the North Sea, sinking one. Theodore Roosevelt is elected US president. The first official speed limit is imposed in the United States. Rolls Royce starts manufacturing cars. The American Tobacco Company is formed. Restrictions on child labour are introduced in the United States. An ultraviolet lamp is made. The photoelectric cell and the tea bag are invented.

Culture

US historian Henry Adams writes *Mont St Michel and Chartres*. Joseph Conrad's *Nostromo*, O. Henry's *Cabbages and Kings*, Henry James's *The Golden Bowl*, Jack London's *The Sea Wolf*, and J. M. Barrie's *Peter Pan* are published. Paul Cézanne paints *Mont Sainte Victoire*, Henri Matisse *Luxe* and Henri Rousseau *The Wedding*. Charles Rennie Mackintosh designs the Willow Tea Rooms, and Frank Lloyd Wright the Larkin Building, New York. Leos Janáček writes his opera *Jenufa*, Gustav Mahler his 'Tragic' Symphony No. 6, and Giacomo Puccini his *Madame Butterfly*. Anton Chekhov writes *The Cherry Orchard*.

Births

Russian choreographer George Balanchine; photographer Cecil Beaton; Soviet premier Alexei Kosygin; Johnny Weissmuller ('Tarzan'); poet Pablo Neruda; musician Count Basie; Chinese communist leader Deng Xiaoping; novelists Graham Greene and Christopher Isherwood; sculptor Isamu Noguchi.

Personalities born in 1904

Uranus-Neptune individuals born in 1904 can be inspired, enlightened or, frankly, deluded. Often creative, especially in music, poetry or the visual arts, they can find it difficult to keep a sense of perspective. They often swing between extreme views. Highly strung, over-sensitive, they can be obstinate in a brittle way. They yearn for what lies beyond surface reality, which can bring an interest in the occult or, paradoxically, new scientific understanding in physics. Their judgements and reactions are often irrational, though not always wrong. With Saturn in Aquarius aspecting Pluto, they have an underlying toughness and stamina, especially in intellectual arguments.

1905

The challenging, disorienting, see-saw influences of 1904 continue with revolutionary Uranus now fully ensconced in traditional Capricorn until 1912, unsettling old business and government power structures. With psychic Neptune in Cancer across the zodiac, there is muddled thinking, high ideals about home and patriotic values but unrealistic hopes. Saturn trine Pluto pushes new scientific ideas into view, but also causes mass suffering. Jupiter in Taurus in gritty contact with the Aquarian Saturn leads to disappointment and failure after short bursts of rapid expansion.

This is a tough, highly strung year with nervy obsessions and a good deal of social unrest. Splitting is a major outcome of Uranus opposing Neptune leading to polarized arguments, with people taking sides often for irrational reasons. Pluto in Gemini continues to promote breakthroughs in technology but it also fosters stubbornly held views with little flexibility. Saturn in Pisces from mid-April to mid-August raises the paranoia level, especially around the March eclipse.

Events

Riots break out in Russia, triggered by the 'Bloody Sunday' massacre of 100 people by Winter Palace guards in St Petersburg. This leads to significant compromises by the Tsar: three days before the March eclipse he promises to undertake religious reforms and call a consultative assembly; and 10 days before the August eclipse he announces the creation of an Imperial parliament. Despite this there is a general strike in Russia, the first 'soviet' (workers' council) is set up, and Moscow workers revolt. There are anti-Jewish pogroms across Russia. More Japanese victories lead to Russia losing two-thirds of the Baltic fleet and territories, including Manchuria. The Russo-Japanese War ends. Japan forcibly makes Korea a protectorate. Norway gains independence from Sweden. Greeks in Crete revolt against the Turks, and there is revolution in Persia. The Trans-Siberian Railway is completed. The Rotary Club is founded in the United States. Albert Einstein publishes his *Special Theory of Relativity*. First cornea transplant takes place.

65

Culture

French artists led by Henri Matisse are dubbed *Les Fauves*, the 'wild beasts'. Paul Cézanne paints *The Great Bathers*, Henri Matisse *Portrait of Madame Matisse, (The Green Line)*, Pablo Picasso *Acrobat and Young Harlequin*, Henri Rousseau *The Hungry Lion* and John Singer Sergeant *The Marlborough Family*. Antonio Gaudi designs the Casa Mila and Casa Batlo in Barcelona, and Frank Lloyd Wright the Unity Temple in Chicago. George Santayana publishes *The Life of Reason* and E. M. Forster *Where Angels Fear to Tread*. August Strindberg writes *Historical Miniatures* and George Bernard Shaw writes *Major Barbara*. In the musical world, Claude Debussy writes *La Mer*, Franz Lehar his *Merry Widow* and Richard Strauss *Salome*. Harry Lauder sings 'I Love a Lassie'.

Births

Composer Michael Tippett; playwright Lillian Hellman; writers Jean-Paul Sartre and Arthur Koestler; actress Greta Garbo; novelist and physicist C. P. Snow; United Nations Secretary-General Dag Hammarskjöld; novelist Anthony Powell; American tycoon Howard Hughes.

Personalities born in 1905

Highly sensitive individuals, personalities born in 1905 have a sentimental attachment to family, country and religious beliefs. They mean well but are often irrational in their thinking, swinging from one extreme standpoint to another, or sticking rigidly to one belief. They can be brittle, and rather fearful of taking on board other points of view, but are also capable of being innovators, keen to move with the times and dispense with what is old and outworn. Often contradictory, they manage to be vulnerable and tough-minded, rather dreamy but very down-to-earth all at the same time. Those born with Saturn in Pisces between 14 April and 18 August have a tendency to be excessive worriers, regretful of past mistakes, and with over-active imaginations. However, they also fight for the underdog in society and the less fortunate. Those born outside those dates have sharp, inquiring, argumentative minds which home in on fundamental truths, although they can be depressive as well.

1906

The unsettled swing continues between innovative Uranus, pushing for business and political change, and intuitive Neptune across the zodiac yearning for otherwordly bliss and emotional contentment. Their divisive effects are heightened as they reach an exact opposition. Stabilizing Saturn, not functioning at its best in timid Pisces, aspects both and tries to provide a balance but often fails as a result of misjudgement, lack of courage and excessive worry. A build-up in the emotional water signs, with Jupiter joining Neptune in Cancer from 31 July, increases sensitivity, making for dramatic mood swings and flamboyant charitable gestures. Pluto in the air sign of Gemini continues to press forward with intellectual investigation.

There is a strong tendency to worry, accompanied by often intangible fears, obsessive thinking, maudlin and misplaced sentimentality. Disagreements, with widely divergent views, continue. Opposing sides hold rigidly to their standpoint with little insight across the gulf. Great kindness is in evidence along with high ambition, but not much steady progress. Everything slips and slides, muddling along with highs and lows of optimism and pessimism.

Events
A colliery disaster in France kills 1800 miners when Uranus reaches its first exact opposition with Neptune. The San Francisco earthquake kills 1000 five weeks later when the aspect is still exact. Later in the year an earthquake in Chile destroys parts of Santiago and 50 other smaller towns four days before the August eclipse. In September a Hong Kong typhoon kills 10,000. Franco becomes dictator in Spain. In France, the verdict against army officer Alfred Dreyfus, convicted of treason, is annulled; he is awarded the Legion of Honour. Women suffragettes lobbying outside Parliament in London are sent to prison. Tsar Nicholas II reaffirms autocratic rule. W. K. Kellogg's Toasted Corn Flake Company launch their new breakfast cereal. Coca-Cola replaces cocaine in its drink with caffeine.

Science and technology
US astronomer Percival Lowell reports seeing 'canals' on Mars from his Lowell Observatory in Arizona (his search for 'Planet X' later led to the discovery of Pluto). The Third Law of Thermodynamics is formulated. The term 'allergy' is first used to describe a medical condition.

Culture
Paul Cézanne paints *The Gardener Valier*, André Derain *Port of London*, Henri Matisse *The Young Sailor II* and Pablo Picasso *Composition: Peasants and Portrait of Gertrude Stein*. Arnold Schoenberg composes his Chamber Symphony No. 1. In France, singer Maurice Chevalier makes his debut. The first volume of John Galsworthy's *Forsyte Saga* is published. Mark Twain publishes *What is Man?* and Maxim Gorky *Enemies*. Paul Valéry writes *Monsieur Teste*. The first-known radio broadcast is made in the United States.

Births
Aristotle Onassis; A. J. P. Taylor; Hugh Gaitskell; Samuel Beckett; John Betjeman; Luchino Visconti; Leonid Brezhnev.

Personalities born in 1906
Contrary, contradictory, highly emotional, often sentimental and kind, but also pushy, domineering and innovative—richly complex individuals characterize the mood of 1906. Creative and imaginative, they are given to psychic hunches, so can be amazingly right and amazingly wrong. Great worriers, they can allow their anxieties to get the better of them. Resentful of past mistakes or hurts, they have a tendency to brood in isolation about what has gone wrong. Those born up to 10 March love the good life, and are indulgent to a fault. Those born between 10 March and 30 July are lighter-hearted, communicative, but can ride roughshod over social niceties to get what they want. Those born with Jupiter in Cancer after 30 July are friendly, generous and dedicated to family stability.

1907

The second year of the exact Uranus–Neptune opposition continues the trend towards high stress, anxiety, polarized swings of opinion and natural disasters. Disruptive Uranus pushes its reforms through the Capricornian arenas of business and government, being distracted at times by Neptune's emotionally based, irrational misjudgements. Saturn, unable to utilize its practical skills to their full potential in vague Pisces, resorts to excessive worry, fretful regret and resentment. Jupiter is in Cancer up to 18 August, promoting kindness, charitable impulses and domestic ideals, then moves into flamboyant, extravagant, colourful Leo. Powerful, argumentative Pluto continues its slow progress through Gemini, forcing academic and intellectual debate and scientific discoveries.

The first eight months of the year are emotionally sensitive, highly strung, rather obsessive, prone to excessive worry and misjudgements. The pull is between the ideal of a happy, protected family life and the need to put new structures in place in the outer world of social institutions, politics and commerce. There is compassion but not enough realism in charitable efforts. The tough Saturn-Pluto square causes mass misery and unyielding circumstances without the drive to overcome problems through hard work; practical solutions are hard to find. Lethargy interferes with common sense and endurance. After 18 August the mood lightens, brightens and becomes more outgoing, and parties are in vogue.

Events

Following the pattern of 1906, Uranus once more in exact opposition to Neptune coincides with an earthquake, this time in Jamaica, which kills 800 people. It occurs on 14 January, the day of the total eclipse in Capricorn, aspected by both planets. The natural disasters and accidents continue with a famine in Russia killing several million, and bubonic plague in India resulting in a death toll of over a million. A serious train accident in California kills 26 people. There are major fires on Coney Island, New York, and the New Zealand parliament buildings are destroyed in Wellington. The Sinn Fein League is formed in Ireland. Japan takes control of Korea. Political upheavals continue in Russia with leading Bolshevik Lenin leaving for the second time. In the United States the stockmarket crashes. In Britain Robert Baden-Powell founds the Boy Scout organization.

Science and technology

Bakelite, the first synthetic plastic, is invented. Physiologist Ivan Pavlov publishes *Conditioned Reflexes*. The first electric washing machine is marketed. Persil, the washing powder, is invented.

Culture

André Derain paints *Blackfriars Bridge* and *The Bathers* and Augustus John paints a portrait of W. B. Yeats. Henri Matisse paints *The Blue Nude* and *Luxe, Calme et Volupte, Memory of Biskra*, Edvard Munch *Amor and Psyche*, Pablo Picasso *Les Demoiselles d'Avignon* and Henri Rousseau *The Snake Charmer*. Constantin Brancusi sculpts *The Kiss*. Construction begins on Charles Rennie Mackintosh's library wing of the Glasgow School of Art. Frederick Delius's opera *A Village Romeo and Juliet* is staged. Gustav Mahler composes his Symphony No. 8

('Symphony of a Thousand'), and Jean Sibelius his Symphony No. 3. Joseph Conrad publishes *The Secret Agent*, E. M. Forster *The Longest Journey*, Maxim Gorky *Mother* and Rainer Maria Rilke *New Poems*. August Strindberg writes *The Dream Play* and J. M. Synge *The Playboy of the Western World*. The film *20,000 Leagues Under the Sea* is shown.

Births

French statesman Pierre Mendès-France; poet W. H. Auden; actors Katherine Hepburn, Laurence Olivier and John Wayne; poet Louis MacNeice; novelist Alberto Moravia; British politician Richard Crossman.

Personalities born in 1907

Emotional, creative, kind and hugely stubborn, personalities born in 1907 are complex individuals with over-active imaginations and a determination to unsettle the status quo. They feel regret over the past and fret over old mistakes, sometimes finding it difficult to live in the present. They can be depressive, often not seeing a way out of unyielding situations. But they can also show a rare understanding of human suffering, and are well constituted to live through a turbulent century of change. Those born before 18 August are family-oriented, compassionate and fond of security. Those born after that date are ostentatious, indulgent and extravagant, and like living life to the full.

1908

The major Uranus-Neptune opposition, occurring only six times in a millennium and still in exact aspect for the third year, continues to coincide with high stress, disasters, confused, polarized disagreements and rather impractical ideas. Experimental Uranus jolts new political and financial ventures into existence, not always wisely, but it refuses to let the status quo remain. In contrast, Neptune in Cancer leans towards idealized home and family values and rather sentimental religious beliefs. Saturn in late Pisces and in restrictive aspect to Pluto initially holds back progressive ideas, fostering discouragement and depression; it also coincides frequently with acts of brutality. Moving into Aries, Saturn then blocks Neptune and Uranus, contributing to a more general contraction and excessive worry. Jupiter in outgoing Leo lifts the mood sporadically until September, before settling into workmanlike Virgo.

Jangled, temperamental, impatient and rather fanatical, the year feels disorienting, very tough, and at times highly confused. Endurance is always a key factor with Saturn-Pluto influences. Jupiter usefully placed towards Pluto in Gemini, however, produces spurts of confidence in scientific thinking and inventions.

Events

King Carlos of Portugal and the Crown Prince are murdered. A school fire in Cleveland, Ohio, kills 180 children. Belgium takes over the Congo. Bulgaria declares independence from Turkey. Austria annexes Bosnia and Herzegovina. An earthquake in Sicily kills 200,000 in December on the exact opposition of Uranus and Neptune, following the pattern of the earthquakes in San Francisco and Jamaica in the previous two years. This one occurred five days after a stressed

Capricorn eclipse, a remarkable rerun of the combination of influences around the Jamaica earthquake of January 1907.

Science and technology
Henry Ford announces the production of the Model T, which sells for $850. Cellophane is patented. The Geiger counter, the electric iron and the paper cup are invented. Helium is liquefied.

Culture
Pierre Bonnard paints *Nude against the Light*, Georges Braque his 'L'Estaques' series (the first fully Cubist landscapes), Marc Chagall *Nu Rouge*, Wassily Kandinsky *Blue Mountain*, Maurice de Vlaminck *The Red Trees*. Maurice Utrillo's White Period begins. Sculptor Jacob Epstein creates his controversial figures for the building of the British Medical Association in London. Béla Bartók writes String Quartet No. 1, Claude Debussy *Golliwog's Cakewalk*, Edward Elgar Symphony No. 1, and Aleksandr Skriabin *Poem of Ectasy*. Arnold Bennett publishes *The Old Wives' Tale*, G. K. Chesterton *The Man Who Was Thursday*, E. M. Forster *A Room With A View*, and Kenneth Grahame *The Wind in the Willows*. The films *Romeo and Juliet*, starring Florence Lawrence, and *Tosca*, starring Sarah Bernhardt, are shown.

Births
Writers Simone de Beauvoir and Ian Fleming; Nelson Rockefeller; US President Lyndon Baines Johnson; comic actor Jacques Tati.

Personalities born in 1908
Contradictory characters, often pioneering in spirit, 1908 personalities have rebellious Uranus in Capricorn looking for excitement, and dreamy, creative Neptune in Cancer looking for artistic, religious or domestic bliss. They find it difficult to decide on their aims. Those born before 20 March, with Saturn not well placed in anxious Pisces grittily aspected by Pluto, feel like outsiders, tending to worry over the past and being passively resentful. They are obsessive, stubborn, and find life a serious business. Those born with Saturn in Aries after 20 March are self-reliant and resourceful, but also defensive and self-absorbed. They often preach what they do not practise, and can be rather contrary. Jupiter in Leo until 13 September encourages an appreciation of the good life, and personalities that are successful, ostentatious and extravagant. People born after that date, with Jupiter in Virgo, are hard workers with a broad overview.

Simone de Beauvoir
Born 9 January 1908, 4 am, Paris, France.
Chart: Sun, Mercury, Uranus in Capricorn ◆ Moon, Mars, Saturn in Pisces ◆ Venus in Aquarius ◆ Pluto in Gemini ◆ Neptune, Moon's North Node in Cancer ◆ Jupiter in Leo ◆ Ascendant in Scorpio

With three planets, including the Sun, in earthy, ambitious Capricorn, Simone de Beauvoir—a curiously masculine figure and the author of highly influential feminist book *The Second Sex*—argued for the liberation of women from their traditional roles. Uranus close to her Sun marked her out as a revolutionary and pioneer, able to pursue her own course, breaking taboos fearlessly and sometimes recklessly. The opposition by both the Sun and Uranus to Neptune in Cancer is highly strung and not always rational. Perhaps because of an unfortunate, repressive childhood, with Mars, Saturn, and the Moon conjunct in resentful Pisces representing a cruel though beloved father, she struggled to break free from conventional bonds. With idealistic Neptune close to the Cancerian Moon's North Node in the chart area of sexual relations, she became for the feminist culture an early, ground-breaking icon fighting for the freedom of women to control their bodies and their sexuality. But with Pluto in the same house, though widely separated, she was destined to remain trapped in a lifelong involvement with an overwhelmingly powerful man, the existentialist writer, Jean-Paul Sartre, who was born in 1905 when the Sun and Pluto were together in Gemini. Ironically she failed always to practise what she preached: she yearned to lose herself in an ecstatic, blissful union but feared the consequences of losing control.

With a well-placed, idealistic Jupiter in the chart area of higher education, she was attracted to philosophy, teaching and writing. In 1929, as a student at the Sorbonne, she met Sartre when Jupiter was starting to move through her chart area of sexuality, opening her up to new depths of intimacy. Uranus then in Aries also attracted her to an open relationship, where challenge and excitement took priority over commitment.

With a close Sun–Venus contact, her relationship chart with Sartre was based on love, but the Mars–Neptune opposition hints at a constant undermining of each other's position, as if there was room only for one ego. The 'false happiness' engendered by the Jupiter–Neptune contact was sufficient to obscure the elements of cruelty and emotional coldness that surfaced throughout their time together. Neither tolerated too much intimacy since he had an Aquarian Moon, and she Venus in Aquarius, placings that suggest a need for space and a wide circle of friends.

When Saturn reached her Virgo midheaven in 1949 at the pinnacle of her chart, she published *The Second Sex*, which marked a peak in her career (Margaret Thatcher reached similar heights as Prime Minister when Saturn reached her midheaven). When Sartre died on 15 April 1980, Neptune at 22 degrees in Sagittarius was opposing her Pluto, pulling her away from the past; Saturn in Virgo was opposing her Mars–Saturn–Moon conjunction in Pisces—planets which represent the disciplinarian masculine—marking a break from a lifetime of never having been fully nurtured. When she died six years later, one day before the anniversary of Sartre's death, Uranus had reached exactly 22 degrees in Sagittarius to free her finally from bondage.

1909

Uranus in Capricorn across the zodiac from Neptune in Cancer continues, for the fourth year running, to maintain an uneasy balance, characterized by extremist views, polarized irrational arguments, natural disasters and confused, worrying situations. Saturn in Aries lends a tougher, materialistic tone, with new ventures being forced into existence through sheer will-power. However, for a second year Saturn is in square aspect to both Neptune and Uranus, causing setbacks and delays so that success comes only after extreme effort. Jupiter in Virgo until 12

October brings hard-working, dutiful and warmer influences. In Libra after that, it leads to a search for fairness, justice and balance. Four of the five outer planets are now in cardinal signs, promoting initiative, entrepreneurial spirit and extreme restlessness.

Still tense, nervy and disorienting, the year bears a sense of anxious anticipation. The old order is gradually altering to give way to a confused future. Old emotional and family values continue to be undermined, but disciplinarian Saturn, poised as a counterbalance to erratic Uranus and unrealistic Neptune, does force through practical solutions.

Events

A Serbo-Austrian war is averted. The great powers accede to Austria's annexation of Bosnia-Herzegovina. Violent snowstorms disrupt the inauguration of US President W. H. Taft. There is alarm in Britain at the growth of the German navy. Earthquakes in Mexico destroy Acapulco. Prince Ito of Japan is murdered by a Korean fanatic. In Illinois, 250 miners are killed in a mine explosion. Civil war breaks out in Honduras. Britain founds the MI5 and MI6 security services. In the United States, the National Association for the Advancement of Colored People is founded. First kibbutz opens in Palestine. Pope Pius beatifies Joan of Arc.

Science and technology

Genetic research begins. DNA is discovered.

Culture

Philosophers Henri Bergson, Benedetto Croce and William James publish, respectively, *Time and Freewill*, *Logic as the Science of Pure Concept* and *The Meaning of Truth*. Georges Braque paints *Violin and Palette*, Wassily Kandinsky *Mountain*, Pablo Picasso his 'Horta de Ebro' landscape series (the first fully defined statements of Analytic Cubism) and Henri Rousseau *Flowers in a Vase*. Architect Edward Lutyens starts St Jude's Church, Hampstead, London, and Frank Lloyd Wright designs Robie House, Chicago. Gustav Mahler writes Symphony No. 9, *Das Lied von der Erde*, Richard Strauss his opera *Elektra*, and Ralph Vaughan Williams *Fantasia on a Theme of Paganini*. Russian impresario Sergei Diaghilev presents a season of Russian opera and ballet in Paris, from which the Ballets Russes develops. André Gide publishes *Strait is the Gate*, Gertrude Stein *Three Lives*, Rabindranath Tagore *Gitanjali*, H. G. Wells *Tono-Bungay*, D. H. Lawrence *A Collier's Friday Night* and Maurice Maeterlinck *The Blue Bird*.

Births

US politicians Barry Goldwater and Dean Rusk; film director Joseph Losey; art historian E. H. Gombrich; bandleader Benny Goodman; philosopher Isaiah Berlin; Ghanaian president Kwame Nkrumah; painter Francis Bacon.

Personalities born in 1909

Tough-minded but contradictory, 1909 personalities swing from one extreme to another, forcing through major changes while at the same time clinging to sentimental notions of the past. With Saturn in Aries, they are forced through hardship to rely on their own will-power and inner strength, so tend to assume that others should be equally strong. With Saturn in square to Uranus, they do not follow their own advice; with Saturn in square to Neptune, they have a tendency to worry excessively, although they have deeply creative imaginations. Those born with Jupiter in Virgo are hard-working, lucky and wish to be of service, but are bad delegators. Those born after 12 October, with Jupiter in Libra, are fair-minded, active, energetic, but unable to sit still, constantly flying around in circles like windmills in a storm.

1910–1919

The main signatures of this decade are Pluto's move into Cancer starting in 1912, marking a time of economic struggle and bringing major transformations in the areas associated with Cancer, such as food production, as well as emotional and family values and women's rights. In opposition to Capricorn, the sign of government, it also promotes—at times destructively—new forms of political control in the rise of communism and fascism. Pluto always involves a destruction of the old before a rebirth. The war-mongering connection to Saturn comes exactly in 1914 at the start of the First World War, and remains until 1916, inflicting misery on the masses.

The catastrophe-ridden Uranus–Neptune opposition, a feature of almost 20 years since the turn of the century and a harbinger of man-made and natural disasters, slides in and out of exact aspect. The 1917 Saturn–Neptune conjunction in Leo promotes worker revolts and uprisings, most noticeably in the Russian Revolution. The Great War reaches its conclusion on the eclipse cycle that also sees the ceasefire in Vietnam years later in 1973. The decade finishes with Uranus revolutionizing art and tearing up the past in Pisces, aspecting Pluto with revolutionary intent.

1910

The continuing exact aspect of the enlightening, confusing Uranus opposition to Neptune, which has held sway since 1904, sees only sporadic disruptions and disasters. The political and business changes forced through in jolting steps over the past years are now becoming accepted, although the high tension continues. Saturn in Aries until May puts the emphasis on self-reliance and individual will-power, and makes for tough conditions. The early months, with four of the five outer planets in cardinal signs, see initiative being rewarded, but there is also a 'windmill-in-a-storm' effect of revolving crisis. Saturn in square aspect still to Uranus and Neptune makes for worry, slow progress and disappointment. Jupiter in Libra until 12 November fosters fairness in justice. After that, in Scorpio, it reaches for financial gain. Halley's Comet returns on 19 May.

The mood is jangled, edgy and rather exhausted after several stressful years, and there is anxiety about an uncertain future. There is also a sense of finality as both Uranus and Pluto near the end of their stay in different signs. The early months witness a restlessness with no real stability, and Saturn moving into Taurus after 18 May hints at a need for austerity and cutbacks, bringing self-discipline and economic tightening.

Events

Boutros Boutros-Ghali, Egyptian premier, is assassinated. An Albanian revolt is suppressed. Louis Botha founds South African Party. In London, King Edward VII dies on 6 May after a brief illness, three days before the total solar eclipse in Taurus. On 11 May, 132 miners in England are presumed killed in an explosion; their bodies are walled in to cut off the fire. Robert Baden-Powell founds the Girl Guides organization. Japan takes over Korea. Portugal is declared a republic, after revolution. US steel magnate Andrew Carnegie founds Endowment for International Peace.

Science and technology

The fluorescent tube is invented. Marie and Pierre Curie isolate radium. Sickle-cell anaemia is discovered.

Culture

Georges Braque paints *Violin and Pitcher*, Henri Matisse *La Danse II* and Henri Rousseau *The Dream*; Pablo Picasso produces portraits of Ambrose Vollard and D. H. Kahnweiler. Wassily Kandinsky produces his first abstract painting. Alban Berg composes *String Quartet*, Gabriel Fauré his song cycle *Le Chanson d'Eve*, Giacomo Puccini his opera *The Golden Girl of the West*, Aleksandr Skriabin his symphonic poem *Prometheus*, and Ralph Vaughan Williams his Symphony No. 1, 'A Sea Symphony'. There is a tango dance craze. John Sousa and his band tour the world. Albert Schweitzer publishes *The Quest of the Historical Jesus*, Evelyn Underhill *Mysticism* and Bertrand Russell and A. N. Whitehead their *Principia Mathematica*. Arnold Bennett publishes *Clayhanger*, E. M. Forster *Howards End*, H. G. Wells *The History of Mr Polly* and John Galsworthy *Justice*.

Births

Japanese film-maker Akira Kurosawa; English biochemist Dorothy Hodgkin; French playwright Jean Anouilh; Mother Teresa; English philosopher A. J. Ayer.

Personalities born in 1910

Hard-working, very resourceful, will-driven and rather materialistic, typical 1910 personalities are interested in a fairer society but need to protect their own security. As it usually does, Saturn in Aries up to 18 May produces people whose early beginnings are tough, with emotional or financial deprivation, but who are able to stand on their own two feet. Still part of the Uranus-Neptune opposition generation, however, they can be contradictory, upsetting the status quo yet wanting religious or family peace. They tend to veer, often irrationally, from one extreme standpoint to another. Deeply creative, they have strong imaginations which can cause excessive worry. Those born between 18 May and 14 December with Saturn in Taurus are careful with money and stubbornly practical. Those born after 12 November with Jupiter in Scorpio are good with money and inspire confidence.

Mother Teresa
Born 26 August 1910, Skopje, Yugoslavia; birth time unknown.
Chart: Sun, Mars, Mercury in Virgo ◆ Moon, Saturn, Moon's North Node in Taurus ◆ Jupiter in Libra ◆ Uranus in Capricorn ◆ Neptune in Cancer; Venus in Leo

A dynamic pairing of the Sun and Mars in earthy Virgo, the feminine sign of service, were the driving force behind Mother Teresa's lifelong desire to help the destitute and dying, which earned her worldwide respect and a Nobel Prize. Virgo is typified as being fastidious and hygiene-conscious, yet Mother Teresa heroically overcame her natural inclinations to nurse those suffering the most appalling poverty and disease. Mars in Virgo made her a rigid perfectionist about detail, a stickler for her own methods of work, and sharply critical of those who failed to come up to her standards or who were unwilling to give total dedication in the orphanages and refuges she set up in India. Virgo is also par excellence a communicator, so she was able to spread the word about her work to bring in much-needed funds.

A tough-minded Saturn–Moon conjunction in practical Taurus gave her the stamina and stubbornness to realize her vision, and perhaps gave her the capacity to cope with the appalling conditions of dirt and physical decay in which she worked. Mars also squared Pluto in her chart, which can indicate that she had a ruthlessness about getting her own way as well as an ability to tolerate the darkness of human existence at its absolute depths.

Mother Teresa's birth (as Agnes Bojaxhiu) coincided with the almost exact oppositon between Uranus and Neptune. Connected to religious and artistic inspiration, the influence of these planets was strongly in evidence when Giotto painted the Padua frescoes in 1305, Michelangelo painted the Sistine Chapel ceiling in 1485 (see Uranus–Neptune, page 29), and William Blake illustrated *The Book of Job* in 1820. In her chart they square onto Jupiter in Libra, giving her the impetus for an intense search for meaning and a greater vision. An emphasized Jupiter suggests an exceptional teacher, spiritual guide and spokesperson for a personal, social and philanthropic vision. It is the keystone of her chart, and resonant at every station in her life where significant events happened. When she founded her Missionaries of Charity in 1950, spiritual Neptune in Libra was transiting this charitable Jupiter, beginning a process that was ultimately to see 50 orphanages set up. In 1971, when Mother Teresa was awarded the Pope John XXIII Peace Prize, pioneering Uranus was in Libra crossing the same pivotal point. Then, in 1979, when she was given the Nobel Prize for Peace, powerfully influential Pluto was in Libra, again sparking off Jupiter.

Mother Teresa died on 5 September 1997, 10 days after her eighty-seventh birthday and only six days after the death of one of her most ardent admirers, Princess Diana. Both had Mars in Virgo catastrophically afflicted by the difficult 1 September eclipse (see *Princess Diana*, page 163). Saturn then in Aries was also opposing the shining light of Mother Teresa's philanthropic Jupiter in Libra, bringing to a final close the amazing cycle of her tremendously influential life.

1911

Inspired, electrifying Uranus in businesslike Capricorn is finally separating after six years from the exact opposition to sentimental Neptune in emotional Cancer, although its disruptive effect is still obvious. Saturn in earthy, materialistic Taurus after 21 January trims off extravagances and hints at economic recession and cutbacks. In positive aspect to Uranus, it puts changes in place slowly, merging the best of the old with the new. Jupiter in cash-hungry Scorpio pushing overfast for gains, and in opposition to restrictive Saturn, leads to disappointments, or success only through hard effort. Failures are obvious. After 10 December Jupiter in optimistic Sagittarius lifts morale.

There is still a see-saw mood with irrational fears, polarized arguments and rather rigidly held positions. The highly strung brittleness is tiring, leading to nervous exhaustion. Jupiter provides moments of high spirits and sudden outbreaks of joy as it aspects Uranus, and promotes charitable impulses when connected to Neptune. Entrepreneurial Jupiter in Sagittarius after 10 December kick-starts new ventures.

Events

Carnegie Trust Company, New York, closed by bank authorities. Birkbeck Bank in London crashes. The coronation of George V takes place in Westminster Abbey. A commercial treaty is signed between the United States and Japan. In Germany, the Reichstag votes to increase the standing army by 515,000 troops. International crisis breaks out as a German gunboat arrives in Morocco. Transport and miners' strikes take place in Britain. The Russian Prime Minister is assassinated. Italy declares war on Turkey and bombards the Tripoli coast. Revolution breaks out in China and a Chinese Republic is declared four days after the October Libra eclipse. There are Suffragette riots in London. Norwegian explorer Roald Amundsen reaches the South Pole. The *Mona Lisa* is stolen from the Louvre.

Science and technology

Cosmic radiation is discovered. The term 'schizophrenia' is first used.

Culture

Wassily Kandinsky and Franz Marc found the *Blaue Reiter* ('Blue Rider') group of artists. Georges Braque paints *The Portuguese*, pioneering the use of stencilled letters. Marc Chagall starts his *Homage to Apollinaire*. Juan Gris paints *Man in a Café*, Henri Matisse *The Red Studio*, and Pablo Picasso *The Accordionist*. Sculptor Jacob Epstein creates the tomb of Oscar Wilde in Paris, and Amedeo Modigliani sculpts *Head*. Edward Elgar writes his Symphony No. 2, Maurice Ravel his opera *L'Heure Espagnole*, Arnold Schoenberg *Gurrelieder*, Jean Sibelius his Symphony No. 4, Richard Strauss the opera *Der Rosenkavalier* and Igor Stravinsky the music for the ballet *Petrushka*. In the world of literature, the first volume of Rupert Brooke's poems is published. Also out are G. K. Chesterton's *The Innocence of Father Brown*, Ivy Compton-Burnett's *Dolores*, Joseph Conrad's *Under Western Eyes*, D. H. Lawrence's *The White Peacock*, John Masefield's *The Everlasting Mercy*, Ezra Pound's *Canzoni*, Saki's *The Chronicle of Clovis*, Rainer Maria Rilke's *Duino Elegies* and H. G. Wells's *The New Machiavelli*. The films *Anna Karenina*, *La Dame aux Camélias* and *Pinocchio* are released.

Births

Opera singer Jussi Björling; US president Ronald Reagan; French president Georges Pompidou; media theorist Marshall McLuhan; economist E. F. Schumacher.

Personalities born in 1911

Creative, imaginative, inspired and innovative, individuals born in 1911 would have strong, though not always well-thought-out, opinions. Experimental in business, they press through changes, though emotionally they are sentimentally attached to the past and to strong family values. Those born after 21 January with Saturn in Taurus are careful, if not tight, with money, and quite materialistic—savers, not spenders. With Jupiter in Scorpio until 10 December, they would be resourceful about money, generally lucky, and good at inspiring confidence and eliciting confidential information. The opposition to Saturn makes them erratic where money is concerned, profligate and stingy at different times. Those born after 10 December, with Jupiter in Sagittarius, are risk-takers—confident, rather colourful characters. Pluto in Gemini all year makes for bright, inquiring, argumentative thinkers.

1912

Three outer planets changing sign makes for a year of transition, some anxiety, and major gear shifts. Uranus finally moves out of Capricorn into the sign of its rulership, Aquarius, on its 84-year cycle (returning in 1996) and away from its accident-prone opposition to Neptune, although this influence brings one last, catastrophic event in the sinking of the *Titanic*.

Neptune resident in Cancer until 1915 continues to foster an emotional attachment to family ideals and religious conservatism. Austere Saturn in Taurus until 8 July and after 8 November tightens the financial grip, but aspecting Uranus pushes through practical reforms. Jupiter in optimistic Sagittarius all year adds a note of luck and confidence; opposing Pluto it emphasizes power. Pluto, slipping into Cancer for six weeks only from mid-September, hints at major emotional changes to come over the next decade.

The mood changes with innovation switching away from business into consciousness-raising ideas. It is challenging, livelier, forward-looking and more focused. There is less irrational swinging between extremes than formerly, as the highly strung brittleness of previous years recedes. Intellectually, debate is springing up and new ideas are bandied around.

Events

New Mexico becomes the forty-seventh state of the United States. Tibet is declared a Chinese republic. The British liner *Titanic* sinks with the loss of 1513 lives, two days before the Aries solar eclipse squared by watery Neptune. An uncanny repetition of this combination of influences occurs in 1987 when the *Herald of Free Enterprise* ferry sinks at Zeebrugge in Belgium, with 187 lives lost, in the same month as an Aries solar eclipse undermined by Neptune. The British parliament rejects the women's franchise bill. There is revolution in Santo Domingo, and hostilities in the Balkans when Turkey declares war on Bulgaria and Serbia. Theodore Roosevelt, US presidential candidate, is wounded by fanatical gunmen. Woodrow Wilson wins US presidential election. There is a run on savings banks in Central and Eastern Europe. The Russian newspaper *Pravda* is founded.

Science and technology

The first parachute jump from a moving aircraft is made. The first sea-plane is built. Stainless steel is invented. X-ray crystallography is used for the first time. The first International Eugenics Conference is held.

Culture

Developments in psychoanalytical theory see the publication of C. G. Jung's *The Psychology of the Unconscious* and Alfred Adler's *The Neurotic Constitution*, while in philosopy G. E. Moore offers *Ethics* and Bertrand Russell *The Problems of Philosophy*. Georges Braque creates his first paper collage, *Fruit Dish and Glass*. Giorgio de Chirico paints *Melancholy, Place d'Italie*, Marcel Duchamp *Nude Descending a Staircase II*, Juan Gris *Homage to Picasso* and Pablo Picasso *Still Life with Chair Caning*, his first collage. Composer Alban Berg writes *Five Altenberg Songs*, Frederick Delius *On Hearing the First Cuckoo in Spring*, Arnold Schoenberg *Pierrot Lunaire*, and Maurice Ravel composes the music for his ballet *Daphnis and Chloë*. The London revue *Hullo Ragtime* encourages the craze for ragtime songs. Jack Judge and Harry Williams give the world 'It's a Long Way to Tipperary.' Max Beerbohm publishes *A Christmas Garland*, Compton Mackenzie *Carnival*, Saki *The Unbearable Bassington*, Arnold Bennett *Milestones* and W. B. Yeats *The Hour Glass*.

Births

Writers Tennessee Williams and Patrick White; British politician James Callaghan; American economist Milton Friedman; Hitler's lover Eva Braun.

Personalities born in 1912

More thinkers than the feelers of the previous years, personalities born in 1912 are open to new ideas and, with Jupiter in Sagittarius, are often pushy about their own beliefs. They are attracted to travel and interested in foreign cultures. Those born between 31 January and 5 September, and after 12 November with Uranus in Aquarius, are pioneers, experimental in some way, or determined to change the status quo in the fields of business and social structures. Saturn in Taurus up to 8 July and after 30 November fosters financial skill, along with caution about spending. Saturn in Gemini between those dates has a less materialistic, more scientific influence. Neptune in Cancer produces emotional attachments to family, and religious beliefs. Pluto in Cancer between 12 September and 20 October hints that there are major changes ahead in family structure, and strong nationalist sentiments. Otherwise Pluto in Gemini encourages inventiveness and argumentativeness.

Eva Braun

Born 6 February 1912, 12.30 am Central European Time, Munich, Germany.
Chart: Sun, Uranus in Aquarius ◆ Mercury, Venus in Capricorn ◆ Moon in Virgo ◆ Jupiter in Sagittarius ◆ Saturn in Taurus ◆ Moon's North Node in Aries ◆ Mars, Pluto in Gemini ◆ Neptune in Cancer; ascendant in Scorpio

A one-time model who became Adolf Hitler's mistress and then his wife the day before both committed suicide, Eva Braun had an understandably disturbed chart.

Extravagantly fond of money, with flamboyant Jupiter in Sagittarius in her financial house, she was dependent first on her father, then on older men friends. With Venus, Mercury and Uranus close together at the time of her birth, she could be gregarious, but an Aquarian Sun placed on the lowest point of her chart indicates that a life away from the public eye, in a grand home that would be the envy of all, was really what she sought. Mars in early Gemini and Pluto, widely separated from it, in the same sign—often a combination that produces criminal tendencies—both share the chart area of sexuality, death, power and joint finances. This is a quite psychotic placing, which means that Braun would have been attracted to danger, black magic and rather perverse sexual behaviour, but with little emotional intimacy. Mercury, which rules the mental processes, close to disruptive Uranus which was opposed to vague, delusional Neptune would lead her to make irrational judgements and have confused thinking.

Her relationship chart with Hitler suggests a common bond of affection and—from her perspective—a lively sense of financial advantage, intermixed with anger and even violence on occasion, as well as a staggeringly unhealthy amount of dominance, deception and destructive interplay between them. Hitler himself was a surprisingly dependent personality, needing the support of partners to function, as well as being driven by deep-seated pathological impulses. It is a moot point which of them was the more psychologically unbalanced.

She was a detached Aquarian with Saturn in Taurus, which is both withholding and low in self-esteem. He was a power-hungry, controlled Taurus with Saturn in Leo, giving him an urgent need for personal recognition. He also had the mesmerizing but delusional Neptune–Pluto conjunction deeply rooted in his chart, attracting him to occult practices, and to their misuse. This combination of planets finds its symbolism in Nietzsche's *Beyond Good and Evil*, published three years before Hitler's birth, and indeed in Nietzsche's own retreat from sanity in the latter part of his life. It is also connected with sexual and other scandals (see Neptune-Pluto, page 27).

When Adolf Hitler and Eva Braun committed suicide in April 1945, Uranus in Gemini was transiting the chart area of death and transformation for both of them. Like J. F. Kennedy, Eva Braun had Mars in this house at birth, hinting at the possibility of a violent end to life. Uranus was opposing Jupiter, bringing to an end her financial ambitions. Hitler, in addition, had Pluto moving across his midheaven towards Saturn, suggesting the destruction of his ambition and the imminent collapse of his power base.

1913

Saturn moving sign at the end of March and heading for the Pluto contact over the following three years, in Gemini, then Cancer, is always a harbinger of tough times; its character is rather dark and unyielding, and frequently a sign of war or mass misery. The influences are still in flux, criss-crossing into new signs and reversing backwards, so changes are unstable. Uranus in Aquarius is lively, challenging and inventive, and plays with inspirational, rather revolutionary ideas. Pluto in Cancer between 10 July and 29 December points ahead to economic hard times, and major changes in food production and domestic values over the next decade. Neptune trails to the end of Cancer, holding fast to old, sentimental religious and family values. Jupiter in Capricorn from 3 January brings a money-oriented and expansive influence, although opposing Neptune can also be given to charitable gestures.

Events
Suffragettes demonstrate in London and in Washington. Bulgaria renews the war with Turkey, and there is civil war in Mexico. King George I of Greece is assassinated. The first Balkan War ends in May; the second one begins in June with Bulgaria attacking Serbia and Greece, then involving Russia and Turkey. The Irish Home Rule Bill is debated in London, but rejected. Mahatma Gandhi is arrested. The *Mona Lisa*, stolen from the Louvre, is recovered. Coco Chanel popularizes casual fashions for women.

Science and technology
Bela Schick discovers a test for immunity from diphtheria. Niels Bohr proposes his theory of atomic structure.

Culture
In the world of ideas, Sigmund Freud publishes *Totem and Taboo*, and philosopher Edmund Husserl publishes *Pure Phenomenology*. Georges Braque paints *Chequerboard*, Giorgio de Chirico *The Uncertainty of the Poet*, Wassily Kandinsky *Improvisation 31—Sea Battle* and Pablo Picasso *Man with a Guitar*. The world of sculpture welcomes Marcel Duchamp's *Bicycle Wheel*, Jacob Epstein's *Rock Drill* and Henri Matisse's *The Back II*. Claude Debussy writes his ballet *Jeux*, Sergei Rachmaninov *The Bells*, Igor Stravinsky the ballet *The Rite of Spring* and Anton Webern *Six Bagatelles*. Kenneth Alford composes the 'Colonel Bogey' march. In the world of literature, D. H. Lawrence publishes *Sons and Lovers*, Compton Mackenzie *Sinister Street*, Thomas Mann *Death in Venice* and *Marcel Proust* the first part of his *A la recherche du temps perdu*. Charlie Chaplin makes 35 films.

Births
US presidents Richard Nixon and Gerald Ford; film star Danny Kaye; bandleader Woody Herman; writers Angus Wilson and Albert Camus; Cypriot politician and Greek Orthodox archbishop Makarios III; Israeli leader Menachem Begin; athlete Jesse Owens; composer Benjamin Britten; German leader Willy Brandt.

Personalities born in 1913
Complex, tough-minded but still rather contradictory personalities as in previous years, individuals born in 1913 push hard for what they want—with Jupiter opposing Pluto—but can be the soul of kindness as well, with Jupiter aspecting Neptune. Those born up to 26 August and after 7 December, with Saturn in Gemini, have sharply inquiring minds, although with Pluto close by they are also prone to obsessions and depression. They have endurance but feel like outsiders and stubbornly resist change. Uranus in Aquarius all year also fosters inventive, rather pioneering types. Saturn in Cancer along with Neptune engenders childhoods of emotional or financial hardship, resulting in dreams of

idealized but unattainable family lives. This is especially true of those born with Pluto in Cancer between 10 July and 29 December. These individuals are very self-protective, and defend against emotional upheavals.

1914

Pluto moves to stay in Cancer for a decade in late May. Cancer is a sign astrologically associated with patriotism, and with power-hungry Pluto in residence a hardening of national sentiments is inevitable, dividing country from country. Saturn heading towards an exact conjunction with Pluto in late summer darkens the emotional mood, with omens of very tough times to come, of mass misery, of the destruction of family and domestic values, and difficulties in food production. Saturn-Pluto contacts happen only three times a century and can be connected to exploration as well as war. This placing in Cancer occurred previously only in 209, when the Romans, having repaired Hadrian's Wall, ravaged Northern Britain; in 710, just before the Arabs and Berbers invaded Spain; and in 1680, when France annexed Strasbourg, and when King Charles II dissolved the 'Cavalier' parliament in England and seized total power. Neptune heads for Leo re-emphasizing its polarized, calamitous opposition to Uranus, with even more delusional overtones. Jupiter in enlightening Aquarius crossing Uranus early on in the year produces joyful breaks and hopeful hints. With none of the five outer planets in earth signs, however, there is a lack of realism so nothing stays rooted.

Events

Ernest Shackleton leads a three-year Antarctic expedition. A Turkish-Serbian peace treaty is agreed one week after the Jupiter–Uranus conjunction. US forces bombard and seize Veracruz in Mexico to prevent German munitions being landed, after the Mexican president has refused a US request to have Mexican guns salute the American flag. British parliament passes the Irish Home Rule Bill. The Women's Enfranchisement Bill is defeated in London. On 28 June, Archduke Franz Ferdinand of Austria-Hungary and his wife are assassinated in Sarajevo, leading to the outbreak in July of the First World War, which escalates rapidly through August. Germany, along with Austria and Turkey, goes to war with Russia, Japan, Belgium, France and Britain; the United States declares neutrality. The August eclipse, interpreted as power-hungry, forceful and manic, belongs to the same cycle that recurred in 1950 with the outbreak of the Korean War; in 1968 with the assassination of Martin Luther King and the Soviet invasion of Czechoslovakia; and in 1986 with the US bombing of Tripoli and the Chernobyl explosion.

Culture

Georges Braque paints *Glass, Bottle and Newspaper*, Giorgio de Chirico *The Enigma of a Day*, Otto Dix *Self-portrait as a Soldier*, and Wassily Kandinsky *Fugue*. Constantin Brancusi sculpts *The Little French Girl* and Ernst Kirchner *Nude Woman Sitting with her Legs Crossed*. Gustav Holst begins composing *The Planets*, which is finished in 1916 and performed in 1918. Richard Strauss writes his ballet *Josephslegende* and Ralph Vaughan Williams his Symphony No. 2, 'The Lark Ascending'. Joseph Conrad publishes *Chance*, Robert Frost *North of Boston*, Hermann Hesse *Rosshalde*, James Joyce *Dubliners*, Gertrude Stein *Tender Buttons* and Rabindranath Tagore *Balaka*. Ivor Novello writes the popular song 'Keep the Home Fires Burning'.

Births
Boxer Joe Louis; British politician George Brown; poet Dylan Thomas; Jonas Edward Salk, inventor of the polio vaccine.

Personalities born in 1914
Stubbornly rigid, rather obsessive personalities, with Saturn close to Pluto, typify those born in 1914. They see themselves as outsiders and are prone to depression, but have amazing endurance and stamina. Those born after 28 May with Pluto in Cancer are emotionally defensive and are destined to live through times of major domestic and national upheaval. Those born after 26 August with Saturn in Cancer show strong signs of having to face a deprived childhood, and are geared for tremendous hardship. Those born with Jupiter in Capricorn until 23 January have a streak of practical compassion. Thereafter, with Jupiter in Aquarius close to Uranus, the over-intense, brooding 1914 temperament is leavened with sporadic joyful moods and tolerance across class and cultural boundaries, and an interest in travelling more widely.

1915
Emotionally deprived Saturn in Cancer from May, crossing destructive Pluto, hardens the mood from 1914, deepening mass misery, destroying homes, family values and fortunes, and laying waste agricultural resources. Connected to hard labour, cruelty, fanaticism, violence, martyrdom and mass murder, this tough-minded influence recurs three times a century but only four times in 2000 years in this sign placing. Neptune, fully in Leo from July, a placing that is to last for more than a decade, boosts grandiosity; in opposition to Uranus it nurtures irrational beliefs and polarized arguments, and usually accompanies man-made or natural disasters. Jupiter moving into compassionate Pisces in early February provides comfort and odd glimmers of balance and hope.

Events
The First World War continues. The Allies invade Turkey. On the Western Front the Germans start using poison-gas. The Turkish government deports 1.8 million Armenians; one third are massacred. Just days before the exact Saturn–Pluto conjunction in May the Germans sink the British liner *Lusitania*; nearly 2000 die. Two weeks later the worst British train disaster to date occurs. Italy joins the war. German Zeppelin airships attack London. Riots break out in Moscow; Tsar Nicholas II takes personal command of the army. The United States lends $500 million to Britain and France. The Allied campaign at Gallipoli fails; as a result Winston Churchill resigns from the Cabinet. British nurse Edith Cavell is executed by the Germans for harbouring Allied prisoners and escapees. In Britain enemy aliens are interned. Denmark introduces universal suffrage, with a voting age of 29. In the United States the Ku Klux Klan is revived.

Science and technology
The first all-metal aeroplane is built. Albert Einstein publishes his *General Theory of Relativity*. The dysentery bacillus is isolated. Tetanus outbreaks in the trenches are suppressed with serum injections.

Culture
Marc Chagall paints *The Birthday*, Wyndham Lewis *The Crowd*, Pablo Picasso *Harlequin*, and Gino Severini *Armoured Train*. Marcel Duchamp creates the sculpture *In Advance of the Broken Arm*. Alban Berg composes *Three Pieces for Orchestra*, Jean Sibelius writes the first version of his Symphony No. 5 and Richard Strauss the tone poem *Eine Alpensinfonie*. Asaff and Powell write the popular wartime song, 'Pack up your Troubles in your Old Kit Bag'. Rupert Brooke has more poems published. John Buchan publishes *The Thirty-Nine Steps*, Joseph Conrad *Victory*, Ford Madox Ford *The Good Soldier*, D. H. Lawrence *The Rainbow*, Somerset Maugham *Of Human Bondage* and Virginia Woolf *The Voyage Out*. D. W. Griffith's film *Birth of a Nation* and Cecil B. De Mille's *Carmen* are released.

Births
Actor and film-maker Orson Welles; actress Ingrid Bergman; novelist Saul Bellow; playwright Arthur Miller; operatic baritone Tito Gobbi; singer and actor Frank Sinatra; Moshe Dayan, Israeli general and politician.

Personalities born in 1915
Tough, enduring, obsessive, and rather brooding, typical 1915 personalities tend to regard themselves as loners. Enforced separations from the time of childhood are the pattern of their lives, with family upheavals and self-destructive emotional relationships a continuing theme. They have extraordinary stamina which enables them to deal with difficult times, but are defended against change so they can seem unduly stubborn. Those born with Jupiter in Aquarius up to 5 February are more socially tolerant; those born after this date, with Jupiter in Pisces, are of a charitable nature. Those born before 12 May with Saturn in Gemini have serious, inquiring minds; those after, with Saturn in Cancer, tend to a melancholy temperament, with an experience of a financially or emotionally deprived childhood. Pluto still in Cancer until 1938 signposts a generation who lived through a revolution in family circumstances and feminine values. Neptune opposing Uranus created see-saw temperaments, often driven by irrational beliefs.

1916
The common suffering caused by the brutal influence of Saturn and Pluto close together for the third year running in Cancer continues. All Cancerian areas—home, maternal behaviour, family relationships, food production—are subject to destructive and violent attack. This Saturn–Pluto aspect accompanies times of self-denial and martyrdom, and brings a need for extreme endurance. Though hardly exuberant, Saturn straying briefly into Leo between 18 October and 8 December does lift the intolerable sense of strain. Rebellious Uranus in cross-cultural Aquarius, in opposition to unrealistic Neptune in flamboyant Leo, makes for wild gestures of grandiosity with little sense of planning, organization or rational

justification. Jupiter in Pisces until 12 February engenders compassion; in Aries thereafter until 27 June and after 27 October, it brings a fiery, adventurous influence, and a sense of hope triumphing over realism. Jupiter in Taurus between 27 June and 27 October emphasizes the need for physical comfort and a yearning for the return of the good life.

Events

The First World War continues, with brutal losses; at the Battle of Verdun, the French and German forces suffer casualties of 400,000 each. The United States threatens to break off diplomatic relations with Germany. In Dublin, the Irish Republican Brotherhood instigates the Easter Rising (15 leaders are later executed). In the Battle of Jutland in the North Sea, the British lose most ships, but the clash results in the German navy remaining in harbour for the rest of the war. Lord Kitchener, the British Minister for War, dies when his ship is sunk by a mine. US troops fight Mexicans at the Battle of Carrizal. On 1 July, on the Cancer New Moon (the one immediately preceding the late July eclipse), close to Venus, Saturn and Pluto in Cancer, the Battle of the Somme begins, in which the British suffer 20,000 casualties on the first day. During the five-month campaign, just five miles of territory are gained and the Allies suffer over 600,000 dead; the Germans lose nearly half a million. A disastrous harvest leads to severe rationing in Germany. Woodrow Wilson is elected US President. In the United States the first Jewish Associate Justice is appointed, and the first woman is returned as a member of the House of Representatives. In Canada, the first women magistrates are appointed. In Britain, British Summer Time is introduced.

Science and technology

Plastic surgery is used in the treatment of war casualties. A theory to explain the condition of shellshock emerges. Liquid nail polish is produced in the United States.

Culture

In the world of art, the term 'Dada' is used to describe a movement of iconoclastic 'anti-art'. Claude Monet works on his series of water-lily paintings. Georg Grosz produces *Metropolis*, Henri Matisse paints *Piano Lesson*, Christopher Nevinson *Troops Resting* and Pablo Picasso designs curtains for *Parade*, a Jean Cocteau play. In the world of music, Manuel de Falla writes *Nights in the Gardens of Spain*, Charles Ives his Symphony No. 4 and Carl Nielsen his Symphony No. 4 'The Inextinguishable'. Nat Ayer writes the hit song 'If You were the Only Girl in the world'. Jazz, an improvisational music of the southern USA, begins to emerge. John Buchan publishes *Greenmantle*, Ronald Firbank *Caprice*, Robert Frost a collection of poems entitled *Mountain Interval*, James Joyce *A Portrait of the Artist as a Young Man*, Franz Kafka *Metamorphosis*; George Bernard Shaw *Prefaces* (to his plays) and H. G. Wells *Mr Britling Sees It Through*. Eugene O'Neill writes *Bound East*, and D. W. Griffith's film *Intolerance* is released.

Births

British premiers Harold Wilson and Edward Heath; violinist Yehudi Menuhin; French president François Mitterrand.

Personalities born in 1916

Tough-minded, emotionally defensive and rather obsessive individuals, personalities born in 1916 rarely let down their guard or display their vulnerabilities. Not having known domestic or social protection early on in life, they are poorly equipped for settled family life, and can be rather self-destructive, although enormously tenacious. Their tremendous stamina can also manifest itself as a resistance to change, since they are able to stand firmly rooted through great disruptions. With the Uranus–Neptune opposition continuing all year, they can be rigidly attached to fanatical and not very rational beliefs, and tend to jump from one extreme viewpoint to the opposite. Those born between 18 October and 8 December, with Saturn in Leo, are proud, with a need to control their circumstances and a tendency to be autocratic. Those born up to 12 February, with Jupiter in Pisces, are more sentimental and sympathetic. Those born with Jupiter in Aries between 12 February and 27 June and after 27 October are confident, tending to rush in where angels fear to tread. Those born with Jupiter in Taurus between 27 June and 27 October like to eat, drink and spend extravagantly.

1917

Saturn heading out of Cancer hints at a gradual easing of the melancholy mood that has prevailed since 1914, although Pluto remaining ensures that the massive family, social and national disruptions will be a long time passing. Saturn heading into Leo and crossing Neptune emphasizes the rights of the underdog and provokes uprisings of the disadvantaged. It can bring practical action to bear on visionary ideals, and promotes creative enterprises, but can also be disorienting and confusing as aspects of reality and old structures are undermined. Uranus in Aquarius, supported by communicative Jupiter in Gemini, promotes radical new inventions, especially after 30 June. With Uranus still polarized across the zodiac to Neptune in Leo, however, the rigid standpoints of previous years, with fanatical adherence to irrational beliefs, continue to cause problems. Jupiter in Aries until 13 February gives a lift of heady confidence. In Taurus between then and 30 June, it adds a note of comfort to unsettled lives.

Events

The First World War continues, with massive casualties. The United States declares war on Germany. Food shortages in central Europe cause many deaths; there are food strikes in Berlin and bread rationing in Britain. News of the proposed German–Mexican alliance is leaked. The 'February Revolution' breaks out in Russia; workers and soliders take over. Tsar Nicholas II abdicates and the Romanov dynasty ends. There are Sinn Fein riots in Dublin. The British Royal Family renounces its German names and titles. The Russian Black Sea fleet mutinies, as do German sailors. Race riots in Illinois result in deaths. In the Battle of Passchendaele, British forces advance eight miles with huge loss of life, starting on 31 July on the first exact conjunction of Saturn and Neptune. There is revolt in Spain for home rule in Catalonia. China declares war on Germany. Mata Hari is executed as a spy. The Balfour Declaration, named after the British Foreign Secretary, favours the establishment of a national home for the Jewish people. In the 'October Revolution' in Russia, Lenin and the Bolsheviks seize the Winter Palace in Petrograd, taking control of the government; large, landed estates are abolished and banks nationalized. In December, two days before the Sagittarius eclipse, a train crash kills 543 in France.

Science and technology
Freezing is introduced as a method for preserving food.

Culture
Giorgio de Chirico paints *Disquieting Muses* and Pablo Picasso *Portrait of Olga in an Armchair*. Dadaist Marcel Duchamp submits *Fountain*—a signed urinal—for an art exhibition. Gabriel Fauré composes his Violin Sonata No. 2, Sergei Prokofiev his Symphony No. 1 (the 'Classical'), Giacomo Puccini the opera *La Rondine*, Ottorini Respighi *The Fountains of Rome* and Erik Satie the ballet *Parade*. Jascha Heifetz, the American violinist, makes his debut. The Original Dixieland Jazz Band takes jazz to New York for the first time, and makes the first jazz record, including 'Original Dixieland One-Step'. In the world of books and poetry, Arthur Conan Doyle's *His Last Bow*, T. S. Eliot's *Prufrock*, Paul Valéry's *La Jeune Parque*, P. G. Wodehouse's *The Man with Two Left Feet*, Luigi Pirandello's *Liola* and J. M. Barrie's *Dear Brutus* are published. Buster Keaton stars in *The Butcher Boy* and Mary Pickford in *A Poor Little Rich Girl*.

Births
Poet Robert Lowell; US president John F. Kennedy; British politician Denis Healey; US historian and Pulitzer Prize winner Arthur Schlesinger Jnr; musician Dizzy Gillespie; Indian premier Indira Gandhi.

Personalities born in 1917
Personalities born in 1917 are determined, rather brooding individuals, especially those born before 25 June with both Saturn and Pluto in Cancer, which suggests deprived childhoods spent in times of major social upheaval. Emotionally defensive, they rarely reveal their inner vulnerabilities to anyone and find change difficult. Those born thereafter, with Saturn in Leo, are also stubborn, but more outgoing and egocentric. With Saturn close to Neptune bringing hope for a fairer society, they can be visionary in their outlook but can also be paranoid, mentally on edge, or highly creative. The inventive, rebellious streak signposted by Uranus in Aquarius sits in an uneasy balance with dreamy, fantasy-prone Neptune in Leo, creating personalities that can be fanatical, sliding from one rigid, irrational belief to the opposite, or holding inconsistent viewpoints simultaneously. Those born with Jupiter in Aries until 13 February are confident, tending to leap before they look; those born with Jupiter in Taurus between 13 February and 30 June are gourmands and lucky with money; those born with Jupiter in Gemini are communicative, open-minded and love travel.

John F. Kennedy
Born 29 May, 1917, 3 pm Eastern Standard Time, Brookline, Massachusetts.
Chart: Sun, Venus in Gemini ✦ Mars, Mercury, Jupiter in Taurus ✦ Pluto, Saturn in Cancer ✦ Neptune in Leo ✦ Moon in Virgo ✦ Uranus in Aquarius ✦ Moon's North Node in Capricorn; ascendant in Libra

Indira Gandhi

Born 9 November 1917, 11.11 pm Indian Time, Allahabad, India.
Chart: Sun in Scorpio ◆ Moon, Venus and Moon's North Node in Capricorn; Mercury in Sagittarius ◆ Jupiter in Gemini ◆ Pluto in Cancer; Neptune, Saturn, ascendant in Leo ◆ Mars in Virgo

Two of the most renowned political leaders of the 20th century, born in the same year, both come from dynastic families with a tradition of political power-broking; both share the same ultimate fate in that they were assassinated.

Indira Gandhi, the daughter of Nehru, with an intense Scorpio Sun in her chart area of family lineage, was proud of her connections and keen to emulate her father. Fortunate Jupiter at her midheaven suggests she would rise to a position of respect; affectionate Venus in Capricorn hints at her interest in child welfare. With Neptune close to Saturn, she had a vision of creating a better society but was impeded by her often dictatorial, uncooperative stance, with disruptive Uranus across the zodiac in Aquarius squaring onto her Sun. An aggressive Mars in Virgo just below the horizon when she was born made her a force to be reckoned with. Saturn, the career indicator, was on the rise in her chart when she was elected Prime Minister for the first time in 1966, and aiming to sink below the horizon of her ascendant in Leo in 1977 when she was resoundingly defeated. Her assassination by Sikh extremists in 1984 after she was returned to office occurred when Jupiter and Neptune in Capricorn were close to her Moon's North Node. The Moon's Node is often a point of destiny in a chart, or a public figure's connection to the collective. Neptune is the planet of sacrifice, and there were murmurs at the time that she knew what was coming and wanted a martyr's death.

Kennedy's chart is also tied into the family, but is of a different order. Four planets, including his communicative Gemini Sun, and Mars, Mercury and Jupiter in indulgent, sensual Taurus, are all buried deep in his chart, suggesting an enclosed, not altogether healthy family dynamic. His political career was manipulated to a great extent by his father Joseph Kennedy. John Kennedy's compulsive sexual addiction stems from the placing of these planets and was a pathological defence against psychological disintegration. Like Eva Braun (see pages 78–9), he had Mars in the chart area of sexuality and death, hinting at the possibility of a violent death.

He shared with Indira Gandhi the Saturn–Neptune contact, which fostered the desire to create a better society, supporting the rights of the disadvantaged and turning ideals into reality (see Saturn–Neptune, page 37). Both also had Pluto in Cancer, bringing a powerful need to transform family values.

When Kennedy became President in 1961, the wildly expansive Jupiter–Saturn conjunction was in place in Capricorn, raising high hopes of a new Camelot—a new, golden age of peace. It crossed the lowest point of his chart, moving him out of obscurity. As in the cases of John Lennon and Princess Diana, however, whose lives moved uncannily to the tune of this 20-year conjunction, such unrealistic inflation can have terrible consequences.

At Kennedy's death in November 1963, the violently disruptive Uranus–Pluto conjunction in Virgo—which fanned the flames of the destructive Vietnam War (which Kennedy started), the Six Day War, and Mao Tse Tung's Red Revolution in

China (see *1960–1969*, pages 159–176, and Uranus–Pluto, page 32)—was rapidly approaching his Virgo Moon. The Moon is often a politician's barometer for sensing the public mood. Perhaps because of his inability psychologically to act as a separate individual from his enmeshed family, John Kennedy was tragically pulled into the epicentre of the storm that was about to wreak such havoc over the following years.

1918

Faster-moving Uranus is drawing away from the calamitous opposition to Neptune, which has been an almost constant feature since the turn of the century. Inventive new ideas continue to spill out, although they are undermined by Neptune's unrealistic grandiosity in Leo. Saturn in Leo stresses the need for individual respect; close to Neptune it promotes the rights of the underclasses and disadvantaged—social reform is afoot. The mood is tense, changes coming abruptly, with Saturn sitting across the zodiac from Uranus producing a swing between conservatism and radical ideas. Expansive Jupiter heading into home-loving Cancer in July promotes a desire for peace. Joining Pluto there, it puts control in the hands of the masses. The long, slow process of healing the emotional, domestic and agricultural catastrophes of the previous years is beginning.

Events

As Jupiter enters Cancer on 13 July the German advance towards Paris is halted. Three days later Tsar Nicholas II and his family are executed. In August, within three days of the exact conjunction of Jupiter and Pluto, British forces break the German lines on the Western Front, an event known as 'the black day of the German army'. The United States and Russia break off diplomatic relations. In November, the armistice is signed on the Western Front, ending the First World War. The Allied occupation of Germany begins in the first few days of December on the Sagittarian eclipse, in the cycle that also marked the two US ceasefires in Vietnam in 1973. In Calcutta, Muslims riot. In India, Europe and the United States, a Spanish 'flu epidemic kills at least 20 million. Bolsheviks form the Russian Communist Party. In Britain, the government abandons Home Rule for Ireland, and women over the age of 30 are given the right to vote.

Culture

Paul Klee paints *Gartenplan* and Paul Nash *We Are Making a New World*. Béla Bartók writes the opera *Bluebeard's Castle*, Giacomo Puccini the opera *Il Trittico* and Anton Webern *Four Songs with Orchestra*. The Original Dixieland Jazz Band records 'Tiger Rag'. Rupert Brooke's *Collected Poems*, the first collection of Gerard Manley Hopkins's poems, Wyndham Lewis's *Tarr*, Siegfried Sassoon's *Counter-Attack*, Rebecca West's *The Return of the Soldier*, James Joyce's *Exiles*, and Luigi Pirandello's *Six Characters in Search of an Author* are all published. Elmo Lincoln's film *Tarzan of the Apes* is released.

Births

South African president Nelson Mandela; Egyptian presidents Gamal Abdel Nasser and Anwar Sadat; Romanian politician Nicolae Ceausescu; singer Ella Fitzgerald; composer Leonard Bernstein; evangelist Billy Graham; writer Aleksandr Solzhenitsyn; German chancellor Helmut Schmidt.

Personalities born in 1918

Not good at practising what they preach, personalities born in 1918 are inconsistent, contradictory but nonetheless idealistic individuals. Emotionally rather cool, secretive and at times self-destructive, they are born into childhoods where settled family lives are not the norm. Saturn in Leo gives them a desire for personal recognition and importance. The opposition to Uranus, across the zodiac in Aquarius, can make them dictatorial on occasion, wanting freedom for themselves but not offering it elsewhere. In outlook and ideas they veer between the traditional and the revolutionary. A kindly, lucky streak benefits those born up to 13 July, with Jupiter in communicative Gemini. Those born with Jupiter in Cancer have the drive to control their destinies—domestic, emotional and social—with force if need be, and have an almost magical ability to turn thoughts into solid results.

1919

Revitalizing, revolutionary Uranus, moving sign for the first time in seven years, heralds a gear change. From 2 April in emotional and idealistic Pisces, it supports causes that struggle to break free from the influences of the past. The approaching aspect to Pluto in Cancer, although not hard, does contribute to outbreaks of violence, mass insurrection and rebellion against the established order. Jupiter in Cancer until 3 August looks for a return to peaceful family values, though force is often the method adopted. Saturn in Leo until 14 August stands proud for the rights of strong individuals, although it can promote dictatorial attitudes. Moving then into Virgo in August, where it remains for three years, it reasserts the work ethic. Disciplined Saturn, uneasily situated across the zodiac from freedom-loving Uranus, accompanies inconsistent, often contradictory arguments.

Events

There is a communist revolt in Berlin, after which the leaders are shot. The Paris Peace Conference opens. Sinn Fein MPs are elected to Westminster; in Dublin, an Irish Republic is proclaimed, with Eamon de Valera as president. The IRA attacks British authorities in Ireland. The League of Nations is proposed. In February, the Emir of Afghanistan is murdered within a day of the assassination of the Bavarian Prime Minister. There are nationalist riots in Cairo. Benito Mussolini founds the Italian Fascist movement. Adolf Hitler attends a meeting of the newly formed German Workers' Party for first time. The 'Weimar Constitution' is adopted in Germany, on the exact Uranus–Saturn opposition. There are riots in Portugal over food shortages. In India, the 'Amritsar Massacre' takes place, in which British troops fire on crowds after riots protesting against the arrest of two leaders of the Indian National Congress. Civil war breaks out in Russia, with the Bolshevik Red Army inflicting a series of defeats on Anton Denikin's counter-revolutionary White Army. There are riots in Beijing when Japanese holdings in China are confirmed by the Paris Peace Conference. Armenia declares independence. Race riots erupt in Chicago, and there are lynchings throughout the United States; there are also steel and dock strikes, and President Wilson breaks down and suffers a stroke.

Science and technology

British aviators J. W. Alcock and A. W. Brown make the first transatlantic flight, lasting 16 hours 27 minutes. The first successful helicopter flight takes place. The first motor scooter is manufactured.

Culture

The influential Bauhaus School of Design, Building and Crafts is founded. Marcel Duchamp paints *L H O O Q*, Fernand Léger *Men in the City*, Amedeo Modigliani *The Blue Nude, Portrait of Jeanne Hebuterne*, Alfred Munnings *Zennor Hill* and Pablo Picasso *Pitcher and Compotier with Apples* and sets for Manuel de Falla's ballet *The Three-cornered Hat*. Edward Elgar writes his cello concerto, and Richard Strauss the opera *Die Frau ohne Schatten*. Vicente Blasco Ibañez's *The Four Horseman of the Apocalypse*, André Gide's *Two Symphonies*, Somerset Maugham's *The Moon and Sixpence*, Ezra Pound's *Quia Pauper Amavi*, and collections of poems by Thomas Hardy and Rudyard Kipling are all published. George Bernard Shaw writes *Heartbreak House*. Charlie Chaplin, Douglas Fairbanks and D. W. Griffith found United Artists. Robert Wiene's *The Cabinet of Dr Caligari*, Abel Gance's *J'Accuse* and Ernst Lubitsch's *Madame Dubarry* are all released.

Births

Italian politician Giulio Andreotti; entertainer Liberace; dancer Margot Fonteyn; British Foreign Secretary and NATO Secretary-General Lord Carrington; novelists Iris Murdoch, Doris Lessing and Primo Levi; mountaineer Edmund Hillary; Canadian Prime Minister Pierre Trudeau; Muhammad Reza Shah Pahlavi, Shah of Iran.

Personalities born in 1919

Highly strung, complex, rather contradictory individuals, personalities born in 1919 tend not to follow their own advice, yet aspire to very high moral or creative ideals. Exasperatingly, they can be both kind and dictatorial, open-minded and dogmatic. Born into troubled times, with Pluto in Cancer aspecting Uranus, they regard upheavals as a way of life, finding settled family lives difficult to handle. They bury their feelings deeply, often appearing rather proud, and sometimes aiming for positions of importance or a grand lifestyle as a way of avoiding their emotional difficulties. Those born with Jupiter in Cancer up to 3 August push hard for an expansive, elegant home; those born with Jupiter in Leo are sociable and flamboyant. Saturn in Leo until 14 August also gives them an added touch of egocentricity, in contrast to those born after that date with Saturn in Virgo, which brings a workaholic, self-effacing and rather retiring influence to bear. Those born with Uranus in Pisces between 2 April and 17 August are pioneers in creative, emotional or visionary ideas.

1920–1929

Creative, illusionary Neptune in flamboyant, romantic Leo until 1928 stokes up the inflationary flames of the Roaring Twenties, both in emotional and financial expectations. Speculation is not based on realism, as becomes apparent when Neptune finally enters earthy Virgo in 1928, undermining employment prospects, the work-base, and health—all Virgo-ruled areas. Pluto continues in home-oriented Cancer, where it remains until 1938, altering for ever the status of women, the face of the family and the production of food. No major outer planet conjunctions mark the 1920s, except for the Jupiter–Saturn conjunction which recurs in a 20-year cycle; this time it is in Virgo, a conjunction that has not been seen since 1861. Again it heralds expansion in feminine lives, perhaps symbolized as well in the tight 'flapper' styles, which fit the fastidious Virgo mood. The catastrophe-prone Uranus–Neptune opposition, which has caused so much devastation for two decades, has waned. The hard Saturn–Pluto aspect in 1921 and 1922, which has a seven-year cycle, leads—as ever—to mass misery, but does pass. Until 1927, Uranus pulls away from the past in Pisces, then roars into reckless Aries, preparing the way for major upheavals. The first year of Neptune's total exit from Leo—1929—coincides with the disruptive and violently destructive Pluto–Uranus aspect and with restrictive Saturn's move into materialistic Capricorn, heralding the Wall Street Crash and the start of the major world crisis in the capitalist economy.

1920

Practical Saturn in hard-working Virgo continues the slow process from the previous year of picking up the pieces, putting together more solid structures, and giving a better deal to the workers and underclasses. Virgo, having archetypally a feminine energy, promotes the feminist movement. The cautiously expansive Jupiter–Saturn contact in Virgo moves closer from August, bringing ideals down to earth and producing solid results in the final, general acceptance of universal suffrage for women. Financial disappointments arise as over-confidence is exposed; fantasy-prone Neptune in grandiose Leo leads to unwise speculations and extravagant living, paving the way for the Roaring Twenties. Uranus heading out of inventive Aquarius into emotional, idealistic Pisces speeds up the separation from the past, and supports worthwhile causes. In aspect to Pluto, it continues to fuel fanatical attitudes and rebelliousness.

The mood of the year is 'betwixt and between'—full of hope but wary of disappointment. Stability is still not a reality.

Events

The League of Nations is formed, with 29 members. The Hague becomes the base for the International Court of Justice. In the Russian Civil War, the Bolsheviks emerge as the winners, and Russia goes to war with Poland. In Germany, the US-born journalist Wolfgang Kapp and military seize Berlin in the 'Kapp Putsch'; the government flees but the conspirators cannot establish their authority in the face of a general strike. The Mexican President is assassinated two days after the May eclipse, coinciding with the birth of Pope John Paul II. There is widespread famine in China. Canada introduces universal suffrage. In the United States, the American Civil Liberties Union is founded. A bomb in Wall Street kills 30 people and injures many more. Sinn Fein supporters and Unionists riot in Belfast. The Government of Ireland Act becomes law; the North and the South now have their own separate governments. Joan of Arc is canonized.

Science and technology
The submachine-gun is invented. The first radio broadcasts are made in Europe. In the United States, 500 radio stations are set up.

Culture
Art historian Antoine Pevsner and sculptor Naum Gabo issue the Realistic Manifesto, stating the principles of European Constructivism. Max Beckmann paints *Carnival* and Pablo Picasso *Seated Woman*. Leos Janácek writes the opera *The Adventures of Mister Broucek* and Maurice Ravel composes *La Valse*. Marie Rambert founds her ballet school in London. Agatha Christie publishes her first Hercule Poirot novel. Colette's *Chéri*, Franz Kafka's *The Country Doctor*, Wilfred Owen's *Collected Poems* and Paul Valéry's *Le Cimetière marin* are all published. Eugene O'Neill writes the play *Beyond the Horizon*. In the world of film, John Barrymore stars in *Dr Jekyll and Mr Hyde* and Douglas Fairbanks in *The Mark of Zorro*.

Births
Writer Isaac Asimov; film-maker Federico Fellini; Karol Wojtyla (Pope John Paul II); jazz pianist and composer Thelonious Monk.

Personalities born in 1920
With dutiful Saturn in Virgo, the work ethic is strong in the perfectionist worriers of 1920. They tend to be tough-minded and suited to difficult times, but a sufficient degree of fortunate circumstances gives them confidence and keeps them cheerful. Those born with Jupiter in flamboyant Leo have expensive tastes, combined with a charitable, compassionate streak. Those born after 28 August with Jupiter in Virgo are purposeful, idealistic and good with details, but have a tendency to attempt too much so that they became overstretched. They all share a concern about failure, pushing hard—though erratically—for success. They can be pioneers in a quiet, unassuming way, although they often espouse principles they do not practise. With controlling Pluto in home-loving Cancer and disruptive Uranus in sentimental, romantic Pisces, their emotional lives are rather tumultuous.

1921
The practical yet idealistic Jupiter–Saturn conjunction in feminist, dutiful Virgo and then in fair-minded Libra signposts changes in working practice, and puts in place social changes that will blossom through the next decade. Such changes are always an economic marker, bringing both success and failure. Falling in rather fastidious Virgo, the conjunction may have triggered the rather tight, boyish fashions of the 1920s. Inventive but rebellious Uranus in creative, emotional Pisces pushes forward the development of the film business, but continues to promote the unsettling pull away from the past. In exact aspect with Pluto, it also provides the spark for social unrest and rebellion. Pluto in Cancer fosters new forms of politically controlled fascist and communist governments. Neptune in Leo brings artistic, romantic trends, but also fuels wild financial speculation.

The mood of the year veers between optimism and pessimism, great sympathy and ruthless fanaticism.

Events

Under Kemal Atatürk, Turkey fights the occupying Greek forces and expels them. Germany fails to pay reparations, set at £6500 million; there is a rapid fall in the value of the German mark, and a state of emergency is declared in the face of economic crisis. The German war trials begin. In Italy there are riots between fascists and communists. In Germany there are communist riots. Famine spreads in Russia; communist principles have failed to create economic stability in the country, and Lenin introduces his New Economic Policy, which allows a limited amount of free-market trading. Fighting in Ireland ceases between the self-declared Irish Republic under Eamon de Valera and the British authorities. The centralized Indian Parliament opens.

Science and technology

Preliminary experiments are made that will lead to the splitting of the atom. The perfume Chanel No. 5 is launched. Sanitary towel products are marketed. Band Aid sticking plasters are introduced.

Culture

Georges Braque completes *Still Life with Guitar*, Max Ernst paints *Celebes*, Fernand Léger *Le Grand Déjeuner*, Paul Klee *The Fish*, Henri Matisse *The Moorish Screen* and *Odalisque with Red Culottes*, Joán Miró *The Farm*, and Piet Mondrian *Composition with Red, Yellow, Blue and Black*. Leos Janácek completes the opera *Katya Kabanova*, Pietro Mascagni the opera *Il Piccolo Marat*, and Sergei Prokofiev the opera *The Love of Three Oranges*. Jazz is outlawed on Broadway. In the world of literature, Walter de la Mare's *Memoirs of a Midget*, John Galsworthy's *To Let*, Aldous Huxley's *Crome Yellow*, D. H. Lawrence's *Women in Love* and Somerset Maugham's *The Circle* are published. In the worlds of theatre and film, Eugene O'Neill writes *Anna Christie*, Charlie Chaplin makes *The Kid*, F. W. Murnau makes *Nosferatu* and Rudolph Valentino stars in *The Sheik*.

Births

Indian film-maker Satyajit Ray; US boxer and world welterweight champion 'Sugar' Ray Robinson (born Walker Smith); sculptor and performance artist Joseph Beuys; Czech politician Alexander Dubcek.

Personalities born in 1921

Fear of failure and the determination to achieve freedom are the two driving forces of those born in 1921. Jupiter together with Saturn in Virgo until 26 September creates practical but workaholic worriers, who have a capacity to succeed through sheer grit and attention to detail, if they do not overstretch themselves. Saturn in Libra after 8 October, together with Jupiter, points to fair-minded attitudes, social aspirations and indecisiveness. Uranus and Pluto in water signs—in 1921 they are in Pisces and Cancer—usually coincide with disruptions in domestic and emotional lives, and suggest that periods of major change and upheaval are to be experienced. Neptune in Leo leads to a too-idealistic view of romance, or wild speculation.

93

1922

Jupiter and Saturn travelling concurrently in socially aware Libra promote idealistic causes, although erratically, with early enthusiasms turning into disappointments; only cautiously realistic ventures succeed. The brutal Saturn–Pluto square, always an intimation of war or mass misery, produces a tough-minded mood. Pluto, continuing its 33-year trek through home-loving Cancer, pushes through changes in family values and the production of food, but these are not always positive. Pluto in exact trine to Uranus for the second year is explosive, given to violent outbreaks of fanaticism. Neptune in unrealistic Leo promotes high hopes for love, money and artistic ventures, but leads to major financial and emotional disappointments.

Events

Civil war breaks out in Ireland; in Dublin rebels seize the Four Courts. In London, two Irishmen murder Sir Henry Wilson, a British field marshal, who favours the reconquest of Ireland. There is heavy fighting in Dublin, and Michael Collins, first prime minister of the Irish Free State, is assassinated. Unemployed workers leave Glasgow, Scotland, on a hunger march to London. Workers go on general strike in Italy, with fascists seizing power in Milan and Genoa. In Germany, the value of the mark falls catastrophically. There is civil war in China. In India, Mahatma Gandhi is sentenced to imprisonment for civil disobedience. In the United States, coal miners go on strike, 'prohibition' is introduced to prevent liquor smuggling, and the first woman senator takes office. There are strikes in South Africa and martial law is introduced.

Science and technology

The self-winding watch is invented. A diabetic patient is given the first insulin injection. Howard Carter, supported by Lord Carnarvon, discovers Tutankhamun's tomb at Luxor. Britain's first mass-produced car, the Austin Seven, is manufactured. Marie Stopes instigates her birth-control campaign in London. The British Broadcasting Corporation (BBC) is founded.

Culture

Giorgio de Chirico paints *Roman Villa* and Pablo Picasso *Dancing Couple*. Constantin Brancusi sculpts *The Fish*. Arthur Bliss composes the 'Colour Symphony', Carl Nielsen his Symphony No. 5, Ralph Vaughan Williams his Symphony No. 3 (the 'Pastoral Symphony') and William Walton *Façade*. John Buchan's *Huntingtower*, T. S. Eliot's *The Waste Land*, F. Scott Fitzgerald's *The Jazz Age*, James Joyce's *Ulysses*, D. H. Lawrence's *Aaron's Rod*, Katherine Mansfield's *The Garden Party*, Virginia Woolf's *Jacob's Room* and A. A. Milne's *The Dover Road* are published. Bertolt Brecht writes *Drums in the Night* and Eugene O'Neill *The Hairy Ape*. D. W. Griffith makes the film *Orphans of the Storm*, starring Lillian Gish.

Births

Novelists Jack Kerouac and Kingsley Amis; Judy Garland; heart surgeon Christiaan Barnard.

Personalities born in 1922

With the Uranus–Pluto aspect bringing a strong-willed but contradictory outlook, personalities born in 1922 are in favour of dynamic reform, in emotional and family values as well as in social attitudes. Hard-driving and tough-minded with Saturn in square to Pluto, they are also stubborn, resisting pressure to change. The disruptive planets in water signs and unrealistic Neptune in romantic Leo suggest adventurous rather than stable emotional lives. Saturn in Libra produces fair-minded individuals who are serious about justice, those born before 27 October with Jupiter in Libra being doubly so; they can also be indecisive and frightened of failure. Those born with Jupiter in Scorpio after 27 October are lucky with money, are natural confidantes, and are good with secrets. Blessed with the ability to turn ideas into reality, they have the ability to prosper.

1923

The entrenched Saturn–Pluto square continues to create tough conditions, brutal events and misery for the masses. The fanatical Uranus–Pluto connection trine in idealistic Pisces and in family-oriented Cancer forces through social reforms, points to scientific discoveries, but also hints at destructive movements. Neptune continues in Leo, creating optimism but not much realism when it comes to speculation. Jupiter in money-conscious Scorpio and then in gambling Sagittarius offers temptations with get-rich-quick schemes. Saturn in fair-minded Libra until 20 December promotes just causes, is serious about workers' rights, and fosters responsible social attitudes.

Events

French and Belgian troops occupy the Ruhr because of Germany's failure to meet reparation payments. Collapse of the German currency leads to strikes and riots and barter exchange in some transactions. In November, with Mars in Libra forming an exact square to Pluto and heading for the conjunction with Saturn, Adolf Hitler and the National Socialists attempt a coup in Munich. There is a coup in Bulgaria and the prime minister is assassinated. Spain becomes a dictatorship. A severe earthquake in Japan destroys most of Tokyo, killing half a million; this occurs in September nine days before a total solar eclipse in the cycle which recurred around the time of the Japanese bombing of Pearl Harbor in 1941. In the United States, president Warren Harding dies suddenly at the age of fifty-seven. There is a strike by American coal miners, and in San Francisco, the first supermarket is opened. In Britain, women are given equality in divorce suits; dock workers strike.

Science and technology

Continuous hot-strip rolling of steel is invented by British metallurgist John B. Tytus, a significant advance in modern technology since steel production is a key factor in the world economy.

Culture

Max Beckmann paints *Self-portrait with Cigarette*, Max Ernst *Pieta* or *Revolution by Night*, Joán Miró *The Tilled Field* and Pablo Picasso *Harlequin and Mirror* and

The Pipes of Pan. Fernand Léger designs costumes and scenery for the ballet *Création du Monde*. Sculptor Constantin Brancusi produces *Bird in Space*. Composer Zoltán Kodály writes *Psalmus Hungaricus* and Igor Stravinsky composes his ballet *Les Noces*. A new dance called the Charleston is introduced in New York. The first recording of 'hillbilly' music is made in the United States. In Harlem, the Cotton Club is opened, providing black music for a white audience. Poet Rainer Maria Rilke writes his two major works, *Die Sonnette an Orpheus* and the *Duino Elegies*. In the world of literature, Arnold Bennett's *Riceyman Steps*, Colette's *The Ripening Seed*, Robert Frost's *New Hampshire* poems, Kahlil Gibran's *The Prophet*, D. H. Lawrence's *Kangaroo*, John Masefield's *Collected Poems*, Dorothy L. Sayers' *Whose Body?*, P. G. Wodehouse's *Leave it to Psmith* and Luigi Pirandello's *The Late Mattia Pascal* are published. George Bernard Shaw writes *Back to Methuselah*. The film production company Warner Brothers is founded. Harold Lloyd stars in *Safety Last*, and Ronald Colman and Lillian Gish star in *The White Sister*.

Births
Film director Franco Zeffirelli; Cardinal Basil Hume; newspaper owner Robert Maxwell; Rocky Marciano, world heavyweight boxing champion; actor and director Sir Richard Attenborough; singer Maria Callas.

Personalities born in 1923
Dynamic, strong-minded, rather obstinate individuals typify those born in 1923. They can be obsessive and sometimes lonely, always feeling themselves to be outsiders, but with Saturn in aspect to Pluto they have tremendous endurance for tough times, and are able to tackle the difficulties of life with great resilience. Disruptive Uranus and controlling Pluto both in water signs present them with the emotional challenge of finding domestic stability. With Saturn in Libra they seek cooperation in group efforts, but can be hard-driving at work. Those born before 25 November with Jupiter in Scorpio are lucky with money, although Neptune in Leo would have attracted them to grandiose schemes. Those born after 25 November with Jupiter in Sagittarius are broadminded, philosophical thinkers, interested in foreign cultures and travel.

1924
A marginally less stressful year than 1923 with Saturn heading into Scorpio and moving into easier aspect to Pluto. Three powerful outer planets in water signs makes for an emotionally self-protective, rather intense mood. Changes are pushed through with vigour, and sometimes fanatical and violent determination, by strong-willed individuals. But the softer aspects of Saturn to Uranus and Pluto do indicate that certain practical reforms see solid results. Jupiter in Sagittarius is high-minded; in aspect to Neptune, it fosters charitable causes, but also encourages financial over-confidence.

Events
Soviet leader Lenin dies. Adolf Hitler is imprisoned for six months following the 1923 failed coup, and writes *Mein Kampf*. There is crisis in the German Cabinet.

In Italy the fascists gain power through widespread intimidation. Denmark becomes the first country to appoint a woman cabinet minister. In Britain, the dock strike continues. Greece becomes a republic. A revolt by Kurds in Turkey is brutally suppressed. There is rioting in Delhi between Hindus and Muslims. J. Edgar Hoover becomes head of the FBI. Native Americans receive full US citizenship, and Learned Hand is appointed as a US Court of Appeals Judge. A military junta takes over Chile.

Science and technology
British astronomer Sir Arthur Eddington discovers that there is a relationship between the mass of a star and its output of light. In France, Nobel Prize-winning physicist Louis de Broglie suggests that particles can behave as waves, laying the foundation for wave mechanics and the development of quantum theory. The first insecticide is developed. Clarence Birdseye sets up a frozen seafood company. Two million radio sets are in use in the United States.

Culture
In the world of art, André Breton publishes the Surrealist Manifesto. Joán Miró paints *Harlequin's Carnival*, and Stanley Spencer begins *The Resurrection, Cookham*. George Gershwin writes *Rhapsody in Blue*. Leos Janácek writes the opera *The Cunning Little Vixen*, and Richard Strauss completes the opera *Intermezzo*. The musical *No, No, Nanette*, with music by Vincent Youmans and lyrics by Otto Harbach and Frank Mandel, has its first successful run in Chicago, and then meets with great acclaim in Europe. E. M. Forster publishes *A Passage to India*, Thomas Mann *The Magic Mountain*, and Katherine Mansfield her *Journal*. Noel Coward writes *The Vortex*, Eugene O'Neill *Desire Under the Elms* and George Bernard Shaw *St Joan*. Columbia Pictures and Metro-Goldwyn-Mayer are founded. Walt Disney makes his first cartoon, *Alice's Wonderland*; John Ford makes *The Iron Horse* and Buster Keaton stars in *Sherlock Junior*.

Births
Zambian president Kenneth Kaunda; comedian Tony Hancock; novelist James Baldwin; American presidents George Bush and Jimmy Carter.

Personalities born in 1924
Talented but intense and rather stubborn individuals express the character of those born in 1924. They have high-flying fantasies, but also the capacity to turn dreams into reality through sheer determination. Those born before 7 April and after 13 September with Saturn in Scorpio forming a grand trine with Uranus in Pisces and Pluto in Cancer—all water signs—are emotionally secretive, will-driven, rather stubborn individuals who are miserly with money and have difficulties with intimacy. Those born between those dates, with Saturn in Libra, are serious about close relationships and work. Those born with Jupiter in Sagittarius until 18 December are high-minded thinkers and keen travellers, with strong charitable impulses. Thereafter those born with Jupiter in Capricorn attract the good life and are lucky with money.

1925

The tough-minded, hard-driving, self-protective mood continues from 1924 as persistent, tight-fisted Saturn continues its three-year sojourn in Scorpio. Disruptive, fanatical Uranus and controlling Pluto also in water signs contribute to an emotionally inward-looking, rather resentful mood. Jupiter in materialistic Capricorn emphasizes the split between the haves and have-nots, fostering greed rather than ideals. Neptune in arrogant, grandiose Leo dreams wonderful dreams but lacks the business qualities to make them work. The approaching hard aspect of Saturn to Neptune exacerbates the disaffections of the underprivileged, leading towards the only general strike ever in Britain in 1926, which occurs when the aspect is exact.

Events

In Italy Mussolini takes dictatorial powers. In the USSR, in the struggle for power following the death of Lenin, leading revolutionary Leon Trotsky is dismissed from the chairmanship of the Revolutionary Military Council. Britain returns to the gold standard, causing increasing problems for industry. The shooting of Chinese students by foreign municipal police in Shanghai provokes a Chinese boycott of British goods. The Geneva Conference debates the use of poison-gas in war. The Locarno Conference agrees European boundaries. Adolf Hitler's *Mein Kampf* is published. The Cabinet crisis continues in Germany. The start of a three-year Druse insurrection in Syria leads to the French bombarding Damascus. Reza Khan deposes the Shah of Persia and becomes Shah of Iran, the new name for Persia. In the United States, the first woman state governor takes office, and Al 'Scarface' Capone becomes head of organized crime.

Culture

In the world of art, Otto Dix produces *Three Prostitutes on the Street*, Pablo Picasso paints *Three Dancers* and Chaim Soutine *Carcass of Beef*. Sculptor Jacob Epstein completes *Rima*. Architect Walter Gropius, condemned as an 'architectural socialist', designs the new Bauhaus in Dessau, and Le Corbusier designs the pavilion of the *Esprit Nouveau* for the Paris Exhibition. Alban Berg writes the opera *Wozzack*, Aaron Copland his Symphony No. 1, Carl Nielsen his Symphony No. 6 ('Sinfonia Semplice'), Sergei Prokofiev Symphony No. 2, Maurice Ravel the opera *L'Enfant et les Sortilèges* and Dmitri Shostakovich his Symphony No. 1. In the United States, country music from Nashville, Tennessee, becomes popular through radio shows like the *Grand Ole Opry*. Louis Armstrong records with the Hot Five. Paul Robeson gives the first recital of negro spirituals. In the world of literature, Ivy Compton-Burnett's *Pastors and Masters*, F. Scott Fitzgerald's *The Great Gatsby*, Ford Madox Ford's *No More Parades*, André Gide's *The Counterfeiters*, Aldous Huxley's *Those Barren Leaves*, Gertrude Stein's *The Making of Americans*, P. G. Wodehouse's *Carry on Jeeves* and Virginia Woolf's *Mrs Dalloway* are published. Noel Coward writes *Hay Fever* and Sean O'Casey *Juno and the Paycock*. Sergei Eisenstein makes the film *The Battleship Potemkin* and Charlie Chaplin makes *The Gold Rush*; Greta Garbo stars in *Joyless Street*.

Births

Film director Robert Altman; composer Pierre Boulez; designer Laura Ashley; actor Peter Sellers; Irish prime minister Charles Haughey; writer and satirist Gore Vidal; British premier Margaret Thatcher; artist Robert Rauschenberg; actor Richard Burton; US politician Robert Kennedy.

Personalities born in 1925

Stubbornly determined and rather obsessive, personalities born in 1925 are prone to bury their intimate feelings and sexuality deep, and to push hard for material security. With the intense outer planets in water signs, they live tumultuous and challenging emotional lives, and find domestic contentment elusive. Neptune in Leo gives them high ideals where romance is concerned, although these often remain fantasies rather than becoming reality. With Jupiter in earthy Capricorn opposing Pluto, they ignore social niceties to aim for what will bring power and money. Saturn in aspect to Neptune fosters creative and artistic talent, accompanied by an inclination towards paranoid worries.

1926

The third year running of the grand trine of Saturn, Uranus and Pluto in water signs continues to toughen the emotional mood and cast shadows on the economic climate. Saturn in square aspect to Neptune, always an indicator of uprisings of the underprivileged, raises worry levels. Controlling Saturn in materialistic Scorpio is will-driven. Feelings are deeply buried as control becomes the key factor. Neptune in Leo promotes unrealistic financial hopes. The Uranus–Pluto trine mutes its violent, fanatical effect, although the underlying rebellious force is still there. Reforms are pushed through with vigour, though not always compassionately. Jupiter in tolerant, enlightened Aquarius from 7 January promotes egalitarian and cross-cultural international agreements.

Events

There is an attempted assassination of Mussolini. The first and only general strike in Britain takes place on the exact Saturn–Neptune square. In Syria, there is continuing revolt by the Druse, a religious sect. In Poland, Jozef Pilsudski and army units march on Warsaw and seize power, forcing the resignation of the president and prime minister. A coup in Portugal deposes the president. A financial crisis in France causes the downfall of the government, and devaluation of the franc. There is financial crisis in Belgium, and a dictatorship is declared. In the Irish Free State, Eamon de Valera resigns from Sinn Fein and founds Fianna Fáil, the 'Soldiers of Destiny'. In China Chiang Kai-shek's nationalist forces set up their capital in Hankou. Germany is admitted to the League of Nations; as a result Spain resigns. In the USSR, Leon Trotsky is expelled from the Politburo following Joseph Stalin's victory. A campaign against the Mafia starts in Sicily. The Cabinet crisis in Germany continues. In the United States, the first 'Book of the Month' club is formed. Charles Atlas opens a gym in New York to promote body-building.

Science and technology

Roald Amundsen flies over the North Pole. A rocket powered by petrol and liquid oxgen is developed. Liver extract is used to treat pernicious anaemia. On 26 January, when the Sun, Venus and Jupiter are all in Aquarius—the astrological signifier of high technology—with a home-oriented Cancer Moon, John Logie Baird gives the first public demonstration of television, in London.

Culture

Otto Dix paints *The Poet Ivan von Lucken*, Arshile Gorky begins *Artist and Mother*, Georg Grosz paints *Eclipse of the Sun* and *Pillars of Society*, Joán Miró *Person Throwing a Stone at a Bird*, Georgia O'Keeffe *Black Iris*, and Stanley Spencer starts on the murals for Burghclere Chapel. Sculptor Alberto Giacometti creates *Spoon Woman*. Architect Le Corbusier publishes *The Coming Architecture*. Béla Bartók composes his ballet *The Miraculous Mandarin*, Alban Berg composes *Lyric Suite*, Paul Hindemith his opera *Cardillac*, and Leos Janácek his opera *The Makrapoulos Case*. The musical *The Desert Song*, by Romberg and Harbach, is performed. Jelly Roll Morton forms the band the Red Hot Peppers. In the world of literature, William Faulkner publishes *Soldiers' Pay*, Ernest Hemingway *The Sun Also Rises*, Rudyard Kipling *Debits and Credits*, D. H. Lawrence *The Plumed Serpent*, Hugh MacDiarmid *A Drunk Man Looks at a Thistle*, Somerset Maugham *The Casuarina Tree*, A. A. Milne *Winnie the Pooh* and Vladimir Nabokov *Mary*. T. E. Lawrence makes a limited edition of his *Seven Pillars of Wisdom* available for private circulation. Sean O'Casey writes *The Plough and the Stars* and Eugene O'Neill *The Great God Brown*. Ramon Novarro stars in *Ben Hur*, F. W. Murnau directs *Faust*, and Laurel and Hardy make *Slipping Wives*.

Births

French president Valéry Giscard d'Estaing; Irish prime minister Garret Fitzgerald; film directors John Schlesinger and Andrzej Wajda; Queen Elizabeth II; playwright Peter Shaffer; actress Marilyn Monroe; poet Allen Ginsberg; writers Alison Lurie and Anthony Sampson; philosopher Michel Foucault.

Personalities born in 1926

Rock-solid, stubborn, fixed individuals, personalities born in 1926 are emotionally self-protective and strong on stamina, but not always flexible. Jupiter in Aquarius makes them tolerant of cultural differences, and interested in new ideas. With Saturn aspecting Pluto, they are tough-minded, slightly obsessive, and set to deal with difficult times, but not good at change. They have a self-willed determination to succeed. With Jupiter in square to Neptune, they can be amazingly kind; with Saturn also in square, they are scared of failure and are great worriers, despite their tremendous endurance. Romantic at heart, they nevertheless do not wear their hearts on their sleeves, but keep their feelings deeply controlled.

Queen Elizabeth II

Born 21 April 1926, London, 2.40 pm.

Chart: Sun in Taurus; Moon, Neptune in Leo ◆ Mercury in Aries ◆ Venus, Uranus in Pisces ◆ Mars, Jupiter in Aquarius ◆ Pluto, Moon's North Node in Cancer ◆ Saturn in Scorpio ◆ Ascendant in Capricorn

Dominated by an over-conscientious, perfectionist Saturn in Scorpio on the midheaven, this is the chart of a workaholic executive, an individual brought up to put duty before pleasure, self-discipline before emotional needs. Her stamina, with six planets in her chart in fixed signs, including the Taurus Sun, is awesome. Speed and flexibility are not her forte, but staying the course over the long haul is. The iron training of her tough, though fey, Scottish mother shows all too clearly, and is perhaps a contributory factor in her own children's inability to find domestic stability. With a Moon–Neptune conjunction in Leo, she has a tendency to become absorbed in a dream world, and can be evasive rather than relating directly. The water grand trine in her chart is a further indication of an impressionable personality with a private inner world, who feels vulnerable to emotional overload and must escape to protect herself.

Her Taurus Sun attracts her to nature, horses and the outdoor life. Placed as it is in the communication area of her chart, she has a bright, inquiring mind which copes well with detail, and she prides herself on her quick uptake. Mercury in fiery Aries can make her remarkably sharp, though she hides it well. Her Capricorn ascendant makes her appear more conservative and duller than she is.

With Venus falling in her chart area of money, her other great love in life is beautiful objects and being able to spend as she pleases. With Saturn in Scorpio, however, she can also be stingy on occasion. Like her mother she is a bundle of contradictions, being fun-loving and even tactile yet distanced, extravagant and parsimonious at the same time.

Her Mars–Jupiter conjunction in Aquarius predisposes her to enthusiastic encounters with Commonwealth and other foreign leaders because she is tolerant of class, colour and creed differences and can be genuinely humanitarian in outlook.

The timing of her marriage in November 1947 to Prince Philip, one week after a highly afflicted Scorpio eclipse at her midheaven, was an inauspicious start to a lifelong partnership. When her father George VI died in 1952, the Moon–Neptune conjunction in her chart was being triggered by the Leo eclipse close to Pluto, which occurred within days of his death. With his passing, the burden of her destiny became inescapable, perhaps causing her to withdraw further emotionally to hide her inner confusion.

From 1983 onwards, Pluto again became a key agent for change—although it was not to her liking—as it began its 12-year journey through Scorpio, unsettling her sense of family stability and making it impossible to sweep tensions out of sight with the steady disintegration of Prince Charles's marriage. The fire at Windsor Castle, a much-loved part of her heritage, came as Pluto approached her midheaven, a symbolic analogy for the near-destruction of her life's work.

The all-too-public family traumas of recent years, involving the marital breakdowns of her children and their surrounding scandals, coincided, at their peak, with the massive triple conjunction of Saturn, Uranus and Neptune in Capricorn in the late 1980s. Initially this opposed the Queen's determined Pluto in Cancer, which partially controls her rather rigid attitudes to work and service. The three planets then crossed her ascendant, which signifies major changes in her public image. She would happily have retired after 1991 had her sense of duty not been so immovable. The continuing turmoil shows no hint of respite with Uranus

101

and Neptune now in fixed Aquarius jolting and jarring their way round the major pivotal fixed points of her chart. Whether the monarchy survives or not will be due to her seemingly unending endurance.

Marilyn Monroe
Born 1 June 1926, Los Angeles, 9.30 am Pacific Standard Time.
Chart: Sun, Mercury in Gemini ◆ Moon, Jupiter in Aquarius ◆ Venus in Aries ◆ Mars, Uranus in Pisces ◆ Saturn in Scorpio ◆ Pluto, Moon's North Node in Cancer; Neptune and ascendant in Leo

A bright-as-a-button Gemini, with the Sun near the midheaven when she was born as Norma Jean Baker, Marilyn Monroe had a flair for public life, which offered a way out of her inner emptiness. With a sugary-sweet, rather comforting Moon–Jupiter conjunction in easy-going Aquarius opposite a seductive Neptune on her flamboyant Leo ascendant, she was every man's dream woman. The underlying realities of having an unbalanced mother, who spent much of Marilyn's early years in mental asylums, and of her unsettled and sometimes abusive childhood, her traumatic adult relationships, and her sad end, are hidden in the deeply buried emotional chart areas. A self-protective water grand trine with ungiving Saturn in intense Scorpio aspecting Pluto in Cancer, which can be destructive of family life, and an explosive, destructive Mars–Uranus conjunction in Pisces, are not hopeful of any kind of ongoing domestic stability.

Queen Elizabeth, born only five weeks earlier, could turn the considerable endurance given her by the fixed planets outwards into the world in a disciplined work schedule, with her escape route being into an inner world of soothing fantasy. Born at a different time of day, Marilyn had the burden of her emotional intensity thrust inwards, where the resentment about not being nurtured gnawed constantly away at her. With Mars–Uranus in the chart area of sexuality, her inner world was dangerous, and she was drawn to walk on the wild side.

Her career, starting as a calendar pin-up, had risen sharply by 1954 to make her Hollywood's sex goddess. Saturn then in Scorpio was pushing her out of the low-profile years and—all things being equal—should have given her 21 years of rising success ahead. Her marriage to baseball player Joe DiMaggio lasted a bare nine months, finishing as she filmed *The Seven Year Itch*. In 1956, with successful Jupiter and Pluto crossing her ascendant and giving her renewed confidence, she married playwright Arthur Miller and made the smash film hits *The Prince and the Showgirl* and *Some Like It Hot*. But Uranus following not far behind made emotional stability difficult to maintain. They divorced in 1961 as Pluto approached the square to her Sun, pulling down old structures.

Her multiple marriages and high-profile liaisons with John Kennedy, another Gemini, and Scorpio Robert Kennedy, can be seen as a sad attempt to find the mothering she had never experienced. Compulsive sexuality was what drew her to both Kennedy brothers—and, where John was concerned, the hope for her of a career boost, inextricably tied up with her need for constant attention. Like John Kennedy (see page 86) and Eva Braun (see page 78), she had Mars in the chart area which can sometimes hint at a violent death, but also points to highly physical sexual needs.

When she was discovered dead from a drug overdose in 1962 (although controversy still surrounds the exact circumstances), expansive Jupiter was moving into her rather overloaded chart area of sexuality and psychological death and rebirth, which might have eased the strain. She was also due for a career boost. But Pluto moving closer to exact aspect with her Gemini Sun was a major transformation she obviously could not make.

1927

The widening Uranus–Pluto trine exerts a less disruptive influence than in the previous few years, although idealistic reforms are still being pushed vigorously through, sometimes with fanatical force. Uranus trailblazing into Aries in April for a seven-year sojourn, not seen here since the mid-1840s, is impulsive, outspoken and creates a mood of missionary zeal. Jupiter initially in Pisces fosters a kindlier, more charitable approach. Then it chases Uranus into Aries mid-year bringing a lively, joyful spirit. Four of the five outer planets are now in fire signs, promoting adventurous, entrepreneurial projects and foreign travel, and boosting confidence, although realism is not always present. Saturn in Sagittarius continues to put weight behind philosophical discussions and educational projects. Pluto continues its long, slow journey through Cancer, revolutionizing agriculture, transforming family values, fostering nationalist sentiments and bringing in new forms of government—fascism and communism.

Events

Allied military control of Germany ends. There is revolt in Portugal against the military dictatorship of General Carmona. The Chinese nationalist movement takes more territory, although Japan intervenes to halt its advance. In Ireland, the assassination of Kevin O'Higgins, a nationalist minister, brings about denunciation of the tactics of Irish Republicans, and the Dáil, the Irish parliament, declares revolutionary societies treasonable. Riots and a general strike occur in Vienna. Leon Trotsky is expelled from the Soviet Communist Party, having been stripped of government office in the previous two years. Iraq's independence is recognized. China and the USSR break off diplomatic relations. Adolf Hitler publishes the second volume of *Mein Kampf*.

Science and technology

Charles Lindbergh flies across the Atlantic, from New York to Paris, in 37 hours. British archaeologist Leonard Woolley makes exciting discoveries at the site of the ancient Babylonian city of Ur. Physicist Werner Carl Heisenberg propounds his Uncertainty Principle. The iron lung is invented. The British Broadcasting Corporation broadcasts the world's first-ever programme of recorded music presented by a disc jockey.

Culture

Giorgio de Chirico paints *Furniture in a Valley*, Edward Hopper *Drug Store*, Fernand Léger *Woman Holding a Vase*, and L. S. Lowry *Coming Out of School*. Sculptor Jacob Epstein creates *Madonna and Child*, and Eric Gill *Mankind*. Oscar Hammerstein collaborates with Jerome Kern on the musical *Showboat*. George Gershwin writes *Strike up the Band*. Robert Graves' *Poems, 1914–1926*, Ernest Hemingway's *Men Without Women*, Hermann Hesse's *Steppenwolf*, Franz Kafka's

America, Sinclair Lewis's *Elmer Gantry*, Henry Williamson's *Tarka the Otter*, Virginia Woolf's *To the Lighthouse*, Somerset Maugham's *The Letter* and Thornton Wilder's *The Bridge of San Luis Rey* are all published. In the world of film, René Clair makes *The Italian Straw Hat*, Sergei Komarov *The Kiss of Mary Pickford*, Abel Gance *Napoleon* and Sergei Eisenstein *October*. In the world of sport, the Harlem Globetrotters are formed. The first Ryder Cup match between professional golfers takes place. In the United States, a new world land-speed record of 203 mph is achieved.

Births
Film-maker Ken Russell; Swedish politician Olof Palme; singer Harry Bellafonte; playwright Neil Simon; artist Andy Warhol; jazz saxophonist and composer Gerry Mulligan.

Personalities born in 1927
Serious thinkers who are well-read and rather intense on philosophical or religious subjects, with a need to be highly praised for their intellectual abilities, typify those born in 1927. Kindly disposed to those who are unfortunate or disadvantaged, they work hard for a better society. Not always realistic, however, they push ahead with confidence and grand ideas. Those born up to 19 January with Jupiter in Aquarius are tolerant and interested in foreign cultures. Those born thereafter up to 6 June with Jupiter in Pisces are doubly compassionate and charitable. Those born thereafter with Jupiter in Aries are impulsive and headstrong and crusade passionately for their pet causes. Uranus also in Aries between 1 April and 5 November makes them bluntly outspoken, daring and resourceful, though occasionally irritable.

1928
Innovative Uranus moves into dynamic, headstrong Aries for seven years, trailblazing the way for the turbulent 1930s, but also promoting scientific and social reform. Neptune eases unhappily into Virgo for a 15-year sojourn, undermining the employment base, militating against creative enterprises, and leading to psychosomatic illnesses and the adulteration of food with chemical additives. Saturn, in aspect to Neptune in Leo, continues to put serious emphasis on philosophical or religious discussions, and pushes for idealistic, though not necessarily realistic goals. Jupiter skips confidently back into Aries after 23 January, giving rise to entrepreneurial enthusiasm; in Taurus after 4 June it lends an indulgent attraction to the good things in life. Only one major aspect between the heavier outer planets makes for a less stressful year, though it is the calm before the storm of the approaching Uranus–Pluto square in 1929.

Events
In the United States, a dam bursts in California killing 450 people. Stalin introduces the first Five Year Plan for a state-driven economy. On the US stock exchange, shares are bought on borrowed money. Over-production of coffee causes an economic crisis in Brazil. The voting age for women in Britain becomes the same as for men. The first African-American Congressman is elected in the United States. Chinese nationalists take Beijing. The French franc is devalued. The Kellogg-Briand pact, outlawing war,

is signed by 65 countries. Herbert Hoover is elected US President. Chiang Kai-shek becomes President in China. Benito Mussolini publishes *My Autobiography*.

Science and technology
Alexander Fleming discovers penicillin. The first marketable peanut butter is produced. The airship *Graf Zeppelin* flies across the Atlantic from Germany to the United States in four and a half days. John Logie Baird makes a transatlantic television transmission and demonstrates colour television.

Culture
Max Beckmann paints *Black Lilies*, Max Ernst *The Virgin Spanking the Infant Jesus Before Three Witnesses*, Henri Matisse *Seated Odalisque* and Pablo Picasso his *Bathers* series. George Gershwin writes *An American in Paris*, Maurice Ravel composes his ballet *Bolero*, and Kurt Weill his musical *The Threepenny Opera*. Al Jolson sings 'Sonny Boy', and Paul Robeson sings 'Ol' Man River' in the musical *Showboat*. Aldous Huxley's *Point Counter Point*, D. H. Lawrence's *Lady Chatterley's Lover*, Ezra Pound's *A Draft of the Cantos*, Siegfried Sassoon's *Memoirs of a Fox-Hunting Man*, Stephen Spender's *Nine Experiments*, Evelyn Waugh's *Decline and Fall*, Virginia Woolf's *Orlando*, and W. B. Yeats's *The Tower* are published. Bertolt Brecht writes *The Caucasian Chalk Circle*, and Eugene O'Neill *Strange Interlude*. In the world of film, George Eastman produces the first moving colour pictures, Jean Epstein makes *The Fall of the House of Usher* and Jean Renoir makes *The Little Matchgirl*. Al Jolson stars in *The Singing Fool*, and Walt Disney makes *Steamboat Willie* featuring Mickey Mouse.

Births
Playwright Edward Albee; Latin American revolutionary Ernesto 'Che' Guevara; film-maker Stanley Kubrick; actress Grace Kelly; linguistics expert Noam Chomsky.

Personalities born in 1928
Bluntly outspoken, freedom-loving and daring, with experimental Uranus in hot-headed Aries, those born in 1928 are adventurous individuals, naively impulsive though not always sensible. Serious about spiritual or political beliefs, they fear disapproval and can be self-righteous. Neptune in Leo until 22 September fosters grandiose fantasies about money and romance. Neptune in Virgo marks individuals born after that with anxiety about employment prospects, with a childhood in the Depression of the 1930s to come. They have a tendency to suffer hard-to-diagnose ailments or to worry about inconsequential details. Those born up to 23 January with Jupiter in Pisces are kind-natured and charitable; those born with Jupiter in Aries between then and 4 June are fiery, energetic, dashing in where angels fear to tread but tending to be lucky; those born with Jupiter in Taurus adore the good life, and are sensual and indulgent.

1929
Disruptive Uranus approaching the turbulent, violent square with Pluto stokes up the revolutionary, fanatical climate, undermining stability and ruthlessly jolting changes through. This is the start of several years of social upheaval. Neptune

firmly, though not happily, now in Virgo undermines employment prospects. Restrictive Saturn heading for businesslike Capricorn in hard aspect to Uranus in the latter part of the year hints at severe economic cutbacks. Pluto, only two thirds through Cancer, continues to change family values, but not always for the better. Even Jupiter in Taurus until 14 June—usually the bringer of the good life—fails to lift the mood. Jupiter in Gemini thereafter is lightweight, cheerful, but superficial.

Events

A dictatorship is established amongst the Serbs, Croats and Slovenes. In Chicago, Al Capone's gang guns down seven of Bugs Moran's gansters in what becomes known as the 'St Valentine's Day Massacre'. The fascists take control in Italy. In Germany, communists clash with the police, leaving 15 dead. Pope Pius XI, no longer a 'voluntary prisoner' following the Lateran Treaty, leaves the Vatican, the first Pope to do so since 1870. Following disputes over the use of the Wailing Wall in Jerusalem, Arabs attack Jews in Palestine. Wall Street shares crash in late October with the Sun and Mars together in Scorpio a few days before the Scorpio solar eclipse, the symbol for the acute crisis in the world capitalist economy. In Mexico, the National Revolutionary Party is formed. In South Africa, the term 'apartheid', meaning the separate development of races, is first used.

Science and technology

The *Graf Zeppelin* flies around the world. Kodak develop a 16-mm colour film. Crease-resisting cotton fabric is developed. The motor industry becomes the largest sector of the American economy.

Culture

New York sees the opening of the Museum of Modern Art, with works by Paul Cézanne, Paul Gauguin, Georges Seurat and Vincent Van Gogh. The Second Surrealist Manifesto is issued, and the group is joined by Salvador Dali. Paul Klee paints *Fool in a Trance*, René Magritte *The Treachery of Images* (or *Ceci n'est pas une pipe*), Piet Mondrian *Composition with Yellow and Blue* and Pablo Picasso *Nude in an Armchair*. Henry Moore sculpts *Mask*. Béla Bartók composes his String Quartets Nos 3 and 4. In the world of popular music, Noel Coward writes the musical *Bitter Sweet*, Franz Lehár the operetta *The Land of Smiles* and Hoagy Carmichael the song 'Happy Days Are Here Again'. *Fifty Million Frenchmen*, Cole Porter's first major success, is staged. Jean Cocteau's *Les Enfants Terribles*, William Faulkner's *The Sound and the Fury*, Robert Graves' *Goodbye to All That*, Ernest Hemingway's *A Farewell to Arms*, Axel Munthe's *The Story of San Michele*, and J. B. Priestley's *The Good Companions* are published. George Bernard Shaw writes *The Apple Cart*. Alfred Hitchcock makes *Blackmail* King Vidor makes *Hallelujah*, and Rowland V. Lee *The Mysterious Dr Fu Manchu*. Louise Brooks stars in *Pandora's Box* and Gary Cooper in *The Virginian*.

Births

Sergio Leone, film director and maker of 'spaghetti' westerns; civil-rights campaigner Martin Luther King; racing drivers Graham Hill and Stirling Moss; athlete Roger Bannister; actress Audrey Hepburn; golfer Arnold Palmer; Australian prime minister Bob Hawke; playwright John Osborne; first lady Jackie Onassis.

Personalities born in 1929

Outspoken, active and rather rebellious individuals characterize those born in 1929. With Uranus in Aries aspecting Pluto, they have daring, courage and initiative, but not always realistic common sense—this is especially marked in those born in the cardinal signs, Aries, Cancer, Libra and Capricorn. They can be fanatically obstinate about their opinions, and very compassionate at the same time. With Neptune in Virgo, they can be chaotic about work, not always trusting their hunches, and occasionally suffering from psychosomatic ailments. Those born with Jupiter in Taurus up to 14 June love the good life, eat well and attract money. Thereafter those born with Jupiter in Gemini have their moments of being light-hearted and talkative. This trait is less evident in those born after 30 November with Saturn in Capricorn, who are overly serious and slightly depressive, have hard childhoods, and are very resistant to emotional change, although their lives tend to be marked by upheavals. They do, however, fight to bring about a fairer society and can be creative.

Martin Luther King

Born 15 January 1929, 12 pm Central Standard Time, Atlanta, Georgia.
Chart: Sun in Capricorn ♦ Moon, Venus in Pisces ♦ Mars in Gemini ♦ Ascendant, Moon's North Node, and Jupiter in Taurus ♦ Saturn in Sagittarius ♦ Neptune in Virgo ♦ Uranus in Aries

A resilient, practical, rather controlling Capricorn with a penetrating style of speech, Martin Luther King had an outer drive and inner peace that many close to him envied. Jupiter above the horizon when he was born gave him a sense of vision and of confidence in his own judgement, which was a constant support. With a sympathetically sensitive Moon–Venus in Pisces conjunction in his chart area of social vision, he had the ability to attract friends among the wider public. He was highly strung, and had an uncertain temper with a frustrating Mars–Saturn opposition squaring onto the Moon, but along with this went a courage to face danger and a self-discipline about sticking to his course. Through the 1960s when his civil-rights movement came to prominence, Saturn was riding high across his Aquarian midheaven as he gave his unforgettable 'I have a dream ...' speech in front of 200,000 African-Americans in Washington. Jupiter in Aries was also boosting his Capricorn Sun and Pluto in Cancer opposition.

In the turbulent years that followed, the Uranus–Pluto conjunction in Virgo (see *1960–1969*, pages 159–176) was the major influence in operation, coinciding with major revolts and rebellions in society at large. It was opposing King's visionary Pisces Moon, bringing emotional turmoil to his personal life, but also connecting him to the Zeitgeist, since the Moon in the charts of political personalities is their barometer of the public mood. Tragically it also inevitably brought the explosive energy closer to his accident-prone Mars–Saturn opposition. In 1968, when the spirit of destructiveness was pervasive—the Vietnam War was at its height, the Soviets invaded Czechoslovakia, the Irish Troubles started—the Uranus–Pluto conjunction finally hit home. Uranus jarring off his Saturn and Pluto squaring Mars became a murderous combination, and he was assassinated—a mere two months before Robert Kennedy was shot.

Jackie Onassis (née Bouvier)
Born 28 July 1929, 2.30 pm Eastern Daylight Time, Southampton, New York.
Chart: Sun, Mercury in Leo ◆ Venus, Jupiter in Gemini ◆ Moon, Uranus in Aries ◆ Moon's North Node in Taurus ◆ Pluto in Cancer ◆ Mars, Neptune in Virgo ◆ Saturn in Sagittarius ◆ Ascendant in Scorpio

A communicative, widely read, well-travelled, rather philosophical Leo is what reflects from Jackie Onassis's chart. Creative, caring, but also deceptive Neptune at her midheaven, contributed to the mystery of her progress through life and her career. With Mars in perfectionist Virgo at her midheaven, she was adept at smokescreening, and hid her undoubtedly ambitious streak behind a veil of vagueness. Expansive, extravagant Jupiter close to spendthrift Venus in the area of joint finances hinted at her expectation that someone else would always provide for her lavish habits. Rather mean with her own money, as indicated by Saturn's position, she could go wild at the expense of a close partner.

Born six months after Martin Luther King, she still shared with him Saturn-in-Sagittarius's seriousness about ideas, and Neptune-in-Virgo's dedication to service. With Uranus in Aries, both had a rather flamboyant need to cut across conventional boundaries regardless of social cost; and squaring onto Pluto in Cancer, they were destined to live through highly unsettled times, personally and publically. They also shared the difficult Moon's Node in Taurus, which brings almost self-chosen emotional turmoil in early adult relationships.

When John Kennedy was shot in Dallas in 1963 beside her, transiting Pluto was exactly on her midheaven Mars in Virgo—a very dark energy from the underworld—bringing acute danger within a hair's breadth. Uranus was aspecting Jupiter exactly, which typically indicates relief from strain, while Neptune was stationed on her ascendant, pointing ahead to a time of confusion.

1930–1939

The grandiose dreams of the 'Roaring Twenties' come crashing down as undermining Neptune is established for more than a decade in Virgo, sign of the worker. Saturn in the business-ruler Capricorn opposing Pluto bodes ill for economic growth in the early years of the 1930s. Uranus in reckless, assertive Aries squaring onto Pluto in nationalist Cancer fans the flames of fanatical fervour. The decade opens with the four outer planets all at awkward angles to each other, indicating disappointments with no immediate solutions. Midway through the decade Uranus heads into Taurus, pushing slowly for financial reforms. Pluto moves out of a 25-year stay in Cancer where it has transformed family values, the status of women and agricultural food production. From 1937 it moves into Leo for 20 years, promoting the individual over family relationships, and coinciding with the development of atomic power. The Saturn-in-Pisces and Neptune-in-Virgo opposition of 1936 and 1937 is deeply creative, but causes obsessive, paranoid worry as well. Saturn returns to hard aspect with Pluto as the Second World War breaks out.

1930

The tough-minded, rather brutal Saturn–Pluto–Uranus triangle makes for a heavy mood. Restrictive Saturn in materialistic Capricorn—always an indicator of economic cutbacks—opposes controlling Pluto in Cancer, hinting at an intransigent situation with no instant answers for business or family life as the world economic crisis bites. The Saturn–Pluto aspect also hints at misery for the masses in war. Squaring onto trailblazing, revolutionary Uranus in daredevil Aries, it paves the way for coups, riots and general insurgence. Fanaticism is fanned; violence is inevitable. Jupiter moving into Cancer after 27 June mitigates the Depression for the lucky few with resources and stamina. Neptune continuing in Virgo is not well placed to push through practical reforms.

Events

Mahatma Gandhi begins his civil disobedience campaign in India. Ras Tafari, regent of Ethiopia, becomes emperor (Haile Selassie) on the death of the empress after a revolt led by her brother. The last Allied troops leave the Rhineland. There is an uprising of Kurds on the Turkish border. A neo-fascist movement starts in Portugal, and in Spain there is a military uprising against the government. In Poland, after the outbreak of centre-left mass protests, Josef Pilsudski forms a new government; 70 opposition members are imprisoned. A military junta takes over Peru, in Argentina there is an army revolt, and martial law is declared in Brazil. A British airship crashes, killing 44 people. Two weeks later, on the day of a strongly aspected total solar eclipse, two separate coal mine explosions in Germany kill 362. There is an attempted assassination of the Japanese prime minister. Pope Pius XI condemns birth control as a grave and unnatural sin. The world population rises above 2 billion.

Science and technology

Amy Johnson makes a solo flight from Britain to Australia. The photoflash bulb and acrylic plastic are invented. The planet Pluto is discovered. Ready-sliced bread is introduced. In Britain, the BBC broadcasts the first televised play.

Culture

Marc Chagall paints *Lovers in the Lilacs*, Paul Klee *The Prophet*, Fernand Léger *La Joconde with Keys*, and Joán Miró *Painting*. Alberto Giacometti sculpts *Suspended Belt*. Igor Stravinsky composes *Symphony of Psalms*, Eric Coates composes 'By the Sleepy Lagoon', Kurt Weill, with Bertolt Brecht, writes the opera *The Rise and Fall of the City of Mahogany*, George Gershwin composes *Girl Crazy* and Marlene Dietrich sings 'Falling in Love Again'. Sigmund Freud's *Civilisation and its Discontents* is published. James Bridie publishes *The Anatomist*, Agatha Christie *Murder at the Vicarage*, T. S. Eliot *Ash Wednesday*, Dashiell Hammett *The Maltese Falcon*, Somerset Maugham *Cakes and Ale* and Evelyn Waugh *Vile Bodies*. In the world of film, Luis Bunuel's *L'Age d'Or*, Jean Vigo's *All Quiet on the Western Front*, Howard Hawks' *Hell's Angels* and Alfred Hitchcock's *Dial M for Murder*. Marlene Dietrich stars in *The Blue Angel*.

Births

Composer and lyricist Stephen Sondheim; West German chancellor Helmut Kohl; artist Jasper Johns; philosopher Jacques Derrida; poet Ted Hughes; playwright Harold Pinter.

Personalities born in 1930

Blessed with awesome stamina and a great deal of initiative, personalities born in 1930 are forced to cope with a tough life and continuing upheavals through their childhoods, which marks them out for challenging, though not always happy, adult lives. With strongly aspected Uranus in Aries, they are often impatient, demanding personal freedom, yet with the Saturn–Pluto opposition they can be enormously stubborn and slightly obsessive. They regard themselves as loners and outsiders, traits that are especially marked in those born under the cardinal signs, Aries, Cancer, Libra and Aries. Those born with Jupiter in Gemini up to 27 June are bright communicators; those born after this date, with Jupiter in Cancer, push hard for a comfortable home, and often succeed in this since their fear of failure drives them on. All have Neptune in Virgo which makes them prone to psychosomatic ailments and distrustful of their intuition.

1931

Nothing comes easily with austere Saturn in businesslike Capricorn in exact opposition to unyielding Pluto, indicating hard labour for the masses with no immediate hope of change, and pointing to a need for stamina. Squaring onto unpredictable Uranus—another signpost of tough economic struggles—it coincides with a time of instability and acute restlessness. Uranus in its revolutionary mood in Aries, drawing closer to the exact aspect with Pluto, brings fanatical fervour to the fore and provokes violent disagreements and macho gestures. There is a tremendous fear of failure with Jupiter in Cancer until 18 July, in opposition to Saturn. Paradoxically, there is a strong success drive, too, since Jupiter also crosses Pluto, producing a 'might makes right' attitude in the strong-minded. After 18 July Jupiter in flamboyant Leo adds a lavish touch, although it also promotes unwise speculation.

Events

In Spain, after republican gains in the municipal elections, Niceto Alcala Zamora, leader of the Madrid Revolutionary Committee, demands the abdication of King Alfonso XIII, who flees; Zamora becomes president of a provisional government. The bankruptcy of the Credit-Anstalt Bank in Austria initiates the financial collapse of Central Europe, with total bank closure in Germany for three weeks. There is a budget deficit of record levels in Britain; government economy measures spark riots in London and Glasgow; Britain receives Franco–US loan. In Korea, there are anti-Chinese riots. In the United States, Al Capone is sentenced to 11 years in jail for tax evasion; a record wheat crop leads to collapsed prices and agricultural discontent, and dire economic problems in Nevada lead the state to raise revenues by becoming a centre for marriage, divorce and gambling. The Black Muslims (Nation of Islam) movement is founded by W. D. Fard in Detroit. A fire in the Vatican destroys 15,000 books.

Science and technology

The Technicolor corporation introduces colour photography, based on the simultaneous exposure of red-, green- and blue-sensitive films. Petrol is produced from coal. British physicists John D. Cockcroft and Ernest Walker develop a high-voltage particle accelerator, which they use to split lithium atoms. The first ascent into the stratosphere is made.

Culture

Salvador Dali paints *The Persistence of Memory*, Edward Hopper *Route 6*, Piet Mondrian *Composition with Two Lines*, and Pablo Picasso *Figures on the Seashore*. Henry Moore sculpts *Composition*. Béla Bartók composes his Piano Concerto No. 2, William Walton writes the oratorio *Belshazzar's Feast*, Noel Coward writes *Cavalcade*, and George and Ira Gershwin *Of Thee I Sing*. Sergei Rachmaninov's music is banned in the USSR as decadent. In Britain, singer and comedian George Formby Jr presents his own variety show, starting a highly successful film and record career. Pearl Buck's *The Good Earth*, William Faulkner's *Sanctuary*, Anthony Powell's *Afternoon Men*, and Vita Sackville-West's *All Passion Spent* are published. Eugene O'Neill writes *Mourning Becomes Electra*. Charlie Chaplin makes *City Lights*. Bela Lugosi stars in *Dracula*, Boris Karloff in *Frankenstein* and Gracie Fields in *Sally in Our Alley*; Greta Garbo plays Mata Hari.

Births

Russian presidents Boris Yeltsin and Mikhail Gorbachev; media magnate Rupert Murdoch; actor Clint Eastwood; South African archbishop Desmond Tutu.

Personalities born in 1931

Rather similar to 1930 personalities, those born in 1931 are determined survivors, with incredible stamina. Three outer planets in the cardinal signs of Aries, Cancer, Libra and Capricorn give those born under these signs a strong sense of initiative. Highly Uranian, they are restless, sometimes reckless, bluntly outspoken, and determined to maintain their personal freedom. Often innovators, they can destabilize what is going on around them. Accustomed from their earliest years to dealing with upheaval, they find stability unfamiliar and difficult to maintain. With strong Saturn–Pluto aspects they can be obsessive, depressive and regard themselves as outsiders, but they can also be very successful because they push hard to rise up from their beginnings. Those born with Jupiter in Cancer until 18 July want comfort at home and so double their determination to succeed. Thereafter those born with Jupiter in Leo love anything lavish and flamboyant, and can be romantic and rather wild with money.

1932

The nationalist sentiments of Pluto in Cancer are stoked up to fanatical levels as Uranus draws into exact hard aspect in Aries, and the Nazis rise to prominence in German elections. The brutally tough, discouraging, war-mongering Saturn–Pluto opposition is just waning as the year opens but still exerts massive economic pressures. These are turbulent, violent times for some, with Uranus in Aries highly active, but miserably depressing for others,

111

especially the disadvantaged, with austere Saturn blocked from recovery by obdurate Pluto. Neptune in Virgo for another 12 years undermines work prospects and creative enterprises. Saturn slides into more tolerant Aquarius on 25 February, remaining there until 13 August, and returning again after 20 November, lightening the intolerable pressures and promoting scientific endeavours and humanitarian ideals. Jupiter in Leo until 11 August produces flashes of flamboyant pageantry; thereafter in Virgo it lends itself to charitable causes, and raises the ideal of service.

Events
Mahatma Gandhi returns to India, resumes civil disobedience, and is arrested again. A fascist coup takes place in Lithuania. Eamon de Valera, leading Fianna Fáil, wins the general election in the Irish Free State. A Japanese puppet republic is proclaimed in Manchuria. A fascist revolt is suppressed in Finland. Adolf Hitler wins 11 million votes in the German elections, but fails to win or to form a coalition, although the Nazis are the largest single party in the Prussian parliament. Germany is given equal rights with other nations and returns to the Geneva Disarmament Conference. There is a bloodless coup in Siam. In Chile a military coup ousts President Davila, and the three-year Chaco War begins between Bolivia and Paraguay. Unsuccessful revolts take place in Brazil and Spain. Financial crisis hits Belgium and Hungary. F. D. Roosevelt wins the US presidential elections. The baby son of aviator Charles Lindbergh is kidnapped and murdered, six days before the March eclipse in Pisces. King George V makes the first Christmas broadcast as British head of state. Aristotle Onassis buys six freight ships and starts his shipping business. There is famine in the USSR.

Science and technology
Amelia Earhart becomes the first woman to fly solo across the Atlantic. 'Heavy hydrogen' is discovered.

Culture
Henri Matisse begins to paint *Dance* and Man Ray his *Observatory Time—The Lovers*. Henry Moore produces his first sculpture with a hole through it. In the musical arena, George Gershwin writes *Cuban Overture*, Maurice Ravel composes Piano Concerto in G, Cole Porter's show *The Gay Divorcee* is performed, Tommy Dorsey's band plays 'I'm Getting Sentimental Over You', and Jay Gourlay's 'Brother, Can You Spare a Dime' is sung. Louis-Ferdinand Celine's *Journey to the End of the Night*, Lewis Grassic Gibbons's *Sunset Song*, Stella Gibbons's *Cold Comfort Farm*, Ernest Hemingway's *Death in the Afternoon*, Aldous Huxley's *Brave New World*, Charles Morgan's *The Fountain*, Boris Pasternak's *Second Birth*, Damon Runyon's *Guys and Dolls*, Bertolt Brecht's *The Mother*, and J. B. Priestley's *Dangerous Corner* are all published. In the film world, Leni Riefenstahl's *The Blue Light*, Frank Lloyd's *Cavalcade* and Rouben Mamoulian's *Doctor Jekyll and Mr Hyde* are released. Gary Cooper stars in *A Farewell to Arms*, Marlene Dietrich in *Shanghai Express* and Johnny Weissmuller in *Tarzan the Ape Man*.

Births
Film directors François Truffaut, Louis Malle and Milos Forman; novelists John Updike and V. S. Naipaul; dramatist and theatre director Athol Fugard; poet Sylvia Plath; playwright Arnold Wesker; French prime minister Jacques Chirac.

Personalities born in 1932
Less awesomely tough than the personalities of the two previous years, individuals born in 1932 are still outspoken, hot-headed, and rather obsessive in their outlook. Living in tumultuous times, they become adapted to conditions of constant upheaval and find stability difficult to maintain. Those born before 25 February with Saturn in Capricorn, and between 13 August and 20 November, struggle to find financial security, and are exceptionally hard-working, though slightly depressive. Those born when Saturn is in Aquarius—from 25 February to 13 August, and after 20 November—have good mental concentration, inquiring minds and are serious about friendships. The Jupiter-in-Leo types born up to 11 August have a dash of optimism, and like to impress. Those born thereafter with Jupiter in earthy Virgo are more practical, kind-hearted, and compassionate.

1933
The violently fanatical Uranus exact square to Pluto, causing destructive disruption, marches in tune to Hitler's rise to power and the opening of the first concentration camp. Uranus in Aries can be trailblazing since it has the courage of its convictions, but its negative effects triggered by power-hungry Pluto in nationalist Cancer lead to extremism, a total rejection of the past, and a dismantling of traditional social structures. Neptune continues its chaotic progress through Virgo, undermining work prospects and health. Saturn in scientific Aquarius is steadier, ambitious for knowledge, and tries to push forward humanitarian schemes. Jupiter in Virgo also puts emphasis on service as an ideal up to 10 September. Then it moves into fair-minded Libra, striving for balanced agreements, though too politely to withstand the blast from the stronger planets.

Events
Adolf Hitler is appointed chancellor of Germany in January. Three days after the February eclipse, the German Reichstag (parliament) is destroyed by fire. Hitler takes dictatorial powers on the exact Uranus–Pluto square in March, and opens Dachau, first of the concentration camps for enemies of the Nazi regime. The official persecution of the Jews begins in Germany, with a national boycott of Jewish shops and businesses. Germany withdraws from the League of Nations and its Disarmanent Conference. In the German election in November, 92 per cent vote for Nazi candidates (on a 96 per cent turnout). Australia claims one third of Antarctica. There is an armistice between China and Japan, and a coup in Thailand. The Cuban army overthrows the government. Brazil becomes a dictatorship.

Science and technology
The first successful removal of a human lung takes place. A round-the-world flight is made, in 7 days 18 hours.

Culture

Wassily Kandinsky, Paul Klee and others leave Nazi Germany, and the Bauhaus design school is closed. Paul Klee paints *Von der Liste Gestrichen* and Max Beckmann paints *Departure*. Olivier Messiaen writes *The Ascension*, Béla Bartók his Piano Concerto No. 2, and Richard Strauss his opera *Arabella*, and Kurt Weill composes *The Seven Deadly Sins*. George Balanchine forms the School of American Ballet. Carl Jung publishes *Modern Man in Search of a Soul*. Other publications include George Orwell's *Down and Out in Paris and London*, H. G. Wells's *The Shape of Things to Come*, Erskine Caldwell's *God's Little Acre*, André Malraux's *Man's Estate*, Thomas Mann's *The Tales of Jacob*, Dorothy L. Sayers's *Murder Must Advertise*, Gertrude Stein's *The Autobiography of Alice B. Toklas*, Nathaniel West's *Miss Lonelyhearts*, Antonia White's *Frost in May* and Federico Garcia Lorca's *Blood Wedding*. In films, Carmen Miranda stars in *A Voz do Carnival*, Jean Harlow in *Dinner at Eight*, the Marx Brothers in *Duck Soup*, Hedy Lamarr in *Ecstasy*, James Cagney in *Footlight Parade* and Mae West in *She Done Him Wrong*. Busby Berkeley choreographs *42nd Street*, George Cukor directs *Little Women* and Alexander Korda directs *The Private Lives of Henry VIII*, starring Charles Laughton.

Births

Akihito, emperor of Japan; composer Henryk Gorecki; playwright Joe Orton; novelist Philip Roth; architect Richard Rogers; film director Roman Polanski.

Personalities born in 1933

Bluntly outspoken, rather unsettled temperaments mark those born in 1933—they are prepared to fight obstinately for their individual freedoms, no matter what disruptions this causes. Acclimatized from early life to upheavals, they do not easily maintain stability. This is especially marked in those born in Aries, Cancer, Libra and Capricorn. Those born with Saturn in Aquarius have steady, inquiring minds, good concentration, and are serious about friendships and group ventures. Those with Neptune in Virgo are idealistic about work, though not always practical. They can suffer from psychosomatic ailments. Those born up to 10 September with Jupiter in Virgo are charitable and compassionate and work in a spirit of service, and can be successful with the helpful aspect to Pluto. Those born thereafter are better balanced, keen on good relationships and justice for all.

1934

The hard, exact Uranus–Pluto aspect for the third year running starts the year on a grimly fanatical note. Extremist measures are pushed forcefully through, with disruptions and violent disagreements. A dark energy, it tends to tear down old structures, and destroy the past without putting positive new foundations in place. Uranus in Aries is headstrong, explosive, trailblazing. Pluto in Cancer promotes nationalist sentiments, continuing its slow overturning of Victorian family values. Uranus starts the move into earthy Taurus between 7 June and 12 October, fostering new business ideas that are practical and original. Neptune limps on through Virgo as it has done since 1928, undermining the business base, employment prospects and general health, with another eight years to run. Saturn in Aquarius for its final full year concentrates scientific endeavours and struggles to put humanitarian ideals into practice. Jupiter in Libra until 12 October is essentially fair-minded, though indecisive. In Scorpio thereafter, it mildly promotes financial affairs.

Events

There are riots in Paris over government corruption, brought to light after the death of a fraudulent financier. Germany signs a 10-year non-aggression pact with Poland. There are general strikes in Austria and in France. The Belgian king dies in a climbing accident, three days after the February total solar eclipse. In Germany, in June, there is the 'Night of the Long Knives', a Nazi purge to break the power of the Storm Troopers; those murdered include over 70 leading Nazis. In July, SS leader Himmler takes control of the secret police, and the SS (Gestapo) becomes an independent organization within the Nazi party. The chancellor of Austria is murdered in an attempted Nazi coup. Hitler, the *Führer* ('Leader'), becomes both president and chancellor of Germany. There are fascist and anti-fascist demonstrations in London. The Geneva Disarmament Conference ends in failure. The USSR is admitted to the League of Nations; in the USSR itself, there are assassinations and executions, with Stalin's connivance: 126 are killed. King Alexander of Yugoslavia is assassinated by Croats. Forced to move under harassment from nationalist forces, the 'Long March' of Chinese communists, led by Mao Tse Tung, begins; 100,00 people walk 6000 miles in a year. The United States police kill robbers Bonnie and Clyde and notorious bank robber John Dillinger. The island of Alcatraz is purchased as a prison site.

Science and technology

The cat's-eye reflector is invented. A bathysphere, used for deep-sea observation, descends 922 metres (3025 feet) into the Atlantic.

Culture

Salvador Dali starts *Mae West* and René Magritte paints *The Human Condition*. Sculptures produced include Max Beckmann's *The Man in Darkness*, Alberto Giacometti's *The Invisible Object* and Picasso's *Woman with Leaves*. Sergei Rachmaninov composes *Rhapsody on a Theme of Paganini*, Franz Schmidt his Symphony No. 4, and Dmitri Shostakovich *The Lady Macbeth of Mtensk*. Cole Porter writes the hit song 'Anything Goes', with lyrics by comic novelist P. G. Wodehouse. Wilhelm Reich's *The Mass Psychology of Fascism* and Bertrand Russell's *Freedom and Civilisation* are published. Other publications include James Cain's *The Postman Always Rings Twice*, F. Scott Fitzgerald's *Tender Is the Night*, Robert Graves' *I, Claudius*, Vladimir Nabokov's *Despair*, William Saroyan's *The Daring Young Man on the Flying Trapeze*, Ben Traven's *The Treasure of the Sierra Nevada*, Evelyn Waugh's *A Handful of Dust*, Lillian Hellman's *The Children's Hour* and Federico Garcia Lorca's *Yerma*. J. B. Priestley writes the play *Eden End* , and Jean Cocteau writes *La Machine Infernale*. Boris Karloff stars in *The Black Cat* and Robert Donat in *The Count of Monte Cristo*. Cecil B. De Mille makes *Cleopatra* and Alexander Korda makes *The Scarlet Pimpernel*. W. S. Van Dyke directs *The Thin Man*.

Births
Playwright Alan Bennett; actress Sophia Loren; murderer Charles Manson.

Personalities born in 1934
Those born in the early months up to 7 June, and after 12 October with the almost exact Uranus-in-Aries and Pluto-in-Cancer aspect, are dynamically outspoken, headstrong, rather disruptive and accustomed to upheavals. Not always settled in their private lives, they are determined to have personal freedom. Saturn in Aquarius all year makes for serious, inquiring minds, good at concentrating, and keen on humanitarian ideals and loyal friendships. Neptune in Virgo can throw up hard-to-diagnose ailments. Those born between 7 June and 12 October with Uranus in Taurus are stubborn, can have artistic talents and inspired ideas about handling money, and tend to be attached to traditional family values. Those born with Jupiter in Libra until 12 October have a strong concern for justice and fairness in relationships. With Jupiter in aspect to Uranus and Pluto, they are lucky, successful and like to travel. Jupiter in Scorpio after 12 October makes for good financiers and trusted confidantes.

Charles Manson
Born 12 November 1934, 4.40 pm Eastern Standard Time, Cincinnati, Ohio.
Chart: Sun, Venus, Jupiter, Mercury in Scorpio ✦ Moon, Moon's North Node and Saturn in Aquarius ✦ Mars, Neptune in Virgo ✦ Uranus in Aries ✦ Pluto in Cancer ✦ Ascendant in Taurus

A clutch of deceptively amiable planets in intense Scorpio gives a hint of where cult murderer Manson's charismatic hold over his teenage followers derives. The rampant sexuality fostered by these is intensified by a highly controlling Pluto in Cancer, but rendered perverse by a total emotional block from the chill Moon–Saturn conjunction in Aquarius. A selfish, domineering personality, he is detached from any real human feeling. His mother was wildly erratic, unpredictable, both over-possessive and rejecting, an impossibly confusing mix for a young child to handle. To compensate he set up his own Manson Family cult, where sexuality and drugs ran rampant under his direct control. Jupiter in Scorpio, which occurs in his chart, can encourage dabbling in psychic phenomena to try to manipulate occult forces for personal gain. There is a degree of psychological disturbance from an unbalanced Uranus above his ascendant in reckless Aries squaring onto an abusive Pluto. But for all that, nothing leaps out of the chart that is as dramatically horrific as his murder of Roman Polanski's wife Sharon Tate, their unborn child and three friends on 10 August 1969.

Manson had been through a tumultuous few years in the mid-1960s, with brutality writ large, especially in 1964 and 1965, followed by a near-paranoid breakdown, possibly drug-induced. But what provides the key to the events of 1969 is the Mars–Neptune conjunction in Virgo, a highly theatrical, publicity-seeking influence which encouraged him to seek fame at any cost. This was being sparked off by Pluto in Virgo, sitting close to a specially violent Virgo eclipse at the end of the month. In the months after the Sharon Tate murder running up to his indictment, the My Lai massacre trial was shocking America to the core, exposing even more horrific atrocities committed by GIs in Vietnam. High-profile murders have occurred before around this particular eclipse cycle, which takes place approximately once every 18 $\frac{1}{2}$ years: in February 1933 in the United States, a failed assassination attempt on president elect Roosevelt resulted in the death of the Mayor of Chicago; next time around, in 1987 in Britain, a gunman ran amok with a machine-gun in the English town of Hungerford, killing 16 people before committing suicide.

In that eerie and totally inexplicable synchronicity of astrology, when two people meet for the first and last time but with hugely significant results, Sharon Tate and Manson are uncannily linked. She had her Aquarian Sun on exactly the same degree as his Moon's Node in Aquarius; and her Virgo Moon falls within two degrees of his Mars–Neptune conjunction.

Born a year earlier than Manson, Roman Polanski—a Leo with an Aquarian–Saturn opposition—also has key links to Manson's chart in the Aquarian and Virgo planets. His own chart all too accurately describes his terrifying early life in the Polish ghetto, his mother being killed in a Nazi concentration camp, and his struggle to survive. His later career, with acclaimed films *Repulsion*, *Rosemary's Baby* and *Chinatown*, not surprisingly reflects his obsession with the darkness of human nature.

1935

The waning Uranus–Pluto square causes less active disruption, although the destructive, fanatical views instilled in previous years have now gained ground. Uranus moving out of hot-headed Aries into earthy Taurus on 29 March, where it stays for seven years, is an instigator of new financial and business ideas. Uranus's urge for freedom is restricted by the stubbornly materialistic Taurus, although it does provide stamina for new ventures. Saturn shifts out of scientific, serious-thinking Aquarius on 5 February to sit uneasily in dreamy Pisces for three years, creating a fretful, worrying mood of paranoia and vain regret for a lost past. Opposing Neptune in Virgo it is highly creative, though prone to moods of Dionysian madness as well as addictions. Jupiter in Scorpio promotes financial ventures until 9 November, largely successfully, in good aspect to Pluto. Moving into Sagittarius thereafter it engenders optimism.

Events

In the USSR, leading Communists are arrested. There is an uprising in Greece. Germany repudiates the disarmament clauses of the Versailles Treaty, and Italy, France and Britain protest at German rearmament. Hitler announces the 'Nuremberg Laws', restricting Jewish activities, and the Swastika becomes the official flag. In Austria, there is a bloodless coup against the Nazis. The Gallup Poll is introduced in the United States. Persia renames itself Iran. In the Irish Free State, the sale of contraceptives is made illegal. There are anti-Catholic riots in Northern Ireland. Alcoholics Anonymous is founded.

Science and technology

A sea crossing of the Atlantic is completed in 107 hours. 'Kodachrome' 35-mm film is invented. The Richter Scale is devised for measuring earthquakes. The first practical radar equipment for detecting aircraft is developed. The longest railway bridge in the world is opened on the Zambezi River.

Culture

Fernand Léger paints *Adam and Eve*, Ben Nicholson paints *White Relief* and Pablo Picasso produces his *Minotaurmachy* etchings. Barbara Hepworth sculpts *Three Forms* and Henry Moore *Family*. George Gershwin writes his opera *Porgy and Bess*, Alban Berg his Violin Concerto, Ivor Novello his operetta *Glamorous Nights*, and Sergei Prokofiev his Violin Concerto No. 2. Count Basie plays at the Famous Door Club, jazz musician Artie Shaw founds his first band, and Victor Sylvester's dance band makes its first recordings. In the literary world, publications include Ivy Compton-Burnett's *A House and Its Head*, Cyril Connolly's *The Rock Pool*, Cecil Day-Lewis's *A Time to Dance*, a collection of poems by Walter de la Mare, T. S. Eliot's *The Four Quartets* and *Murder in the Cathedral*, Christopher Isherwood's *Mr Norris Changes Trains*, John Steinbeck's *Tortilla Flat* and Emlyn Williams's *Night Must Fall*. In the film world, the 20th Century Fox corporation is formed. At the cinema, audiences see *Anna Karenina* with Greta Garbo, *The Bride of Frankenstein* with Boris Karloff, *Cyrano de Bergerac*, David O. Selznick's *David Copperfield*, *Hopalong Cassidy* with William Boyd, *Les Misérables* with Fredric March, *Mutiny on the Bounty* with Charles Laughton and Clark Gable, *A Night at the Opera* with the Marx Brothers, Alfred Hitchcock's *The Thirty-nine Steps* and *Top Hat* with Fred Astaire and Ginger Rogers.

Births

Singer and actor Elvis Presley; architect Norman Foster; novelist Françoise Sagan; racing jockey Lester Piggott; film-maker Woody Allen; religious leader the Dalai Lama.

Personalities born in 1935

Less hard-edged and outspoken than those born in 1932, '33 or '34, individuals born this year can still be disruptive when they feel their personal freedom is being restricted. Those born with Saturn in Pisces after 15 February are great worriers, especially about past mistakes, and need periods of peace to wind down. With Saturn opposing Neptune in Virgo, they can be paranoid, and prone to addictions or psychosomatic ailments, although they can also be massively creative. Jupiter in Scorpio until 9 November luckily adds a more confident streak, helping them attract money. Those born after 29 March with Uranus in Taurus are determined to push forward practical new ideas, but can be held back by an overly materialistic approach. Jupiter in Sagittarius after 9 November lends a philosophical note, producing good thinkers, great travellers and confident optimists.

Dalai Lama

Born July 6 1935, 4.45 am Greenwich Mean Time, Tengster, Tibet.
Chart: Sun, Pluto in Cancer ◆ Moon's North Node in Capricorn ◆ Moon, Neptune in Virgo; Mercury in Gemini ◆ Venus in Leo ◆ Saturn in Pisces ◆ Mars, ascendant in Libra ◆ Jupiter in Scorpio ◆ Uranus in Taurus

A controlled Cancer with formidable courage and stamina in the face of overwhelming odds, the Dalai Lama acts as mother to his flock of Tibetan Buddhists worldwide in a typically water-sign way. With powerful Pluto close to his Sun squaring onto Mars, he was destined to feel trapped by the darker elements in human nature, and even to brush with death, but this placing has also given him the grit to withstand such experiences. The emphasized Mars in Libra gives him initiative, and fuels his fight for social justice for his people, who have been brutalized since the Chinese invasion in 1950; however, it also tends to make him feel he should operate within the rules and with a grace that at times prevents him from being sufficiently assertive. The Capricorn Moon's Node also hints at a tendency to see life through rose-coloured glasses, when in reality there is a need for him to act more like the disciplinarian father.

His Moon–Neptune conjunction in Virgo opposing Saturn is the hallmark of a life sacrificed to duty and patriotism, making him too detached or immersed in his religious vocation to desire the intimacy of close relationships. With this creative opposition, he could, in different circumstances, have been an artist, and it also hints at a deeper level of nervous worry than his calm demeanour suggests. Like Mother Teresa, he has the key elements of his chart in either Libra or Virgo, and the major turning points for him also occur when there are major planetary transits in the cardinal signs, Aries, Cancer, Libra and Capricorn (see page 74). In his chart he also has sociable Venus in flamboyant Leo aspecting Jupiter, which attracts him to a degree of celebrity and to showbusiness friends. Richard Gere, an ardent supporter, is Virgo, drawn to the Dalai Lama personally as a visionary leader because of the compatibility of their Sun and Moon signs.

In 1940, at the age of five, when both Jupiter and Saturn were passing through Aries, giving him hopes and fears of his path ahead, he was installed as the 14th Dalai Lama. In 1951, at the age of 16, when undermining Neptune in Libra was close to Mars, bringing a panicky sign of failure, and when disruptive Uranus in Cancer was approaching his Sun, he surrendered control of the army and foreign affairs to Peking in return for religious freedom. In 1959, when he finally fled the Chinese oppressors, talking of the 1000 monasteries that had been destroyed and many dead, Saturn in Capricorn was moving to oppose his Cancer Sun, separating him from his homeland, and was also crossing his Node, forcing him to carry heavier burdens than before.

When he was awarded the Nobel Peace Prize in 1989, influential Pluto was in Scorpio exactly on his expansive Jupiter and aspecting his Sun, bringing his cause much-needed recognition and public acclaim; and transiting Jupiter—always a luck and confidence bringer—was approaching his Sun. Following not far behind, the gathering triple conjunction of Saturn, Uranus and Neptune in Capricorn was preparing to trigger key parts of his chart, hinting at a bumpy road ahead.

1936

Three of the outer planets are uncomfortably sited in signs that do not suit their basic energy. Businesslike Saturn, midway through its three-year stay in dreamy Pisces, continues to raise worry levels, create paranoid fears and give rise to major regrets over the past. Sitting opposite undermining Neptune in dutiful Virgo, it raises levels of mistrust and creates morbid fears, though it can be highly creative. Innovative Uranus is in solidly earthy Taurus, pushing through financial reforms, but with difficulty. Pluto nears the end of its 25-year stay in Cancer which has erased old family ways, transformed agriculture and food production, and roused nationalist sentiments. Jupiter in optimistic Sagittarius until 3 December offers a ray of hope, although, as weakest of the influences, it succumbs more often than not to disappointment. Moving into materialistic Capricorn in December, it gives business confidence a minor boost.

Events

In Britain, King George V dies in January and is succeeded by Edward VIII; in December, two days before the Sagittarian eclipse, Edward abdicates to marry Wallis Simpson. The Crystal Palace in London is destroyed by fire, 10 days before Edward's abdication. The Spanish Civil War begins, and the three-year siege of Madrid; General Franco is appointed chief of state. German troops occupy the demilitarized Rhineland, breaking the Treaty of Versailles. In the German elections, 99 per cent of the electorate vote for official Nazi candidates. Austria becomes a one-party state. There is Arab unrest in Palestine, and Jews are murdered. The IRA is declared illegal in the Irish Free State. Martial law is proclaimed in Greece and Belgium. The French fascist party is suppressed. British fascists under Oswald Mosley stage an anti-Jewish march. The Jarrow March, from Jarrow in the north-east of England to London, takes place, in protest at high unemployment. F. D. Roosevelt is re-elected US president. Jesse Owens, the US African-American athlete, wins four gold medals at the Berlin Olympics.

Science and technology

The first diesel-electric vessel is launched. The first Volkswagen car factory opens.

Culture

Arshile Gorky paints *Organization*, Wassily Kandinsky *Dominant Curve* and Piet Mondrian *Composition in Red and Blue*. Salvador Dali creates his three-dimensional 'lobster telephone'. Architect Frank Lloyd Wright designs his 'Falling Water' house in Pennsylvania. Olivier Messiaen composes *Poèmes pour Mi*, and Sergei Prokofiev *Peter and the Wolf*. Composer Richard Rodgers and librettist Lorenz Hart write the musical *On Your Toes*, and Arthur Johnston the popular song 'Pennies from Heaven'. Jazz bandleader Benny Goodman is labelled the 'King of Swing'. Dale Carnegie publishes *How to Win Friends and Influence People* and Leon Trotsky *The Revolution Betrayed*. Literary publications include W. H. Auden's *Look, Stranger!*, James Cain's *Double Indemnity*, William Faulkner's *Absalom, Absalom!*, Aldous Huxley's *Eyeless in Gaza*, Margaret Mitchell's *Gone with the Wind*, Federico Garcia Lorca's *The House of Bernarda Alba* and Terence Rattigan's *French Without Tears*. Cinema audiences go to see *The Charge of the Light Brigade* with Errol Flynn, Jean Renoir's *A Day in the Country*, *Flash Gordon* with Buster Crabbe, Robert Leonard's *The Great Ziegfeld*, Frank Capra's *Mr Deeds Goes to Town*, *Modern Times* with Charlie Chaplin, and Alexander Korda's *Things to Come*.

Births

Racing driver Jim Clark; South African president F. W. de Klerk; cricketer Gary Sobers; Czech playwright and politician Vaclav Havel.

Personalities born in 1936

A rather delicate psychological balance with the Saturn–Neptune opposition makes those born in 1936 highly creative, sometimes spiritual, but rather distrustful individuals who allow irrational fears to guide their actions and responses; Jupiter in Sagittarius until 3 December does, however, add an optimistic streak. Those born this year tend also to be restless wanderers, and can be indecisive or easily distracted. Those whose birthdays fall from April onwards with Saturn aspecting Pluto have more staying power and the ability to endure. Uranus in Taurus makes for a curious mix of the inventive and the rather placid: great value is placed on financial security but there is fascination, too, with new techniques at work. Those born with Jupiter in Capricorn from 3 December are good with money and blessed with luck.

1937

Saturn edges out of an anxious, rather paranoid three-year run in Pisces, into defensive, grimly self-reliant Aries. Pluto starts to hover at the end of a 25-year stay in Cancer for a move into Leo, hinting at an era of energy and power ahead which—with the coming of atomic energy and new technology—may be viewed as creative, or totally destructive. Inventive though disruptive Uranus in fixed Taurus forces through economic change with difficulty, increasingly propelled into violent change as Pluto moves into another fixed sign. Neptune wavers in Virgo for another five years, undermining employment prospects and general levels of health. Jupiter in Capricorn until 21 December supports traditional values and pushes for financial gain.

Events

Leon Trotsky arrives in Mexico; in the USSR, former comrades are imprisoned and three are executed. There is a further purge in the USSR of high-ranking army generals said to have collaborated with Germany. In Britain, left-wing parties oppose German rearmament. The Spanish Civil War continues. The German airship *Hindenburg* explodes over the United States, killing 36 people. King George VI is crowned in London; in France, his brother—formerly Edward VIII and now the Duke of Windsor—marries Mrs Wallis Simpson. Japan invades China, takes Beijing, attacks Shanghai, and follows this victory with the 'Rape of Nanjing', when a quarter of a million Chinese are killed. The dictator of Iraq, General Bake Sidqui, is assassinated. Pope Pius XI brands Nazism as anti-Christian. In Germany, the preacher Martin Niemöller is arrested, acquitted, rearrested, and sent to a concentration camp. Mussolini confers with Hitler, as does British cabinet minister Lord Halifax. Italy withdraws from the League of Nations. In the United States, major floods in the Midwest leave a million people homeless.

Science and technology

A prototype of the jet engine is made.

Culture

Salvador Dali paints *Sleep*, Max Ernst *The Angel of the Hearth* and Pablo Picasso *On the Beach*. Käthe Kollwitz begins the sculpture *Pieta*, and Barbara Hepworth creates *Conicoid: Sphere and Hollow*. Benjamin Britten composes his *Variations on a Theme by Frank Bridge*, Carl Orff *Carmina Burana*, and Dmitri Shostakovich his Symphony No. 5. Karen Horney publishes *The Neurotic Personality of Our*

Times. George Orwell's *The Road to Wigan Pier*, Karen Blixen's *Out of Africa*, Ernest Hemingway's *To Have and Have Not*, Christopher Isherwood's *Sally Bowles*, Rudyard Kipling's *Something of Myself*, Jean-Paul Sartre's *Nausea*, John Steinbeck's *Of Mice and Men*, J. R. R. Tolkien's *The Hobbit,* Bertolt Brecht's *A Penny for the Poor*, and J. B. Priestley's *Time and the Conways* appear in the literary and theatre worlds. In the cinema, *Camille* with Greta Garbo, *Captains Courageous* with Spencer Tracy, Michael Powell's *The Edge of the World*, Sydney Franklin's *The Good Earth*, David O. Selznick's *The Prisoner of Zenda*, Walt Disney's *Snow White and the Seven Dwarfs* and *A Star is Born* with Judy Garland and James Mason go on release.

Births
Actors Vanessa Redgrave, Jack Nicholson, Robert Redford and Sir Anthony Hopkins; composer Philip Glass; Anita Desai; playwright Tom Stoppard; artist David Hockney.

Personalities born in 1937
With Jupiter in materialistic Capricorn, Uranus in possessive Taurus and Neptune in hard-working Virgo, those born in 1937 are earthier, more practical individuals than those born in preceding years. Those born up to 25 April, with the creative, though distrustful, Saturn–Neptune opposition, can have see-saw personalities with erratic mood swings, pulled between fantasy and reality, between new innovations and old, conventional ways. Those born with Saturn in Aries between 25 April and 20 October are tougher, more self-reliant, and hardened by circumstances to help themselves. Pluto in Leo between 8 October and 26 November marks the start of the 'me first' generation, determined to achieve personal power and growth. For those born after 21 December, Jupiter in Aquarius adds a streak of tolerance and humanitarian ideals.

Jack Nicholson
Born 22 April 1937, 11 am Eastern Standard Time, Neptune, New York.
Chart: Sun, Uranus, Mercury in Taurus ◆ Venus in Aries ◆ Mars, Moon's North Node in Sagittarius ◆ Moon, Neptune in Virgo ◆ Jupiter in Capricorn ◆ Pluto in Cancer ◆ Saturn in Pisces ◆ Ascendant in Leo

Sir Anthony Hopkins
Born 31 December 1937, 9.15 am, Port Talbot, Wales.
Chart: Sun, Mercury, Venus and ascendant in Capricorn ◆ Moon, Moon's North Node in Sagittarius ◆ Jupiter in Aquarius ◆ Mars, Saturn in Pisces ◆ Neptune in Virgo ◆ Pluto in Cancer ◆ Uranus in Taurus

Two highly acclaimed, very earthy actors from the same year, both Hopkins and Nicholson live out similar energy in entirely different ways. Hopkins, with his Capricorn Sun and two other planets just above the horizon when he was born, is rather isolated and deeply buried in his inner world. His creativity, like that of Laurence Olivier who shared the same placings, is largely unconscious, emerging with effort from layers below his rational mind. He needs a good deal of personal space, easily becoming psychologically overloaded from too much social contact.

A rather wild, untamed Sagittarian Node and Moon keep him wandering, at times directionless, unsure of what his career ambitions are. His workaholic Capricorn planets, however, never let him linger for long, and tend to repress his capacity for relaxation. Only occasionally does he let down his emotional guard. The roots of his rather desperate drinking years were in part a Capricornian trait—shared by Elvis Presley (born in 1935), among others—of seeking to go beyond the confines of the body through over-indulgence. Money is a driving force, with Mars in Pisces in the financial area of his chart, perhaps fuelled by resentment from his Welsh childhood. He is chaotic with money, being both parsimonious and over-trusting.

Jack Nicholson, in contrast, with a midheaven Taurus Sun, wants to glitter in the spotlight, seeking through career and public acclaim the attention he lacked as a child. With a dramatically impulsive Mars in adventurous Sagittarius, he throws himself wholeheartedly into the enjoyment of life, romance and fun. Taurus is a sign connected to the body, which wants constant sensual, tactile stimulation, and to the voice, which is often noteworthy. With rebellious Uranus close to his Sun, Nicholson goes his own rather eccentric way, not caring for convention, nor being well suited to long-term cooperation.

What both share is the bullish Jupiter–Pluto opposition, often an indication of a success drive that can ride roughshod over social niceties. Their Sagittarian Node hints at a lack of commitment in both men, of a chameleon-like quality of constantly trying to fit into a variety of surroundings without ever really settling. More crucially, they also have the spiritual, creative and slightly paranoid Saturn–Neptune opposition, which allows each of them, in his own characteristic style, to play rather tortured characters—Hopkins with his run of Stalin, Adolf Hitler, Nixon, Kellogg and Hannibal Lecter; and Nicholson with *One Flew Over the Cuckoo's Nest*, *As Good As It Gets* and *The Shining*, among many others. They both have a Dionysian ability to merge with their roles, sometimes to the detriment of their personal lives. Nicholson shares with the Dalai Lama (see page 118) the Moon–Neptune–Virgo opposition to Saturn, but opts to direct his emotional energies and needs towards an artistic rather than a spiritual vision.

With substantial careers behind them, both actors look set to go on and on.

1938

Both Saturn and Pluto in aspect, moving backwards and forwards over a sign change, gives a tough-minded but ambivalent feel to the year. On 15 January Saturn makes the final transition out of anxious Pisces into coldly resourceful, will-driven Aries for a three-year stay. Having transformed family values and not always helpfully boosted national dogmas, Pluto finishes its 25-year run in Cancer and, from 3 August, moves for 19 years into self-aggrandizing Leo, promoting the power of the individual and harnessing the power of the universe, for good or ill, in atomic energy. Uranus finds its innovative powers rather stifled in solid Taurus, though new financial methods are put into place. Aspecting vague Neptune in earthy Virgo, it can bring enlightening new ideas in spirituality and creative enterprises, although it can also support outlandish beliefs. Jupiter in Aquarius until 15 May and after 30 July is tolerant and open-minded. Jupiter in Pisces between these dates is compassionate, charitable and rather weak-willed.

Events
The Spanish Civil War and the Sino-Japanese War continue. Hitler declares himself commander of the German army; troops enter Austria, which is declared part of the German Reich. Germany mobilizes armed forces, as does France; in Britain the Royal Navy is mobilized. In Italy, the fascist government passes anti-Semitic legislation. There are more executions in the USSR of former leading communists. Soviet troops clash with Japanese. British prime minister Neville Chamberlain advocates appeasement of Hitler. In Germany on 9 November, two days after the lunar eclipse, Jewish houses, synagogues and schools are burned in 'Kristallnacht'. (A similar eclipse cycle was in place in November 1957 when the IRA pub bombing in Birmingham took place, provoking the Prevention of Terrorism Act; and again in November 1956 when the Cambodian navy seized an American liner.) In the United States, the House Un-American Activities Committee is set up which, after the war, will lead to an anti-communist witch-hunt. American tycoon Howard Hughes flies around the world in a monoplane in 3 days 19 hours.

Culture
Max Beckmann paints *Birds' Hell*, Augustus John a portrait of Dylan Thomas, Paul Klee *Dark Message*, Joán Miró *Head of a Woman*, and Jackson Pollock begins his *Man with a Knife*. Aaron Copland writes the music for his ballet *Billy the Kid*, Sergei Prokofiev his ballet *Romeo and Juliet*, Richard Strauss the opera *Daphne* and Anton Webern his String Quartet. Irving Berlin composes the popular hit 'God Bless America', Artie Shaw 'Begin the Beguine'. Samuel Beckett's *Murphy*, Cecil Day-Lewis's *Overtures to Death*, Lawrence Durrell's *The Black Book*, William Faulkner's *The Unvanquished*, Graham Greene's *Brighton Rock*, Christopher Isherwood's *Goodbye to Berlin*, Daphne du Maurier's *Rebecca*, Vladimir Nabokov's *Invitation to a Beheading*, Jean Anouilh's *Traveller without Luggage*, Jean Cocteau's *Les Parents terribles*, and Thornton Wilder's *Our Town* appear in the world of literature and theatre. Cinema audiences see *The Adventures of Robin Hood* with Errol Flynn, *Angels with Dirty Faces* with James Cagney, Alfred Hitchcock's *The Lady Vanishes*, Leni Riefenstahl's *Olympiad* and *Pygmalion* with Leslie Howard.

Births
King Juan Carlos of Spain; tennis player Rod Laver; Ian Brady; Herb Elliot; stuntman Evel Knievel; actor Sir Derek Jacobi; film star Jon Voight; dancer Rudolf Nureyev.

Personalities born in 1938
Inventive, idealistic, hard-driving, self-sufficient and rather independent, personalities born in 1938 veer between self-promotion (especially those born after 3 August with Pluto in Leo) and kindness. To those born up to 15 January, Saturn in Pisces gives a tendency to worry excessively and to regret the past, but thereafter, in Aries, it produces a determined ambition to survive and succeed. Uranus and Neptune aspecting in earth signs merge the spiritual with the practical, although they can also produce rather erratic mood swings. Jupiter in Pisces between 15 May and 30 July is sympathetic and charitable; in Aquarius outside those dates, it makes for bright, confident minds, and an interest in different cultures.

1939

Chill Saturn travels in square aspect to power-hungry Pluto throughout this bleak year. A regular seven- or eight-year occurrence, its brutal effect is emphasized by the April Aries eclipse, which carries difficult aspects to both planets as Hitler denounces his non-aggression pacts. Saturn reaches the exact square when it enters Taurus in July, as war becomes increasingly inevitable: in 1914, at the outbreak of the First World War, Saturn had just reached the exact conjunction with Pluto in Cancer, so it is often an indicator of very tough times ahead—although in 1939 astrologers had over-hopefully predicted peace. Saturn in Taurus hints at cutbacks and austere living, and—with the approaching triple conjunction with Uranus and Jupiter in Taurus in two years' time—is a definite indication of a major economic recession. Pluto now in self-aggrandizing Leo from 15 June, where it will stay for 18 years, promotes individual and atomic power. Uranus continues its long, slow trine to Neptune in Virgo, undermining employment prospects and slowing down financial growth. Jupiter dashes into headstrong Aries after 12 May.

Events
The Spanish Civil War ends with the nationalists taking Madrid. The Sino-Japanese War continues. Germany occupies Czechoslovakia, signs a treaty with Mussolini, and invades Poland. Paris is evacuated. Britain and France declare war on Germany. British warships are sunk. The deportation of Polish Jews begins. German Jewish refugees are turned back by US authorities at Havana; many are captured back in Europe by the Nazis. Britain restricts Jewish immigration to Palestine.

Science and technology
The VS300, the first helicopter, invented by Igor Sikorsky, makes a successful flight. The first Messerschmitt military jet plane is built. Albert Einstein outlines the possibility of creating atomic power. Otto Hahn discovers nuclear fission.

Culture
Paul Klee paints *La Belle Jardinière*, and Pablo Picasso *Bust of a Woman with Striped Hat*. William Walton writes his Violin Concerto, Zoltán Kodály *Peacock Variations*, Arnold Schoenberg his Chamber Symphony No. 2, Béla Bartók String Quartet No. 6, and Heitor Villa-Lobos his *Bachiana Brasiliera* No. 5. Raymond Chandler's *The Big Sleep*, T. S. Eliot's *The Family Reunion* and *Old Possum's Book of Practical Cats*, James Joyce's *Finnegans Wake*, Richard Llewellyn's *How Green Was My Valley*, Henry Miller's *Tropic of Cancer*, Dorothy Parker's *Here Lies*, and John Steinbeck's *The Grapes of Wrath* are published. In the film world, *The Adventures of Sherlock Holmes* with Basil Rathbone, *Gone with the Wind* with Vivien Leigh and Clark Gable, *Goodbye Mr Chips* with Robert Donat, *The Hunchback of Notre Dame* with Charles Laughton, *The Wizard of Oz* with Judy Garland, and *Wuthering Heights* with Laurence Olivier and Merle Oberon, are all released.

Births
Canadian politician Brian Mulroney; film director Francis Ford Coppola; playwright Alan Ayckbourn.

Personalities born in 1939

With the Saturn–Pluto stamp strongly emphasized, individuals born in 1939 feel that they carry the weight of the world on their shoulders. They always feel like outsiders, can be obsessive, have enormous stamina, and are resistant to change. Saturn in Aries up to 7 July and after 23 September gives self-reliance; in Taurus between these dates it indicates care with money. Uranus in Taurus suggests a curious mix of inventiveness and attachment to conventional values. Pluto in Cancer between 8 February and 15 June is reflected in those who cling possessively to family values. Those born outside these dates with Pluto in Leo value self above relationships, and desire personal power. Jupiter in Pisces up to 12 May is sympathetic and charitable; in Aries thereafter it is recklessly impetuous.

1940–1949

The triple conjunction of Jupiter, Saturn and Uranus together for only the fourth time in this millennium—it previously occurred in 1307, 1623, and 1762—and not for more than 2000 years in Taurus, is a sign of unique times. Being in fixed Taurus, the conjunction is heavyweight in energy and exerts massive physical pressure, as well as pushing—though not always smoothly—for major financial reforms. Neptune and Pluto, the two outermost planets, also change focus in this decade. Established in Leo since 1939, where it will stay for almost two more decades, Pluto promotes individual power, as man plays god in releasing awesome atomic power. In 1942, Neptune slithers out of Virgo into Libra for 14 years, raising unrealistic expectations of relationships. As Uranus and Saturn both move out of Taurus in 1942 into lighter-weight Gemini, the tide of the war turns and new scientific ideas leap ahead. The bleakly tough Saturn–Pluto contact of 1946–48 signposts a difficult path for the new states set up post-war.

1940

The triple conjunction of Jupiter, Saturn and Uranus in fixed, possessive Taurus makes a battle of wills inevitable. Taurus is a sign of great determination with deep reserves of endurance for whom mastery of the physical universe is of prime importance. The downside of Taurus (Hitler's sign) is very black. But whatever the difficulties of the Nazi advances in Europe, the Jewish Holocaust and the bombardment of Britain—which owe their devastation also partly to the Saturn–Pluto square—this triad does, over two years, hint at the seeds of major new developments being sown in science, agriculture and business. Uranus and Saturn crossing tend to dismantle old structures, often joltingly; they seem to occur at significant points in Jewish, French and Russian history. Pluto, firmly established in self-promoting Leo, slows down any hopes of progress to a standstill for another year, inflicting misery and reinforcing personal and national defences. Dreamy Neptune still placed in workmanlike Virgo continues to aspect Uranus, hinting that ideals are being striven for but are not yet realized.

Events

Germany invades Denmark and Norway, and occupies France, the Netherlands and Belgium. In Britain, Winston Churchill takes over as prime minister, local defence volunteers are formed into the Home Guard, and food rationing begins. At

Dunkirk on the north-east coast of France, 300,000 British and French soldiers are evacuated. Italy declares war on Britain and France. France, under Prime Minister Pétain, signs an armistice with Hitler; General Charles de Gaulle, leader of the Free French, flees to Britain. As the Jupiter–Saturn contact becomes exact, the five-week Battle of Britain rages, with German planes attacking shipping and ports; the Royal Air Force shoots down 180 enemy planes. The Blitz—the bombing of London and other cities—begins; in the first week 6000 civilians are killed in bombing raids. Hitler postpones his planned invasion of Britain. In the United States, F. D. Roosevelt is elected for an unprecedented third term as president.

Science and technology
The first electron microscope is produced. Nylon stockings are an instant success. Kentucky Fried Chicken is launched. The first Jeep is manufactured.

Culture
Many artists flee Paris after the Nazi occupation of France, but Picasso remains. In Britain Paul Nash and Stanley Spencer are among the officially appointed war artists. An Augustus John exhibition is held at the Tate Gallery. Max Ernst paints *Europe After the Rain, II*, Wassily Kandinsky *Sky Blue*, Paul Klee *Death and Fire*, Willem de Kooning *Seated Woman*, Joán Miró his *Constellation* series, and Stanley Spencer starts his *Shipbuilding on the Clyde* series. In the world of music, Benjamin Britten composes his *Sinfonia da requiem*, Aram Khatchaturian his Violin Concerto, and Sergei Prokofiev his Piano Sonata No. 6. Jazz musician Stan Kenton's band is formed. In Britain, the BBC launches the *Sincerely Yours* radio show, with Vera Lynn singing 'We'll Meet Again' and 'White Cliffs of Dover'. Carl Jung publishes his *Psychology and Religion*. Raymond Chandler's *Farewell, My Lovely*, Graham Greene's *The Power and the Glory*, Ernest Hemingway's *For Whom the Bell Tolls* and *The Fifth Column*, C. P. Snow's *Strangers and Brothers*, Howard Spring's *Fame is the Spur*, and Dylan Thomas's *Portrait of the Artist as a Young Dog* are published. Eugene O'Neill writes the play *Long Day's Journey into Night*. In the cinema, audiences see Walt Disney's *Fantasia* and *Pinocchio*, John Ford's *The Grapes of Wrath*, *The Great Dictator* with Charlie Chaplin, *The Road to Singapore* with Bing Crosby, Bob Hope and Dorothy Lamour, and *A Wild Hare* with Bugs Bunny.

Births
US golfer Jack Nicklaus; Italian film director Bernardo Bertolucci; pop singers John Lennon, Cliff Richard and Frank Zappa; Brazilian footballer Pele; English novelist Angela Carter.

Personalities born in 1940
Strong, sturdy, stubborn and blessed with stamina, those born in 1940 are designed for the long haul. With Pluto in Leo they are concerned with personal power rather than relationships, and with Pluto in hard aspect to Saturn, they resist change. Rather obsessive, they see themselves as outsiders, always struggling against the odds. Those born with Saturn in Aries before 21 March are determinedly self-reliant; thereafter those born with Saturn in Taurus are cautious with money. Jupiter in Aries up to 17 May makes for headstrong, dynamic and not always

sensible personalities. Those born after this, with three planets in Taurus and Neptune in Virgo, are earthy, practical, possessive, obstinate, jealous, good at acquiring possessions but erratic with money, being both spendthrift and stingy, and often creative. Occasionally they suffer from psychosomatic ailments.

1941

The triple conjunction of Jupiter, Saturn and Uranus, only occurring four times a millennium (though not in Taurus in the first millennium AD), continues to exert unpredictable effects, with highs and lows, abrupt changes, and hugely determined efforts for the first few months. Physical mastery is the keynote, with Taurus— Hitler's sign—involved, although the waning Pluto square makes the mood less bleak than in the previous year. Pluto in Leo pushes for power, both personal and atomic. The seeds of future economic reform are being sown, although the effects are hidden in the recessionary effect of austere Saturn in Taurus. The shift of both Jupiter (on 26 May) and Uranus (from 7 August to 6 October) into air sign Gemini lifts the leaden mood temporarily, opening up a cooperative dialogue between the United States and Britain. Uranus in Gemini for seven years heralds a new phase of thinking and exposure to new ideas, and pioneers new concepts in communications. As Uranus heads back into Taurus for the remaining three months to approach Saturn again, the bombing of Pearl Harbor takes place, escalating the worldwide conflict, with the United States now actively involved in the war.

Events

The North African campaign is fought. Germany invades Yugoslavia and Greece. Rudolf Hess, deputy German leader, flees to Scotland. Heavy bombing in London destroys part of the Houses of Parliament. The *Bismarck*, a German battleship, is sunk. Germany invades the USSR; and half a million Jews are rounded up and slaughtered. In France, the pro-Nazi Vichy regime hands Jews over to the Nazis. Winston Churchill and Franklin Roosevelt meet in a ship off Newfoundland to sign the Atlantic Charter. The Germans advance towards Moscow. In December, the Japanese make a surprise attack on Pearl Harbor, destroying eight battleships and 300 aircraft. The United States declares war on Japan; Germany and Italy declare war on the USA. The Japanese army forces a British retreat to Singapore; their aircraft sink two British ships, and they take Hong Kong.

Science and technology

Research on the atomic bomb begins in the United States.

Culture

Henry Moore makes crayon drawings of refugees in air-raid shelters during the London Blitz, Renato Guttuso paints *Crucifixion* and Pablo Picasso *Boy with a Crayfish*. Richard Addinsell composes the *Warsaw Concerto*, Olivier Messiaen his *Quartet for the End of Time*, and Noel Coward writes his song 'London Pride'. James Agee's *Let Us Now Praise Famous Men* is published, with photographs by Walker Evans. Ivy Compton-Burnett's *Parents and Children*, John Masefield's *The Nine Days Wonder*, an account of the Dunkirk evacuation, and Stephen Spender's *Ruins and Visions* are also published. Bertolt Brecht writes his play

Mother Courage. The Big Store with the Marx Brothers, *Citizen Kane* with Orson Welles, Michael Powell's *19th Parallel, High Sierra* with Humphrey Bogart, John Ford's *How Green Was My Valley,* and John Huston's *The Maltese Falcon* with Humphrey Bogart, are shown at the cinema.

Births
Singers Bob Dylan, Joan Baez and Richie Haven; Serbian president Slobodan Milosevic; writer Stephen Jay Gould; American dancer Twyla Tharp; Nigerian writer and activist Ken Saro-Wiwa.

Personalities born in 1941
Practical, earthy, rather contradictory individuals, those born in 1941 do not always practise what they preach, with conventional Saturn close to innovative Uranus. Keen on change, but attached to material possessions, they are both extravagant and rather stingy with money. Pluto in Leo makes them self-focused and keen on personal power, which they value more highly than relationships. Neptune in Virgo aspecting Uranus gives an otherworldy, slightly visionary streak; it can also produce rather hard-to-diagnose ailments and a lethargy about day-to-day working routines. Jupiter in Gemini for those born after 26 May is lighter-hearted, chatty and rather restless. Those born between 7 August and 6 October are fidgety, lucky, travel suddenly, are very open to new ways of thinking, and not very self-disciplined.

Joan Baez
Born 9 January 1941, 10.45 am Eastern Standard Time, Staten Island, New York.
Chart: Sun, Mercury in Capricorn ◆ Moon in Gemini ◆ Venus, Mars in Sagittarius ◆ Jupiter, Saturn, Uranus in Taurus ◆ Pluto in Leo ◆ Neptune in Virgo ◆ Moon's North Node in Libra ◆ Ascendant in Aries

Bob Dylan
Born 24 May 1941, 9.05 pm Central Standard Time, Duluth, Minnesota.
Chart: Sun, Venus, Mercury in Gemini ◆ Saturn, Moon, Uranus, Jupiter in Taurus ◆ Mars in Pisces ◆ Neptune, Moon's North Node in Virgo ◆ Pluto in Leo ◆ Ascendant in Sagittarius

Born less than five months apart, the two most influential folk singers of the turbulent 1960s flower-power, anti-Vietnam War generation loved and sang together.

Joan Baez, a creative Capricorn (like Janis Joplin, David Bowie and John Denver), practical and visionary, has a chart dominated by earth signs with dreamy Neptune in Virgo and and the triple conjunction of Saturn, Jupiter and Uranus in Taurus, sign of the voice. Her aims have always been tangible: she wants to see a solid result. Her distinctive soprano voice singing the anthem of the protest movement 'We Shall Overcome' was the symbol for non-violence. Although kindly, she can also be hugely stubborn, reflecting the fixed Taurus planets. Jupiter and Saturn together hint at a strong need to put self-discipline behind ideals in order to make them real, a characteristic she shared with John Lennon as well. Artistic, flamboyant Venus and dynamic Mars in crusading Sagittarius gave her the vehicle and medium for her message. They were triggered by the rebellious, revolutionary Uranus–Pluto conjunction of the 1960s (see 1960–1969, page 159), as was her restless Gemini Moon. She and Dylan had a strong, affectionate compatibility with her Gemini Moon close to his Sun and Venus in Gemini suggesting a real love, and his Taurus Moon nurturing her earth planets. At the time it was a beautiful connection.

Prepared for the long haul, with her singing career disappearing into sporadic dips over the years, she maintained her humanitarian activities throughout. When Saturn, always a career indicator, disappeared below her Aries ascendant in the late 1960s she lost her momentum, but when it reached her midheaven again in 1989 she released an acclaimed album celebrating 30 years of singing, with other successes following.

Bob Dylan, renowned for culture-shifting hits like 'Blowin' in the Wind' and 'The Times They Are a-Changin', shares the same stubborn, sensuous Taurus planets and sympathetic, creative Neptune in Virgo as Joan Baez. But he is a lighter personality, with the Sun, Venus and Mercury in Gemini, a sign present in numerous popular singers, from Paul McCartney and Julie Felix to Tom Jones. He also has active Mars uneasily situated in lethargic Pisces, not helpful for the long haul. By 1966 his increasingly frantic career was starting to overload, and a motorbike accident gave him a much-needed break from singing and allowed him to move away from campaigning. At that time Saturn in late Pisces was opposing his Neptune and Moon's Node in Virgo, an anxiety-provoking influence, pulling him away from the public domain. Neptune was also sitting on his natal Saturn, doubling his paranoid feelings. As if that was not enough, Uranus and Pluto in Virgo were sending shock waves around his chart.

Dylan's career has always been erratic, with huge early acclaim being followed by considerable hostility. In 1979 he became a born-again Christian as the idealistic, expansive Jupiter–Saturn conjunction in Libra moved across his midheaven. What should have been a high-flying few years thereafter followed his earlier pattern of short bursts of popularity, some awards and criticism.

1942

A general shift of planetary influence out of fixed, controlling, power-hungry earth sign Taurus begins as Saturn and Uranus both head for Gemini, a communicative air sign. The drive for physical mastery and control of territory no longer receives so much support from the astrological energies. Undermining Neptune also finishes a debilitating 13-year stay in employment-oriented Virgo to move into Libra, producing the yearning for the ideal of perfect relationships. The tide of the war starts to turn, although slowly, with painful losses, especially in the Far East. The erratic, abruptly reforming Uranus–Saturn conjunction is focused after early May on developing new ideas and better information systems. It brings sudden tensions, then a release of tensions, and tends to dismantle old structures without warning. In aspect to Pluto and Neptune, as are all three eclipses, it causes major disruption and dictatorial behaviour. Often it occurs at key points in Jewish, Russian or French history. Pluto in Leo inexorably propels the development of atomic power. Jupiter in restless, expansive Gemini until 11 June lifts the mood; in Cancer thereafter it suggests moments of emotional calm and hints at domestic contentment.

Events

In the United States, the 22 war allies make a joint pledge, calling themselves the United Nations. Germany fights to take Stalingrad, but the German force is surrounded. Germany retreats in the North African campaign. The Japanese land in Singapore; 70,000 British soldiers and airmen surrender. In the Philippines, US and Filipino forces surrender to the Japanese; 10,000 die on a forced march. The Japanese bomb Ceylon and Darwin in North Australia; they advance through Burma, and take Mandalay, but an American victory turns the tide against them. British bombing raids are launched on Lubeck and Hamburg. The Germans step up large-scale murder of Jews at six 'death camps', including Auschwitz, Bergen-Belsen, Treblinka and Majdanek. In the United States, civilian car production is halted for the duration of the war; the number of working women increases by 50 per cent.

Science and technology

The first V2 rocket is launched in Germany. Magnetic tape is invented. Pure uranium is produced for use in the atom bomb. The first electronic computer is developed.

Culture

Piet Mondrian starts work on his painting *Broadway Boogie-Woogie*, and Pablo Picasso paints *Woman with a Hat in the Shape of a Fish*. Composer Aaron Copland writes his ballet *Rodeo*, Sergei Prokofiev writes the score for Sergei Eisenstein's film *Ivan the Terrible*, Arnold Schoenberg his Piano Concerto, Dmitri Shostakovich his 'Leningrad' Symphony No. 7, and Richard Strauss his opera *Capriccio*. Irving Berlin writes his song 'White Christmas', made into a hit by Bing Crosby. Frank Sinatra makes his first stage appearance, and is greeted with adulation. Albert Camus' *The Outsider*, T. S. Eliot's *Little Gidding*, John Steinbeck's *The Moon is Down*, Jean Anouilh's *Antigone*, Sean O'Casey's *Red Roses for Me* and Thornton Wilder's *The Skin of our Teeth* appear in the worlds of literature and theatre. Cinema audiences go to see *Casablanca* with Ingrid Bergman and Humphrey Bogart, *Holiday Inn* with Bing Crosby, Orson Welles's *The Magnificent Ambersons*, *Mrs Miniver* with Greer Garson and Luchino Visconti's *Ossessione*.

Births

Physicist Stephen Hawking; boxer Muhammad Ali; film directors Derek Jarman, Werner Herzog and Martin Scorsese; musician Jimi Hendrix; singers Paul McCartney, Carole King and Barbra Streisand; actor Harrison Ford; American novelist Michael Crichton.

Personalities born in 1942

Complex, richly diverse personalities characterize those born in 1942—an intriguing mix of restless adaptabilty and stubborn resistance to pressure. They can be dictatorial and do not always follow their own advice. Those born before early May are earthy, practical, very obstinate, and inventive about practical matters, especially money, although sometimes stingy. With Pluto in Leo they are self-centred and keen on personal power, although Neptune in Virgo up to 3 October

131

often makes it difficult for them to put theories into practice or find the energy to push ahead over the long term. Those born after early May, with Saturn and Uranus in Gemini, have sharply inquiring minds, and highly strung nervous systems. Those born up to 11 June with Jupiter in Gemini are communicators par excellence; thereafter Jupiter in Cancer points to a need for a full and contented home life.

1943

The lightening of the general mood with the move of Saturn and Uranus out of dictatorial Taurus into inquiring Gemini coincides with increasing defeats for German and Italian forces. Still a difficult time with tension and sudden releases of tension, the old structures fostered by Saturn continue to be destroyed by Uranus to pave the way for long-term changes. Since self-aggrandizing Pluto in Leo, signifier of atomic power, is in aspect to both these planets, albeit in a milder fashion, there are still brutal experiences, mass suffering and pockets of fanatical fervour. Just before the crash of the late 1920s, Neptune moved out of an uneasy 13-year stay in Virgo, sign of the worker, and brought hope of relief. Now in Libra for 14 years, it raises hopes of better agreements and fairer relationships. Jupiter in Cancer until 30 June is emotionally more settled; then in Leo, it brings a taste for flamboyant gestures and extravagant living in bleak times. When it crosses Pluto in late July, Mussolini falls, and the Soviet army effectively halts the German offensive on the eastern front for good.

Events

German advances in the USSR are repulsed by the Soviet army. General Dwight Eisenhower takes over the Allied armies in North Africa; the German army in Tunisia surrenders. There is round-the-clock bombing of Germany by American and British planes, and an Allied air-raid on Rome. Italy surrenders and declares war on Germany, Mussolini is toppled, and Allied troops enter Italy. The 'Katyn' massacre is discovered, involving the killing of 4500 Polish officers in the USSR. There is an uprising in the Warsaw ghetto. Severe famine affects Bengal. Japan has the worst rice harvest in 50 years. Danish Jews are evacuated to Sweden to save them from the death camps.

Science and technology

The hallucinogenic properties of LSD are discovered.

Culture

Arshile Gorky paints *Waterfall*, Paul Nash *Vernal Equinox* and Jackson Pollock *Mural*. Béla Bartók composes his *Concerto for Orchestra*, Benjamin Britten his *Serenade for Tenor, Horn and Strings*, Aaron Copland *Fanfare for the Common Man* and Ralph Vaughan Williams his Symphony No. 5. Leonard Bernstein makes his first appearance as an orchestral conductor in New York. Oscar Hammerstein's musicals *Carmen Jones* and *Oklahoma* are staged. Hermann Hesse's *The Glass Bead Game*, Antoine de Saint-Exupery's *The Little Prince* and Jean-Paul Sartre's *The Flies* are published. Bertolt Brecht writes *The Good Woman of Setzuan*.

Births

Fashion designer Mary Quant; British prime minister John Major; American tennis stars Arthur Ashe and Billie Jean King; British theatre director Sir Richard Ayre; Polish politician and freedom fighter Lech Walesa; playwright Sam Shepard; singer John Denver.

Personalities born in 1943

With lighter-weight temperaments than in the previous two years, individuals born in 1943 think fast, talk a great deal and never sit still. Pioneers in their own way, they are good at welding together the best of the old with the best of the new. With Saturn close to Uranus, they are sometimes dictatorial, do not always practise what they preach, but expect others to do what they avoid doing themselves. Rather centred on themselves with Pluto in Leo, they yearn for bright passions and ideal relationships, yet find disappointments because they are rather detached emotionally and not always rooted in their bodies. With Neptune in Virgo, those born between 18 April and 2 August are the last of the old generation: they can be lethargic about heavy work routines and sometimes suffer from psychosomatic ailments. Those born prior to 30 June, with Jupiter in Cancer, want happy home lives as a priority; those born thereafter with, Jupiter in Leo crossing Pluto, need to live a five-star life in grand style.

1944

Uranus and Neptune in communicative air signs aspecting Pluto in fire sign Leo completes the reversal of the influences from the bruising, brutal start to the decade where a concentration of fixed earth energy promoted a drive for physical mastery. New ideas, some profound and some extreme, new scientific concepts, especially in the development of atomic power, now move expectations in a different direction. Saturn moving out of aspect to Pluto also lifts the general outlook; starting to square Neptune after the middle of the year, however, it does create a degree of paranoia and excessive worry. Saturn in Cancer from 22 June can be emotionally isolating and rather defensive about feelings. Jupiter in Leo until 27 July brings flashes of flamboyance and hopes for the disappearance of austerity. In Virgo thereafter, it points to a revived work ethic.

Events

General Dwight Eisenhower is appointed supreme commander of the Allied forces in Europe on the day of the total solar eclipse in Aquarius. Germany resumes heavy bombing of mainland Britain, using the first V1 flying bombs. In one month over 80,000 tonnes of bombs are dropped on Germany and occupied Europe. Hungarian Jews are rounded up by the Nazis; 400,000 are gassed. The D-Day landings in Normandy take Germany by surprise. France and Greece are liberated. The Soviet army continues to push back German forces and enters Czechoslovakia. On the day of the second solar eclipse of the year on 20 July, an assassination attempt against Hitler fails. Rommel, German commander-in-chief in Europe, commits suicide. In the Pacific, in the greatest naval battle in history, US ships destroy the Japanese fleet; the United States also starts bombing Tokyo. F. D. Roosevelt wins a fourth term as president.

Science and technology

A second uranium pile is built in the United States for the manufacture of plutonium for the atomic bomb. The kidney dialysis machine is invented.

Culture

Francis Bacon paints *Three Studies for Figures at the Base of a Crucifixion*, Jean Dubuffet *Vue de Paris—Le Petit Commerce* and Willem de Kooning *Pink Lady*. Sculptor Barbara Hepworth creates *Wood and Strings*. Leonard Bernstein composes his 'Jeremiah' Symphony, Aaron Copland his ballet *Appalachian Spring*, Sergei Prokofiev Symphony No. 5, Richard Strauss his opera *Die Liebe der Danaë* and Michael Tippett *A Child of Our Time*. Jazz musician Dizzy Gillespie writes his 'Groovin' High'. Bandleader Glenn Miller is presumed killed in a plane crash. In the world of literature, Jorge Luis Borges's *Fictions*, Joyce Cary's *The Horse's Mouth*, T. S. Eliot's *The Four Quartets* and Aldous Huxley's *Time Must Have a Stop* are all published. Theatre audiences see Terence Rattigan's *The Winslow Boy* and Tennessee Williams's *The Glass Menagerie*. Cinema audiences see Frank Capra's *Arsenic and Old Lace*, Billy Wilder's *Double Indemnity*, *Henry V* with Laurence Olivier, Sergei Eisenstein's *Ivan the Terrible* and Clarence Brown's *The White Cliffs of Dover*.

Births

Star Wars producer George Lucas; novelist Alice Walker; Indian politician Rajiv Gandhi; Australian politician Paul Keating; English composer John Tavener.

Personalities born in 1944

Open to new ideas, even wild flights of fancy, those born in 1944 are communicative thinkers, interested in new ideas, even the occult. With Pluto in Leo, they are self-centred and keen on personal power. Neptune in Libra makes them yearn for perfect relationships, so they can be dissatisfied with the reality of what they have. Those born before 22 June with Saturn and Uranus in Gemini have sharp, inquiring minds, are especially restless, sometimes dictatorial, and inventive, but tend to practise what they preach. Those born after this date, with Saturn in Cancer, are emotionally defensive and guarded against family warmth; they can be both highly creative and rather given to neurotic worry. Those with Jupiter in Leo up to 27 July have an indulgent, extravagant streak; in contrast, Jupiter in Virgo thereafter signifies individuals who work willingly in service to others.

1945

Uranus and Neptune in air signs, still within aspect of Pluto in Leo, point the way ahead to developments in communications, scientific breakthroughs in nuclear physics, and an understanding of what lies beyond surface reality. Pluto, the power planet, in Leo is self-aggrandizing, with a capacity for making men feel like gods. It has an awesome but double-edged force, resulting in either constructive or destructive effects. Pluto is close by when, in August, on the Leo New Moon after the July eclipse, the first atom bomb is dropped on Hiroshima. Saturn in Gemini up to 22 June is serious-minded, self-disciplined in mathematical thinking and clear about agreements. Thereafter in Cancer squaring onto Neptune, it throws up an emotionally confusing mood—anxious, defensive, rather paranoid. Jupiter in Virgo up to 26 August is concerned with practical service to others; in Libra thereafter it promotes fair agreements and legal and social justice.

Events

Soviet forces take Warsaw and liberate the Auschwitz death camp. At the Yalta conference, Roosevelt, Churchill and Stalin plan for Germany's surrender and divide up Berlin. The Allies bomb Dresden, killing 60,000 people. In the Pacific, there is heavy loss of life as US forces capture several islands. Roosevelt dies, aged 63, and is succeeded by Harry Truman. Mussolini and his entourage are shot in Italy by partisans. Hitler marries Eva Braun in his Berlin bunker, then shoots himself the next day; Berlin surrenders to the Soviets. The first atomic explosion occurs on 16 July, a week after the total solar eclipse in Cancer, with Saturn close by, squared by Neptune. After VE (Victory in Europe) day, Allied troops occupy Berlin. The United States drops atomic bombs on Hiroshima and Nagasaki. The USSR declares war on Japan. The United Nations comes into formal existence. The International Military Tribunal at Nuremberg rules that following orders is not a defence for those accused of atrocities. Churchill is defeated in the British elections. Tito heads Yugoslavia, de Gaulle France, and Salazar Portugal. Middle Eastern countries warn the United States that the creation of a Jewish state in Palestine will lead to war. Coptic Christian manuscripts are discovered at Nag Hammadi in Egypt.

Culture

Balthus paints *Les Beaux Jours*, Willem de Kooning *Pink Angels*, Pablo Picasso *The Charnel House*, and Graham Sutherland *Thorn Trees*. Henry Moore sculpts *Family Group*. Béla Bartók composes his Piano Concerto No. 3, Benjamin Britten the opera *Peter Grimes*, and Richard Strauss his *Metamorphosen*. Rodgers and Hammerstein's musical *Carousel* is staged in New York. Perry Como sings 'Till The End of Time'. 'Bluegrass' country music becomes popular in the United States. George Orwell's *Animal Farm*, Jean-Paul Sartre's *The Age of Reason*, John Steinbeck's *Cannery Row* and Evelyn Waugh's *Brideshead Revisited* are published. *Brief Encounter*, written by Noel Coward and starring Celia Johnson and Trevor Howard, Marcel Carné's *Les Enfants du Paradis*, Billy Wilder's *The Lost Weekend* and Roberto Rossellini's *Rome, Open City* are released at the cinema.

Births

Cellist Jacqueline du Pré; opera singer Jessye Norman; reggae musician Bob Marley; actor Henry Winkler (best known for his TV character 'The Fonz').

Personalities born in 1945

With bright, inquiring minds, though at times rather otherworldly, personalities born in 1945 adore exploring new ideas and are restless. With Pluto in Leo they are charismatic, but fairly self-centred. With Neptune in Libra they have unrealistically high expectations of partners. Emotionally defensive with Saturn in Cancer, they can be isolated within their families, or neurotic, building protective shells around themselves. The square onto Neptune makes for obsessive preoccupations and paranoid anxieties. Those born up to 26 August with Jupiter in

135

Virgo are hard-working, warm-hearted, and wish to be of service; those born thereafter with Jupiter in Libra close to Neptune have a charitable, compassionate streak and a strong concern for fairness.

1946

This year sees the start, in August, of three years of Saturn beside Pluto in Leo, always an indicator of tough times, which produces resilient, obsessive, self-contained and sometimes self-destructive individuals and violent events. This placing occurs only three times a century: in the 20th century it occurred in Cancer in 1914–16, then in Libra in 1981–82, but it has not occurred in Leo since 1211. Uranus in Gemini aspects Neptune in Libra and Pluto in Leo—a mystical or spiritual counterbalance offering challenging new ideas and ideals during the years 1943 to 1949. The Saturn–Pluto effect is intense, tough, fanatical, sometimes brutal, making it a hard struggle to achieve success and submerging personal individuality in mass movements. Uranus, Neptune and Pluto in more harmonious contact produce an explosion of new and inspired scientific discoveries and philosophies. Probing deeply into the core of reality, there are developments in nuclear power and the new physics; there is also a need to escape the harsher aspects of life. Four eclipses contribute to a sense of heightened anxiety. Jupiter in Libra until 26 September stresses the need for social justice; thereafter in Scorpio it promotes financial ventures.

Events

The first session of the UN General Assembly takes place; New York is chosen as the organization's permanent headquarters. After the War Crimes Trials in Nuremberg and Tokyo, 10 leading Nazis are hanged. In a speech in the United States, Winston Churchill coins the term 'Iron Curtain' to describe the barrier between communist East and capitalist West, and signals the formal start of the Cold War. French troops bomb Vietnam, killing 20,000: the French-Indochina war begins, lasting until 1954. A Zionist terrorist bomb in Jerusalem (still in Palestine) kills 91 people. Juan Peron is elected president of Argentina. Jawaharlal Nehru is elected Indian vice-president. There is an anti-Jewish pogrom in Poland. The post-war baby boom begins. The world is hit by a wheat shortage. The first bikinis cause a sensation.

Science and technology

The USSR's first nuclear reactor goes into operation. The first electronic computer is built in the United States. A pilotless radio-controlled rocket missile is developed.

Culture

Mark Rothko paints *Sacrifice* and sculptor Barbara Hepworth produces *Pelagos*. Aaron Copland composes his Symphony No. 3 and Sergei Prokofiev the first version of his opera *War and Peace*. Kurt Weill writes his musical *Street Scene*, and the musical *Annie Get Your Gun* opens in New York. Edith Piaf sings 'La Vie en Rose'. Jean Genet's *Our Lady of the Flowers*, Nikos Kazantzakis's *Zorba the Greek*, Paramahansa Yogananda's *Autobiography of a*

Yogi, and Eugene O'Neill's *The Iceman Cometh* appear in the worlds of literature and theatre. Jean Cocteau's *La Belle et la Bête* ('Beauty and the Beast'), William Wyler's *The Best Years of Our Lives*, David Lean's *Great Expectations*, Alfred Hitchcock's *Notorious* and Tay Garnet's *The Postman Always Rings Twice* are released on film.

Births
US president Bill Clinton; German film and theatre director Rainer Werner Fassbinder; singer and actress Dolly Parton; singer-songwriter Freddie Mercury; German immunologist George Kohler.

Personalities born in 1946
With Uranus and Neptune in air signs connecting to Pluto in fiery Leo, personalities born in 1946 are unconventional thinkers, not always realistic, who like to explore alternative ways of looking at the universe. They are psychic, tuned into the intangible, intrigued by occult phenomena and by the new physics—anything that lies beyond surface reality. The air signs Gemini, Libra and Aquarius, and the adaptable, mutable signs Virgo, Sagittarius and Pisces are, in 1946, attuned to this mystical, highly strung energy. Those born with Saturn in Cancer until 2 August have an emotionally difficult early life, and struggle to find home and family contentment. Those born thereafter, with Saturn and Pluto in Leo, are immensely strong, slightly obsessive and compulsive personalities, who defend themselves against intimate emotional involvement, often in a rather destructive way. They regard themselves as outsiders who do not walk to the same drumbeat as the majority, so they can be highly original. They can have an almost magical capacity to manipulate situations. Supremely resourceful in crisis, they have amazing perseverance, but often create difficulties to give life an air of adventure. Those born with Jupiter in Libra up to 26 September are fair-minded; those born with Jupiter in Scorpio have skill with money and are trusted with confidential information.

Bill Clinton
Born 19 August 1946, 8.51 am Central Standard Time, Hope, Arkansas.
Chart: Sun, Mercury, Saturn, Pluto in Leo ✦ Moon in Taurus ✦ Ascendant, Mars, Neptune, Venus, Jupiter in Libra ✦ Uranus, Moon's North Node in Gemini

A clutch of sociable, charming planets were on the horizon in diplomatic Libra when Bill Clinton was born. The ascendant sign—Clinton's is in Libra—shapes the outer image, an individual's façade. Libra's strength is in its innate sense of fairness and justice, but its negative traits run to superficiality and lack of integrity. Mars and Neptune attract him to publicity and showbusiness, Venus and Jupiter to the indulgent, good life. As a Leo, he is the entertainer par excellence, thriving in group situations, out in society. An audience is essential for his self-esteem, the mirror that compensates for his sense of inner emptiness. He is a quixotic mix of light and dark, both unstable and profoundly powerful. Like Mick Jagger, another flamboyant Leo, he has a sensual Taurus Moon which craves physical, sexual contact. But Clinton is drawn beyond this to the more perverse by Mars, Neptune and Venus all together in Libra. He is both attracted to and repelled by the body, so his sexuality is often ungrounded.

With Saturn and Pluto in Leo aspecting both his Sun and his Moon he has strongly self-destructive emotional traits. Stemming from disturbed relationships in childhood to parents who both over-controlled but could not love him, he has continued the pattern in a highly ambitious business marriage where opportunism outweighed intimacy.

With Uranus in Gemini aspecting the Libra planets 120 degrees from the horizon, he is a truly pioneering thinker and communicator with the courage to stand up for his beliefs. The tragedy of Clinton, the louche sensualist, is that he has allowed his desire to 'walk on the edge' to destroy his undoubted potential for revolutionizing America's outlook.

The years of his political crisis from 1993 coincided initially with Pluto in late Scorpio aspecting his Leo Sun. This started to deconstruct his power base, although with potential for rebirth if he could change. When Uranus moved into Aquarius in 1995 the bars of his highly defended cage were not to be just rattled, but actively broken open. His attempt to keep control was brought to an end in 1998 when Uranus, having jarred against Saturn, finally came into alignment across the zodiac with Pluto at 11 degrees Leo. Like Richard Nixon, Clinton was disgraced at the height of his power, when astrologically he could have been facing many years of eminent service. He will not disappear from public view, but will reinvent himself after an emotionally traumatic couple of years between 2000 and 2002.

1947

The tenacious, cold-hearted, emotionally destructive Saturn–Pluto effect makes for a difficult year when success comes sparingly after great struggle. Exacerbated by fiery Mars through October and November the mood is ruthless, the need is for endurance and extreme self-discipline in difficult circumstances. Flare-ups in the aftermath of Indian independence and the partition of Palestine are one of the results. Inventive Uranus in sharp-thinking Gemini continues to push ahead exciting new scientific concepts. In aspect to otherworldly Neptune in Libra, it promotes advances in nuclear physics and new levels of consciousness. The yearning is for a more meaningful purpose in life and relationships. None of the outer planets in earth signs makes for a lack of practical common sense. Jupiter in Scorpio until 25 October is helpful to financial ventures; in Sagittarius thereafter it boosts morale.

Events

The partition of India and Pakistan leads to massacres and killings. Lord Mountbatten oversees Indian independence. Kashmir is invaded by Pathan tribesmen. Fighting breaks out between Jews and Arabs as the UN adopts the plan to divide Palestine. In Britain, Princess Elizabeth marries Philip Mountbatten (created Duke of Edinburgh) one week after the November solar eclipse in Scorpio, which is aspected by a formidably unfriendly, high-tension array of Mars, Saturn and Pluto in Leo. A fuel and economic crisis affects Britain, hit by a hard winter. Major strikes occur in France. The Dead Sea Scrolls are discovered at Qumran.

Science and technology

The first supersonic flight takes place. A round-the-world flight is made in 73 hours. The printed circuit board is developed. Britain's first atomic pile becomes operational. Holography, the production of three-dimensional images, is invented. The first microwave ovens go on sale. The first recorded UFO sightings are made.

Culture

The theories of existentialism are popular in Paris, with Alberto Giacometti and Wols following the ideas of the Jean-Paul Sartre. Arshile Gorky paints *Agony*, Jackson Pollock *Full Fathom Five*, and Diego Rivera starts work on *Alameda Park*. Architect Le Corbusier designs 'Unité d'Habitation' in Marseilles, and Frank Lloyd Wright the Unitarian Chuch in Madison, Wisconsin. In the world of music, Benjamin Britten composes his opera *Albert Herring*, Alan Jay Lerner and Frederick Loewe stage their musical *Brigadoon*, and the musical *Finian's Rainbow*, with lyrics by Harburg and Sady, and music by Burton Lane, is staged in New York. Albert Camus' *The Plague*, Anne Frank's *The Diary of Anne Frank*, Malcolm Lowry's *Under the Volcano* and Alberto Moravia's *The Woman of Rome* are all published. Jean Genet completes *Querelle de Brest* and Tennessee Williams *A Streetcar Named Desire*. Elia Kazan founds the 'Method' school in the Actors' Studio, New York. New films include Michael Powell's *Black Narcissus*, John Boulting's *Brighton Rock*, John Ford's *The Fugitive* and Charlie Chaplin's *Monsieur Verdoux*.

Births

Writer Salman Rushdie; playwright and film-maker David Mamet; US politician Dan Quayle; US TV host David Letterman; racing driver James Hunt; German political activist Petra Kelly.

Personalities born in 1947

Immensely strong and built for the long haul, those born in 1947 have abundant endurance but can be resistant to change. Intensely independent, slightly obsessive, rather brooding individuals, who feel the need to pit themselves against extreme circumstances, they always feel like outsiders. The tough Saturn–Pluto contact in fiery Leo, the sign of the burning heart, makes them emotionally self-destructive, and not good at allowing their vulnerabilities to show. With restless, inventive Uranus in inquiring Gemini, they are good communicators, always pushing the frontiers of knowledge and limits, and wanting to know what lies beyond surface reality. Neptune in Libra makes them yearn for ideal relationships, though unrealistic expectations lead to disappointment. Those born with Jupiter in Scorpio before 25 October attract both money and confidential information; those born with Jupiter in Sagittarius thereafter are high-minded, widely read, serious thinkers.

1948

The waning contact between restrictive Saturn and power-hungry Pluto, together in fixed Leo since 1946, continues to exert a bleak influence. Times are tough, made more so by aggressive Mars's presence in Leo from mid-February to mid-May, during the creation of the state of Israel. The mood is self-defensive, stubborn, with changes occurring only after extreme resistance, and then sometimes self-destructively. Inventive Uranus in inquiring Gemini still in aspect to Neptune in Libra promotes new scientific ideas and new technology and sows the seeds for the information revolution. After 30 August, Uranus starts the move into Cancer for a seven-year stay, which promotes emotional freedom and an unconventional approach to family life. Self-disciplined Saturn in hard-working Virgo for two and a half years places emphasis on efficiency and issues related to health. Expansive Jupiter is in high-minded Sagittarius until 15 November, then moves into materialistic Capricorn.

Events

Mahatma Gandhi is assassinated. Popular protests in Czechoslovakia are crushed. Chiang Kai-shek is granted dictatorial powers in China. The state of Israel is established one week after a violently aspected solar eclipse. The Nationalist Party, which advocates apartheid, wins the South African elections. The USSR blocks road and rail traffic between Berlin and the West. Harry Truman wins the presidential election in the United States. The World Health Organization is founded.

Culture

Willem de Kooning paints *Mailbox*, Jackson Pollock *Composition No. 1*, and Max Ernst produces the sculpture *Capricorn*. Richard Strauss writes *Four Last Songs*; the musical *Kiss Me Kate*, with music by Cole Porter and lyrics by Bella and Samuel Spewack, is performed in New York. Ella Fitzgerald sings 'My Happiness'. Publications include Thor Heyerdahl's *The Kon-Tiki Expedition*, F. R. Leavis's *The Great Tradition*, Truman Capote's *Other Voices, Other Rooms*, Graham Greene's *The Heart of the Matter*, Norman Mailer's *The Naked and the Dead*, Alan Paton's *Cry the Beloved Country*, Georges Simenon's *Pedigree*, Gore Vidal's *The City and the Pillar* and Thornton Wilder's *The Ides of March*. Albert Camus completes *State of Siege*, and Jean Genet *The Maids*. Cinema audiences see *Abbot and Costello Meet Frankenstein*, Vittorio De Sica's *Bicycle Thieves*, Akira Kurosawa's *Drunken Angel*, John Ford's *Fort Apache* starring Henry Fonda, John Huston's *Key Largo* starring Humphrey Bogart, and Laurence Olivier's *Hamlet*.

Births

Popular composer Andrew Lloyd Webber; Prince Charles, heir to the British throne; Soviet dancer and choreographer Mikhail Baryshnikov; US politician Al Gore.

Personalities born in 1948

Enormously strong-minded, slightly obsessive, very determined personalities with formidable stamina, who tend to regard themselves as being outside the mainstream, typify those born in 1948. Highly resistant to change, especially in their emotional lives, they find intimacy difficult, and remain fairly defended, sometimes becoming depressed. Good communicators and bright thinkers, with a wide-ranging curiosity for new ideas, they rarely sit still but are continually exploring new horizons. Those born between 30 August and 13 November with

Uranus in Cancer demand freedom of expression in their family lives, and sometimes total independence. Those born with Saturn in Virgo after 19 September are hard-working worriers, concerned with health. Jupiter in Sagittarius up to 15 November lends an optimistic streak; to those born with Jupiter in Capricorn thereafter, it brings financial success.

Prince Charles
Born 14 November 1948, 9.14 pm, London, England.
Chart: Sun, Mercury in Scorpio ◆ Moon, Moon's North Node in Taurus ◆ Mars, Jupiter in Sagittarius ◆ Venus, Neptune in Libra ◆ Saturn in Virgo ◆ Ascendant, Pluto in Leo ◆ Uranus in Gemini

A highly spiritual introvert and an intensely secretive Scorpio with strong Pluto aspects to both Sun and Moon, Prince Charles has a birth chart on which imprisonment is writ large. Trapped by inner family dynamics and outer circumstances, he feels a pawn on the chessboard of life. With a tactile Taurus Moon at the midheaven when he was born, Charles does care deeply about satisfying public needs and yearns in return for the emotional sustenance that was lacking in an over-dutiful, absent mother. But showing his vulnerabilities is not easy—Scorpio guards its privacy jealously. As frequently happens with caesarean births, Pluto was on the horizon when he was born, giving him an ingrained, suspicious defensiveness. With a Leo ascendant, he should appear flamboyant, colourful, the entertainer, but Pluto close by represses the fire, making him seem uncooperative and resentful. The plus side is a tremendous staying power and psychological stamina.

With Neptune close to his hidden Sun, he sees his restless Gemini father, Prince Philip, as a figure of pity, despite his controlling nature. He is the real source of Charles's indecisiveness. His relationship with his mother (see *Queen Elizabeth II*, page 100) is where the power struggles are largely played out. Emotionally cold and a disappointment to them both, this is an essentially unstable relationship which can only thrive if each gives the other maximum freedom. Yet there is an equally strong control-and-dominate dynamic. Charles's relationship to his own children is easier, with a confident pairing of Mars and Jupiter in adventurous Sagittarius giving him an escape route from duty and bringing to life his own restricted spontaneity (see *Prince William*, page 194, and *Prince Harry*, page 198).

What was lacking in Prince Charles's childhood is benevolently fulfilled in his enduring relationship with Camilla Parker-Bowles. They are able to express affection warmly and easily, and yet they do need adversity to bring out the best in each other. Camilla, like the Princess of Wales, is a Cancerian, the sign that brings out the archetypally mothering nature. Even more so than Charles, she dislikes constant limelight, preferring to stay close to her comfortable home surroundings.

In the broad sweep of Prince Charles's life, he is at a career peak from now until 2006, when he will be hard-working and have a more prominent profile. Pluto throws him into intensely romantic feelings for years ahead; these can be rather obsessive at times, and can also create power struggles with children. Uranus and Neptune travelling opposite his ascendant for the next few years are hardly ideal influences for committed, long-term relationships. Uranus wants freedom; Neptune lacks decisiveness. When Uranus enters Pisces post-2002, a major change in financial circumstances is likely for Charles as well as major emotional changes. A bumpy ride to 2006 sees his old ambitions losing fire, and his desire to fulfil his inner needs growing ever stronger.

1949

Both Saturn and Uranus continue to hover between two signs, causing an ambivalent mood, and leading to a back-and-forth pattern of progress. Saturn reversing into Leo between 3 April and 29 May in wide aspect to Pluto is tough, resistant and bleak, and demands endurance, but with less intensity than in the previous three years. Pluto in the midst of a 19-year stay in Leo, starting in 1938, continues to promote atomic research, with its grandiose implications of human omnipotence, and focuses on individual power rather than collective values. Uranus moving into Cancer for seven years on 10 June puts emotional freedom above family ties. Saturn in Virgo before 3 April and after 29 May is efficient, dutiful and concerned with health. Neptune in Libra looks for fairness, justice and ideal relationships. Jupiter in Capricorn up to 12 April and between 28 June and 30 November supports traditional business ventures; otherwise in Aquarius it promotes racial and religious tolerance and humanitarian ventures.

Events

NATO (the North Atlantic Treaty Organization) is founded. The Republic of Ireland is proclaimed in Dublin. In South Africa, apartheid legislation is passed. The Berlin blockade by the USSR is lifted. Greek Civil War ends. Communists win the civil war in China. France gives sovereignty to Vietnam. The first atomic bomb tests in the USSR take place.

Culture

Willem de Kooning paints *Asheville*, Graham Sutherland paints *Somerset Maugham*, and Wols paints *Bird*. Henri Matisse creates the maquette for the famous stained glass for the Chapel of the Rosary of the Dominican Nuns in Vence, France. Sculptor Jacob Epstein creates *Lazarus*, and Pablo Picasso *Pregnant Woman*. Leonard Bernstein composes *The Age of Anxiety*, and Benjamin Britten *Spring Symphony*. The musical *Gentlemen Prefer Blondes*, with music by Jule Styne and lyrics by Leo Robins, is first performed in New York. Rodgers and Hammerstein's musical *South Pacific* also makes its debut in New York. Rhythm and blues is the rage in the United States. Simone de Beauvoir's *The Second Sex*, H. E. Bates's *The Jacaranda Tree*, Enid Blyton's *Noddy* (the first version), Paul Bowles' *The Sheltering Sky*, Jean Genet's *The Thief's Journal*, Fitzroy Maclean's *Eastern Approaches*, George Orwell's *Nineteen Eighty-Four*, T. S. Eliot's *The Cocktail Party* and Arthur Miller's *Death of a Salesman* are among the year's literary and theatrical works. Film releases include *All the King's Men* with Broderick Crawford, *The Blue Lamp* with Jack Warner, *The Heiress* with Olivia de Havilland, *Kind Hearts and Coronets* with Alec Guinness, *The Third Man* with Orson Welles and *White Heat* with James Cagney.

Births

Singer Bruce Springsteen; British novelist Ken Follett; American photographer Annie Leibovitz.

Personalities born in 1949

Extremely hard-working individuals, prone to worry, personalities born in 1949 can be emotionally erratic, demanding total freedom from home and family ties one moment, and digging in for the long haul the next. With Pluto in Leo they tend to be rather self-centred; with Neptune in Libra they dream of wonderful partnerships but find the practice of relating tricky. Those born with Saturn in Virgo are concerned with efficiency and health, are slightly over-dutiful, but good at detailed writing. Those born with Uranus in Gemini up to 10 June have restless, inquiring minds, and a great deal of curiosity; those born thereafter, with Uranus in Cancer, adore unusual homes filled with gadgets. Jupiter in Capricorn before 12 April, and between 28 June and 30 November, attracts money and material status to those born then; those born with Jupiter in Aquarius have a broadminded streak, but this planetary placing can make these individuals scatter their energy too much.

1950–1959

Possibly the easiest decade of the century so far, with fewer highly stressed outer planet aspects. The defining characteristic of the early 1950s is Saturn and Neptune in Libra square to Uranus, giving a highly strung quality accompanied by a strong motivation for social justice and the rights of the under-privileged. Enlightening, inspired, though at times fostering frankly wild beliefs, this is where the seeds of the hippie, 'flower-power' generation are sown. Both revolutionary Uranus and idealistic, dreamy Neptune are passing through emotional signs, altering attitudes to sexual behaviour for ever. Uranus aims for freedom in family relationships in Cancer until midway through the decade, then dashes into hot-headed, theatrical Leo, making a firm stand for free love. Neptune, having put romance on a pedestal in Libra since 1942, slides into intensely passionate Scorpio in 1955, fostering the search for bliss through the body and music—sex, drink, drugs and rock-'n'-roll have arrived. Pluto also changes midway out of self-focused Leo—also a promoter of atomic-energy development—where it has been since 1938. Once into Virgo it fosters a profound transformation of medicine, health and attitudes to work. However, its devastating entry in 1956, squaring Saturn, a bleak energy, coincides with the decade's worst hotspot with the Soviet invasion of Hungary, the Suez crisis and a Middle East flare-up all in quick succession.

1950

A betwixt and between year with few aspects between outer planets. Austere Saturn in hard-working, over-worrying Virgo aspects both eclipses, handing out heavy responsibilities and focusing on health; almost in opposition to Jupiter, it hints at disappointments in hopes or ventures which were launched on the Jupiter–Saturn conjunction of 1941. Neptune at a minor angle to Pluto promotes fey ideas, looks beyond reality, and supports advances in nuclear physics, with Pluto promoting godlike powers in the field of atomic energy. Uranus in Cancer revolutionizes attitudes to family life and aims for independence; in approaching square to Saturn late in the year it hints at jolting economic changes to come the following year. The highly strung Uranus–Saturn–Neptune connection starting to form signals the birth of those who will be the future hippie generation. Jupiter in Pisces between 15 April and 15 September is charitably inclined; in Aquarius otherwise it is humanitarian and tolerant.

Events

The Korean War starts, with North Korea invading the South. UN forces under General MacArthur invade North Korea, then retreat as China enters the war. China invades Tibet. In the United States, Senator Joseph McCarthy starts his anti-communist witch-hunt. The Republic of India is formed. There are race riots in South Africa over apartheid. The USSR shoots down a US plane. American tycoon Howard Hughes becomes a recluse. Pope Pius XII issues the dogma of the bodily assumption of the Virgin Mary into Heaven. The Scottish Stone of Scone is stolen from Westminster Abbey.

Science and technology

The United States develops the hydrogen bomb. Regular colour TV broadcasts begin in the United States.

Culture

Jackson Pollock paints *Autumn Rhythm*, Robert Rauschenberg paints *White Painting*—the first monchrome by an American artist—and Mark Rothko paints *Number One*. Sculptor Alberto Giacometti produces *Falling Man* and Pablo Picasso *The She-goat*. Opera star Maria Callas makes her debut at La Scala, Milan. Irving Berlin's musical *Call Me Madam* has its first performance in New York, as does *Guys and Dolls* by Frank Loesser and Abe Burrows. Fats Domino sings 'The Fats Man'. Publications include E. H. Gombrich's *The Story of Art*, G. I. Gurdjieff's *Beelzebub's Tales*, Ernest Hemingway's *Across the River*, Doris Lessing's *The Grass is Singing*, P. D. Ouspensky's *In Search of the Miraculous*, C. P. Snow's *The Masters*, Richard Wilhelm's *I Ching* and Christopher Fry's *Venus Observed*. Cartoon character Charlie Brown appears in the first syndicated cartoon. The year's films include *All About Eve* with Bette Davis, the film version of Irving Berlin's musical *Annie Get Your Gun*, John Huston's *The Asphalt Jungle*, John Ford's *Rio Grande*, *Sunset Boulevard* with Gloria Swanson and William Holden, and Luis Buñuel's *The Young and the Damned*.

Births

Princess Anne, the Princess Royal; Olympic swimmer Mark Spitz; singer David Cassidy; violinist Eugene Fodor; US TV host Jay Leno; Canadian actor John Candy.

Personalities born in 1950

Extremely hard-working, fair-minded though emotionally erratic individuals, personalities born in 1950 are a contradictory mix of the conventionally dutiful and the rebellious. Saturn in Virgo until 20 November signposts a conscientious streak, with a practical interest in health; in Libra thereafter it brings a serious concern for justice in society and relationships. Uranus-in-Cancer types are rule-breakers where family and romantic relationships are concerned—freedom is their watchword. With Neptune in Libra they have over-high expectations of romance, and are continually dissatisfied with the reality of what they choose. Neptune angled at Pluto brings a fey, otherworldly streak and an interest in what lies below surface reality. Jupiter in Pisces between 15 April and 15 September, and after 1 December, is compassionate and charitable; in Aquarius it brings a humanitarian tolerance.

Princess Anne

Born 15 August 1950, 11.50 am, London, England.

Chart: Sun, Pluto and midheaven in Leo ✦ Ascendant and Neptune in Libra ✦ Moon, Mercury, Saturn in Virgo ✦ Jupiter in Pisces ✦ Uranus and Venus in Cancer ✦ Mars in Scorpio ✦ Moon's North Node in Pisces

A secretive Leo with a need for a public career, she is better designed for a life of royal service than her more introverted older brother (see *Prince Charles*, page 141). Pluto at her midheaven close to her Sun damps some of Leo's more flamboyant tendencies but will make her hugely influential, if rather controlling, the older she gets. Three planets, including self-disciplined Saturn, give her a strong work ethic, inherited from her over-dutiful, emotionally distant mother. With a midheaven Sun, her identity is wrapped up in fulfilling her mother's ambitions for her, while leaving a sense of inner emptiness that can make intimate relationships difficult to sustain. Despite her own lack of nurturing as a child, charitable Jupiter in Pisces focuses her practical energies towards helping the world's disadvantaged youth through the charity Save the Children, and gives her a good rapport with her own children. Jupiter, well placed in her chart and in good aspect to Venus in Cancer, stimulates her love of sport (in particular racing and three-day eventing) and the entertainment business.

A water grand trine (of Cancer, Scorpio and Pisces planets) often indicates a healing personality keen to support the sick, the troubled or the socially rejected, while at the same time protecting their own inner vulnerabilities. Princess Anne learned to toughen up early on, and uses her stinging Mars in Scorpio, prominently placed at her birth, to good effect when invasions of her privacy are threatened. With pioneering Uranus in Cancer in the chart area of travel, she thrives on foreign adventures, happily volunteering to go on uncomfortable tours for her children's-charity work.

Her colourful choice of dress for formal occasions comes from her sociable Libra ascendant; but when at work on famine relief her understated Virgo–Sun–Saturn contact turns her out in practical, often drab clothes.

Venus in Cancer close to her midheaven, being ruler of her ascendant, is pivotal, both to her public diplomatic life and her marriages. Uranus on her ascendant in Libra was aspecting Venus in 1973 when she first married, hinting at the need for freedom rather than close contact. During the years of her separation and divorce from Mark Phillips, Pluto in Scorpio was squaring her career-driven Sun–Pluto conjunction, pulling her painfully away from the past, and transforming her public image. When she remarried in 1992, Uranus and Neptune in Capricorn were approaching the opposition to Venus, again hinting at frequent separations and the need for distance. Her public profile will remain high for many years to come as she takes on more duties, perhaps easing her mother's burden.

1951

Disruptive, unconventional Uranus in emotional Cancer approaching the hard aspect to Neptune in Libra creates a highly strung, wilful mood which continues throughout the decade. Social and psychic confusion lead to polarized arguments and promote extreme beliefs and secret societies. A new way of relating is being advocated which throws conventional family life into turmoil. Fairness and total

145

freedom are the incompatible ideals. Pluto in Leo emphasizes personal self-interest. Neptune in easy aspect to aggrandizing Pluto continues to foster developments in nuclear physics and an interest in what lies beyond reality. Saturn in hard-working, dutiful Virgo up to 20 November focuses on efficiency and improving health. Jupiter in compassionate Pisces up to 21 April in opposition to Saturn throws failures into sharp relief; it moves on thereafter into impetuous, hot-headed, entrepreneurial Aries.

Events

General MacArthur is relieved of his command of the UN forces in the Korean War on the exact Saturn–Jupiter opposition, as he advocates war with China using atomic bombs. Chinese forces advance. The prime ministers of Pakistan and Iran, the King of Jordan, and the British high commissioner of Malaya are all assassinated by different local fanatics. British diplomats Guy Burgess and Donald Maclean go to Moscow, having been warned by art historian and Soviet spy Anthony Blunt that they are under suspicion for spying. In the United States, the Rosenbergs are sentenced to death for passing atomic weapon secrets to the Russians. In Britain, Winston Churchill again becomes prime minister; the Witchcraft Act is repealed.

Science and technology

In the United States, electrical power is satisfactorily produced from atomic energy, and the transcontinental dial telephone service begins.

Culture

Henri Matisse paints *Blue Nude 1*, Jackson Pollock his *Echo No. 25*, and Robert Rauschenberg starts his *Black Painting*. Henry Moore sculpts *Reclining Figure* and Pablo Picasso *Baboon and Young*. Benjamin Britten composes his opera *Billy Budd*, Dmitri Shostakovich *Twenty-four Preludes and Figures* and Igor Stravinsky his opera *The Rake's Progress*. Rodgers and Hammerstein's musical *The King and I* is first performed in New York, as is Lerner and Loewe's *Paint Your Wagon*. Johnnie Ray sings 'Cry'. Ray Bradbury's *The Illustrated Man*, Albert Camus' *The Rebel*, James Jones's *From Here to Eternity*, Carson McCuller's *The Ballad of the Sad Café*, Nicholas Monsarrat's *The Cruel Sea*, Anthony Powell's *A Question of Upbringing*, J. D. Salinger's *The Catcher in the Rye* and John Wyndham's *The Day of the Triffids* are published. Tennessee Williams writes his play *The Rose Tattoo*. Cinema audiences see *The African Queen* with Humphrey Bogart and Katharine Hepburn, *An American in Paris* with Gene Kelly and Leslie Caron, *Bedtime for Bonzo* with Ronald Reagan, Orson Welles's *Othello*, John Huston's *The Red Badge of Courage* with Audie Murphy and Elia Kazan's *A Streetcar Named Desire* with Vivien Leigh and Marlon Brando.

Births

Irish politician Bertie Aherne; chess champion Anatoly Karpov.

Personalities born in 1951

Hard-working, high-minded and rather nervy individuals, those born in 1951 have a good deal of initiative. On the cusp of the hippie, flower-power generation, they are concerned with creating a better society, particularly those born before 7 March and after 14 August with Saturn and Neptune in fair-minded Libra. They can be indecisive and rather paranoid at times. Creative, they are also highly strung and sometimes wilful, setting their minds and refusing to budge from what may prove to be rather eccentric beliefs. Those born between those same dates with Saturn in Virgo are exceptionally dutiful and concerned with health. With Uranus in Cancer, they demand emotional freedom from their family ties to live as they want, and adore homes with unusual features or gadgets. Jupiter in Pisces up to 21 April gives a kindly outlook, although in opposition to Saturn it also brings a fear of failure; those born thereafter with Jupiter in Aries are reckless.

1952

The Saturn–Neptune contact in Libra raises hopes of improving the lot of the disadvantaged, and of promoting the rights of the working classes. High-minded, though often paranoid, it can bring inspired new ideas in social justice or frankly mad beliefs. The square to wilful, impatient Uranus in Cancer, which is determined to have emotional freedom, creates a mood of high tension and polarized, irrational arguments. Pluto continuing in self-promoting Leo raises individual needs over relationship or family values. Jupiter in fiery Aries until 29 April is reckless; in Taurus thereafter it promotes good living and helps financial ventures.

Events
King George VI dies in London, five days before the February lunar eclipse, which was only one degree away from Pluto; Queen Elizabeth II accedes to the throne while visiting Kenya. No lynchings are reported in the United States for the first time since records began in 1881. Winter smog in London leads to 2000 deaths. Hussein, still a minor, becomes King of Jordan, as his father retires with poor mental health. The United States bombs North Korea. Eva Peron, wife of Argentinian president Juan Peron, dies of cancer. A state of emergency is declared in Kenya as nationalist Mau Mau power erupts. Dwight D. Eisenhower becomes US president in a Republican landslide.

Science and technology
The United States explodes the first hydrogen bomb in the Pacific.

Culture
In the world of art Balthus starts his *Le Passage du Commerce Saint André*, Willem de Kooning paints *Woman with Lipstick* and Henri Matisse *The Swimming Pool*. Sculptor Henry Moore produces *King and Queen*. In the world of music John Cage composes *4' 33"*, Hans Werner Henze his opera *Boulevard Solitude*, Michael Tippett his opera *The Midsummer Marriage* and Ralph Vaughan Williams his *Sinfonia Antarctica* (Symphony No. 7). The year's publications include Flannery O'Connor's *Wise Blood*, John Steinbeck's *East of Eden*, Laurens Van der Post's *Venture to the Interior*, Angus Wilson's *Hemlock and After*, George Axelrod's *The Seven Year Itch*, Truman Capote's *The Grass Harp* and Agatha Christie's *The Mousetrap*. In the world of film, *The Bad and the Beautiful* with Kirk Douglas, Cecil B. De Mille's *The Greatest Show on Earth*, Fred Zinnemann's *High Noon*

with Gary Cooper and Grace Kelly, *Limelight* with Charlie Chaplin and Clare Bloom, Walt Disney's *Peter Pan*, and *Singin' in the Rain* with Gene Kelly are all released.

Births
Novelist Vikram Seth; actor Dan Aykroyd; tennis player Jimmy Connors.

Personalities born in 1952
Well-meaning but not always sensible or practical, individuals born in 1952 can be wilful and highly strung. They push for better social agreements, although they often hold slightly irrational views. Good communicators, they are intrigued by new ideas, and are sometimes attracted to the occult or spiritual beliefs. Contradictory and rather restless, they are good at starting new projects and have initiative, but often delude themselves about what will work well. Although they are serious about relationships, they demand emotional freedom and can be fairly self-centred. They love unusual homes filled with gadgets. Those born with Jupiter in Aries before 29 April are impetuous and inclined to dash ahead; in Taurus thereafter it attracts the good life, and usually brings money and possessions for those born then.

1953
The year when major aspects become exact intensifies the mood and leads to events that symbolize the year's energy. Saturn and Neptune come together in Libra, leading to anxiety but also highlighting better social justice for the disadvantaged. Impatient, wilful Uranus in Cancer is also in exact hard aspect to Neptune, causing social unrest and psychic confusion. Emotional excitement is high at certain points in the year, with change and freedom being the watchwords. Irrational arguments or extreme beliefs flourish. Neptune and Pluto continue to link up, promoting an interest in otherworldly subjects, nuclear physics and what lies beyond reality. Jupiter in Taurus up to 11 May supports the good life; then in Gemini it is light-hearted and communicative. Saturn in Scorpio after 23 October is obsessively conscientious and rather tight financially.

Events
There are riots in Pakistan. Egypt becomes a dictatorship. In South Africa, the minister of justice is given power to declare a state of emergency. Joseph Stalin dies. Jomo Kenyatta and others are convicted of organizing Mau Mau terrorism in Kenya. In the United States the Rosenbergs are executed for spying. Widespread flooding in the Netherlands and England kills 1500 people just after the late January lunar eclipse aspected by Pluto. British serial murderer John Christie is executed four days after the solar eclipse in Cancer, exactly conjunct Uranus, squared by Saturn and Neptune. Edmund Hillary and Tenzing Norgay climb Mount Everest, three days before the coronation of Queen Elizabeth II. Myxomatosis spreads from continental Europe to Britain, killing millions of rabbits. The Piltdown Man is found to be a fraud. Jacqueline Bouvier marries John F. Kennedy.

Science and technology

In the United States a woman is impregnated with frozen sperm. The first successful open-heart operation is performed.

Culture

Henri Matisse paints *The Snail*, Jackson Pollock *Blue Poles No. II* and Robert Rauschenberg *Untitled* (Red painting). Composer Benjamin Britten writes his opera *Gloriana*, Dmitri Shostakovich Symphony No. 10, and Michael Tippett *Fantasia Concertante on a Theme by Corelli*. In London, Sandy Wilson's musical *The Boyfriend* is first performed, and in New York the musical *Kismet*, based on the music of Alexander Borodin and with lyrics by Charles Lederer and Luther Davis, makes its debut at the Ziegfeld Theatre. Tom Lehrer records his *Songs by Tom Lehrer* and Marty Robbins *Sing the Blues*. James Baldwin's *Go Tell It on the Mountain*, Saul Bellow's *The Adventures of Augie March*, William Burroughs's *Junky*, Raymond Chandler's *The Long Goodbye*, William Faulkner's *Requiem for a Nun*, Ian Fleming's *Casino Royale* and T. S. Eliot's *The Confidential Clerk* are published. Arthur Miller's *The Crucible* is performed. Film releases include *The Big Heat* with Glenn Ford, *The Cruel Sea* with Jack Hawkins, Fred Zinnemann's *From Here to Eternity* with Deborah Kerr, Burt Lancaster and Frank Sinatra, *Gentlemen Prefer Blondes* with Marilyn Monroe and Jane Russell, Jacques Tati's *Monsieur Hulot's Holiday* and *Shane* with Alan Ladd.

Births

British prime minister Tony Blair; prime minister of Pakistan Benazir Bhutto; Haitian president Jean-Bertrand Aristide; American comedienne Roseanne Barr; actress Kim Basinger.

Personalities born in 1953

With temperaments similar to those of the previous two years' births, people born in 1953 are the future hippie, flower-power generation, drawn to wild and way-out ideas but driven by a need for social justice and fairer relationships. Rather self-centred and keen on total emotional freedom, they do not settle easily to monogamy or conventional domestic situations. Great worriers, they can be impatient, highly strung and at times rather irrational. They are keen on unusual, modern homes with all the new gadgetry. Those born with Jupiter in Taurus up to 9 May attract money and possessions and adore the good life; those with Jupiter in Gemini thereafter are chatty, versatile and broadminded. Saturn in Scorpio after 23 October adds a dedication to duty to those born then, along with a fear of intimacy and a frugality with money.

1954

Another year of the excitable Uranus-in-Cancer square to undermining Neptune in Libra causes emotional confusion and unrest. Wildly inspired ideas float side by side with irrational beliefs. With Neptune in Libra, there are still high expectations of better social agreements and ideal relationships, but little practical idea of how to achieve them. Self-disciplined Saturn in secretive, obsessive Scorpio lends a hard-working though rather over-controlled approach to money and sex. In good aspect to Uranus it does promote some well-balanced reforms, although approaching the square to Pluto at the year's end it builds up to a tough, bleak, rather miserable mood, when nothing comes simply or easily. Jupiter in light-hearted, chatty Gemini up to 25 May gives way to a more settled, domestic Jupiter in Cancer thereafter.

Events
Ministers from the United States, the USSR, Britain and France meet to discuss reducing world tension, but the USSR refuses to consider reunifying Germany. Racial segregation in schools in the United States is deemed unconstitutional. French forces surrender to the Vietminh at Dien Bien Phu, Vietnam; the French government falls as a result. Armistice for Indochina is signed. The United States, Britain and France agree to end the occupation of Germany. France sends 20,000 troops to Algeria following disturbances there. The US Senate censures Joseph McCarthy. There are riots in Greece over Cyprus. The McDonalds hamburger chain starts to expand worldwide. American evangelist Billy Graham holds meetings in the United States and Europe. Roger Bannister runs the first under-four-minute mile.

Science and technology
The United States tests the hydrogen bomb—500 times more powerful than that used on Hiroshima; the fall-out causes concern. The first nuclear submarine is launched. The link between smoking and lung cancer is suggested.

Culture
Robert Rauschenberg paints *Pink Door*, Mark Rothko paints *Untitled, Yellow, Orange, Red on Orange* and Graham Sutherland paints a portrait of Sir Winston Churchill, which is later destroyed by Lady Churchill. Sculptor Barbara Hepworth produces *Two Figures, Menhirs* and Henry Moore *Internal and External Forms*. Benjamin Britten writes the opera *The Turn of the Screw*, Aram Khatchaturian the ballet *Spartacus* and William Walton the opera *Troilus and Cressida*. The musical *The Pajama Game*, by Richard Adler and Jerry Ross, has its debut performance, as does the musical *Salad Days* by Julian Slade. Eddie Calvert records 'Oh, My Papa' and Doris Day sings 'Secret Love'. Bill Haley's 'Rock Around the Clock' is a hit, as is Elvis Presley's 'That's All Right'. The cha-cha-cha is all the rage in the United States. The year's publications include Kingsley Amis's *Lucky Jim*, Peter de Vries's *The Tunnel of Love*, William Golding's *Lord of the Flies*, John Masters's *Bhowani Junction*, Françoise Sagan's *Bonjour Tristesse* and J. R. R. Tolkien's *The Lord of the Rings*. Tennessee Williams' *Cat on a Hot Tin Roof* is performed. Among the year's film releases are *Bad Day at Black Rock* with Spencer Tracy, *The Belles of St Trinians* with Alastair Sim and *The Caine Mutiny* with Humphrey Bogart.

Births
Actor John Travolta; tennis players Vitas Gerulaitas and Chris Evert Lloyd; American TV host Oprah Winfrey; singers Reba McEntire, Yanni and Elvis Costello.

Personalities born in 1954
Highly strung, impatient, wilful, emotionally excitable and determined to have personal freedom, those born in 1954 are strongly individualistic. With Saturn in

Scorpio, they are perfectionists at work, sparing with money, resentful if they are ill used, and often wary of too much intimacy. With Neptune in Libra they have high hopes of wonderful relationships, but Pluto in Leo puts self-interest before family values. Inventive, they like introducing new ideas, which weld the best of the old to the best of the new. Those born up to 25 May with Jupiter in Gemini are chatty, sociable, and lighter-hearted; thereafter those born with Jupiter in Cancer are attracted to expansive, comfortable home lives with unusual gadgetry. They want to be conventional and independent at the same time.

Oprah Winfrey

Born 29 January 1954, 7.51 pm Central Standard Time, Kosciusko, Mississippi.
Chart: Sun, Venus and Mercury in Aquarius ◆ Moon in Sagittarius ◆ Ascendant in Virgo ◆ Mars, Saturn in Scorpio ◆ Jupiter and midheaven in Gemini ◆ Uranus in Cancer ◆ Pluto in Leo ◆ Neptune in Libra ◆ Moon's North Node in Capricorn

A lively, charming Aquarian with a dedication to work and service, she has triumphed over difficult early beginnings to become America's best-paid entertainer with a talk show watched by millions in 100 different countries.

An air–fire chart makes her a dynamo of a personality with energy to spare, a real steam-roller who races on when others fall by the wayside. With the Sun, Venus and Mercury in Aquarius, she is friendly and sociable, though rather detached, with a knack of being able to speak to anyone, and tolerating differences easily. At times, however, she needs to retreat into privacy to settle her feelings. These planets situated in the chart area of hard work and health indicate that she needs to look after her body, trimmed down now from a time of serious obesity, and also needs to be proud of doing an exceptionally good job. Integrity is more important to her than ego or—surprisingly—money, of which she has made a great deal. With Neptune in her financial area, she is vague to the point of carelessness with cash.

A restless, wandering, colourful Sagittarian Moon gives her a longing for a colourful, slightly exotic home. She is not domestic, or keen to feel tied down. Jupiter in communicative Gemini on her midheaven, aspecting her Aquarian planets—a doubly lucky placing for career matters—will bring her increasing respect and acclaim the older she gets. Uranus, often connected astrologically to television, is in nurturing Cancer, in the chart area linking her to the wider society.

The difficulties of her childhood—born to unmarried teenage parents, raised by a grandmother, abused and raped by a relative—are starkly outlined in the cruel Mars–Saturn conjunction in Scorpio squaring onto brutal Pluto. This mirrors the rage, fear and powerlessness of her experiences, contributing to her defensive weight gain in adult life, and perhaps her drive for success. In 1968, when, as a 14-year-old, she had her only child, undermining Neptune was crossing Mars in sexual Scorpio, giving rise to a panicking sense of failure and disorientation. In 1978 her chat show debut as a 24-year-old came as enlightening Uranus transitted through her chart area of journalistic communication. Her career has risen steadily from then as Saturn moves slowly on a 29-year upward cycle, not peaking until 2002 and remaining there for another seven years.

1955

Starting on a lucky, relief-giving Uranus–Jupiter contact in Cancer, the mood is lighter-hearted. Both Uranus and Neptune change signs for the first time in years, lending an ambivalent, anticipatory note to the year. Uranus, having spent seven years in Cancer promoting freedom from domestic ties, moves into creative, theatrical Leo from August, stressing unconventional approaches to romance—free love is in the air. After idealizing relationships in Libra for 13 years, Neptune—a creative, though escapist, energy—moves in December into intense Scorpio for 15 years, hinting at a forthcoming period of sexual confusion, and of a search for life's deeper meanings through experimentation with drugs and rock music. Self-disciplined Saturn in its second and final full year in Scorpio keeps a tight control of feelings and money; in hard aspect to Pluto it is defensive and tough-minded, although its brutal effects do not emerge until its final station on the exact aspect in 1956.

Events

There is an amnesty for Mau Mau rebels in Kenya. In Britain, Ruth Ellis is the last woman to be hanged for murder. In the United States, Dr Martin Luther King leads 50,000 African-Americans in a boycott of local buses, demanding an end to segregation. L. Ron Hubbard establishes the Church of Scientology. In Britain, Winston Churchill resigns as prime minister because of ill health. Juan Peron resigns as Argentinian president. President Eisenhower suffers a heart attack. Heart-throb James Dean is killed in a car crash. Tight jeans become fashionable in the United States and Europe. In Britain Princess Margaret decides not to marry Captain Peter Townsend.

Science and technology

The United States and the USSR announce that they will attempt to launch earth satellites in two years' time. In Britain, commercial television is introduced.

Culture

Jasper Johns paints his *First Flag*, *Target* and *Number* paintings, Willem de Kooning *Composition*, Pietro Annigoni a portrait of Queen Elizabeth II, and Robert Rauschenberg *Bed*. Pierre Boulez composes *Le Marteau sans Maître*. Richard Adler and Jerry Ross's musical *Damn Yankees* has its debut. Chuck Berry records 'Maybelline' and 'Roll over Beethoven', Tennessee Ernie Ford 'Sixteen Tons', and Slim Whitman 'Rosemarie'. J. P. Donleavy's *The Ginger Man*, Graham Greene's *The Quiet American* and Vladimir Nabokov's *Lolita* are published. Samuel Beckett's *Waiting for Godot* and Arthur Miller's *A View from the Bridge* are performed. Cinema audiences see *The Blackboard Jungle*, *The Dam Busters* with Michael Redgrave and Richard Todd, *The Ladykillers*, *Rebel Without a Cause* starring James Dean and *The Seven Year Itch* starring Marilyn Monroe.

Births

Computer-software developer Bill Gates; actors Kevin Costner, Whoopi Goldberg and Margot Hemingway; Japanese cult leader Shoko Asahara, whose followers released nerve gas on the Tokyo subway in 1995.

Personalities born in 1955

With the controlled, money-conscious Saturn–Pluto aspect, strong-minded, slightly obsessive individuals who walk their own road and who regard themselves as outsiders typify those born in 1955. Defensive, with formidable stamina, they do not find emotional intimacy easy, and are resistant to change. With Uranus in aspect to Neptune, they can be highly strung, inventive, and not always rational in their arguments, but at best truly enlightened. Those born before 24 August with Uranus in Cancer want unusual homes and family lives without too many ties; those born thereafter with Uranus in Leo are stubbornly determined to create their own standards, are artistic, have leadership ability, and strive for emotional freedom. Those born with Jupiter in Cancer up to 14 June have a need for expansive, comfortable homes; those with Jupiter in Leo from then until 17 November like living the five-star way; and those with Jupiter in Virgo thereafter are hard-working individuals who are warm-hearted about service to others. Neptune in Scorpio after 24 December brings the next generation of experimenters in sex, drink, drugs and rock-'n'-roll.

Bill Gates

Born 28 October 1955, 9.15 pm Pacific Standard Time, Seattle, Washington.
Chart: Sun, Venus, Saturn in Scorpio ◆ Mars, Mercury, Neptune in Libra ◆ Uranus, Jupiter, Pluto in Leo ◆ Moon in Aries ◆ Moon's North Node in Sagittarius ◆ Ascendant in Cancer

The outstanding business phenomenon of the computer age, Bill Gates has a surprisingly subjective, inward-looking chart, with only a fiery Aries Moon in his career house channelling his formidable talents out into the world. Not surprisingly Uranus, associated astrologically with high-tech computer energy, was close to the horizon when he was born, aspecting his Scorpio Sun, and making him not only cyber-literate, but also zany, rebellious and freedom-loving. A megaton combination of lucky Jupiter and powerful Pluto falls in his chart area of money in flamboyant Leo, hinting at the billion-dollar empire he has spawned. This combination, often described as 'might makes right', gave him the confidence, drive and determination to increase his wealth by putting the considerable weight of his personality behind his ambitions. These financial planets square onto Venus and Saturn in Scorpio. Thus he is conscientious to a perfectionist degree, a hard taskmaster, and over-intense about his responsibilities, at times to the point of fanaticism. Once he has involved himself in a project, he never lets go. With this heavy concentration of Scorpio planets, his resentment runs deep if he thinks he has been unfairly dealt with.

Like Rupert Murdoch, Prince Charles and David Bowie, Bill Gates was born when the Sun was at the furthest point from midheaven, suggesting not a life of obscurity but one in which domestic privacy is fiercely sought. He needs to feel master of his home, is proud of his family lineage, and wants comfortable, intimate surroundings. In typically expansive style, his custom-built main residence is a hugely expensive, gadget-laden enterprise. His excitable Aries Moon opposing Mars hints at a rather fiery presence at home and in family relationships. Neptune close to his Sun could have made him indecisive and rather dreamy, but he has

153

been able to turn his inner vision into a tangible outer reality with the help of the unshiftably determined Scorpio planets and powerful Pluto.

When he left Harvard at the age of 19, without graduating, to set up Microsoft with a friend, successful Jupiter was moving across his midheaven and inventive Uranus was crossing his Sun in Scorpio. In 1980, when he licensed his computer system to IBM, Uranus had reached his Venus–Saturn conjunction, and was emotionally unsettling but was opening up new opportunities. By 1986 he had become a billionaire, with influential Pluto in Scorpio now crossing his Sun, and successful Jupiter back on its 12-year cycle at his midheaven. In 1996, when he launched his initiative to take a large slice of the Internet market, Uranus was squaring his Sun, a jolting influence with unpredictable results. Disciplined Saturn was then at his midheaven, hinting that only well-laid plans would succeed. He will continue to ride the doubtless bumpy crest of his phenomenal career, pausing only when Saturn reaches his ascendant in 2004.

1956

All five outer planets hover on the cusp of a sign change, making for unsettled times. Unconventional, inventive Uranus moves into Leo for seven years, bringing an uncompromising demand for freedom in emotional expression, in free love and wilder music. In hard aspect to dreamy, escapist Neptune now in intense Scorpio, it fuels the drive for sex, drugs and rock-'n'-roll, and promotes irrational standpoints and a highly strung mood politically. Austere Saturn moving out of Scorpio loosens up financial restrictions; entering Sagittarius for three years, it promotes intellectual disciplines, although it also leads to self-righteous religious or political stances. Pluto moves out of self- and power-centred Leo where it has been since 1938 during the period of the development of atomic energy, and enters Virgo (for the first time since 1712) in late October, still in hard aspect to Saturn—always a signifier of brutality or misery—and to the forthcoming Sagittarian eclipse, as political affairs in Suez, Hungary and the Middle East all hot up. This 15-year stay coincides with major changes in the Virgo areas of employment, health and medicine, combining in the Plutonic areas of sexuality with the widespread use of birth control.

Events
Khrushchev denounces Stalin's policies. British authorities deport Archbishop Makarios from Cyprus on suspicion of involvement with EOKA terrorists. British troops leave the Suez Canal. Colonel Nasser is elected president of Egypt, and nationalizes the Suez Canal, owned partly by France and Britain. On 20 October Pluto enters Virgo in aspect to Saturn in Sagittarius, both afflicting the approaching December solar eclipse in Sagittarius; in quick succession thereafter Soviet troops invade Hungary, Israeli troops invade the Sinai Peninsula, and British and French planes bomb Egyptian airfields. In December Fidel Castro lands in Cuba to begin a guerrilla war.

Science and technology
In the United States, a visual telephone is developed, as is FORTRAN, the first computer-programming language.

Culture

In the world of art Yves Klein produces his first blue monochrome, and Antoni Tapies creates *Earth + Paint*. Composer Hans Werner Henze writes his opera *König Hirsch*, and Karlheinz Stockhausen writes *Gesang der Junglinge*. Frederick Loewe's musical *My Fair Lady*, with lyrics by Alan Jay Lerner, has its debut in New York, as does Leonard Bernstein's musical *Candide*. Doris Day sings 'Que Sera Sera', Pat Boone records 'I'll Be Home', Fats Domino 'Blueberry Hill' and Elvis Presley 'Heartbreak Hotel'. The first part of Anthony Burgess's *The Malayan Trilogy*, Albert Camus' *The Fall*, Gerald Durrell's *My Family and Other Animals*, Laurie Lee's *Cider With Rosie* and Angus Wilson's *Anglo-Saxon Attitudes* are published. Jean Genet completes his play *The Balcony* and John Osborne *Look Back in Anger*. Notable films of the year are *Anastasia* with Ingrid Bergman, *Baby Doll* with Carroll Baker, the film version of Rodgers and Hammerstein's musical *Carousel*, *The King and I* with Yul Brynner and Deborah Kerr, *Reach for the Sky* with Kenneth More, Laurence Olivier's *Richard III*, Ingmar Bergman's *The Seventh Seal* and *A Town like Alice*.

Births

Tennis players Martina Navratilova and Bjorn Borg; actor Tom Hanks.

Personalities born in 1956

Complex, rather highly strung personalities born in 1956 can be incredibly stubborn and have formidable endurance. More of a mixed crop than in most years because of the changing signs, they are still all inventive, and, on occasion, even inspired, and tend to regard themselves as outside the mainstream. With Saturn in Scorpio until 12 January, then again between 15 May and 11 October, they are sparing with money and emotional intimacy, and highly conscientious about work; outside those dates in Sagittarius they are intellectually serious, at times self-righteous. With Uranus in Leo up to 28 January, and after 10 June, they are romantic revolutionaries and highly creative; otherwise in Cancer they love unusual homes and freedom from family ties. With Neptune in Libra between 13 March and 19 October, they are romantic idealists like the previous generation; outside those dates with Neptune in Scorpio, they seek transcendental bliss through sex, drugs or escapist music. Pluto in Leo until 20 October gives a self-centred approach to life and relationships; in Virgo after that it brings an intense attitude to body, health and work.

1957

Saturn and Uranus now firmly established in fire signs give a boost to scientific confidence and inventions and push ahead developments in new areas, notably space travel. Both Uranus in heart-centred Leo and Neptune in sexual Scorpio slant relationships in new and not always constructive directions, with great emphasis on total freedom and experimentation. The hard aspects of two different pairs of the outer planets continue to keep the tension levels high. Saturn in waning aspect to Pluto is lessening its bleak effect, though still promoting self-righteous ideological disagreements. Uranus at right angles to Neptune is highly strung, and promotes outlandish beliefs and inspirational music. Both Neptune and Pluto are still, as in 1956, hovering on the cusp of a sign change, leading to an ambivalent, uncertain mood. Pluto moves from the power base of Leo into work- and health-oriented Virgo for 15 years. Neptune, having over-idealized relationships in Libra for 13 years, now in Scorpio focuses its escapist dreams on sex, drugs and music. Jupiter in Virgo between 20 February and 7 August emphasizes the virtues of hard work and service; otherwise in Libra it promotes concerns over social and legal fairness.

Events
Israeli forces withdraw from the Sinai Peninsula in Egypt. The Treaty of Rome is signed bringing Belgium, France, West Germany, Italy, Luxembourg and the Netherlands into the European Economic Community or Common Market. King Hussein of Jordan proclaims martial law after an attempted coup. Turkey concentrates troops on the Syrian border. In Britain, there is a radiation leak after a serious accident at the Windscale atomic energy reactor on the full moon immediately before the October solar eclipse, closely aspected by Neptune in Scorpio and Uranus in Leo.

Science and technology
The USSR launches the artificial satellites Sputnik I and II into space, the second carrying a live dog.

Culture
Francis Bacon paints *Screaming Nurse* and Mark Rothko paints *Browns*. Sculptor Jacob Epstein produces *Christ in Majesty* and Alberto Giacometti *Buste aux Grands Yeux*. Composer Francis Poulenc writes his opera *Les Dialogues des Carmelites* and Igor Stravinsky his ballet *Agon*. The musical *West Side Story*, with music by Leonard Bernstein and lyrics by Stephen Sondheim, is performed in New York. Hit records include Harry Belafonte's 'Mary's Boy Child', Pat Boone's 'Love Letters in the Sand', the Everley Brothers' 'All I Have to Do Is Dream', Buddy Holly's 'Peggy Sue', and Elvis Presley's 'All Shook Up'. In the world of books and theatre, newcomers include Richard Hoggart's *The Uses of Literacy*, John Braine's *Room at the Top*, Jack Kerouac's *On the Road*, Lawrence Durrell's *Justine*, Alan Watts's *The Way of Zen*, and Samuel Beckett's *Endgame*. In the cinema, audiences see Otto Preminger's *Bonjour Tristesse*, David Lean's *The Bridge on the River Kwai*, *Gunfight at the OK Corral* with Burt Lancaster, *The Prince and the Showgirl* with Laurence Olivier and Marilyn Monroe, *Twelve Angry Men* with Henry Fonda, and Ingmar Bergman's *Wild Strawberries*.

Births
Golfers Severiano Ballesteros of Spain, Nick Faldo of Britain and Nick Price of South Africa.

Personalities born in 1957
With Saturn in Sagittarius, those born in 1957 have a serious outlook and are high-minded about education and their religious or political beliefs. Often innovative and curious about new discoveries, they have a way of combining the best of the

old with the best of the new, and are a contradictory mix, being both stubborn and pioneering. Uranus in Leo gives them a theatrical flair, with a strong determination to express themselves emotionally as they please. Neptune in Scorpio brings a rather psychic, otherworldly streak, an openness to new sexual ideas and an attraction to drugs. Otherwise Neptune in Libra fosters an idealization of close relationships. Pluto in Leo between 16 January and 19 August encourages a focus on self-development; in Virgo otherwise it brings slight obsession with health and work. Jupiter in Virgo between 20 February and 7 August creates a desire to be of service; in Libra otherwise it fosters fair-mindedness and a concern with justice.

1958

The weakening hard aspects from Saturn to Pluto and Uranus to Neptune ease the tensions from their peak in 1956. Pluto makes its final sally in reverse into Leo for a couple of months, ending 20 years of power-directed effort in self-development and atomic energy. Now establishing itself in Virgo, it starts the long, slow transformation of methods of industrial production, the employment base and medical techniques. Spiritual, creative, escapist Neptune now in Scorpio for 12 years looks for deeper meaning in sex and drugs—transcendence through the body. Uranus in Leo stands for romantic rebellion: free love is chic. Saturn for the last of its three years in Sagittarius continues to promote education and a serious intellectual approach. Jupiter hovers between fair-minded Libra (up to 14 January, and between 21 March and 7 September) and financially oriented Scorpio, where it benefits business.

Events

Egypt and Syria become the United Arab Republic with Nasser as head of state. Netherlands, Belgium and Luxembourg become an economic union. French forces bomb Tunisia. There are serious race riots in London. Pope Pius XII dies three days before the October solar eclipse; John XXIII is elected pope two days before the lunar eclipse that follows. A British expedition under Vivian Fuchs makes the first crossing of Antarctica. In Hungary, former prime minister Imre Nagy is executed after a secret trial. In a coup in Iraq, the king and his prime minister are murdered. Prince Charles, aged nine, becomes Prince of Wales. China bombs Quemoy, an island ruled by Formosa (now Taiwan). Martial law is declared in Pakistan after unrest. There is a military coup in Thailand.

Science and technology

The United States puts five satellites into orbit. The first scheduled transatlantic jet services begin between the United States and Britain.

Culture

The painting *Garçon au Gilet Rouge* by Paul Cézanne sells for £220,000 at auction in London, double the highest price ever paid for a single picture. Lucian Freud starts *Woman Smiling* and Mark Rothko is commissioned to paint the Seagram murals, donated to the Tate Gallery in London. Composer Benjamin Britten writes *Noye's Fludde*. Hit records include Perry Como's 'Magic Moments', Connie Francis's 'Stupid Cupid', and Phil Spector's 'To Know Him is to Love Him'. H. E. Bates's *The Darling Buds of May*, Brendan Behan's *Borstal Boy*, Truman

157

Capote's *Breakfast at Tiffany's*, Giuseppe di Lampedusa's *The Leopard*, Iris Murdoch's *The Bell*, Boris Pasternak's *Dr Zhivago*, Leon Uris's *Exodus*, and T. H. White's *The Sword in the Stone* are all published. The Beatnik movement of Californian poets spreads worldwide. *Gigi* with Audrey Hepburn, Jacques Tati's *Mon Oncle*, Rodgers and Hammerstein's *South Pacific* and Alfred Hitchcock's *Vertigo*, with James Stewart and Kim Novak, are among the year's film releases.

Births
Singers Madonna and Michael Jackson; actress Michelle Pfeiffer.

Personalities born in 1958
Highly strung, with determined but not always rational standpoints, those born in 1958 are inventive, inspired, innovative and good at pushing through reforms. Saturn in Sagittarius adds a serious touch to their communications, whether writing or speaking. Uranus in flamboyantly theatrical Leo encourages them to fight for romantic freedom. Neptune in intense Scorpio brings psychic abilities, especially emphasized by the aspect to Pluto, and a determination to explore the fundamental meaning of the universe through sex, drugs, music or the body. Pluto itself in Virgo, except between 12 April and 12 June, signals the new generation of those deeply concerned with health and new techniques at work. Pluto in Leo between those dates brings more of a focus on self-development. Jupiter in Libra, up to 14 January and between 21 March and 7 September, encourages a more balanced view of relationships and fosters sociability; in Scorpio otherwise it attracts money and the sharing of confidences.

1959
Easier aspects between the outer planets make for less stressful events and smoother transitions. Creative Neptune in sensual Scorpio continues to promote the search for bliss through sex, drugs and rock-'n'-roll. Rebellious Uranus in flamboyant, romantic Leo advocates total freedom in relationships. The waning hard aspect between Uranus and Neptune still throws up highly strung situations but with less catastrophic effects. Irrational and sometimes inspired opinions are the norm. Saturn moving out of high-minded Sagittarius on 6 January for a three-year stay in Capricorn hints at economic cutbacks in preparation for a better structured business economy. Pluto now settled in Virgo for 13 years is exerting its slow transformation of medicine, attitudes to health, industrial production and work methods. Jupiter in Scorpio promotes financial ventures, then in Sagittarius turns its expansive focus on intellectual activities.

Events
Alaska and Hawaii become part of the United States. There are disturbances in the Belgian Congo (now Zaire) and in British Nyasaland (now Malawi). Archbishop Makarios returns to Cyprus from exile and is elected president. There are crop failures in China, and a Tibetan uprising takes place against the Chinese, who have destroyed 1000 Buddhist monasteries since 1956; the Dalai Lama is smuggled out. Fidel Castro becomes prime minister of Cuba and nationalizes US-owned sugar mills and plantations. Solomon Bandaranaike, prime minister of Ceylon, is assassinated. Buddy Holly dies in a plane crash.

Science and technology

Mark Leakey discovers the 1.77 million-year-old fossil remains of a hominid in Africa. American astronomer Harold Babcock discovers that the Sun reverses its magnetic polarity. The structure of haemoglobin is discovered.

Culture

Francis Bacon paints *Sleeping Figure*, Jasper Johns *False Start* and Robert Rauschenberg *Canyon*. Francis Poulenc writes his opera *La Voix Humaine*, and Karlheinz Stockhausen *Gruppen*. The musical *Gypsy*, with lyrics by Stephen Sondheim and music by Jule Styne, makes its debut on Broadway; Rodgers and Hammerstein's *The Sound of Music* also opens in New York. Hit records include Shirley Bassey's 'As I Love You' and Cliff Richard's 'Living Doll'. Berry Gordy founds Motown Records and launches the Tamla record label. Saul Bellow's *Henderson the Rain King*, William Burroughs's *The Naked Lunch*, Günther Grass's *The Tin Drum*, Norman Mailer's *Advertisement for Myself*, Anaïs Nin's *Cities of the Interior*, Alan Sillitoe's *The Loneliness of the Long Distance Runner* and Edward Albee's *The Zoo Story* are all published. New theatrical works include Tennessee Williams's *The Sweet Bird of Youth* and Harold Pinter's *The Caretaker*. In the world of film, *Anatomy of a Murder*, *Ben Hur* with Charlton Heston, *Black Orpheus*, *Hiroshima Mon Amour*, *Look Back in Anger* with Richard Burton, *Rio Bravo* with John Wayne, and *Some Like It Hot* with Marilyn Monroe, Jack Lemmon and Tony Curtis, are notable new releases.

Births

Tennis player John McEnroe; actor-director Kenneth Branagh; singers Bryan Adams and Sheena Easton.

Personalities born in 1959

With a mini grand trine of Saturn, Pluto and Neptune, individuals born in 1959 have tremendous willpower, relentless stamina and a strong sense of mission in their lives. Compassionate and concerned with the underdog, they are also materialistic and keen to build their own security. With Saturn in Capricorn they experience either emotional or financial deprivation in childhood and are determined to end their days in better circumstances. Uranus in Leo gives them a touch of flamboyant colour, a rebelliousness in their emotional lives which is not easy to reconcile with their more conventional traits. Neptune in Scorpio brings a fey, almost psychic quality, and encourages a yearning for an escape from reality through sexual experiences. Jupiter in Scorpio up to 11 February and after 5 October promotes a high-minded outlook, and an interest in religion or foreign countries; in Scorpio otherwise it makes for good confidantes and attracts material resources.

1960–1969

One of the more tumultuous decades of this century, the 1960s are in sharp contrast to the 1950s. Starting on the Jupiter–Saturn conjunction in Capricorn, which recurs every 20 years but has not been seen in this sign since 1842, the initial mood is jubilant and expansive with J. F. Kennedy's election and the musical phenomena of the Beatles, Elvis Presley and the Rolling Stones. However, the Uranus–Pluto conjunction—an explosively rebellious and at times destructively violent combination—starts to make its presence felt from 1962. Not seen since 1850, when there were widespread liberal and nationalist revolutions in Europe, when the flames of Irish nationalism were being fanned by the Irish Potato Famine, and when the Taiping Rebellion took place in China, this is the first time this conjunction has fallen in Virgo for more than two millennia. Its powerful effect is exacerbated from 1965 to 1967 by the bleak, misery-inducing Saturn-in-Pisces opposition. The years of the 1960s see the Vietnam War, the Six Day War between the Arabs and Israelis, the assassinations of J. F. and Robert Kennedy and of Martin Luther King, major black civil rights and anti-Vietnam demonstrations and race riots, the brutal Cultural Revolution in China, and student riots in France. The decade finishes with the beginning of the Northern Ireland troubles.

1960

The build-up towards the Jupiter–Saturn conjunction in Capricorn, exact in 1961 and a harbinger of sudden, expansive change, is the only major astrological event, although the March Aries eclipse afflicted by Saturn does throw up a troublesome few months in Africa and in the Cold War. Pluto continues to push forward the frontiers of medical knowledge in Virgo, favouring its own interests in promoting widespread access to contraception. Neptune in Scorpio blisses out on sex and pop music. Uranus in dramatic Leo makes a stand for emotional freedom in free love. Disciplined Saturn in earthy, businesslike Capricorn favours the traditional virtues of hard work and financial security. Jupiter veers between adventurous though high-minded Sagittarius and materialistic Capricorn.

Events

Harold Macmillan, British prime minister, talks of 'winds of change' blowing through the African continent. French settlers riot in Algeria over fears of self-determination there. Queen Elizabeth II gives birth to Prince Andrew, becoming the first reigning monarch to bear a child in 100 years. Princess Margaret marries Anthony Armstrong-Jones (later Lord Snowdon). An earthquake in Agadir in Morocco, the worst recorded in Africa, kills 12,000 people; it occurs in late February on the Aries Moon immediately before the Aries solar eclipse in late March, aspected by Saturn, which is the focus for major unrest. It also coincides with a state of emergency being declared in South Africa. In the Sharpeville Massacre the police panic and kill 69 Africans, wounding almost 200. The ANC is banned. Hendrik Verwoerd, the South African prime minister, is shot and wounded. In the USSR, an American spy plane piloted by Gary Powers is shot down. Adolf Eichmann is brought to Israel to face trial for Nazi war crimes. The Congo troubles escalate; UN forces go in. Sirimavo Bandaranaike, widow of the late assassinated prime minister of Ceylon, becomes the first woman prime minister in the Commonwealth. There is a coup in Laos, and martial law is imposed. J. F. Kennedy is elected president, defeating Richard Nixon.

Science and technology

The oral contraceptive pill is introduced in the United States for general use. Pacemakers are developed for heart patients.

Culture

Andy Warhol paints *Superman*, David Hockney *Adhesiveness* and Yves Klein the first *Anthropométries*, a happening in which women's bodies are used as paintbrushes. Benjamin Britten writes his opera *A Midsummer Night's Dream* and William Walton his Symphony No. 2. Alan Jay Lerner's musical *Camelot* is first performed in New York and Lionel Bart's *Oliver* opens in London. Hit records include Ray Charles's 'Georgia on My Mind', Edith Piaf's 'Je Ne Regrette Rien', and Johnny Mathis's 'The Shadow of Your Smile'. In Hamburg, the Beatles give their first performance. The Twist is all the rage. New books and plays include John Updike's *Rabbit Run*, R. D. Laing's *The Divided Self* and Robert Bolt's *A Man for All Seasons*. Lawrence Durrell completes *The Alexandria Quartet* (four novels). *Lady Chatterley's Lover* by D. H. Lawrence is ruled not obscene in Britain. Cinema audiences go to see Federico Fellini's *La Dolce Vita*, *The Entertainer* with Laurence Olivier, *The Magnificent Seven* with Yul Brynner and Steve McQueen, *Never on Sunday* with Melina Mercouri, and Alfred Hitchcock's *Psycho*.

Births

Prince Andrew; actor Sean Penn; jockey Steve Cauthen; racing driver Ayrton Senna; rock singer Michael Hutchence.

Personalities born in 1960

Rather contradictory traits make those born in 1960 strait-laced and rebellious at the same time. Saturn in Capricorn imbues them with traditional, hard-working values and a need for security, stemming from an early life of either financial or emotional austerity. Pluto in Virgo, in aspect, gives strength and stamina, but also a tendency to pessimism and a strong resistance to change. Independent Uranus in romantic Leo in aspect to spaced-out Neptune in sensual Scorpio hints at a highly unconventional emotional life; under its influence, people born this year can be highly strung, rather nervy and at times inspired, but also prone to irrational arguments. Those born with Jupiter in Sagittarius up to 2 March, and between 11 June and 27 October, have wide-ranging interests and are well read; otherwise with Jupiter in Capricorn they attract money, possessions and social respectability.

1961

The Jupiter–Saturn conjunction, a 20-year occurrence, though not seen in Capricorn since 1842, marks major new beginnings and expansion in business, government and creative arenas. Jupiter brings the social ideals and vision, Saturn the practical application, but the balance is crucial: too much Jupiterian over-confidence and new ventures can collapse. J. F. Kennedy was inaugurated close to the conjunction with high hopes; when the Beatles made their British debut at the Cavern Club in Liverpool, their visionary impact was spearheaded by John Lennon, born on the Jupiter–Saturn conjunction in Taurus in 1940, and tragically and eerily killed on the Jupiter–Saturn conjunction in Libra in 1980. Uranus late in the year moves into Virgo for seven years to join Pluto there, a combination that heralds revolutions and major destructive upheavals through the mid-1960s, of which the Vietnam War and the Six Day War between Israel and the Arab states are the most notable. Jupiter floats between tolerant, humanitarian Aquarius and materialistic Capricorn.

Events

The United States severs relations with Cuba, and sponsors an invasion of Cuban exiles, which fails. South Africa leaves the Commonwealth. There is serious unrest in the Congo, Angola, Algeria and Syria. Iraq threatens Kuwait. Khrushchev, Soviet leader, wages a campaign against Dag Hammarskjöld, UN Secretary-General, who is subsequently killed in an air crash in the Congo. East Germany seals the border between East and West, and begins building the Berlin Wall, on the day Jupiter reverses back into Capricorn close to Saturn. In Israel, Adolf Eichmann is executed for Nazi war crimes. The first successful hijacking of an aircraft takes place; the aircraft lands in Cuba. In Britain, George Blake is sentenced to 42 years in prison for spying. Tristan da Cunha, islands in the South Atlantic, are evacuated after a volcanic eruption.

Science and technology

The USSR puts cosmonaut Yuri Gagarin into space; he returns from Earth orbit after 108 minutes.

Culture

David Hockney paints *Typhoo Tea* and Jasper Johns *Map*. Hans Werner Henze writes his opera *Elegy for Young Lovers*. Sixteen-year-old cellist Jacqueline du Pré makes her debut in London, as does Bob Dylan in Greenwich Village. The Rolling Stones are formed. Russian ballet dancer Rudolf Nureyev defects to the West. Hit records include Billy Fury's 'Halfway to Paradise', Elvis Presley's 'Are You Lonesome Tonight?' and Neil Sedaka's 'Happy Birthday, Sweet Sixteen'. Joseph Heller's *Catch 22*, Iris Murdoch's *A Severed Head*, J. D. Salinger's *Franny and Zooey*, Muriel Spark's *The Prime of Miss Jean Brodie* and Irving Stone's *The Agony and the Ecstasy* are all published. Notable cinema releases are *Breakfast at Tiffany's* with Audrey Hepburn, *El Cid* with Charlton Heston, François Truffaut's *Jules et Jim*, *The Misfits* with Marilyn Monroe and Clark Gable, Walt Disney's *One Hundred and One Dalmatians*, and the film version of the musical *West Side Story* with Natalie Wood.

Births

Lady Diana Spencer, later Princess of Wales; actor George Clooney; pop singer Boy George; athlete Fatima Whitbread; boxer Frank Bruno.

Personalities born in 1961

As in the previous year, those born in 1961 are contradictory individuals, highly strung with rather whacky ideas, but also practically ambitious. Relentlessly will-driven with the earthy Saturn–Pluto aspect, they have the capacity to withstand great pressures and make far-reaching changes. Often they are psychic, and have a sense of mission or destiny. Childhoods that are deprived, financially or emotionally, make them struggle to better their situation; life eases in its latter half. Aspects between spaced-out Neptune in sensual Scorpio to rebellious Uranus in romantic Leo, and to stubborn Pluto, make for uneven emotional responses. Pluto in Virgo brings an interest in medicine. Jupiter in Capricorn up to 16 March, and between 13 August and 4 November promotes the ability to attract wealth; in Aquarius otherwise it fosters broadminded, humanitarian interests.

Diana, Princess of Wales
Born 1 July 1961, 7.45 pm, Sandringham, England.
Chart: Sun, Mercury in Cancer ◆ Moon, Jupiter in Aquarius ◆ Ascendant in Sagittarius ◆ Venus in Taurus ◆ Mars, Pluto in Virgo ◆ Uranus, Moon's North Node in Leo ◆ Neptune in Scorpio ◆ Saturn in Capricorn

An emotional Cancerian Sun with strong dependency needs, coupled with a detached Aquarian Moon, always hinted at the difficult balance Diana had to maintain between intimacy and space in her tragically short life. Tactile, fun-loving Venus in earthy Taurus needs active social and romantic outlets, contact with children for whom there will be genuine affection, and a theatrical stage on which her charm could be allowed to sparkle. Neptune opposing Venus hints at an idealization of love, a yearning for the impossible—a blissful partnership with no rough edges. The Aquarian Moon in contrast finds one-to-one relationships and too much physical contact threatening; there is safety and support in numbers, being one of a crowd. Added to which the Uranian opposition to the Moon, a sign of the absent mother in her childhood, gave her unpredictable mood swings, and an inability to stay close or still for long. Highly argumentative with aggressive Mars and intolerant Pluto together in Virgo, she had an attraction for the darker side of human life, volunteering for causes associated with death or mutilation.

Genuinely tolerant of all classes, colours and creeds, with Jupiter in humanitarian Aquarius close to Saturn at her birth, she lived out the messianic qualities of this placing, though in typically contradictory manner, swinging from Jupiter's expansive over-optimism to the depths of Saturnine despair. This aspect, a 20-year occurrence and covering roughly an 18-month period, is key to her life, as it was to John Lennon, appearing at her birth and marriage to Prince Charles in 1981.

When Diana was killed in the Paris car crash with Dodi al-Fayed in 1997, the afflicted September eclipse close to her threatening Mars–Pluto conjunction in Virgo (in her chart placing of foreign travel) was only one day away. This highly stressed eclipse was around just after her birth, in the period when Dag Hammarskjöld, the UN Secretary-General, was killed, and again in 1979 when Lord Mountbatten was killed in an IRA explosion (see *1961, 1979* and *1997,* pages 162, 189 and 215; see also *1934* and *Charles Manson,* pages 114, 116).

When she married in 1981 the Jupiter–Saturn conjunction had moved around to Libra, raising unrealistic expectations of a beneficial new influence (see John F. Kennedy, *1963,* page 166), in this case in the area of perfect relationships. The aftermath of the fairy-tale marriage brought an identity crisis for her, with undermining Neptune crossing her ascendant and unsettling her fragile sense of self. Disruptive, explosively enlightening Uranus started to blast open psychological fears from 1981, at the same time as Pluto started a seven-year trek across her midheaven, promising great influence or total destruction of reputation. When Uranus crossed her ascendant in 1986 she was rebellious and ready to dash for freedom.

Through the 1990s, as Saturn on the ebb pushed her deeper into her psyche, she struggled hard to cope with her inner demons in various therapies, but the overload of her resentment and rage continually spun her back onto the superficial celebrity circuit. Her Cancerian jealousy could not handle her ex-husband's seeming

163

happiness with his long-time mistress Camilla Parker-Bowles. Her short life carried the quality of Marilyn Monroe's, bitterly unhappy in childhood, loved by the public as an adult, but unable to find personal peace.

George Clooney

Born 6 May 1961, birth time unknown, Lexington, Kentucky.
Chart: Sun, Mercury in Taurus ◆ Venus in Aries ◆ Moon, Jupiter in Aquarius ◆ Saturn in Capricorn ◆ Mars, Uranus in Leo ◆ Pluto in Virgo ◆ Neptune in Scorpio

Born, like Princess Diana, with the heady mix of a Jupiter–Saturn close contact, in the days of Kennedy's optimistic presidency where expectations ran high, Clooney was destined to try hard for success, having to overcome years of obstacle. A determined though charming Taurus Sun gives him a strong physical presence, softened by dreamy Neptune in sensual Scorpio, and a lazy, indulgent Jupiter aspect, which looks for success with little effort. Dynamic, competitive Mars in Leo demands personal recognition and opposing Jupiter in friendly Aquarius gives high confidence, though not always common sense.

Saturn in late Capricorn suggests that the early years were a struggle, financially or emotionally, with rewards coming through in mid-life, and a mellowing in maturity. The son of a broadcaster and nephew of singer Rosemary Clooney, he served a long apprenticeship in showbusiness, doing TV pilots and sitcom for years. Taurus is the sign often connected to the voice, and also to medicine, fitting him for the role that shot him to fame in *ER* as Dr Doug Ross. Intriguingly, in his chart influential Pluto is close to the public-conscious Moon's Node in Virgo, the planet associated with health.

A fixed grand square in his chart of Taurus, Leo, Scorpio and Aquarian planets hints at tremendous endurance but also a deep-rooted inflexibility and difficulty in cooperating, with inner hostilities being kept continually under wraps. With only Pluto in mutable signs, he does not find it easy to adapt. He will need to release his inner resentments, otherwise they will become stored in the body. The Moon close to Saturn and Jupiter poses an ambivalence about the nurturing he received as a child; and opposing Mars can provoke angry, emotional outbursts. Venus in Aries is dashingly romantic, open about whom he is attracted to, although also prone to short-lived emotional attachments. Ultimately Taurus, however, is a possessive, rather placid sign which opts for domestic security over constant variety and excitement.

His move into films with *One Fine Day* and then *Batman and Robin* in 1997 coincided with powerful Pluto aspecting his competitive Mars, and then lucky Jupiter, although Neptune undermining Saturn in late Capricorn made them less than total smash-hits.

1962

Revolutionary Uranus in Virgo drawing closer to Pluto, a contact that will cause major disruption through the next six years, starts with the Bay of Pigs crisis as John Kennedy risks a war with the USSR over Soviet bases in Cuba. Uranus–Pluto conjunctions, historically connected to massacres, persecutions and crusades, occur only eight times a millennium, and have not done so for several thousand years in Virgo. In more benign mode, Pluto in Virgo continues to push the frontiers of medical knowledge. Saturn moving out of Capricorn into Aquarius for three years promotes mental concentration and serious humanitarian efforts, although in square to Neptune it also raises anxiety levels considerably. Jupiter moves out of tolerant Aquarius into compassionate, charitable Pisces in late March.

Events

Disarmament conferences fail to meet agreement. There is a coup in Burma, fighting in Laos, and there are riots in British Guyana. UN forces continue to be involved in the Congo. Chinese troops cross into India. President Kennedy imposes a naval blockade on Cuba; Khrushchev, the Soviet leader, orders the withdrawal of Soviet weapons. In South Africa, Nelson Mandela is imprisoned for five years. Tanzania becomes independent under the leadership of Julius Nyerere. In Britain six members of the CND (Campaign for Nuclear Disarmament) are imprisoned. In Britain, Admiralty clerk John Vassall is imprisoned for 18 years for spying.

Science and technology

Twenty years after the start of the nuclear age, the United States has 200 atomic reactors in operation. US spacemen John Glenn and Scott Carpenter go into orbit. The drug Thalidomide, a sedative used by pregnant women, is established as a cause of congenital deformities.

Culture

Andy Warhol produces his Campbell's soup cans, 210 Coca-Cola bottles and the first of the Marilyn Monroe series. Sculptor Eduardo Paolozzi creates *Four Towers*. Benjamin Britten composes *War Requiem* and Dmitri Shostakovich his Symphony No. 13 ('Babi-Yar'). Stephen Sondheim's *A Funny Thing Happened on the Way to the Forum* makes its debut in New York. Hit records include Tony Bennett's 'I Left My Heart in San Francisco', Bob Dylan's 'Blowin' in the Wind', Elvis Presley's 'Return to Sender' and Neil Sedaka's 'Breaking Up is Hard to Do'. New books include Hugh Hefner's *The Playboy Philosophy*, James Baldwin's *Another Country*, Ken Kesey's *One Flew Over the Cuckoo's Nest*, Doris Lessing's *The Golden Notebook* and Vladimir Nabokov's *Pale Fire*. Films include Alfred Hitchcock's *The Birds*, the first James Bond film, *Doctor No*, with Sean Connery, David Lean's *Lawrence of Arabia*, Stanley Kubrick's *Lolita*, John Frankenheimer's *The Manchurian Candidate* and *To Kill a Mockingbird* with Gregory Peck.

Births

Actress Jodie Foster; country music star Garth Brooks.

Personalities born in 1962

These are the first of the mid-sixties Uranus–Pluto generation, who are rebellious, anarchic and prone to upsetting the status quo. Psychologically restless, they do not find settled emotional relationships easy, but in their own way are pioneers of change, experimenting with new approaches to work and to their bodies. With Saturn in Aquarius they are cool but reliable friends, serious thinkers, with inquiring minds. The creative Neptune aspect can make them great worriers and slightly paranoid. They yearn for bliss through sex but find it difficult to let go. Jupiter in Aquarius until 25 March creates a tolerance for race, colour, creed and class; in Pisces thereafter it lends a sympathetic, though also lively and at times pushy streak.

1963

The disruptive Uranus–Pluto conjunction, not exact until 1965, is beginning to make its presence felt. Historically connected to persecutions, revolutions, the Jewish diaspora, the slave trade and black civil rights, it carries with it a threatening mood. Disciplined Saturn in scientific Aquarius promotes serious discussions, but in square to deceptive Neptune in secretive Scorpio it causes disorientation and anxiety; the assassination of J. F. Kennedy happened in November on the final Saturn–Neptune aspect. Jupiter in kindly Pisces up to 4 April promotes charitable concerns; in Aries thereafter it is hot-headed, fostering reckless acts.

Events

Britain is refused entry into the EEC. The prime minister of Iraq is assassinated. A typhoid epidemic breaks out in Zermatt, Switzerland. In Britain, sex scandal engulfs the government as the secretary of state for war, John Profumo, misleads the House of Commons, denying that he knew Christine Keeler, a model, who was also friendly with a Soviet embassy attaché. He resigns; so later does Harold MacMillan, the prime minister, because of ill health. A hotline is established between the White House in Washington and the Kremlin in Moscow. Indonesia attacks Malaysia. There is an earthquake in Skopje, Yugoslavia. In Britain, the Great Train Robbers get away with £2.5 million in bank notes. In the United States, 200,000 African-Americans attend a peaceful demonstration for civil rights, addressed by Martin Luther King, who makes his famous 'I have a dream' speech. There are riots in Birmingham, Alabama, over school desegregation. J. F. Kennedy is assassinated in Dallas; Lee Harvey Oswald, his alleged killer, is shot dead. Zanzibar and Kenya become independent. Pope John XXIII dies, and is succeeded by Pope Paul VI. Harvard University lecturer Timothy Leary is sacked for running experiments into the effects of psychedelic drugs. Weight Watchers is started in New York.

Science and technology

A vaccine for measles is perfected. The dangers of chemical pesticides are pointed out.

Culture

Andy Warhol creates *Ambulance Disaster*, his *Electric Chair* series and his *Race Riot* series. Composer Leonard Bernstein writes *Kaddish*. In London, Luciano Pavarotti makes his Covent Garden debut. The musical *Half a Sixpence*, with lyrics and music by David Heneker, has its first performance, as does *Oh What a Lovely War*, directed by Joan Littlewood. Hit records include Gerry and the Pacemakers' 'You'll Never Walk Alone' and the Beatles' *Please, Please Me* album. Carl Jung's *Memories, Dreams, Reflections* and Betty Friedan's *The Feminine Mystique* are published. Other publications include Sylvia Plath's *The Bell Jar* and John Updike's *The Centaur*. John Schlesinger's *Billy Liar*, *Cleopatra* with Liz Taylor and Richard Burton, *From Russia With Love* with Sean Connery, Luchino Visconti's *The Leopard* and Tony Richardson's *Tom Jones* are among the year's film releases.

Births
Film director Quentin Tarantino; singer and actress Whitney Houston; Soviet chessmaster Gary Kasparov.

Personalities born in 1963
Challenging, unsettled personalities who follow their own path, often pioneering new methods in their working lives or in health, typify those born in 1963. Determinedly unconventional and rather anarchic with the Uranus–Pluto contact in Virgo, they can be psychologically restless, finding stability unattractive. Saturn in Aquarius does provide a balancing factor in the capacity for serious concentration. These are serious thinkers and reliable friends, if a touch cool emotionally. The Saturn–Neptune aspect adds creative flair, although also paranoid worries. Neptune in Scorpio adds an attraction for the seeming bliss offered by sex, drugs and rock-'n'-roll. Jupiter in Pisces before 4 April adds a softer, more compassionate streak; in Aries thereafter it gives courage, confidence and daring, although often not much foresight as to the consequences of actions.

Whitney Houston
Born 9 August 1963, 8.55 pm Eastern Daylight Time, Newark, New Jersey.
Chart: Sun, Venus in Leo ◆ Moon, Jupiter in Aries ◆ Ascendant in Pisces ◆ Uranus, Mercury, Pluto in Virgo ◆ Mars in Libra ◆ Neptune in Scorpio ◆ Saturn in Aquarius ◆ Moon's North Node in Cancer

A hard-working though colourfully flamboyant Leo, Whitney Houston has her Sun and Venus aspecting dreamy, creative Neptune in sensual Scorpio. Pisces and its ruler, Neptune, are, along with Taurus, the musical energy signs of the zodiac. The cousin of Dionne Warwick, she started as a gospel singer before moving into pop music. A fiery, restless Aries Moon close to expansive Jupiter in the chart area of money hints at wealth and huge extravagance. She needs financial security to feel emotionally settled, but tends to attract unreliable business advice. Her close emotional relationships are unsettled, with an explosive combination of Uranus, Pluto and Mercury in Virgo attracting her to powerful, though unpredictable partners; and with Mars in Libra close by, she needs a strong, masculine partner.

When her first major success came in the mid-1980s, her personal life was stormy. Uranus in Sagittarius was causing disruptions to her emotional planets in Virgo; Saturn crossing Neptune brought confusion; but Jupiter in Capricorn surrounded her with good friends. When in 1992 she married Bobby Brown and her film *The Bodyguard* with Kevin Costner came out to good reviews, Jupiter in Virgo was softening her emotional responses and boosting her self-confidence, although Uranus and Neptune both squaring the Moon–Jupiter conjunction were causing mood swings. Her success of the 1980s will not return for some years, but she can expect a career upswing from 2002 onwards.

1964

Not an easy year with major influences tightening the screw of tensions in various hotspots, notably in Africa and Vietnam. The destructive, revolutionary Uranus–Pluto conjunction, not exact until 1965, draws closer, its persecutory effect multiplied as austere Saturn moves into Pisces in opposition. The Saturn–Uranus opposition coincides with jolting changes, dictatorial behaviour and economic drawbacks; Saturn–Pluto is bleakly miserable and tough in the extreme, demanding endurance. Four eclipses instead of the usual two heighten those formidable pressures. Jupiter is in reckless Aries up to 12 April, then moves into indulgent, possessive Taurus.

Events

There are anti-US riots in Panama. Riots also occur in Southern Rhodesia; nationalist parties are banned. There are coups in South Vietnam and Brazil. A US destroyer is attacked by the North Vietnamese; the United States drops bombs in reprisal. In Cyprus, fighting breaks out between Greeks and Turks. There is violence in Guyana; British troops are flown in. The PLO (Palestine Liberation Organization) is formed. In a football riot in Peru, 135 people die. Nelson Mandela is imprisoned for life in South Africa on the day after the June solar eclipse, afflicted by Saturn, Uranus and Pluto. Martin Luther King is awarded the Nobel Peace Prize. There are race riots in Harlem, New York, disturbances in Northern Rhodesia, and anti-Muslim violence in India. In the United States, Lyndon Johnson is elected president.

Culture

Andy Warhol produces his *Most Wanted Man*. 'Op' art, in which geometric designs give the illusion of movement, becomes fashionable. Jasper Johns paints *Watchman* and Robert Rauschenberg *Retroactive*. The musical *Fiddler on the Roof*, with lyrics by Sheldon Harnick and music by Jerry Bock has its first performance in New York, as does *Hello Dolly*, with lyrics and music by Jerry Herman. Hit records include the Animals' 'The House of the Rising Sun', Louis Armstrong's 'Hello Dolly', the Beatles' 'A Hard Day's Night', Roy Orbison's 'Oh, Pretty Woman' and the Supremes' 'Baby Love'. New to the world of literature and theatre are Saul Bellow's *Herzog*, Christopher Isherwood's *A Single Man*, Hubert Selby's *Last Exit to Brooklyn*, John Osborne's *Inadmissible Evidence*, Harold Pinter's *The Homecoming*, Peter Shaffer's *The Royal Hunt of the Sun*, and Peter Weiss's *Marat/Sade*. New to the world of cinema are Stanley Kubrick's *Doctor Strangelove*, *A Fistful of Dollars* with Clint Eastwood, *Goldfinger* with Sean Connery, *A Hard Day's Night* with the Beatles, Peter Brooks' *Lord of the Flies*, *Mary Poppins* with Julie Andrews and *Zorba the Greek* with Anthony Quinn.

Births

Actor Nicolas Cage; British royal Prince Edward.

Personalities born in 1964

Rebellious but rather battened-down individuals, those born in 1964 tend to feel injustice keenly, dislike being crowded and regard themselves as outsiders. Rather obsessive, stubbornly resistant to pressure, but blessed with formidable endurance, they regard difficult struggles as a normal way of living. Slightly prone to depression, they can be highly creative or anxious worriers. Those born with Saturn in Pisces between 25 March and 17 August, and after 16 December, have humility but tend to be resentful about past mistakes or misfortunes. Those born outside these dates with Saturn in Aquarius have good minds, and a serious approach to education and friendships. Jupiter in Aries up to 12 April lends an entrepreneurial, optimistic streak, though not always common sense. Jupiter in Taurus for those born after that attracts money, and gives a taste for the good life.

1965

This is the start of the three-year revolutionary and at times destructive Uranus–Pluto contact, exacerbated by resentful Saturn in Pisces. Uranus–Pluto pulls down old structures to clear the ground for new growth, supports the rebellion of the young, seen in the anti-Vietnam demonstrations in the United States, but often destabilizes in a quite unconstructive way. Historically it has been associated with the slave trade, black rights and oppression. Now in Virgo for the first time in several millennia, it has its effect in physical and material ways. Saturn–Pluto in flat contrast often toughens brutal attitudes, and is rigid and misery-inducing for those on the underbelly of society. Saturn in opposition to Uranus is economically testing and can be dictatorial.

Events
Winston Churchill dies; 350,000 worldwide watch his televised state funeral. Malcolm X, Black Muslim African-American leader, and other black civil-rights workers are killed; Martin Luther King leads mass demonstrations. Heavy bombing continues in Vietnam; there is a mass student march in the United States in protest, at which the poet Allen Ginsberg coins the term 'flower power'. An earthquake in Chile kills 400 people, and tornadoes devastate the American Midwest on the first exact opposition of Saturn and Uranus; cyclones in Bangladesh follow close to the Gemini eclipse afflicted by the outer planets. In Indonesia political violence leads to massacres. India invades West Pakistan and bombs Lahore. There is civil war in Dominica. Ian Smith, prime minister of Rhodesia, declares unilateral independence from Britain.

Science and technology
Soviet and US astronauts walk in space.

Culture
Francis Bacon paints his *Study from a Portrait of Pope Innocent X* and Joseph Beuys his *How to Explain Pictures to a Dead Hare*. Composer Leonard Bernstein writes *Chichester Psalms*, and Pierre Boulez composes *Eclat*. Hit records include the Beach Boys' 'California Girls', the Beatles' 'Help', 'Ticket to Ride' and 'Daytripper', Tom Jones's 'It's Not Unusual', the Rolling Stones' 'satisfaction' and the Temptations' 'My Girl'. Günter Grass's *Dog Years*, Jerry Kosinski's *The Painted Bird*, Norman Mailer's *An American Dream*, Frank Marcus's *The Killing of Sister George* and John Osborne's *A Patriot for Me* are among the year's new

books and plays. Cinema audiences see *The Cincinnati Kid* with Steve McQueen, *Darling* with Julie Christie, David Lean's *Dr Zhivago*, Roman Polanski's *Repulsion* and *The Sound of Music* with Julie Andrews.

Births
Movie actor Charlie Sheen.

Personalities born in 1965
Strong, rather challenging individuals, personalities born in 1965 do not find settled working or domestic lives easy to handle, preferring to walk on the wild side or at least be experimental. Defensive and not always cooperative, they regard themselves as outsiders, can be obsessive, but also have formidable endurance. They can be real pioneers, able to develop new techniques in work or in health, with the determination to push against mainstream attitudes. With Saturn in Pisces they can be resentful or excessive worriers, regretting past mistakes, although Saturn aspecting Neptune makes them charitable, creative and often rather spiritual. Jupiter in Taurus up to 22 April brings a fondness for the good life; in Cancer between 22 September and 17 November it fosters the need for a happy, expansive home life; and in Gemini at other periods it makes for chattiness, restlessness and broad thinking.

1966
The violently disruptive Uranus–Pluto contact in the middle of its three-year exact crossing continues to wreak havoc globally, with additional intensity as Mars joins them in earthy, physical Virgo in mid-October. Saturn across the heavens in Pisces locks entrenched attitudes in a brutally bleak way. This year sees the start of the Cultural Revolution in China, the heaviest bombing yet in Vietnam, the birth of Mike Tyson, and the gruesome trial in London of child torturers and murderers Ian Brady and Myra Hindley. Neptune in intense Scorpio, one of the decade's markers, continues to promote escapism through sex, drugs and pop music.

Events
Indira Gandhi becomes Indian prime minister; food riots and unrest follow. There are coups in Syria, Ghana and Nigeria, and Israeli-Syrian clashes. South African prime minister H. F. Verwoerd is stabbed to death. An earthquake in Turkey kills 2000. There are race riots in the United States. The purge of the Chinese leadership starts, followed by violent removal of the intelligentsia. As Mars enters Virgo in October, a mine slag heap buries a school in Aberfan, Wales, killing 116 children; and the United States steps up bombing in Vietnam. In November, a week before the Scorpio eclipse, conjunct Neptune, severe floods in Italy devastate Florence.

Science and technology
US and Soviet spacecraft make Moon orbits and landing. LSD is withdrawn in the United States as a prescribed drug after widespread misuse.

Culture

Hans Werner Henze composes his opera *The Bassarids*. Hit records include the Beach Boys' 'Good Vibrations', the Beatles' 'Eleanor Rigby' and 'Yellow Submarine', Bob Dylan's 'Blonde on Blonde', Tom Jones's 'Green Grass of Home', Simon and Garfunkel's 'The Sound of Silence' and Frank Sinatra's 'Strangers in the Night'. W. Fullbright's *The Arrogance of Power*, Konrad Lorenz's *On Aggression*, Truman Capote's *In Cold Blood*, John Fowles's *The Magus*, Graham Greene's *The Comedians* and Sylvia Plath's *Ariel* are all published. Playwright Edward Bond writes *Saved* and Joe Orton writes *Loot. Alfie* with Michael Caine, *Georgy Girl* with James Mason and Lynn Redgrave, and *A Man for All Seasons* with Paul Scofield are among the year's film releases.

Births

Italian opera singer Cecilia Bartoli; heavyweight boxer Mike Tyson.

Personalities born in 1966

One-off individuals, those born in 1966 have an intensity, a brooding obsessiveness, and a tendency to destabilize that makes ordinary working or domestic lives difficult for them to maintain. However, they are also strong, tough-minded, good at pioneering new approaches, and able to plough their own furrow without mainstream support. They are a contradictory mix of stubborn resistance to change and open-mindedness to anything experimental or adventurous. Prone to depression, and often resentful about the past, they can escape through music, and sometimes drink or drugs. They have a charitable side, and a willingness to fight for a better society. Those born with Jupiter in Gemini up to 5 May are good communicators and widely read; those born with Jupiter in Cancer from then until 27 September want a happy home life; those with Jupiter in Leo thereafter like living the five-star way, rather flamboyantly.

Mike Tyson

Born 30 June 1966, birth time unknown, New York.
Chart: Sun, Jupiter in Cancer ◆ Mars, Venus in Gemini ◆ Moon in Sagittarius ◆ Saturn in Pisces ◆ Neptune in Scorpio ◆ Uranus, Pluto in Virgo ◆ Moon's North Node in Taurus

With the Sun in home-loving, protective Cancer close to confidently lucky Jupiter, Mike Tyson should be a pussy-cat. But his driving force, and the root of his rage problem, stems from the disruptive Uranus–Pluto conjunction in Virgo opposing depressive, rigid Saturn. This axis is tricky enough, but here it additionally squares at one side onto a restless, narrow-minded, arrogant Sagittarian Moon, and on the other side to an aggressively irritable Mars in Gemini. To say he has problems with women and mood swings is the understatement of the century! Stemming from a rough, unloved, battered childhood practically from the day of his birth, he cannot control the overwhelming anger that has swept him to success in a brutal sport and into outbursts of violent attack outside the ring. In 15 of his first 25 fights he knocked his opponent out in the first round with the sledgehammer blow that became his trademark.

This grand square in mutable signs gives him poor concentration, extreme restlessness and nervousness, and the tendency to be constantly reacting to external pressures rather than finding his own centre. Always described as a windmill in a storm, this rather extraordinary planetary configuration demands that the individual learns to be more reflective, to keep his mind under control, rather than letting it fly off in all directions at once.

In 1986, at the age of 20, Tyson became the youngest-ever heavyweight boxing champion when explosive Uranus in Sagittarius was bouncing erratically around the grand square in his chart, though Jupiter in Pisces was mellowing the effect. When he was sentenced to 10 years in prison for rape and other charges in 1992, Pluto was crossing Neptune in Scorpio, a major disorienting psychological influence, with the highly strung Neptune–Uranus conjunction in Capricorn triggering his own rebellious tendencies. The years since his early release in 1995, with one opponent's ear bitten off and a road-rage incident that sent him back to prison, give no indication that he has the capacity to resolve what are deep-rooted psychological problems. His next major transition comes as Pluto comes to square Uranus–Pluto from 2002 onwards. That he can negotiate towards a more sociable attitude may be too much to contemplate.

1967

Now in its third year, the Uranus–Pluto contact in earthy Virgo, which is revolutionary, disruptive, destabilizing and usually violent, keeps tension levels high, most visibly in Mao's Red China, Vietnam and the Middle East. Occurring only eight times in a millennium, it tears down old structures, sometimes constructively, though not always; it can turn into explosive change for change's sake. Saturn is leaving its three-year opposition across the heavens in weak-willed Pisces, which has created a neurotic mood. Moving into Aries in March, it promotes a cold self-sufficiency and resourcefulness, although usually difficult circumstances to go with these. Fey Neptune linking to Pluto and Uranus is otherworldly and yearns to escape beyond reality, its influence manifesting in a growth in consciousness and in a desire to delve more deeply into nuclear physics and to explore outer space, as well as in the search for bliss through sex, drugs and rock-'n'-roll. Jupiter floats through heart-centred, colourful Leo from 25 May to 20 October for what is designated the 'summer of love'.

Events

There is a major offensive in Vietnam; Stockholm International War Crimes Tribunal finds the United States guilty of aggression, and there are international demonstrations against US involvement in Vietnam. There is a military coup in Greece, and there are riots in Hong Kong and serious race riots in the United States. The Six Day War between Arab states and Israel takes place. Red Guards in China run amok. Donald Campbell is killed attempting the world water-speed record. Che Guevara, revolutionary guerrilla, is executed in Bolivia. In the United States, Albert de Salvo, the 'Boston strangler', is given a life sentence. An outbreak of foot-and-mouth disease begins in the United Kingdom immediately before the Scorpio solar eclipse close to Neptune.

Science and technology
Dr Christiaan Barnard performs the first heart transplant.

Culture
David Hockney paints *A Neat Lawn* and Andy Warhol his silkscreen prints of Marilyn Monroe. Richard Rodney Bennett writes his opera *A Penny for a Song*, and Karlheinz Stockhausen composes *Hymnen*. The musical *Hair*, with lyrics by Gerome Ragni and music by Galt MacDermot, has its first staging in Greenwich Village, New York. Hit records include the Beatles' 'Sergeant Pepper's Lonely Hearts Club Band', Glenn Campbell's 'Gentle on My Mind', Engelbert Humperdinck's 'The Last Waltz', Procul Harum's 'A Whiter Shade of Pale' and Sandie Shaw's 'Puppet on a String'. The Jimi Hendrix Experience makes its debut. New to the world of books and theatre are Desmond Morris's *The Naked Ape*, J. P. Donleavy's *The Saddest Summer of Samuel F*, Thornton Wilder's *The Eighth Day*, Peter Nichols's *A Day in the Death of Joe Egg*, Harold Pinter's *The Homecoming* and Tom Stoppard's *Rosencrantz and Guildenstern Are Dead*. In the cinema, audiences see *Bonnie and Clyde* with Warren Beatty and Faye Dunaway, *The Dirty Dozen,* and *Far from the Madding Crowd* with Alan Bates, Julie Christie and Terence Stamp.

Births
American athlete Michael Johnson; tennis player Boris Becker; singer Kurt Cobain.

Personalities born in 1967
Strong-minded, challenging individuals, those born in 1967 dislike a conventional lifestyle, preferring to walk on the wild side or to be pioneers or reformers. Often feeling like outsiders, they can be obsessive or prone to depression, but they have stamina in abundance. Neptune in Scorpio brings a yearning for transcendence through sex, music or other escapist addictions. Those born with Saturn in Pisces up to 4 March can be worriers and resentful about past misfortunes; those born with Saturn in Aries thereafter are resourceful and hard-driving to succeed, without help if necessary. Jupiter in Leo up to 17 January, and between 25 May and 20 October, makes those born then flamboyant and extravagant; in Cancer from 17 January until 25 May it brings a desire for a settled, comfortable home life; and in Virgo after 20 October it lends a hard-working and charitable streak.

1968
The final year of Pluto and Uranus in Virgo continues on a disruptive and violent course, with revolutionary intent as the young and the oppressed fight for freedom in France, Ireland and the United States, and there is violence in Czechoslovakia. As Uranus moves sign—for the first time in seven years—into Libra, a shift of emphasis occurs on the political scene, but it also promotes new forms of emotional partnerships where freedom is the watchword, and pioneers electronic music. Austere Saturn in dynamic Aries favours a hard-driving, self-sufficient mood, where willpower is the keynote to successful action. Jupiter hovers between flamboyant Leo, workaholic Virgo and fair-minded Libra.

173

Events

Martin Luther King is assassinated one week after the late March eclipse, afflicted by Saturn; riots follow. Racing driver Jim Clark is killed three days later. The My Lai massacre of Vietnamese civilians by US troops also occurs in March. There are riots in West Berlin. Student riots in Paris flare up in the 'Night of the Barricades' on the day that Mars moves into Gemini, aspecting the Uranus–Pluto conjunction. Robert Kennedy is assassinated one month later in Los Angeles as Mars comes directly in square to Pluto. Czechoslovakia, heading for political reform, is invaded by Soviet troops. An earthquake in Iran kills 12,000. In Londonderry, on the day of the October lunar eclipse in Aries, aspected both by Uranus in Libra, and by Saturn, police clash with civil-rights marchers, initiating the latest manifestation of the Northern Ireland troubles. In the United States, Richard Nixon becomes president.

Science and technology

The remains of amino-acids are discovered in rocks that are 3 billion years old.

Culture

Harrison Birtwistle composes his opera *Punch and Judy* and John Tavener *The Whale*. Hit records include James Brown's 'Say It Loud, I'm Black and Proud', Marvin Gaye's 'I Heard It Through the Grapevine', Joni Mitchell's *Songs To A Seagull*, and Simon and Garfunkel's 'Mrs Robinson'. The musical *Joseph and the Amazing Technicolor Dreamcoat* is first performed, in London. Lawrence Durrell's *Tunc*, Ursula Le Guin's *A Wizard of Earthsea*, Alexander Solzhenitsyn's *The First Circle* and *Cancer Ward*, John Updike's *Couples* and Gore Vidal's *Myra Breckinridge* are published. Arthur Miller completes *The Price*. In the cinema, *Butch Cassidy and the Sundance Kid* with Paul Newman and Robert Redford, the 'spaghetti western' *The Good, the Bad and the Ugly*, *The Graduate*, *In the Heat of the Night* with Rod Steiger and Sydney Poitier, Lindsay Anderson's *If*, *The Lion in Winter* with Peter O'Toole and Katharine Hepburn, Franco Zeffirelli's *Romeo and Juliet*, and Stanley Kubrick's *2001, A Space Odyssey* are among the year's new releases.

Births

French-Canadian singer Celine Dion.

Personalities born in 1968

The last of the mid-1960s highly strung, rather rebellious individuals, they are not designed for a settled domestic or working life. They are resourceful, self-sufficient, will-driven and determined to walk their own independent path. With Neptune in intense, sexy Scorpio they want to lose themselves in music, dance or other escapist trips. Those born after 28 September have new ideas about marriage, partnerships and how society fits together. They are insightful about behaviour, and very inventive with their creative talents. Those born with Jupiter in Virgo up to 27 February, and between 15 June and 15 November, are hard-working but lucky, usually finding sudden opportunities to travel, and are successful because they push. Jupiter in Leo (27 February to 15 June) makes for flamboyant, extravagant tastes; in Libra after 15 November it brings a fair-minded approach to social justice and relationships.

1969

The last flickering moments of the Uranus–Pluto conjunction in Virgo coincide with sporadic flare-ups of violence, but there is a shift of emphasis as Uranus makes its settled seven-year move into Libra, bringing a dynamic new approach to marriage and the justice system. Change is generally in the air as both Pluto and Neptune, much slower planets, also near the end of their 15-year stay, prepare for a major move over the turn of the next decade. Saturn also makes a three-year move, this time into Taurus, a placing that is always a hint of economic slowdown and belt-tightening. Jupiter passes through hard-working Virgo, then fair-minded Libra, and finally into financially resourceful Scorpio.

Events

There are clashes between Roman Catholics and Protestants in Northern Ireland; bombing starts. A Czech student burns himself to death in protest at the Soviet occupation of his country. Martial law is declared in Spain. A White House press aide coins the term 'photo-opportunity' as Richard Nixon is inaugurated. Nixon announces the phased withdrawal of US troops from Vietnam. Yasser Arafat becomes PLO chairman. Palestinian terrorists attack an El Al airliner at Zurich airport. London gangsters Ronnie and Reggie Kray are imprisoned for life. In the United States James Earl Ray is convicted for killing Martin Luther King; Charles Manson's 'cult-gang' murders Sharon Tate and three others; and Mary Jo Kopechne, the passenger in a car driven by Senator Edward Kennedy, drowns when it goes into a river at Chappaquiddick. Military government takes over Pakistan. There is unrest between Arabs and Israelis. The 'gay rights' movement starts after police harassment in New York. Half a million people attend the Woodstock music festival in the United States.

Science and technology

American astronaut Neil Armstrong becomes the first man to walk on the Moon. The Internet is established by the US Department of Defense.

Culture

Georg Baselitz paints *The Wood on its Head*. Composer Peter Maxwell Davies writes *Eight Songs for a Mad King*, Henryk Gorecki *Old Polish Music*, and Dmitri Shostakovich his Symphony No. 14. Musical hits include Johnny Cash's 'A Boy Named Sue', Led Zeppelin's *Led Zeppelin I*, the Who's *Tommy* and Frank Zappa's *Hot Rats*. New books and plays include Michael Crichton's *The Andromeda Strain*, John Fowles's *The French Lieutenant's Woman*, Mario Puzo's *The Godfather*, Philip Roth's *Portnoy's Complaint*, Kurt Vonnegut's *Slaughterhouse Five*, Athol Fugard's *Boesman and Lena* and Joe Orton's *What the Butler Saw*. Notable film releases include Dennis Hopper's *Easy Rider*, John Schlesinger's *Midnight Cowboy*, Richard Attenborough's *Oh What a Lovely War*, *The Prime of Miss Jean Brodie* with Maggie Smith, and Ken Russell's *Women in Love*.

Personalities born in 1969

Quite fey and otherworldly with some psychic talents, they are interested in exploring beyond reality. Rather self-reliant individuals, who push to make their presence felt and are driven to protect their security, they nonetheless feel as though they hover in the space between two groups of people, not quite fitting. Those born between 21 May and 25 June are part of the rebellious sixties pioneers. Otherwise with Uranus in Libra they are forward-looking, more devoted to forging new frameworks for relationships. Saturn in Aries up to 29 April produces will-driven, rather resourceful people; in Taurus thereafter it gives a more materialistic slant, with a need to protect their money. Jupiter in Libra until 31 March, and between 16 July and 16 December brings a desire for fairness in relationships; in Virgo (31 March to 16 July) it promotes the willingness to work hard; in Scorpio after 16 December it brings skill with money and attracts the confidences of others.

1970–1979

The tumultuous 1960s give way to a decade in which the waning Uranus–Pluto contact causes less violent disruption by comparison. Spiritual Neptune moves into Sagittarius to stay for the decade, heightening interest in religion. Religious gurus, both genuine and fake, flourish. The new focus on spirituality is reflected in popular culture in the hit musicals *Jesus Christ Superstar* and *Godspell*. Cult leader Jim Jones leads 913 followers to their deaths in a suicide pact. In the Islamic world, religious leader Ayatollah Khomeini takes up power in Iran. The Roman Catholic/Protestant divide in Ireland is the cause of great disruption and many killings. Neptune is the searcher for ultimate meaning, and Sagittarius is connected to long-distance travel, so there is delightful symbolism in the first satellite aimed outside the solar system, launched in 1972; it leaves the solar system only in 1983, as Neptune finishes its stay. Pluto and Uranus in Libra—where Uranus stays until 1975—foster new kinds of marital relationships; the gay-rights movement gets under way. Pluto and Uranus in Libra also push hard for legal reform and social justice, culminating in the Freedom of Information Act in the United States in the wake of the Watergate scandal. High-tech Uranus moves into Scorpio, promoting ingenious scientific inventions in the year that 19-year-old Bill Gates sets up Microsoft. Uranus in sexual Scorpio also jolts into the open with devastating AIDS, which surfaces in 1977.

1970

The Jupiter–Saturn opposition is the midway point of a 20-year cycle, when the high hopes and perhaps over-optimistic expectations of 1960 start to fade. The Beatles, who resonate strongly with these cycles, with John Lennon's birth (1940), debut (1960) and death (1980) all occurring on Jupiter–Saturn conjunctions—now split and go their separate ways. Nixon steps up the withdrawal from Vietnam, a failure tacitly acknowledged. Neptune starts the move out of Scorpio (1956 to 1970), an emotionally confusing time when ecstasy and escapism are sought through sex, drugs and pop music. Now shifting into Sagittarius (1970 to 1984), the search is on for higher spiritual and mystical values, fostering the growth of cults, especially those based on foreign religions.

Events

There are serious clashes on the Golan Heights between Israel and Syria; Israel bombs Cairo. Terrorist plane hijackings proliferate—Palestinian, Japanese and Russian. British forces are reinforced in Northern Ireland as riots and bombings increase. Nixon withdraws more troops from Vietnam. An earthquake in Peru kills 50,000; a cyclone and tidal wave kill 150,000 in East Pakistan. Jimi Hendrix dies from a drug overdose.

Culture

David Hockney paints *Mr and Mrs Ossie Clark and Percy*. Michael Tippett writes his opera *The Knot Garden*. Hit records include the Beatles' 'Let It Be', the Carpenters' 'We've Only Just Begun', the Grateful Dead's 'American Beauty', and Simon and Garfunkel's 'Bridge Over Troubled Water'. Maya Angelou's *I Know Why the Caged Bird Sings*, Richard Bach's *Jonathan Livingston Seagull*, Iris Murdoch's *Bruno's Dream*, Germaine Greer's *The Female Eunuch*, Kate Millett's *Sexual Politics*, and Studs Terkel's *Hard Times* are published. Notable films include Bernardo Bertolucci's *The Conformist*, Ken Loach's *Kes*, *Love Story* with Ali McGraw and Ryan O'Neal, and *M*A*S*H* with Donald Sutherland and Elliott Gould.

Births

Actor River Phoenix (brought up as a member of the Children of God cult).

Personalities born in 1970

Good with money and trusted with secrets, they handle confidential matters well but, with the Jupiter–Saturn opposition, are scared of failure to a critical degree. For some this creates a strong drive for success, but others are so afraid of failing that they never try. Finding a balance between ideals and practical material security is vital to their fulfilment. They can be spendthrift and tight with money at the same time. With Uranus in Libra they demand freedom in marriage and close relationships. Those born with Neptune in Sagittarius (4 January to 3 May, and after 6 November) can travel extensively, searching for deeper meaning in their lives. Otherwise those born with Neptune in Scorpio close to Jupiter are intense but charitable, keen on music, and seek bliss through the body.

Claudia Schiffer

Born 25 August 1970, 12.10 pm Central European Time, Dusseldorf, Germany.
Chart: Sun in Virgo ◆ Mars, midheaven in Leo ◆ Moon in Gemini ◆ Ascendant, Jupiter, Neptune in Scorpio ◆ Venus, Uranus in Libra ◆ Pluto, Mercury in Virgo ◆ Saturn in Taurus ◆ Moon's North Node in Pisces

A seductively beautiful Virgo, international model Claudia Schiffer further contradicts the myth of Virgo's stereotype, the fastidious spinster, for she stands in the same ranks as Sophia Loren, Greta Garbo, Ingrid Bergman and Raquel Welch. With Sean Connery and Richard Gere among the male of the Virgo species, it is one of the top sex-symbol signs.

A midheaven Sun, close to flamboyantly determined Mars in Leo, pushes her into a successful public career. She works conscientiously, paying close attention, in Virgoan fashion, to health and diet, and putting up with considerable discomfort and a punishing schedule to achieve the results she wants. A Mars–Saturn square fosters an attitude of military discipline, suggesting almost a touch of masochism.

With dreamy Neptune in sensual Scorpio on the horizon when she was born— a placing that often produces what are described as 'bedroom eyes'—Schiffer exudes an ethereal charm. However, with her emotional planets in air signs, both well hidden in the chart, she does not find public displays of emotion easy, nor finds real romantic fulfilment, having never felt totally loved in childhood. Saturn also hints at an attraction to rather distanced, older partners. A deeply buried, restless Gemini Moon makes mood swings inevitable—what she wants one moment is not what she wants in 10 minutes' time. Happily she also has a hidden Jupiter giving her a self-contained inner calm that others often envy. She can be at peace with herself and her own company.

A tumultous collection of disruptive Uranus in Libra, close to intense Mercury and Pluto in late Virgo, makes friendships a mixed blessing. She knows powerfully influential and rather unpredictable people, which is also the image she projects out into society. Her long-term, long-distance, on-off relationship with magician David Copperfield, another meticulous Virgo 14 years her senior, picked up this Uranus–Pluto energy. Very much a blow-hot, blow-cold affair, it has deep-rooted, passionate jealousies running side by side with a tremendous need for space.

Not likely to fade from public view for many years, she has recently shifted gear into a new phase, which will push her upwards until she reaches a peak in her forties.

1971

The Saturn-in-Gemini opposition to Neptune in Sagittarius contributes to a paranoid, worrying mood. This is the low point midway through a 40-year cycle starting in 1953, concerned with improving the rights of the disadvantaged and creating a fairer society. Although artistic, it can make reality seem bleaker than it really is. On its two exact stations through the year, Margaret Thatcher stops the granting of free milk to British schoolchildren, and Richard Nixon announces the end of the much-criticized US aggression in Vietnam. Saturn also aspects Pluto as both planets hover on the cusp of sign changes, pushing monumental changes through, slowly and with great effort. Pluto is now heading into Libra for 13 years, joining Uranus now midway through. A major transformation of attitudes to close relationships and agreements, on personal, social and international levels, is under way.

Events

In Scotland, a stampede at a Glasgow football match crushes 66 people to death. Anarchists bomb the home of a British cabinet minister. There are serious riots, shootings and bombings in Ulster. The conflict between Jordan and the Palestinians is renewed; the Jordanian prime minister is murdered. Violent rebellion disrupts Ceylon. François Duvalier—'Papa Doc'—the right-wing Haitian dictator—dies. A mass anti-Vietnam War march takes place in the United States; Nixon withdraws more troops. Charles Manson and accomplices are given life imprisonment for the killing of Sharon Tate. American Lieutenant Calley is given life for the My Lai massacre in Vietnam. Riots in a New York prison result in 42 dead. The Indo-Pakistan War ends. The United Nations votes to admit Communist China. Disney World opens in Orlando, Florida, at a cost of $500 million.

Science and technology
The computer microprocessor chip is introduced.

Culture
David Hockney paints *Rubber Ring Floating in a Swimming Pool* and Anselm Kiefer paints *Mann im Wald*. Benjamin Britten writes his opera *Owen Wingrave*, Dmitri Shostakovich his Symphony No. 15, and Karlheinz Stockhausen *Trans*. Stephen Sondheim's *Follies* makes its debut in New York. Stephen Schwartz's rock musical *Godspell* and Tim Rice and Andrew Lloyd Webber's *Jesus Christ Superstar* are both premiered. Hit records include David Bowie's 'The Man Who Sold the World', Carole King's 'Tapestry' and Rod Stewart's 'Maggie May'. New additions to the world of books and theatre include Albert Camus' *A Happy Death*, Jerzy Kosinski's *Being There*, Aleksandr Solzhenitsyn's *August 1914* and Edward Bond's *Lear*. Major film successes include Stanley Kubrick's *A Clockwork Orange*, Luchino Visconti's *Death in Venice*, Francis Ford Coppola's *The Godfather*, Sam Peckinpah's *Straw Dogs* and John Schlesinger's *Sunday Bloody Sunday*. Clint Eastwood stars in *Dirty Harry* and Gene Hackman in *The French Connection*.

Births
American tennis player Pete Sampras.

Personalities born in 1971
Tough-minded, rather stubborn, occasionally obsessive, these are individuals able to withstand pressure. With Uranus in Libra, they rebel tactfully against conventional forms of relationships, preferring freedom to security. Fearful of failure, they either push exceptionally hard for success, or are too timid to risk anything. They are contradictory in attitudes to money, being spendthrift and stingy at the same time. This is especially true of those born before 18 June with Saturn in Taurus; thereafter Saturn in Gemini creates inquiring minds, although with a tendency to worry excessively. They can be highly creative. Neptune in Sagittarius fosters a yearning for spiritual enlightenment. Jupiter in Scorpio (up to 14 January, and between 5 June and 11 September) attracts money and the divulging of confidences; in Sagittarius otherwise it produces individuals who are widely read and rather philosophical.

1972
The Saturn–Neptune opposition for a second year running is uneasily anxious and rather paranoid. Nothing is quite what it appears. High expectations run side by side with disappointments. Pluto now established in early Libra is slowly forging a new approach to agreements and relationships. Although widely separated from Uranus (also in Libra), it still manages to provoke a degree of revolutionary

disruption. Disciplined Saturn in inquiring Gemini focuses mental concentration on scientific and educational matters. The outer planets are shifting into air and fire signs, a lighter, more thoughtful energy than the physically weighted earth–water emphasis of the 1960s.

Events

On 'Bloody Sunday' in Northern Ireland—the day of the January lunar eclipse—British troops shoot dead 13 civilians; in response the British embassy in Dublin is burned down. The bombing continues in Ulster and mainland United Kingdom; there are 467 killings in 1972. German police round up the Baader-Meinhof urban guerrilla group. Arab and Palestinian terrorists attack Lod Airport, Israel, killing 26, and kill 11 members of the Israeli Olympic team at Munich. There is an attempted assassination of King Hassan of Morocco. Idi Amin expels Ugandan Asians. High-ranking US diplomat Henry Kissinger says peace is at hand in Vietnam. An earthquake hits Nicaragua. The USSR refuses visa to allow Aleksandr Solzhenitsyn to receive the Nobel Prize for Literature.

Science and technology

The United States launches a spacecraft to travel beyond the solar system; it reaches the boundary in 1983. The first home video-cassette recorders are introduced.

Culture

The Tate Gallery, London, makes a controversial purchase of Carl André's 'bricks' (*Equivalent 8, 1966*). Peter Maxwell Davies writes his opera *Taverner* and Michael Tippett his Symphony No. 3. Jim Jacobs and Warren Casey's musical *Grease* opens in New York. Popular music hits include Chuck Berry's 'My Ding-a-ling', David Bowie's 'The Rise and Fall of Ziggy Stardust', Roberta Flack's 'The First Time I Ever Saw Your Face', Gladys Knight and the Pips' 'Help Me Make It Through The Night', Don McLean's 'American Pie' and Helen Reddy's 'I Am Woman'. This is the age of the 'teenyboppers', created by such bands as the Bay City Rollers, the Jackson Five, the Osmonds and singer David Cassidy. New books include Margaret Drabble's *The Needle's Eye*, Frederick Forsyth's *The Day of the Jackal* and V. S. Naipaul's *In A Free State*. US dramatist Sam Shepard writes *The Tooth of Crime* and British dramatist Tom Stoppard writes *Jumpers*. *Cabaret* with Liza Minnelli, Pier Paolo Pasolini's *The Decameron* and Bernardo Bertolucci's *Last Tango in Paris* are among the year's new film releases.

Births

Actress Gwyneth Paltrow.

Personalities born in 1972

Fire-air individuals, those born in 1972 are bright, fast-moving, ambitious, inspired and rather fun. They demand the freedom to live out unconventional relationships, with more personal independence. They can be deeply creative, although also tend to worry too much. Those born between 11 January and 12 February are more practical, and tight-fisted with money; otherwise Saturn in Gemini lends those born then an inquiring mind with rather detached emotional responses. Neptune in Sagittarius gives an attraction for faraway places and, in particular, foreign religious belief systems. Those born with Jupiter in Capricorn (6 February to 25 July, and after 26 September) attract money and have more traditional values; otherwise those born with Jupiter in Sagittarius are high-minded, widely read and rather philosophical.

1973

Three eclipses in Capricorn and Cancer, all aspected by Pluto, Uranus or Saturn, make a significant impact. The January eclipse, in the same cycle as occurred in December 1918 at the end of the First World War, now sees the end of the Vietnam War; the second eclipse in June on the exact day of the Cancer eclipse sees the final second ceasefire agreement. Saturn entering Cancer in August to square Pluto—always an indicator of brutal conditions, usually war—reaches exact aspect as the full-scale Yom Kippur War flares up in the Middle East in October; political tension is at its height in the US Watergate scandal with President Richard Nixon facing impeachment; and, in a CIA-backed coup, Augusto Pinochet's military junta violently seizes power in Chile.

Events
IRA bombing campaign continues on the UK mainland. Palestinian and Arab terrorists attack US and Israeli embassies, and Athens and Rome airports; Israel replies with bombs. Middle East unrest flares up into a full-scale war as Egypt and Syria attack Israel. Richard Nixon's complicity in the Watergate bugging scandal is gradually uncovered; vice-president Spiro Agnew resigns over tax evasion. Terrorists capture 273 people from a mission school in Rhodesia; there are race riots at a university. Drought in Ethiopia causes 100,000 deaths. In Britain, a three-day working week is introduced to save energy. Skateboarding becomes popular.

Science and technology
A calf is produced from a frozen embryo. The parents of children suffering birth defects as a result of Thalidomide receive compensation from the pharmaceutical company that made the drug.

Culture
The world of art mourns the death of Pablo Picasso, widely regarded as the 20th century's greatest painter. Benjamin Britten composes his opera *Death in Venice* and Aaron Copland writes *Night Thoughts*. Stephen Sondheim's musical *A Little Night Music* opens. Hit songs include Roberta Flack's 'Killing Me Softly With His Song', Gary Glitter's 'I'm The Leader of the Gang', Elton John's 'Goodbye Yellow Brick Road', Mike Oldfield's 'Tubular Bells', Pink Floyd's 'The Dark Side of the Moon' and Stevie Wonder's 'I Believe'. Richard Adams' *Watership Down*, Graham Greene's *The Honorary Consul*, Thomas Pynchon's *Gravity's Rainbow*, Tom Sharpe's *Riotous Assembly* and Erich Fromm's *The Anatomy of Human*

Destructiveness are all published. Peter Shaffer's play *Equus* is performed. Cinema audiences see Pier Paolo Pasolini's *The Canterbury Tales*, William Friedkin's *The Exorcist*, Robert Altman's *The Long Goodbye* and Martin Scorsese's *Mean Streets*.

Births
Tennis player Monica Seles.

Personalities born in 1973
Communicative, thoughtful, inquiring, emotionally rather cool individuals, those born in 1973 want freedom to speak, act and relate as they please. Settling to conventional domesticity is not easy, since they constantly want to upset the status quo. Those born with Neptune in Sagittarius are attracted to mystical religions, and often to long-distance travel in search of meaning. Those born before 2 August with Saturn in Gemini have especially inquiring minds; thereafter Saturn in Cancer can produce a rather reserved, slightly gloomy and obsessive streak. Jupiter in Capricorn up to 23 February attracts money; in Aquarius thereafter it brings a tolerant, humanitarian outlook.

1974
The tough Saturn–Pluto aspect extends its influence from 1973 through the year with difficult struggles, but the emphasis on mainly air signs adds a communicative, thoughtful feel to the general mood. Revolutionary Uranus makes a once-every-seven-years change out of relationship-oriented Libra into intense Scorpio in the late part of the year. Powerfully charged emotions will come to the surface, and new ways of handling financial resources, with computerized techniques being developed. Cool, disciplined Saturn moves between inquiring Gemini and home-loving Cancer, where it tends to have a dampening effect on feelings. Jupiter is in humanitarian Aquarius until March, then moves into charitable Pisces.

Events
The USSR deports Aleksandr Solzhenitsyn. In the United States, President Richard Nixon, facing impeachment for the Watergate bugging scandal, resigns. The US Congress passes the Freedom of Information Act. 'Lucky' Lord Lucan disappears after the murder of his children's nanny. In the United States Karen Silkwood dies in mysterious circumstances after expressing concern over safety at nuclear plants. Inflation is a serious problem. Princess Anne escapes a kidnap attempt in London. There is a military coup in Portugal. IRA bombs explode on mainland Britain at Westminster and the Tower of London; the Prevention of Terrorism Bill is passed. Violent unrest between Palestinians and Israelis continues. Hurricane Fifi kills 8000 in Honduras; a cyclone devastates Darwin, Australia. At Xian in China, the Terracotta Army— more than 6000 life-sized model soldiers guarding the tomb of China's First Emperor—is unearthed.

Culture
Anselm Kiefer paints *Resumption*. Joseph Beuys stages his performance *I Like*

America and America Likes Me. Composer Hans Werner Henze writes *Tristan* and Karlheinz Stockhausen writes *Inori*. David Bowie composes and sings 'Diamond Dogs'. Pop hits include Status Quo's 'Down, Down' and Barbra Streisand's 'The Way We Were'. Abba win the Eurovision Song Contest with 'Waterloo'. Erica Jong's *Fear of Flying* and John Le Carré's *Tinker, Tailor, Soldier, Spy* are published; Tom Stoppard's *Travesties* is staged. Poet Anne Sexton commits suicide. Roman Polanski's *Chinatown*, Francis Ford Coppola's *Godfather II* with Al Pacino and Robert de Niro, and *Papillon* with Dustin Hoffman and Steve McQueen, are among the year's new films.

Births
Actor Leonardo di Caprio; supermodel Kate Moss.

Personalities born in 1974
Communicative, detached, rather determined individuals, they think and read a good deal, are keen on new ideas and like freedom in close relationships. Rather fey with the Neptune–Pluto aspect, they can be psychic, interested in the paranormal and keen on mystical spiritual belief systems. Those born with Uranus in Libra before 21 November are especially keen on developing new forms of marriage agreements. Those born later, with Uranus in Scorpio, are decisisve, cannot tolerate laziness and can be highly resourceful. Saturn in Gemini (8 January to 18 April) lends a scientific streak; in Cancer at other dates it makes for an emotionally defensive temperament, prone to depression. Those born with Jupiter in Aquarius up to 8 March are friendly and tolerant; in Pisces thereafter they are charitable and kindly disposed.

Leonardo di Caprio
Born 11 November 1974, 2.47 am Pacific Standard Time, Los Angeles.
Chart: Sun, Mars, Venus in Scorpio ◆ Moon, Pluto, Uranus, Mercury, ascendant in Libra ◆ Jupiter in Pisces ◆ Saturn in Cancer ◆ Neptune, Moon's North Node in Sagittarius

Leonardo di Caprio's slightly bland appearance, signposted by a sociable Libra ascendant, is misleading. He is a highly determined Scorpio, masked by controlling Pluto on the horizon when he was born. This is often an indication of a Caesarean or difficult birth, resulting in a suspicious defensiveness about meeting people and a reluctance to listen to feedback. His innate secrecy is doubly emphasized by an ultra-charming Libra Moon close to Pluto, hinting at a fear of opening up to intimacy. His three powerfully emotional Scorpio planets also guard privacy with a ferocity that repels invaders: he needs to be in control. A water grand trine in his chart of Scorpio, Cancer and Pisces planets makes him vulnerable to atmosphere and prone to being overloaded with other people's problems, causing him to retreat into his shell, in an effort to become emotionally self-contained. He does have an extraordinary capacity to sympathize and could become a hidden comforter to those who are troubled, sick or rejected. (See also *Princess Anne*, page 145.)

His main drive in life is money, which he handles erratically, making and

183

spending large quantities. The influence of Mars in Scorpio is intensely competitive in this area, determined to protect his rights against all comers; Venus favours lavish spending on luxuries and beautiful objects, while the Sun has real lessons to learn about the prudent handling of his long-term security. Luckily Saturn in Cancer at his midheaven hints at growing self-discipline with age, and a talent for practical organization which may take a few years yet to flourish fully.

Although he likes to project, in Libran fashion, a rather light, bright and cheerful persona, he is given to Scorpionic jealousy and resentment. He finds it difficult to forgive when he has been hurt, emotionally or financially, and never forgets. It is a struggle for him not to be vengeful. Highly passionate in his approach to love and lust, he takes nothing superficially.

His early Academy Award nomination in 1993 for *What's Eating Gilbert Grape?*, when he was 19, happened as Jupiter in Libra crossed his ascendant, boosting confidence, and disciplined Saturn moved into Pisces, his chart area of work, laying the foundations of future success. *Romeo and Juliet* followed as Saturn reached his descendant in Aries, giving him the expected career boost. He is now on an upward spiral through the gigantic *Titanic* success of 1998, which temporarily threw him off the rails as Pluto aspected his rather spaced-out Jupiter–Neptune square. He will peak at around the age of 30 and in the years following.

1975

An emotionally self-protective mood starts the year, with three outer planets in water signs. Neptune and Pluto in subtle aspect contribute to an interest in otherworldly, spiritual or psychic phenomena. There are no major aspects until September when Uranus is finally established in intensely charged Scorpio, and Saturn moves into Leo, fostering self-important, dictatorial attitudes. Saturn in square to Uranus through until the November Scorpio eclipse is, as always, an indicator of economic cutback, as well as jarring events. Uranus in Scorpio promotes ingenious mechanical or scientific discoveries. Jupiter is in kindly Pisces until mid-March, then moves into headstrong Aries.

Events

President Nixon's aides are imprisoned for Watergate offences. The IRA declares a ceasefire in Ireland. Bombings continue on mainland Britain; the Birmingham Six are sentenced to life for bombing (freed on appeal in 1991); the Guildford Four are also given life (cleared in 1989). The first North Sea Oil comes ashore in Britain. Indira Gandhi declares a state of emergency in India. Greek colonels are found guilty of treason. As the Saturn–Uranus square becomes exact two attempts to assassinate president Gerald Ford fail; the Cod War begins as Iceland increases its territorial waters. American heiress Patty Hearst is arrested for armed robbery, and financial crisis erupts in near-bankrupt New York. Margaret Thatcher is elected leader of the British Conservative Party. King Faisal of Saudi Arabia is assassinated. There is civil war in Lebanon, and Communist victory in Vietnam.

Science and technology

The first clone of a rabbit is produced. Microsoft is founded by 19-year-old Bill Gates and a friend. The first personal computer is marketed.

Culture

Composer Pierre Boulez writes *Rituel in Memoriam Bruno Maderna*. Marvin Hamlisch and Edward Kleban's musical *A Chorus Line* has its debut in New York. Hit records include the Bay City Rollers' 'Bye Bye Baby', the Bee Gees' 'Jive Talkin', the Carpenters' 'Only Yesterday', Bob Dylan's 'Blood on the Tracks', Elton John's 'Captain Fantastic', Queen's 'Bohemian Rhapsody', Bruce Springsteen's 'Born to Run' and Rod Stewart's 'Sailing'. New literary and dramatic works include Saul Bellow's *Humboldt's Gift*, Ruth Prawer Jhabvala's *Heat and Dust*, Primo Levi's *The Periodic Table*, Athol Fugard's *Statements*, David Mamet's *American Buffalo*, and Harold Pinter's *No Man's Land*. Sydney Lumet's *Dog Day Afternoon*, Steven Spielberg's *Jaws*, Robert Altman's *Nashville*, Milos Forman's *One Flew Over the Cuckoo's Nest* and Jim Sharman's *The Rocky Horror Picture Show* are among the year's new films.

Births

American golfer Tiger Woods.

Personalities born in 1975

A mixed year, with three sign changes, produces a variety of temperaments. All have Pluto in Libra, keen to forge new kinds of relationships, and Neptune in Sagittarius, which has a mystical interest in foreign travel and belief systems. Those born with Jupiter in Pisces up to 18 March are sympathetic and well-balanced; in Aries thereafter it creates a reckless confidence. Saturn in Cancer up to 15 September is emotionally defensive, and often causes separation in families. Uranus in Scorpio up to 2 May and after 8 September is emotionally intense, intolerant but highly resourceful; in Libra otherwise it fosters unconventional views about romance and marriage.

Tiger Woods

Born 30 December 1975, 10.50 pm Pacific Standard Time, Long Beach, California.
Chart: Sun, Mercury in Capricorn ◆ Moon, Neptune in Sagittarius ◆ Ascendant in Virgo ◆ Venus, Uranus, Moon's North Node in Scorpio ◆ Jupiter in Aries ◆ Pluto in Libra ◆ Mars in Gemini ◆ Saturn in Leo

A highly determined, ambitious Jupiter–Pluto opposition across the main axis of his chart, the inheritance of his supportive though controlling father, is the drive-shaft of Woods' success. The youngest-ever winner of the US Masters golf tournament, he has become a sporting phenomenon. He will push aside social niceties to get to where he wants to be (See also *Jack Nicholson* and *Sir Anthony Hopkins*, page 122). His earthy Capricorn Sun at the furthest point from his midheaven suggests a pride in his family, a need for secure roots, and a wish to steer clear of public limelight (see also *Prince Charles*, page 141). An emphasized Jupiter in Aries makes him fiery, go-ahead, and rather impulsive. Self-confidence is not in short supply—a helpful trait for a world-class sportsman. Saturn in Leo increases his need for personal recognition, adding discipline to his ambitions; in the house of friendship, it suggests his social circle is small, loyal and mainly older. With a tidy, understated Virgo ascendant, his image is quietly workmanlike; with Jupiter above the descendant he attracts enthusiastic respect from everyone he meets.

Golfers tend to come in all varieties of signs, with Sevvy Ballesteros born in Aries, Arnold Palmer in Virgo, Lee Trevino in Sagittarius and Jack Nicklaus in Aquarius. Tiger Woods is an earthy, practical Capricorn with a fire grand trine in his chart, a real steam-roller of a personality, with the energy of ten! A restless, adventurous Sagittarian Moon keeps him constantly on the go. Close to dreamy Neptune, it gives him the dream of the perfect home life, which he aims to create when he finally stops roaming the world. A publicity-loving Mars–Neptune opposition in key position gives him constant impetus to try harder, though at times even his super-control breaks out into odd moments of irritability at home. Mars in Gemini tends to drive too fast, is sharply outspoken, and certainly does not suffer fools, or slow-coaches, gladly. Money is an erratic quantity in his life, always coming and going in large lumps, and always will be on a rollercoaster.

Venus in passionate, jealous, secretive Scorpio will not allow him to take his feelings lightly, no matter how much the Sagittarian Moon wants to skip free of entanglements. He can be mesmerizingly charming when it suits him, utterly evasive when it does not.

His meteoric rise to success in April 1997 came as Saturn, the career indicator, swung above his descendant, sending him into an ambitiously successful 15-year phase. Saturn was opposing Pluto as he won, a rather held back, trapped influence, indicating the tremendous effort that was required to break through. But lucky Jupiter close to Uranus in his chart area of sport, clearly boosted his confidence, giving him the break he needed.

1976

Saturn in Leo again squares Uranus in Scorpio, always a hint of economic cutbacks, with jolting changes and inconsistent attitudes prevailing. Saturn in Leo is proud and rather autocratic; Uranus in Scorpio is intensely charged, not tolerant of inactivity and dynamically determined on pushing through changes, especially in the development of scientific equipment. Pluto continues its 15-year swing through Libra, transforming close relationships and the legal system. Neptune in Sagittarius fosters exotic spiritual belief systems. Saturn reversing into Cancer from mid-January until early June is not supportive of contented family values. Jupiter is in headstrong Aries until late March, then moves into indulgent Taurus.

Events
Sectarian murders are perpetrated in Northern Ireland; peace marches are held. Margaret Thatcher is dubbed the 'Iron Lady'. In a UK court case, a male model alleges that he was the homosexual lover of the leader of the Liberal Party, Jeremy Thorpe. Former British cabinet minister John Stonehouse is convicted of fraud, theft and forgery. In July, when the Saturn–Uranus square is exact again, the IRA assassinates the British ambassador in Dublin; £6 million is stolen from a Nice bank; the former Japanese prime minister is charged with accepting bribes in the Lockheed

scandal; and an earthquake in China kills 242,000. South African police kill 76 students in a riot. Crisis hits the British economy as the pound falls; an IMF loan for $4 billion is sought. Chairman Mao dies. Jimmy Carter is elected US president.

Science and technology
Concorde begins its supersonic transatlantic flights. Legionnaire's disease is diagnosed for the first time.

Culture
Composer Malcolm Arnold writes *Philarmonia Concerto*, Benjamin Britten his String Quartet No. 3, Philip Glass his opera *Einstein on the Beach*, and Henryk Gorecki his Symphony No. 3 (of 'Sorrowful Songs'). Pop hits include Abba's 'Dancing Queen', the Eagles' 'Hotel California', Elton John and Kiki Dee's 'Don't Go Breaking My Heart' and Rod Stewart's 'Tonight's the Night'. Shere Hite's *The Hite Report: On Female Sexuality*, Lisa Alther's *Kinflicks*, Alex Haley's *Roots* and Barry Humphries' *Housewife-Superstar* are published. Cinema audiences see Nicholas Roeg's *The Man Who Fell to Earth*, *Marathon Man* with Laurence Olivier and Dustin Hoffman, *The Outlaw* with Clint Eastwood and *Rocky* with Sylvester Stallone.

Personalities born in 1976
Fairly stubborn, rather intense, highly charged individuals, those born in 1976 intend to make a difference, pushing through major changes in their own and others' lives. Rather psychic and interested in the paranormal and foreign belief systems, they also have an otherworldy streak. Those born with Saturn in Cancer (14 January to 5 June) are emotionally defensive, often separated from their family; in Leo otherwise they can be egocentric and driven to gain recognition. Those born with Saturn in square to Uranus can also be unpredictable, not practising what they preach. Jupiter in Aries until 26 March lends a reckless streak; in Taurus thereafter it attracts money and a liking for the good life.

1977
A generally quieter year, with only one major aspect, the final exact station of Saturn in Leo square to Uranus (running since 1975). This coincides with a Romanian earthquake, destroying most of Bucharest, and the world's worst aircrash as two jumbo jets collide over Tenerife. Otherwise the Pluto–Neptune aspect continues its subtle spiritual influence. Saturn heads into Virgo in mid-November, bringing a workaholic, perfectionist mood and interest in medicine. Expansive Jupiter, in indulgent Taurus up to 3 April, moves into communicative Gemini.

Events
An IRA gang is sent to prison for 30 years; violent deaths in Northern Ireland fall by almost a third from the previous year. Indira Gandhi loses power in India, as does Zulfikar Ali Bhutto in Pakistan. Baader-Meinhof terrorists assassinate the West German chief prosecutor. Elvis Presley dies at home of a drug overdose. South African black leader Steve Biko dies in police custody.

Science and technology

AIDS becomes a reality in the West as two homosexual men in New York are diagnosed as having the disease.

Culture

Michael Tippett writes his opera *The Ice Break* and Thea Musgrave her opera *Mary, Queen of Scots*. Martin Charnin and Charles Strouse's musical *Annie* has its debut in New York. Pop hits include Abba's 'Knowing Me Knowing You', Elvis Costello's 'My Aim Is True', Iggy Pop's 'Lust for Life', Barbra Streisand's 'Evergreen' and Wings' 'Mull of Kintyre'. New literary and dramatic works include Bruce Chatwin's *In Patagonia*, Olivia Manning's *Fortunes of War*, Paul Scott's *Staying On*, Steven Berkoff's *East* and Peter Nicholls' *Privates On Parade*. *The Last Waltz* with Bob Dylan, *Saturday Night Fever* with John Travolta, and George Lucas's *Star Wars* are among the year's new films.

Personalities born in 1977

Emotionally intense, yet determined to have freedom in their relationships, those born in 1977 can be intolerant, though also highly resourceful, individuals. Pluto aspecting Neptune leans them towards mystical spiritual interests and travel. Those born with Saturn in Leo up to 17 November can be proud, at times autocratic, and keen for personal recognition. With the square to Uranus, they can also be unpredictable and rather contradictory, failing to practise what they preach. Those with Saturn in Virgo (after 17 November) tend to over-work and worry too much. Those born with Jupiter in Taurus up to 3 April are fond of sensuous pleasures and good living; with Jupiter in Gemini thereafter they are widely read and communicative.

1978

An absence of major outer planet aspects makes for a relatively calm year on the global front. Pluto in Libra continues to have an impact on legal reform and high-profile court cases. Spiritual Neptune in far-travelled Sagittarius throws the search for enlightenment further afield, though it also raises false prophets and fake gurus. Revolutionary Uranus in intense Scorpio is highly charged. Two eclipses aspected by Pluto hint at the need to clear out decay and corruption. Saturn hovers between egocentric Leo and Virgo, planets of employment and health.

Events

Two popes die in quick succession, and a Pole, as John Paul II, becomes the first non-Italian pope in centuries. The Camp David summit achieves a peace treaty ending 30 years of hostility between Israel and Egypt. Violent unrest in Iran leads to military government; an earthquake also kills 21,000. In the Jim Jones cult mass suicide in Guyana, 913 cult followers die. Sweden bans aerosol sprays because they cause environmental damage. Mao's *Little Red Book* is denounced in China after the fall of the Gang of Four. The oil tanker *Amoco Cadiz* runs aground off France. Terrorists kidnap and kill the former Italian prime minister Aldo Moro. The death sentence is passed on the former prime minister of Pakistan, Zulfikar Ali Bhutto. In Britain, the former Liberal Party leader is charged with conspiracy to murder. The presidents of both North and South Yemen are assassinated. In India, Indira Gandhi is imprisoned. Vietnam invades Cambodia. Princess Margaret divorces Lord Snowdon.

Science and technology
In Britain, the first 'test-tube' baby is born by means of IVF.

Culture
Anselm Kiefer paints *Untitled*. Popular composers Tim Rice and Andrew Lloyd Webber's musical *Evita* opens in London. Pop music hits include Abba's 'The Album', Kate Bush's 'Wuthering Heights' and Donna Summer's 'McArthur Park'. Graham Greene's *The Human Factor*, John Irving's *The World According to Garp*, Brian Clark's *Whose Life Is It Anyway?*, David Hare's *Plenty* and Harold Pinter's *Betrayal* are among the year's new books and plays. New films include Michael Cimino's *The Deer Hunter* with Robert de Niro and Meryl Streep, Alan Parker's *Midnight Express* and *Superman* with Christopher Reeve.

Personalities born in 1978
Blessed with no major stress points in their chart, personalities born in 1978 are in tune with otherworldly interests and fascinated by spiritual journeys or paranormal happenings. Emotionally intense, they are highly resourceful and intolerant of inactivity, quite often provoking change rather abruptly. Saturn in Leo between 5 January and 26 July brings pride and a need for personal recognition to those born then; in Virgo otherwise it promotes a hard-working, perfectionist temperament. Those born with Jupiter in Gemini until 12 April are communicative and well read; in Cancer (12 April to 6 September) home-loving; and in Leo after 6 September flamboyant and extravagant.

1979
The approaching Saturn-in-Virgo square to Neptune in Sagittarius creates a worrying, paranoid mood. Both planets aspect the February Pisces solar eclipse and the September lunar one. Workers' rights are typically one focus of attention with these influences, as well as a generally discouraging mood. Neptune in Sagittarius highlights religious beliefs, expressed by both false prophets and genuine spiritual leaders. Uranus in Scorpio, a dynamically disruptive combination, produces outbursts of intolerance, although it also forces through positive reforms. Jupiter flits between home-loving Cancer, flamboyant Leo and hard-working Virgo.

Events
In Britain, the 'winter of discontent', with its serial strikes, leads to the election of Margaret Thatcher as the first woman prime minister. The Shah of Iran flees; Ayatollah Khomeini's Islamic Revolutionary Council takes over government. China launches attacks across Vietnamese borders. Irish terrorists, in separate incidents, kill the British ambassador to the Netherlands; Conservative MP Airey Neave; and Earl Mountbatten. The last incident happens five days after the total solar eclipse in late Leo aspected by Uranus, in the same cycle that next occurs in

September 1997, two days after Princess Diana is killed in Paris. In the Dominican republic, Hurricane David kills 1100 people. There is a serious accident at a US nuclear power station. Zulfikar Ali Bhutto is executed in Pakistan. Jerry Rawlings leads a successful military coup in Ghana. Saddam Hussein becomes president of Iraq. In the Fastnet Race sailing disaster in Britain, 17 die in a hurricane. The rebel parliament in Rhodesia winds up, and Britain formally ends its rule. Oil prices are nearly 90 per cent higher at the end of year than at the beginning.

Science and technology
Motorola produces a microprocessor which leads to the production of the Macintosh computer.

Culture
Velazquez's protrait of Juan de Pareja is sold at Christie's for $5.5 million, making it the most expensive painting ever bought at auction. A Joseph Beuys retrospective at the Guggenheim Museum, New York, is installed by the artist. Stephen Sondheim's musical *Sweeney Todd* is staged for the first time. Pop hits include Abba's 'Voulez Vous', the Boomtown Rats' 'I Don't Like Mondays', Gloria Gaynor's 'I Will Survive' and Pink Floyd's 'Another Brick in the Wall'. New books and plays include Norman Mailer's *The Executioner's Song*, Peter Matthiessen's *The Snow Leopard*, V. S. Naipaul's *A Bend in the River*, William Styron's *Sophie's Choice* and Peter Shaffer's *Amadeus*. In the cinema, audiences see Ridley Scott's *Alien*, Robert Benton's *Kramer vs Kramer*, *Mad Max* with Mel Gibson, Monty Python's *The Life of Brian* and Roman Polanski's *Tess*.

Personalities born in 1979
Hard-working, perfectionist worriers, those born in 1979 are often creative, or concerned with social reform. Well-read and literate, they like to see details in place. With Uranus in Scorpio they are ingenious and resourceful, and dislike laziness or inactivity. Quite psychic, they are intrigued by what lies beyond reality. Jupiter in Leo (up to 28 February, and between 20 April and 29 September) makes for proud, colourful, extravagant individuals; Jupiter in Cancer (28 February to 20 April) produces home- and family-loving types; and Jupiter in Virgo after 29 September encourages the desire to be of practical service.

1980–1989
An astonishing decade, it opens with the Jupiter–Saturn conjunction, a 20-year occurrence and always a signpost for a blossoming of high (though not necessarily realistic) hopes and ideals. In Libra this time around, it emphasizes relationships, symbolized in the fairy-tale marriage of the Prince and Princess of Wales; previously it coincided with John Kennedy's all-too-brief reign. In 1983 powerful, transforming Pluto moves into intensely sexual and financially oriented Scorpio for 12 years. It accentuates the greed of the yuppie boom, and both promotes and clears out corruption. It also coincides with the devastating AIDS plague, forcing changes in sexual attitudes, and brings child sexual abuse into the open. The bleak Saturn–Pluto conjunction, seen only three times a century, creates a brutal mood

through 1982 and 1983. In 1984 idealistic but undermining Neptune moves into materialistic Capricorn for 12 years, initially supporting the wild dreams of the money dealers but eventually undermining old financial and government institutions and bringing scandals to light. Its effect in 1986 could be connected to the first major radiation disaster with the Chernobyl meltdown. The momentous congregation of Saturn, Uranus and Neptune together for the first time in 500 years in the late 1980s sees the end of the Cold War, the dismantling of the Berlin Wall and the start of a major Western economic depression.

1980

The Saturn-in-Virgo square to Neptune in Sagittarius brings a good deal of paranoid anxiety from 1979. This pairing also typically highlights workers' rights, most notable now in the formation of the Solidarity movement in Poland. The Jupiter–Saturn conjunction, a 20-year occurrence, which starts tragically with John Lennon's death (and also marked his birth and public debut as a Beatle), is both the end and beginning of an era. The two planets draw closer through work-related Virgo, but reach exact contact only in sociable Libra. Here for only the first time since 1306, this conjunction highlights a search for new meaning and an outpouring of questioning about the Libran areas of marriage, close relationships, the legal system and social justice.

Events

Martial law is declared in Afghanistan as a major Soviet invasion continues. US commandos fail to rescue hostages held in Tehran; eight die. Terrorists seize the Iranian embassy in London. There is a failed military coup in Pakistan. President Tito of Yugoslavia dies. There are violent clashes in South Africa and India. Basque terrorists bomb Spanish holiday resorts; Italian terrorists bomb Bologna railway station. The Polish Solidarity organization is formed. Ronald Reagan becomes US president. The treason trial of the Gang of Four opens in China. In Algeria, an earthquake kills 20,000. Beatle John Lennon is murdered in New York. In Washington state, Mount Saint Helens volcano erupts.

Science and technology

The Sony Walkman is introduced. A communication satellite is launched, capable of relaying telephone calls and TV channels.

Culture

Composer Peter Maxwell Davies writes his opera *The Lighthouse* and Philip Glass his opera *Satyagraha*. The musical *Barnum*, with music by Cy Coleman and lyrics by Michael Stewart, opens, as does *Les Misérables* with lyrics by Herbert Kretzmer and music by Claude-Michel Schoenberg. Pop music hits include David Bowie's 'Ashes to Ashes', Joy Division's 'Love Will Tear Us Apart', Bruce Springsteen's 'The River' and UB40's 'Signing Off'. Anthony Burgess's *Earthly Powers*, Truman Capote's *Music for Chameleons*, Umberto Eco's *The Name of the Rose* and John Le Carré's *Smiley's People* are published. Howard Brenton's play *The Romans in Britain* causes controversy because of nudity and sexual violence. John Hurt stars in the film *Elephant Man*; other new

191

films include Irvin Kershner's *The Empire Strikes Back*; Michael Cimino's *Heaven's Gate*, Martin Scorsese's *Raging Bull* and Stanley Kubrick's *The Shining* with Jack Nicholson.

Births
American child actor Macaulay Culkin.

Personalities born in 1980
They belong to a generation (born from 1975 to 1981) that has with Pluto in Libra, Neptune in Sagittarius and Uranus in Scorpio. Highly resourceful, rather intolerant of inactivity and quite ingenious, they are intense and unconventional about relationships. Rather psychic, they search for meaning in foreign-based spiritual belief systems. Those born with Saturn and Jupiter in Virgo before 21 September are focused and keen on being of practical service, especially in the area of health, and are perfectionists and worriers. Saturn in Libra makes those born after this date seriously concerned with justice and fairness but gives them a cool emotional approach. Jupiter in Libra after 28 October makes for sociable and considerate individuals.

1981
The expansive and idealistic Jupiter–Saturn conjunction ushers in a new order of high expectations. Now in Libra, the relationship sign, it is symbolized in the fairy-tale marriage of the Prince of Wales and Lady Diana Spencer; the previous occurrence 20 years previously saw the 'Camelot' reign of the newly elected J. F. Kennedy. Both were highly Jupiterian events, but unrealistic, causing the pendulum to swing towards Saturn in its 'Grim Reaper' aspect. The conjunction's darker undertones of destabilization, marked at its start in 1980 by the murder of John Lennon, are emphasized this year by its approach to Pluto in late Libra. It continues to reap its grim results with several assassination attempts—on Ronald Reagan, the Pope, and the Egyptian and Iranian presidents. The previous occurrence of this conjunction in 1961 saw the supposedly accidental death of Dag Hammarskjöld, UN Secretary-General, as well as Princess Diana's birth.

Events
Iran releases American hostages. The treason trial of the Gang of Four continues in China. There are attempted assassinations of President Ronald Reagan and Pope John Paul II, and a successful assassination of President Sadat of Egypt. Serious race riots hit London. The Prince of Wales marries Lady Diana Spencer. In Teheran, a bomb kills the Iranian president and prime minister. The USSR denounces Solidarity in Poland; martial law is imposed. The IRA hunger strikes end after 10 deaths. Israel bombs Baghdad.

Science and technology
AIDS is officially recognized.

Culture
Picasso's *Guernica* is taken from New York to the Prado in Spain to celebrate the return of democracy. In music, popular composer Andrew Lloyd Webber's

musical *Cats*, based on poems by T. S. Eliot, opens in London. Pop hits include Phil Collins' 'In The Air Tonight', the Police's 'Everything She Does Is Magic', and Diana Ross and Lionel Richie's 'Endless Love'. William Golding's *Rites of Passage*, Alasdair Gray's *Lanark*, Salman Rushdie's *Midnight's Children*, Paul Theroux's *The Mosquito Coast* and Andrea Dworkin's *Pornography* are published. In the cinema, audiences see *Chariots of Fire*, John Boorman's *Excalibur*, *The French Lieutenant's Woman* with Meryl Streep, *On Golden Pond* with Katharine Hepburn and Henry Fonda, and Warren Beatty's *Reds*.

Personalities born in 1981

Determined, communicative, deep-thinking and rather resourceful individuals, those born in 1981 want to make a difference to their world. Scared of failure, they sometimes retreat into their shells, but once they start to apply their talents, they have initiative, stamina and courage. Fairly controlling in close relationships, they do not find it easy to open up to intimacy and can seem cool and rather detached. They are also kind, charitable, and rather creative. Those born with Uranus in Scorpio up to 18 February and between 20 March and 16 November are intolerant of laziness and rather dynamic. Otherwise with Uranus in Sagittarius they adore foreign travel, are widely read and fascinated by new forms of religion. Jupiter in Libra up to 27 November lends a fair-minded approach; in Scorpio thereafter it attracts money and confidential information.

1982

The tough, rather bleak Saturn–Pluto conjunction, occurring only twice before during this century, in 1914 and 1947, but not since 1480 in Libra, is always accompanied by heavy, often brutal events that demand endurance. The Sabra Chatila massacre occurs close to the exact aspect. Inventive Uranus also now established in Sagittarius for seven years is bringing interest in unorthodox religious matters and some fanatical adherence to dogmatic views. Promoting a more scientific approach to spiritual matters, it seeks also to incorporate astrology and other paranormal happenings into belief systems. Saturn heads into Scorpio in late November, bringing an intense focus on financial and other confidential matters.

Events

Argentine troops invade the Falkland Islands; British troops recapture the territory, and destroyers are sunk. Israel invades Lebanon in retaliation for the wounding of the Israeli ambassador in London. In Beirut refugee camps 800 Palestinians are killed by Christian militiamen. In Poland, riots break out as food prices increase by 400 per cent; there are demonstrations against martial law; and Solidarity is banned. Military coups occur in Bangladesh and Guatemala. Grace Kelly dies after a car crash. A bomb in an Irish pub kills 17. A burglar breaks into Buckingham Palace and enters the Queen's bedroom. In Britain, at Greenham Common, women demonstrate against the US nuclear cruise-missile site. There is a record day's trading on the New York stock exchange.

193

Science and technology
Compact discs (CDs) go on sale.

Culture
Georg Baselitz paints *Last Supper in Dresden* and Anish Kapoor *White Sand, Red Millet, Many Flowers*. Luciano Berio composes his opera *La Vera Storia*. Pop hits include Abba's 'The Visitors', ABC's 'Lexicon of Love', Culture Club's 'Do You Really Want To Hurt Me?', Michael Jackson's 'Thriller', and Paul McCartney and Stevie Wonder's 'Ebony and Ivory'. Isabel Allende's *The House of Spirits*, Saul Bellow's *The Dean's December*, Thomas Keneally's *Schindler's Ark*, Primo Levi's *If Not Now, When?* and John Updike's *Rabbit is Rich* are all published. *Bladerunner* with Harrison Ford, Steven Spielberg's *ET*, Werner Herzog's *Fitzcarraldo*, Richard Attenborough's *Gandhi*, *An Officer and a Gentleman* with Richard Gere, and *Tootsie* with Dustin Hoffman are among the year's new films.

Births
Prince William, eldest son of the Prince and Princess of Wales.

Personalities born in 1982
Tough-minded, quite stubborn, slightly obsessive personalities, those born in 1982 regard themselves as outsiders. Blessed with formidable stamina, they can withstand a good deal of pressure but find change difficult. Restless, inventive and full of initiative, they will seek to forge new forms of relationship, though they will find too much intimacy rather threatening. Interested in religion, or at least rather philosophical by inclination, they think and read a great deal, and like to travel widely. With Jupiter in Scorpio, they are resourceful with money, and invite the divulging of secrets; with Jupiter in Sagittarius after 26 December they are broadminded, with wide interests.

Prince William
Born 21 June 1982, 0.03 pm, London, England.
Chart: Sun, Moon, Moon's North Node in Cancer ◆ Mars, Saturn, Pluto in Libra ◆ Jupiter, midheaven in Scorpio ◆ Neptune, Uranus, ascendant in Sagittarius ◆ Venus in Taurus ◆ Mercury in Gemini

Born on the day of a solar eclipse, Prince William has Sun and Moon in Cancer, and is a paradoxical mix of the self-contained and highly emotional, and very dependent on close partners or the public for support. Like Harrison Ford, who also has a Cancer New Moon, he will be family-oriented but able to function as an individual. The fated quality of an eclipse birth is emphasized by the fact that this particular eclipse cycle comes to an end in 2036, suggesting that he will outlive the monarchy, at least in its present form. Despite his teenage shyness, with Jupiter in Scorpio on the midheaven—an inheritance from his dramatically theatrical mother—he will grow into the pomp and circumstance of royal life with a good deal more ease than his introverted father, Prince Charles (see page 141).

194

Mysterious, charismatic Neptune on an adventurous Sagittarian ascendant (which he also shared with his mother (see *Princess Diana*, page 163) gives him an attractive appearance, including rather sexy eyes, which he uses to hide his personal uncertainty. An affectionate Venus in tactile Taurus happily situated in his chart will give him a sunny love of light-hearted social events, romance, children and sport, although as an unaspected planet it will only operate sporadically. He will meet the love of his life when he is around 30 years old.

A formidable group of Mars, Saturn and Pluto gives him the courage and stamina to face a gruelling royal career, with the personal dangers that accompany it. He could be accident-prone. It will make him every bit as violently opinionated and at times hot-tempered as his mother. Falling in Libra, it hints at a difficulty in settling to the domestic stability that Cancer craves. These rather frightening planets squaring onto his Sun and Moon in Cancer hint at a deep-seated resentment of the role thrust on him, which he will have to be overcome before expansive Jupiter can fully flourish. He will have temper tantrums, the result of over-disciplined or thoughtless treatment from the adults in his life. He will feel deeply hurt that his own personal needs were ignored.

There is a strong core of friendship between William and his father, though duty constantly intrudes. It is a rugged relationship, able to withstand adversity, always destined to live through times of great change and the creative birth of a new order. William is stepping out to take a more prominent role after 2003; taking on a heavier schedule in 2006; and undergoing pressured changes in the years after as Pluto moving into Capricorn starts to aspect his Sun and Moon. This coincides with the time his father moves into a lower-profile phase, perhaps hinting at what has always been predicted—that William may take over the throne early. He will reach his peak in the years after after 2012, when he is in his thirties.

1983

The bleak Saturn–Pluto conjunction, occurring only three times a century, continues from the previous year in Libra and Scorpio, toughening attitudes. Pluto also starts the shift into a 12-year journey through Scorpio, having been in Libra since 1970. This is an intense, dark energy concerned with death and regeneration, bringing decay, the clearing out of corruption and sleaze, and an obsessive drive to acquire money. It revolutionizes attitudes towards sex, and brings the focus onto child sexual abuse, and onto AIDS and other sexually transmissible diseases; but it also has considerable impact on attitudes towards money in the 'yuppie' decade. Saturn also moves into Scorpio for three years, adding a note of obsessive caution. Jupiter in Sagittarius in contrast, along with Uranus and Neptune, fosters a high-minded, philosophical and essentially spiritual mood.

Events
The Israeli government is condemned for the Beirut massacre. Violent political unrest in India results in 1500 dead. Reagan proposes the Star Wars defence system for the United States, using satellites to detect enemy missiles. Ayatollah

195

Khomeini declares Islam a 'religion of the sword'. Libyan planes bomb Chad. There is a purge of the Chinese Communist Party. Military coups occur in Guatemala and in Grenada; in the latter the prime minister is killed, and US marines invade to topple the new government, attracting international criticism. A Soviet fighter plane shoots down a Korean airliner, killing 269. An IRA bomb explodes at Harrods store in London, killing six people. Lech Walesa is awarded the Nobel Peace Prize.

Science and technology
The first woman is launched into space. The first successful transfer of a human embryo is made.

Culture
Sculptor Joseph Beuys creates *Untitled Vitrine*. Leonard Bernstein composes his opera *A Quiet Place* and Harrison Birtwistle his opera *The Mask of Orpheus*. The musical *La Cage aux Folles*, created by Jerry Herman and Harvey Fierstein, premieres. Musical hits include Phil Collins' 'You Can't Hurry Love', Duran Duran's 'Is There Something I Should Know?', Marvin Gaye's 'Sexual Healing' and Madonna's 'Madonna'. New books include Isaac Asimov's *Foundation's Edge*, Malcolm Bradbury's *Rates of Exchange*, Anita Brookner's *Look At Me*, Gabriel Garcia Marquez's *Chronicle of a Death Foretold*, Andrew Harvey's *A Journey in Ladakh*, Salman Rushdie's *Shame* and Alice Walker's *The Color Purple*. In the cinema, audiences see Andrzej Wajda's *Danton*, Martin Scorsese's *The King of Comedy* with Robert de Niro, and Bill Forsyth's *Local Hero*.

Personalities born in 1983
Similar to those born in 1982, these are tough-minded, rather defensive and fairly stubborn individuals with a good deal of stamina. With the Saturn–Pluto conjunction, they can be obsessive and at times gloomy, regarding themselves as outsiders. They can withstand great pressures but find change difficult. They have a lighter, brighter side, with Uranus and Neptune in Sagittarius, which gives them an inquiring interest in religion and spiritual beliefs, and a love of foreign travel. This is especially marked since Jupiter is also in Sagittarius, which is high-minded, widely read, rather philosophical, though also occasionally self-righteous. Those born with Saturn in Scorpio after 25 August are serious about money and wary of emotional intimacy. Those with Pluto also in Scorpio born after 5 November are intense, rather brooding and very strong.

1984
The Saturn–Pluto conjunction in Scorpio, although separating, still wreaks a grim toll of violence and intransigent disagreements. Tensions in war zones are heightened, but it also exerts its bleak effect in the AIDS plague, changing the face of sexual attitudes for more than a decade to come, and dragging the wide extent of child sexual abuse into the open. Neptune, also on the cusp of a move for the next 14 years into Capricorn, is an unsettling influence, undermining settled government structures and inflating financial expectations. Jupiter flitting across Neptune before it leaves Sagittarius gives moments of spiritual uplift. The

Brighton Bombing, aimed at killing Margaret Thatcher, falls within the same eclipse cycle as the one that occurred at the Aberfan Disaster, killing 116 children.

Events

There is violence between Iran and Iraq, with claims that the Iraqis are using chemical weapons. Iran bombs oil tankers off Saudi Arabia. In Beirut, the US embassy is bombed, killing 23. There is unrest in India; Sikh extremists are killed when Indian troops storm the Golden Temple at Amritsar. Indira Gandhi is assassinated by Sikh bodyguards; Rajiv Gandhi succeeds. Also in India, the Bhopal chemical plant leakage of toxic gas kills 2500 and injures 200,000. An IRA bomb explodes in Brighton during the Conservative Party Conference, nearly killing Margaret Thatcher. Tamils clash violently in Sri Lanka. There is rioting in South Africa. In London, in the Libyan Embassy siege, a policewoman is killed. Ronald Reagan wins a second term as US president. San Francisco bath-houses are closed to slow the spread of AIDS. *The Yuppie Handbook* is published, defining attitudes towards material success in the mid-eighties.

Science and technology

A child is born from a frozen embryo; another child is born to a woman by IVF using her husband's sperm and the implanted egg from another woman.

Culture

Prince Charles causes controversy by describing the extension to the National Gallery in London as a 'carbuncle'. Luciano Berio writes his opera *Un Re in Ascolta*, Philip Glass his opera *Akhnaten* and Michael Tippett *The Mask of Time*. Stephen Sondheim's musical *Sunday in the Park with George* opens in New York. Pop hits include Band Aid's 'Do They Know It's Christmas?', Frankie Goes To Hollywood's 'Welcome to the Pleasure Dome', Madonna's 'Like A Virgin' and Bruce Springsteen's 'Born in the USA'. New literary and dramatic works include Martin Amis's *Money*, J. G. Ballard's *The Empire of the Sun*, Milan Kundera's *The Unbearable Lightness of Being*, Stephen Poliakoff's *Breaking the Silence* and Neil Simon's *Biloxi Blues*. Wes Craven's *A Nightmare on Elm Street*, Wim Wenders's *Paris, Texas*, David Lean's *A Passage to India*, and *Terminator* with Arnold Schwarzenegger are among the year's films.

Births

Prince Harry, second son of the Prince and Princess of Wales.

Personalities born in 1984

A mixed year, with several sign changes, makes for a varied set of individuals. Saturn in Scorpio throughout creates a perfectionist, over-conscientious streak, with the ability to handle money carefully, but a reluctance to be emotionally open. Uranus in Sagittarius gives an interest in new forms of spiritual belief, and foreign travel. Pluto in Scorpio, except between 18 May and 29 August, is especially intense and determined. In Libra otherwise it is keen to develop new forms of relationship. Neptune in Sagittarius (up to 20 January, and between 23 June and

197

22 November) is mystically inclined; in Capricorn otherwise it is idealistic about money and business. Jupiter in Sagittarius up to 20 January makes for widely read, thoughtful individuals; its influence in Capricorn thereafter attracts money.

Prince Harry
Born 15 September 1984, 4.20 pm, London, England.
Chart: Sun, Mercury in Virgo ✦ Moon, Moon's North Node in Taurus ✦ Jupiter, ascendant in Capricorn ✦ Venus in Libra ✦ Saturn, Pluto in Scorpio ✦ Uranus, Mars, Neptune in Sagittarius

A secretive Virgo, with a rebellious streak of reckless adventure and a need for a peaceful home life, Prince Harry is dramatically different from his more public elder brother. His deeply buried Sun hints at an emotional intensity, a strong need to stay in control, and possible talent in handling money as a career in adult life. A tactile Taurus Moon situated opposite his determined Scorpio midheaven suggests that his father was always the nurturing element in his life, though it can be a sparky relationship at times. Home is where he will always be happiest, and his Taurus Moon will insist that it will be a sumptuously comfortable retreat. With affectionate Venus in social Libra in the chart area of foreign countries, he is likely to marry a partner from overseas, and will meet the love of his life when he is around 23 years old. However, with the Taurus Moon's Node he may find that the aftermath of a troubled childhood makes emotional stability in his intimate relationships a challenge. He can be hugely stubborn, resisting change with extraordinary stamina, which can be a strength in difficult times but makes flexibility in close partnerships hard to achieve.

Dynamic, competitive Mars close to electrifying, pioneering Uranus in exotic Sagittarius hints that he has inherited his father's love of dangerous outdoor sports and challenging travel. He will certainly be attracted to hot-headed friends. Like his brother and both parents, he has strong, outspoken opinions and will crusade for his pet causes without regard for the consequences. The visionary, rather mystical Jupiter–Neptune conjunction just above the horizon when he was born is both inwardly calming and escapist. In time he may connect to its deeper religious meaning, although it can also be addiction-prone.

Disciplined Saturn in over-conscientious Scorpio close to his midheaven, a chart placing shared with his grandmother Queen Elizabeth II (see page 100), will make an executive career a possibility as he matures. Deeply serious about his sense of service, he has inherited the family characteristic of suppressing emotional needs at times in favour of duty.

An affectionate though noisy relationship with his elder brother has helped both through tough times. Harry's public profile will be at its highest through his thirties after his Saturn returns at the age of 29, when he takes on board more serious responsibilities.

1985

Neptune now established for 14 years in Capricorn turns its idealism to practical financial use in the Live Aid concerts for famine relief, although its delusions of yuppie heaven in aggressive stock-market dealing also begin to take hold. Pluto in Scorpio continues to wreak devastation in the sexual plague of AIDS, and to focus attention on child sexual abuse. The May Taurus eclipse aspected by both Mars and Saturn in Scorpio occurs within days of the Belgian football disaster, with 39 killed as Liverpool fans riot. Saturn moves towards Sagittarius in November, taking off the financial brakes in preparation for the Big Bang deregulation of 1986. Jupiter moving into open-minded Aquarius in February promotes humanitarian activities.

Events
President Reagan triples defence expenditure. Mikhail Gorbachev becomes Soviet first secretary; he calls for 'glasnost' openness, and pursues reconstruction. The Polish secret police are found guilty of the murder of a pro-Solidarity priest; violent clashes with police occur at the May Day workers' march. A state of emergency is declared after violent unrest in South Africa. There are coups in Sudan, Uganda and Nigeria. Deaths occur in India as Sikh extremists bomb, and in Sri Lanka as Tamils attack. The World Bank sets up a fund for Africa. The use of 'junk bonds' is pioneered in the United States. There is major famine in Ethiopia; Live Aid televised concerts in Britain and the United States raise funds for famine relief. Rock Hudson is the first celebrity to die of AIDS; to date, 8000 Americans have died from the disease. The skeleton of Auschwitz doctor Josef Mengele is exhumed in Brazil. Shi'ite Muslim gunmen hijack a TWA jet; Palestinian guerrillas hijack an Italian cruise liner, the *Achille Lauro*. An Air India Boeing crashes off the Irish coast, killing 329; a bomb is suspected. An explosion sinks the Greenpeace ship *Rainbow Warrior* in New Zealand; French agents are responsible. An earthquake in Mexico City kills 7000. Inner-city race riots break out in London. The day after the Scorpio eclipse, a volcanic eruption in Colombia kills 25,000.

Science and technology
The earliest amphibian, 340 millions years old, is found in Scotland. In the US, a supercomputer is developed which can perform one billion floating point operations per second.

Culture
Andrew Lloyd Webber composes *Requiem*, and André Previn his piano concerto. Pop hits include Phil Collins' 'No Jacket Required', Whitney Houston's 'Saving All My Love For You', Tears for Fears' 'Songs From the Big Chair' and Live Aid's 'We Are The World'. Julian Barnes' *Flaubert's Parrot*, Angela Carter's *Nights at the Circus*, Doris Lessing's *The Good Terrorist* and Kurt Vonnegut's *Galapagos* are all published. Howard Brenton and David Hare's *Pravda* is staged. *Kiss of the Spider Woman* with William Hurt, *Out of Africa* with Robert Redford and Meryl Streep, and Akira Kurosawa's *Ran* are among the year's films.

Births
Athina Roussel, daughter of Tina Onassis.

Personalities born in 1985
Intense, secretive, rather obsessive individuals, those born in 1985 are over-conscientious about their duties, and rather wary of emotional intimacy, especially those born before 17 November with Saturn as well as Pluto in Scorpio. Interested in

199

unconventional spiritual beliefs, they are also attracted by adventurous travel. Those born with Neptune in Capricorn have a vague and sentimental streak, and are careless about money, but also idealistic. Those with Jupiter in Capricorn (up to February 6) like the good life and are extravagant; thereafter, with Jupiter in Aquarius, they have a wide-ranging tolerance. Saturn in Sagittarius after 17 November brings serious mental concentration, and a concern for education and religion.

Athina Roussel

Born 29 January 1985, 2.50 am Central European Time, Neuilly-sur-Seine, France.
Chart: Sun in Aquarius ◆ Moon, Moon's North Node in Taurus ◆ Ascendant, Pluto, Saturn in Scorpio ◆ Mercury, Jupiter, Neptune in Capricorn ◆ Mars, Venus in Pisces ◆ Uranus in Sagittarius

A secretive, defensive Scorpio ascendant with self-disciplined Saturn close by give a misleading impression to outsiders. Not surprisingly, the richest little girl in the world, daughter of Tina Onassis who died tragically young from an accidental drug overdose, builds a wall round her privacy and vulnerabilities. To much loved half-brothers and sisters, she is a bright, chatty, confident personality, with a good deal to say that is intelligent, sensible and entertaining. To the superficial observer she may seem cool to the point of unfriendliness, but to long-term friends she is exceptionally loyal. She prides herself on her mental quickness, her intellectual abilities, is well-read, and curious. She could become an academic, a writer or, in different circumstances, might have been a journalist.

Her Aquarian Sun makes her friendly and rather detached, although a sense of enclosed circumstances with a hidden Pluto may dampen her spontaneity. She has a hidden, perhaps unacknowledged, sense of being trapped, over-controlled by both parents, who are perceived as possessive. The Sun–Moon square is an aspect often found where there has been a divorce or split of two quite incompatible parents. The legacy for her is never to feel totally satisfied. Her head will pull one way and her heart another. Her tactile Taurus Moon needs constant nurturing. Placed as it is in the chart area of work and health, she could direct her career energies to a helping profession, although it also suggests her physical well-being is more than usually dependent on her emotional happiness. With a hidden Pluto, she will need time on her own to clear out the turmoil of feelings that too much company brings up in her. A passionately enthusiastic, rather romantic pairing of affectionate Venus and dynamic Mars in sensitive Pisces will bounce her back into social circulation after periods of isolation. The Taurus Moon's Node ruling her close relationships hints that settling into marriage may not be simple, though since Princess Grace of Monaco shared the same aspect, she may meet her fairy-tale prince along the way; the real love of her life may not appear until she is into her forties.

With erratic Uranus and careless Neptune in her chart area of finances, money is not a key focus for her. There will, however, be major changes in her situation when Pluto reaches Uranus in her financial house in 2002 and 2003 as she reaches her 18th birthday. At that point she will receive all of her late mother's £2 billion inheritance.

1986

Saturn draws closer to the conjunction with Uranus, which becomes exact in 1988; this is always an indicator of economic swings, and was last seen in 1942, although it has not been in Sagittarius since 1398. Self-righteous religious beliefs hold sway. Neptune in materialistic Capricorn aspecting both eclipses has an undermining effect on financial institutions and government. Neptune is traditionally associated with oil and intangibles like radiation, the devastating effects of which are seen in the Chernobyl fall-out. The April Aries eclipse, in the same cycle as the one holding sway when Martin Luther King was assassinated in 1968, is clearly of special significance to American events, undermining national morale with the *Challenger* space-shuttle disaster. Jupiter moves out of tolerant Aquarius into charitable, creative Pisces in late February.

Events
US space shuttle *Challenger* explodes after take-off, killing seven of the crew. Sweden's prime minister is assassinated. In the month of the Aries eclipse aspected by Neptune, the United States bombs Tripoli after suspected Libyan involvement in terrorist bombing; Brian Keenan and John McCarthy are taken hostage in Beirut; and a major accident occurs at the Chernobyl nuclear power station, with radiation leakage spreading across Europe as far as Britain. Over-supply of oil leads to a slump, with prices down by four-fifths. Deregulation in the London Stock Exchange leads to the 'Big Bang', resulting in wild inflation in the property market. US national debt reaches $2 trillion; there is the largest fall of share prices on Wall Street since 1929 because of fears of inflation; and a US securities dealer is fined $100 million for insider dealing. There is violent unrest in South Africa as 30,000 blacks are expelled from their squatter-camp homes. The Iran-Contra scandal starts to emerge; Oliver North is dismissed. Halley's Comet returns.

Science and technology
The first lap-top computer is produced. The first heart, lung and liver transplant is performed. Genetic fingerprinting is developed to identify crime suspects.

Culture
Frank Auerbach paints *Head of Catherine Lampert* and Lucian Freud *Painter and Model*. Harrison Birtwistle composes his opera *Yan Tan Tethera*. The musical *Chess*, created by Tim Rice, Bjorn Ulvaeus and Benny Anderson, opens, as does Andrew Lloyd Webber's *Phantom of the Opera*. Pop hits include Genesis's 'Invisible Touch', Madonna's 'True Blue' and Paul Simon's 'Graceland'. Peter Ackroyd's *Hawksmoor*, Günter Grass's *The Rat*, Andrew Harvey's *Burning Houses*, Garrison Keillor's *Lake Wobegone Days* and Vikram Seth's *The Golden Gate* are all published. The year's film successes include Jean-Jacques Beneix's *Betty Blue*, Derek Jarman's *Caravaggio*, Claude Berri's *Jean de Florette*, Stephen Frears' *My Beautiful Launderette*, Oliver Stone's Platoon, and *Top Gun* with Tom Cruise.

Personalities born in 1986
Inquiring, rather scientific minds with fairly set opinions, those born in 1986 have wide interests, especially in spiritual or philosophical areas. Rather contradictory, they do not always practise what they preach, and can be

dictatorial. They are idealistic about money and business, preferring to avoid strictly materialistic aims. Intense, resourceful and very stubborn when it comes to sexual matters, they can also be amazingly tolerant, especially those born with Jupiter in Aquarius before 21 February. Thereafter Jupiter in Pisces lends a kindly trait.

1987

The Saturn–Uranus conjunction, not seen since 1942 and not exact until 1988, gives impetus to economic changes, forcing through a restructuring of old institutions, though not necessarily smoothly. It is a jolting, jarring combination, amplified now because of the approaching massive triple conjunction in Capricorn, which signposts the end of the 1980s as a truly pivotal point in 500 years of history. Both eclipses are aspected by idealistic, unrealistic Neptune in materialistic Capricorn. Neptune is traditionally associated with water, a fact that led one British astrologer, Derek Appleby, to write to shipping companies warning of a sea disaster three months before the Zeebrugge sinking. In March, Jupiter moves from kindly Pisces into headstrong Aries.

Events
The Archbishop of Canterbury's envoy, Terry Waite, is taken hostage in Beirut. The Iran-Contra scandal leads to censure of Ronald Reagan for abuse of the law. A cross-Channel ferry sinks at Zeebrugge, killing 187 people, three weeks before the Aries eclipse aspected by Neptune—exactly the same combination of influences as surrounded the *Titanic* disaster in 1912. Iran bombs Baghdad; Syrian troops enter Beirut. IRA bombs and killings continue in Northern Ireland and mainland Britain. In Tibet, violent demonstrations are staged against the Chinese. The Soviets and United States agree to dismantle medium-range missiles. The world population is now 5 billion, double the 1950 level. The Vatican condemns artificial methods of fertilization and experiments on living embryos; the Church of England suggests that homosexuals should repent. A gunman shoots 16 in the English village of Hungerford. The 'Great Storm', the worst in 300 years, sweeps across England, felling 15 million trees. In London, 30 die in a fire at King's Cross underground station. In the Philippines, 2000 are killed in a ferry disaster. The US dollar reaches an all-time low.

Science and technology
The first knee-transplant operation takes place. A South African woman gives birth to triplets from her daughter's implanted embryos.

Culture
Auctioneers Christie's sell Vincent Van Gogh's *Irises* for £30 million, a world record sale price for art of any kind. Andres Serrano paints *Piss Christ*. Pop hits include Whitney Houston's 'I Wanna Dance With Somebody', Los Lobos' 'La Bamba', Prince's 'Sign of the Times' and U2's *The Joshua Tree*. New literary and dramatic works include Bruce Chatwin's *Songlines*, Nadine Gordimer's *A Sport of Nature*, Kazuo Ishiguro's *An Artist of the Floating World* and Caryl Churchill's *Serious Money*. In the cinema, audiences see *Fatal Attraction* with Michael

Douglas and Glenn Close, Bernardo Bertolucci's *The Last Emperor*, *The Untouchables* with Kevin Costner, Oliver Stone's *Wall Street* and Wim Wenders' *Wings of Desire*.

Personalities born in 1987

High-minded, fiery, restless individuals, with a determination to bring changes into their own lives and society, typify those born in 1987. They hold strong spiritual beliefs and seek new ways of doing business or handling money based more on ethics than greed. Rather guilty of failing to practise what they preach, they can on occasion be dictatorial. Intense about sexual matters, they either repress their instincts or can be controlling of a partner's behaviour. Those born with Jupiter in Pisces up to 2 March are charitable and rather vague; those born with Jupiter in Aries thereafter tend to dash in where angels fear to tread.

1988

Saturn and Uranus travelling together in late Sagittarius shift sign in February into Capricorn, joining Neptune there for a major congregation of these three planets, not seen since together since the 15th century. Saturn brings solidity to new agreements, with several ceasefires and the US–Soviet nuclear treaty in place. The economic indicators of Saturn–Uranus are always sharp swings before settling on a new track. Neptune in Capricorn upholds ideals in government and business practice. The combination of all three running through to 1991 portends a major transition period—a political, financial and social meltdown and restructuring.

Events

The New York stock market registers its third-largest one-day fall. Disagreements between Margaret Thatcher and her Chancellor unsettle the money markets. Reagan and Gorbachev sign the intermediate-range nuclear treaty. The Soviets withdraw from Afghanistan. A peace agreement is reached between Ethiopia and Somalia (after 11 years); Chad and Libya end their war; Egypt and Algeria restore diplomatic relations; and Iraq and Iran agree a ceasefire. In South Africa, simultaneous elections to white, black, coloured and Indian councils are held for the first time. In the United States, George Bush is elected president. Benazir Bhutto becomes prime minister of Pakistan. Flooding leaves 25,000 homeless in Brazil; 1 million homeless in Sudan; and 25 million homeless in Bangladesh. The United States bombs Iranian oil platforms and shoots down an Iranian civilian airliner. The *Piper Alpha* North Sea oil explosion kills 167. A terrorist bomb results in the Lockerbie plane crash. The Clapham Junction train crash, the worst for 20 years, occurs. The Holy Shroud of Turin is carbon-dated to the 14th century. In the United States, the Anglican Church elects the first woman bishop. A US stealth bomber goes on display.

Science and technology

Stephen Hawking's *A Brief History of Time* is published. Damage is done to computer systems by viruses and hackers.

Culture
Karlheinz Stockhausen composes his opera *Montag aus Licht*. Pop hits include Bros' 'I Owe You Nothing', Guns n Roses' 'Appetite for Destruction', k d lang's 'Shadowland', Def Leppard's 'Hysteria' and Sonic Youth's 'Daydream Nation'. Rock stars do a world tour for Amnesty International. Saul Bellow's *More Die of Heartbreak*, Gabriel Garcia Marquez's *Love in the Time of Cholera*, Thomas Harris's *The Silence of the Lambs*, Salman Rushdie's *The Satanic Verses* and Tom Wolfe's *The Bonfire of the Vanities* are all published. Major film releases include *Die Hard* with Bruce Willis, *A Fish Called Wanda* with John Cleese and Jamie Lee Curtis, Martin Scorsese's *The Last Temptation of Christ*, *Rain Man* with Dustin Hoffman and Tom Cruise, and Pedro Almodovar's *Women on the Verge of a Nervous Breakdown*.

Personalities born in 1988
Highly individualistic, rather intense personalities, those born in 1988 will turn out to have an obsessiveness about rather narrow areas of life, but a few geniuses will emerge as a result. They are essentially traditional in outlook but with innovative ideas and high ideals. Financial security will be a driving force, especially for those born after 29 March, who will attract money and be forcefully successful. They can be dictatorial, and rather erratic, and do not always practise what they preach. Rather creative, they are practical as well as interested in otherworldly areas, either paranormal events or spiritual sub-beliefs.

1989
The first complete year of the massive triple conjunction of Saturn, Uranus and Neptune, not seen together since the late 15th-century, brings momentous events in the ending of the Cold War and the break up of the communist hold over the USSR and Eastern Europe. This is a pivotal moment in history, whose full consequences may not be clearly seen for decades to come. The Saturn–Neptune contact, historically associated with workers' rights and the struggle for a fairer society, makes its third station on the exact aspect (astrologically when resolution is expected) as the Iron Curtain between East and West is lifted. Pluto continues its own intense course, plumbing the depths in Scorpio, and Jupiter moves from indulgent Taurus, through communicative Gemini and into home-loving Cancer from late July.

Events
Ayatollah Khomeini of Iran issues a death threat, or *fatwa*, against Salman Rushdie for blasphemy in his book *The Satanic Verses*; the Ayatollah dies. China imposes martial law in Tibet. The *Exxon Valdez* oil tanker runs aground, spilling 11 million gallons of oil off Alaska. The South African Law Commission calls for the abolition of apartheid. In China, troops put down a student demonstration in Tiananmen Square, killing 2000. Solidarity achieves a landslide victory in Poland. Hungary and Poland allow East Germans to cross to the West. As the Saturn–Neptune conjunction becomes exact for the last time in November, the Berlin Wall comes down and Gorbachev and Bush declare the end of the Cold War. An earthquake in San Francisco kills 273.

Dissident writer Vaclav Havel becomes Czechoslovakia's first non-Communist leader for 41 years. US troops invade Panama to overthrow its leader, Manuel Noriega. In Britain, 96 fans of Liverpool football team are crushed to death at the Hillsborough football stadium.

Science and technology
A foetus is temporarily removed from womb for an operation. The US space probe reaches Neptune.

Culture
John Tavener composes *The Protecting Veil*. Don Black and Andrew Lloyd Webber's musical *Aspects of Love* opens in London. Pop hits include the Fine Young Cannibals' 'The Raw and the Cooked', Madonna's 'Like a Prayer' and the Neville Brothers' 'Yellow Moon'. In the world of words, new works include Shusha Guppy's *The Blindfold Horse*, Kazuo Ishiguro's *The Remains of the Day* and Amy Tan's *The Joy Luck Club*. Bruce Beresford's *Driving Miss Daisy*, Jim Sheridan's *My Left Foot* with Daniel Day-Lewis, Steven Soderbergh's *Sex, Lies and Videotape* and Rob Reiner's *When Harry Met Sally* are among the year's film releases.

Personalities born in 1989
Intense, rather strong-minded and earthy, personalities born in 1989 have a practical sense about money, and inventive ideas about how to handle resources. They can be chaotic and rather contradictory in outlook, being both traditional and rather eccentric. They can be minor geniuses in their own field, with initiative and ambition. Cool and at times controlling where emotion and their sex lives are concerned, they will demand their own way. Cooperation may not come easily. Jupiter in Taurus up to 11 March gives a taste for the good life; in Gemini until 30 July makes for widely read, chatty individuals; and in Cancer thereafter promotes a liking for a good home life.

1990–1999
The massive triple conjunction of Saturn, Neptune and Uranus—a rare occurrence not seen since the 15th century, and one that spanned the end of the 1980s—continues into the 1990s. Undermining old political and financial structures, it coincides with the end of the Cold War, the dismantling of the Iron Curtain and apartheid in South Africa, and the economic recession that brought the 'Big Bang' 1980s to a sharp confrontation with financial realities. As disruptive Uranus draws to exact aspect with undermining Neptune, Iraq's invasion of Kuwait results in an Allied counter-attack, and the former Yugoslavia disintegrates into brutal chaos. As the Uranus–Neptune conjunction passes into Aquarius in the second half of the decade, the information revolution hots up, and levels of nervous tension are palpably higher. The difficult eclipses of 1998 and 1999 coincide with world criticism of ethnic cleansing in the Balkans, resulting in 1999 in the largest NATO exercise since the Second World War, against the Serbs. Transforming Pluto moves out of sexually obsessed Scorpio in 1995 to shift into Sagittarius, associated with the law and religion. High-profile legal cases dominate the second half of the

decade with the Rosemary West trial, the Oklahoma Bombing trial, Bill Clinton's multifarious legal suits, both financial and sexual, and the O. J. Simpson murder trial. Fundamentalist religious arguments again hold sway. The decade finishes with heavily aspected eclipses in 1999, and the approaching Jupiter–Saturn conjunction, a 20-year occurrence which brings expansive—but not always realistic—new hope, as in John Kennedy's presidency in 1960, and the Prince and Princess of Wales' marriage in 1980. This conjunction falls in Taurus, as did that of 1940.

1990

The second year of the rare congregation of Saturn, Uranus and Neptune in traditional, materialistic Capricorn continues to dismantle old political structures, throwing Eastern Europe and Russia into a melting pot of change, and also coinciding with the end of apartheid in South Africa, Margaret Thatcher's 'iron' premiership in Britain and Benazir Bhutto's in Pakistan. The boom eighties end with financial scandals unveiled. The same triple conjunction aspecting the July Cancer eclipse also spurs Iraq into invading Kuwait, an action that ends in failure the following January as the US-led coalition retaliates on the day of the Capricorn eclipse. Three outer planets in earth signs make for a heavy mood as the financial, social and political foundations of everyday life are shaken. Pluto continues to focus obsessive interest on sexual matters.

Events

After 30 years, South Africa officially ends apartheid; Nelson Mandela is released from prison. East and West Germany reunify. There are riots in London at the imposition of Poll Tax, and in British jails 1000 prisoners riot. The Guinness trial in London, on charges of theft and false accounting, is the most expensive in British history. Leading US junk-bond dealers file for bankruptcy. Margaret Thatcher resigns as British prime minister. In Britain, home-produced beef is banned as a result of concern over BSE ('mad-cow disease'). Boris Yeltsin is elected Soviet president. The USSR starts to fragment into independent countries. Three days before the July Cancer eclipse Iraqui troops under Saddam Hussein start to mass on the Kuwait border; on the day of the lunar eclipse two weeks later the UN Security Council imposes sanctions; the following day George Bush sends US troops to Saudi Arabia; two days later Iraq annexes Kuwait and Western hostages are held as shields at military installations. In the same two weeks around these eclipses the IRA explodes a bomb at the Stock Exchange in London, and murders politician Ian Gow. Hostage Brian Keenan is released.

Science and technology

A link is established between radiation and leukaemia in the children of nuclear plant workers.

Culture

In the world of art Damien Hirst produces his sculpture *My Way*, and Rachel Whiteread produces *Valley*. Hans Werner Henze writes his opera *Das Verratene Meer*. Pop hits include Babes in Toyland's 'Spanking Machine' and Sinéad O'Connor's 'Nothing Compares to You'. New publications include Martin Amis's

London Fields, A. S. Byatt's *Possession*, Ian McEwan's *The Innocent*, V. S. Naipaul's *India*, Thomas Pynchon's *Vineland* and Piers Paul Read's *On The Third Day*. Cinema audiences see Jean-Paul Rappeneau's *Cyrano de Bergerac* with Gerard Depardieu, *Dances with Wolves* with Kevin Costner, Denys Arcand's *Jesus of Montreal* and *Silence of the Lambs* with Jodie Foster and Anthony Hopkins.

Personalities born in 1990
Intensely focused but rather contradictory and unpredictable individuals, those born in 1990 will leave their mark in new ways of handling financial and political affairs. Creative in a tangible way, they have a good deal of initiative, and are restless and resourceful. Concerned with ideals of a better society, they will be high-minded but their actions may sometimes be inconsistent with their principles. Rather obsessively controlling about sex, they will either over- or under-indulge themselves. Those born before 18 August with Jupiter in Cancer are home-loving and rather more conventional; those with Jupiter in Leo thereafter enjoy flamboyant extravagance.

1991
Uranus and Neptune remain together in materialistic Capricorn, a highly strung, enlightening though unsettling combination, affecting political structures and financial dealings. Neptune is idealistic but can also be undermining, and is associated with deception and the emergence of financial scandals. Saturn moves away from the triple conjunction that has had such a profound effect since 1988, but not before the trio powerfully aspect the January eclipse at the start of the Desert Storm operation as Allied forces defeat Saddam Hussein's attempt to annexe Kuwait. Saturn shifts into scientific, humanitarian Aquarius, laying the groundwork for the information revolution to come. Uranus and Neptune will be travelling together for the several years to come, an occurrence seen only 11 times in 2000 years and traditionally associated with spiritual and artistic revelation. Pluto in intense Scorpio in the last third of its 12-year stay continues to project an uncomfortably over-sexual energy into the culture. In September, Jupiter flits from colourful, extravagant Leo into hard-working Virgo.

Events
The US-led operation Desert Storm, against Saddam Hussein's invasion of Kuwait, starts on the January eclipse, ending in defeat for Iraq, although only after widespread oil-slick and oil-well fire damage; Iraqi-Kurdish violence occurs. In South Africa, the legal framework supporting apartheid is dismantled; Winnie Mandela is sentenced to six years in prison for kidnap and complicity in assault. Edith Cresson becomes the first woman prime minister of France. In Britain, marital rape is ruled to be a crime. MI5, the security services organization, gets it first woman head. Pan Am airline closes down with massive debts. Rajiv Gandhi is assassinated. Lebanon hostages, John McCarthy, Terry Waite, John Cicipio, Alan Steen and Terry Anderson are released. Floods in China submerge 50 million acres of farmland in one week after the July eclipse. Mikhail Gorbachev resigns, the Soviet government is dismissed; and the USSR continues to fragment and

officially ceases to exist. Yugoslavia starts to disintegrate. Rock star Freddie Mercury dies of AIDS. Robert Maxwell, British publishing tycoon, dies in a yachting accident; his empire collapses with debts and allegations about the misuse of pension funds.

Science and technology
British geneticists discover the gene in the Y chromosome that determines sex. Charcoal drawings more than 27,000 years old are discovered in caves near Marseilles in France.

Culture
Composer Malcolm Arnold writes his Symphony No. 9 and Harrison Birtwistle his opera *Sir Gawain and the Green Knight*. Pop hits include Bryan Adams' 'Everything I Do, I Do For You', Guns n' Roses' 'Use Your Illusion', Nirvana's 'Nevermind' ('grunge' music) and Primal Scream's 'Screamadelica'. William Boyd's *Brazzaville Beach*, Angela Carter's *Wise Children*, Bret Easton Ellis's *American Psycho* and Ben Okri's *The Famished Road* are published. Joel and Ethan Cohen's *Barton Fink*, Walt Disney's *Beauty and the Beast*, Oliver Stone's *JFK*, Zhang Yimou's *Ju Dou* and Ridley Scott's *Thelma and Louise* are among the year's notable cinema releases.

Personalities born in 1991
Fairly focused individuals, those born in 1991 carry an intense, rather determined energy, especially in sexual matters. Highly strung, inspirational about business and financial matters, yet also erratic and rather contradictory, they are movers and shakers for change. Practical and rather traditional in outlook, they also want to open new doors. They can be artistic, turning ideas into reality, and will do so in a very physical way. Those born after 7 February with Saturn in Aquarius are less frugal with money, are focused on scientific ideas, and have a cool, detached emotional approach. Jupiter in Leo up to 12 September fosters a liking for a five-star lifestyle; in Virgo thereafter it promotes a desire to be of service and a rather workaholic approach.

1992

The highly strung conjunction of disruptive Uranus and undermining Neptune becomes exact in Capricorn for the first time in April as the Serb bombardment of Sarajevo begins in the escalating Balkans civil war. Its second station occurs in December, as the formal announcement of the Prince and Princess of Wales' separation is made. All three eclipses in Capricorn and Cancer were triggered through what Queen Elizabeth II dubbed her 'annus horribilis', with the marriages of three of her four children ending and Windsor Castle substantially damaged in a major fire. Financial scandals continue to appear with the materialistic business connection of Capricorn. The approaching, bleakly tough Saturn–Pluto square adds to the heavy mood. It does not become exact until March of 1993 when the civilian evacuation of Srebrenica in Bosnia-Herzegovina occurs after a year's siege. Jupiter moves through helpful, hard-working Virgo until October, then shifts into sociable, fair-minded Libra.

Events

Croatia, Slovenia and Bosnia-Herzegovina are recognized as independent states. Serb army forces begin their bombardment of Sarajevo; the United Nations condemns ethnic cleansing by the Serbs as a war crime. Economic sanctions on South Africa are lifted; Nelson Mandela separates from his wife, Winnie; and the Goldstone Commission exposes evidence of state 'dirty tricks' against the ANC. In Britain the Barlow Clowes £113 million fraud ends in conviction; the Lloyd's Insurance market in London reveals losses of £2 billion, the first in a series of big losses. John Gotti, head of the largest Mafia family in New York, is convicted of murder and racketeering. There are race riots in Los Angeles after four white policemen are acquitted of beating an African-American motorist, despite video evidence. Hurricane Andrew, which hits the Bahamas and Florida, is the United States' most expensive natural disaster. In France, flash floods kill 80. In Britain, the Church of England votes to allow women priests. The Prince and Princess of Wales separate, as do the Duke and Duchess of York; Princess Anne divorces and remarries. Bill Clinton is elected US president.

Science and technology

Sperm cells are discovered to have odour receptors. The oldest sea vessel in the world, dating from 1400 BC, is discovered in England.

Culture

In the world of art Damien Hirst creates *The Physical Impossibility of Death in the Mind of Someone Living*. Michael Tippett composes his String Quartet No. 5. Pop hits include Genesis's 'We Can't Dance', Whitney Houston's 'I Will Always Love You' and Simply Red's 'Stars'. Jung Chang's *Wild Swans* and Ian McEwan's *Black Dogs* are published. Film releases include James Ivory's *Howards End* with Anthony Hopkins and Emma Thompson, Sally Potter's *Orlando* and Baz Luhrmann's *Strictly Ballroom*.

Personalities born in 1992

Individuals born in 1992 will be inspirational, rebellious, rather highly strung and practically determined to change every settled situation they come across. Rather intense with Pluto in Scorpio, they will control their feelings and sexuality, have a good deal of stamina and will resist pressure. With Saturn in Aquarius, they have good mental concentration and inquiring scientific minds, but will appear cool emotionally. With Jupiter in Virgo, a hard-working, helpful influence aspecting Uranus and Neptune, they will be lucky, travel unexpectedly and be charitable. Those born after 10 October with Jupiter in Libra will be keen on social justice, want good close relationships, and be socially charming.

1993

A complex, challenging year with the jangled Uranus–Neptune conjunction, exact through the first three and last six months, bringing inspired changes and disruptive chaos simultaneously. Although typically coinciding with natural disasters and revolutionary violence, this combination can produce artistic or scientific inspiration, as in the solving of Fermat's Last Theorem, a mathematical puzzle posed in the 17th century during the Uranus–Neptune conjunction in Sagittarius. The tough Saturn–Pluto square hangs heavily over the Bosnia-Herzogovina disputes and elsewhere, bringing misery to the masses as its typical effect. In late May, Saturn shifts into Pisces for a few weeks, its initial foray of an uneasy three-year stay, bringing old resentments to the surface, dampening creative efforts and leading to bad financial decisions. Jupiter in fair-minded Libra until November is pushing for better agreements; sitting beside dynamic Mars in September it is almost exactly in aspect to Uranus and Neptune when the Israel–Palestine Peace Agreement is signed.

Events
The European Community's single market comes into force; the Exchange Rate Mechanism comes close to collapse seven months later. Bill Clinton runs into arguments over his appointees for government jobs, and homosexuals in the armed forces. The Bosnia-Herzegovina crisis continues; Serbs attack Goradze and Srebrenica; civilians are evacuated. The United States launches a missile attack on Baghdad. In Washington, a peace agreement is signed between Palestine and Israel. Boris Yeltsin suspends the Russian parliament and declares a state of emergency after rebels hold the parliament building. California bush fires cause $1000 million damage. In Waco, Texas, the FBI besiege the Branch Davidian cult, ending in the death of leader David Koresh and others. In England, an IRA bomb kills two children; two 11-year old boys are convicted of the murder of two-year-old Jamie Bulger. In the United States, a doctor who performs abortions is killed. British mathematician Andrew Wiles solves Fermat's Last Theorem, a mathematical puzzle posed by French mathematician Pierre de Fermat, when the Uranus–Neptune conjunction was in place (see *Uranus–Neptune*, page 32). A bomb attack in Florence damages paintings. Tsar Nicholas and his family's remains are genetically fingerprinted to prove their authenticity

Science and technology
Genetic samples taken from the Duke of Edinburgh and other relatives of the Russian royal family are compared to prove that the remains of Tsar Nicholas II and his family, assassinated in 1918, are genuine. The first pictures of individual atoms are published.

Culture
On the popular music scene, hits include Phil Collins' 'Both Sides', Meat Loaf's 'I'd Do Anything for Love' and Take That's 'Everything Changes'. Isabel Allende's *The Infinite Plain*, Roddy Doyle's *Paddy Clarke Ha Ha Ha*, Gita Mehta's *A River Sutra*, and Vikram Seth's *A Suitable Boy* are published. Cinema audiences see Martin Scorsese's *The Age of Innocence*, *Groundhog Day* starring Bill Murray, Steven Spielberg's *Jurassic Park* and *Schindler's List*, *Philadelphia* with Tom Hanks, and James Ivory's *The Remains of the Day*.

Personalities born in 1993
Rather intensely determined, stubborn, slightly obsessive individuals, those born in 1993 regard themselves as outsiders. Controlling in their approach to emotional and

sexual relationships, they can repress their feelings, coming across as cool and detached. Sharp, scientific, inquiring minds direct them towards mental activities. A curious mix of highly strung, slightly zany and very practical, they will pursue interesting, eventful careers. Those born before 11 November with Jupiter in Libra are tolerant, concerned with social justice, and keen to make fair agreements in close relationships; those born with Jupiter in Scorpio thereafter attract money and are entrusted with secrets.

1994

The year starts heavily with the intense Saturn–Pluto square exact, always a hint of tough times, running into the US earthquake. Although it is starting to separate, the highly strung, disruptive Uranus–Neptune conjunction is still in close aspect through January, sitting beside the Sun, Venus and Mars in Capricorn when the Southern California earthquake occurs. Elsewhere it continues to unsettle financial and political structures. Jupiter in pushy, resourceful Scorpio makes a useful connection with Saturn in Pisces as South Africa's first non-racial elections take place in late April, and again as Russia withdraws from Latvia and Estonia in August. Then expansive Jupiter crosses power-hungry Pluto in December as Russian troops invade Chechnya.

Events

A major earthquake in California kills 57 and makes 25,000 homeless. Despite a ceasefire in Bosnia-Herzegovina the hostilities continue; NATO launches airstrikes on Serb positions. The European Union is enlarged to include Sweden, Finland, Austria and Norway. Fifty Palestinians are massacred in an attack by an Israeli settler. In the 'Whitewatergate' affair, allegations of improper financial dealings are made about the Clintons; Paula Jones files a sexual harassment case against Bill Clinton; Clinton's healthcare reforms collapse. The first non-racial elections in South Africa result in an overwhelming victory for the ANC; Nelson Mandela is sworn in as president on the day of the May solar eclipse in Taurus aspecting Jupiter and Pluto in Scorpio (his life sentence on 11 June 1964 started on a Gemini solar eclipse, and his release on 11 February 1990 took place two days after the Leo lunar eclipse). Yasser Arafat sets foot on Palestinian territory for the first time in 25 years; violent clashes occur in the Gaza Strip. There is genocide in Rwanda; 2 million refugees have fled, and there is cholera in the camps. The Solar Temple cult is connected to a series of suicides and murders in Switzerland and Canada. Riots break out in East Timor. Russia invades Chechnya.

Science and technology

Hundreds of Paleolithic cave drawings, more than 30,000 years old, are discovered in France. A new species of kangaroo, weighing just 7 lbs, is discovered in Australia. Fragments of the Shoemaker-Levy comet collide with Jupiter.

Culture

Artist Damien Hirst creates his controversial work *Away From The Flock*, consisting of a sheep preserved in formaldehyde. Composer Harrison Birtwistle writes his opera *The Second Mrs Kong*, Peter Maxwell Davies composes his Symphony No. 5, and John Tavener writes *The Apocalypse*. Pop hits include the

211

Beastie Boys' '111 Communication', Blur's 'Park Life', Oasis' 'Definitely Maybe' and the Rolling Stones' 'Voodoo Lounge'. New literary and dramatic works include Shusaka Endo's *Deep River*, Joseph Heller's *Closing Time*, John Irving's *A Son of the Circus*, V. S. Naipaul's *A Way in the World*, Edward Albee's *Three Tall Women*, and Arthur Miller's *Broken Glass*. Among the year's film successes are *Forrest Gump* with Tom Hanks, Mike Newell's *Four Weddings and a Funeral*, Oliver Stone's *Natural Born Killers* and Quentin Tarantino's *Pulp Fiction*.

Personalities born in 1994

Earthy and emotional, 1994's personalities can be radical in their approach but rather conventional revolutionaries, wanting to keep the best of the old and add to it the best of the new. Secretive and rather controlling about their feelings, they will stubbornly resist exposing their vulnerabilities except as a last resort. This is especially true of the cool Saturn-in-Aquarians born before 28 January, who are slightly obsessive and regard themselves as outside the mainstream of the population. Those born with Saturn in Pisces thereafter need peace and solitude to calm their worries. Jupiter in Scorpio up to 9 December lends financial skills and the ability to invite secrets; in Sagittarius thereafter it makes for widely read, philosophical and travel-loving individuals.

1995

The separating Uranus–Neptune conjunction still coincides with natural upheavals, crossing the Capricorn Sun and Cancer Moon as the Japanese earthquake occurs in January. This is a year of major change as two outer planets shift sign, inventive Uranus moving into scientific, high-tech Aquarius for seven years, and fanatical Pluto moving into Sagittarius, connected to both religious and legal matters, for 13 years. The gruesome murder and child-abuse trial of Rosemary West, which rocked Britain to the core, started on an afflicted Scorpio eclipse with Mars close to Pluto in late Scorpio. As Pluto heads finally for Sagittarius, always a hint of fundamentalist arguments, Yitzhak Rabin, Israel's prime minister, is shot dead. The peace agreement reached for the warring factions in former Yugoslavia, falling just after the unstable Jupiter–Saturn square offers uneasy hope.

Events

In a bomb explosion in Oklahoma, 168 die; a US army veteran is charged with the bombing in what, it is suggested, was a revenge attack on the US government for the Waco siege killings. O. J. Simpson walks free from his trial for the murder of his wife after months of televised high-drama court scenes. Rosemary West, Britain's worst woman serial killer, is sentenced to life 10 times over for the murder of 10 girls, including her own daughter; her husband Fred West commits suicide in prison. In Japan, an earthquake kills 5000, and reduces 50,000 buildings to rubble. Israel's Prime Minister Yitzhak Rabin is killed because of his commitment to a peaceful resolution of the Middle East conflict. The Dayton Peace Agreement seems to end the bitter three-year war in Yugoslavia, which has left 200,000 dead or missing. A financial dealer who lost more than £800 million on unsupervised trading is convicted in Singapore. Princess Diana opens her heart on BBC television about her unhappy marriage. A Japanese religious cult releases poison-gas into the Tokyo underground system, making 5000 severely ill and killing 12. The deadly Ebola virus rampages through Zaire.

Science and technology
Windows 95, the new Microsoft computer system, is launched amid great publicity, but initial teething troubles follow

Culture
In the world of art American painter Delmas Howe paints *Liberty, Equality, Fraternity*. The music industry sees the rise of 'Britpop', led by such British boy-bands as Blur, Oasis and Pulp. Michael Jackson's 'You Are Not Alone' becomes the first single to enter the US charts at No. 1. In the world of literature Pat Barker publishes the final part of her regeneration triology, *The Ghost Road*, which wins the Booker Prize. Martin Amis publishes his novel *The Information*, Salman Rushdie *The Moor's Last Sigh*, and Philip Roth *Sabbath's Theater*. The top-grossing movies in the United States are *Batman* starring Val Kilmer and *Apollo 13* starring Tom Hanks. Other notables movies are *The Bridges of Madison County* with Clint Eastwood and Meryl Streep, Mike Radford's *Il Postino*, Oliver Stone's *Nixon*, Nicholas Hytner's *The Madness of King George*, *Sense and Sensibility* starring Emma Thompson, and Kevin Costner's *Waterworld*.

Personalities born in 1995
Those born in 1995 are a mixed bunch of individuals with changing signs. All have Jupiter in Sagittarius, which is sharp-witted, sometimes self-righteous and usually well-read. Saturn in Pisces lends a worrying strain, with a great fear of failure, resentment or regret about mistakes of the past. The Uranus–Neptune contact is highly strung and keen on change but within conventional bounds. Those born with Uranus in Aquarius between 1 April and 9 June are part of the new generation of inquiring thinkers and high-tech whizz kids. Those born with Pluto in Sagittarius between 18 January and 21 April, and after 10 November, hold strong opinions on politics, religion and education. Otherwise those with Pluto in Scorpio tend to over-control their feelings and sexual needs.

1996
Uranus and Pluto now both settle into the signs which will see them into the new millennium. Inventive, scientific Uranus, ruler of Aquarius which is astrologically connected to astrology as well as to computers, communications and global cooperation, is setting the pace for the information revolution with the rapidly spreading Internet and new business technology. Influential, though fanatical, Pluto in Sagittarius intensifies religious beliefs and promotes legal reforms. Expansive Jupiter in materialistic Capricorn encourages financial ventures. Saturn in Aries from 7 April is self-reliant and tough-minded; in square to Jupiter it induces a panicky sense of failure at times.

Events
British beef farmers face ruin as fears that beef from animals with BSE ('mad-cow disease') can cause CJD (Creutzfeldt-Jakob disease) in humans leads to a

ban on British beef in continental Europe. Prince Charles and Princess Diana finally divorce; she gets a £17 million settlement. A bomb at the Atlanta Olympic Games kills one person and injures 100. A gunman murders 16 children in Dunblane, Scotland. A TWA flight explodes after take-off from New York, killing 230. In the southern states of America, churches with black congregations are targeted by arsonists. Violent clashes between Soviet troops and rebels in the breakaway republic of Chechnya end in a peace deal. China stages military exercises in the Taiwan Strait in an effort to intimidate voters in the first free elections. Hillary Clinton, wife of the US president, testifies before the Grand Jury and is heavily criticized for her dealings in the Whitewater affair. The War Crimes Tribunal opens in The Hague to examine atrocities in the Yugoslavian civil war. There is outrage in Belgium at the negligent police investigation of the paedophile Marc Dutroux's involvement in the death of young girls. The bloody civil war in Rwanda results in a major refugee crisis. Swiss banks admit holding Holocaust gold, taken from victims of the Nazis during the Second World War.

Science and technology

The death rate from AIDs drops for the first time in 15 years in the United States and Europe. US scientists announce the first decline in levels of ozone-depleting chemicals in the air.

Culture

In the world of pop music Jarvis Cocker, lead singer of the British band Pulp, makes fun of Michael Jackson during a song in which Jackson mimics Christ. In the United States, Robert Miles releases his single 'Children', a dance instrumental which goes on to sell nearly 5 million copies. Hits include Celine Dion's 'Falling into You', Boyzone's 'A Different Beat' and George Michael's 'Jesus to a Child'. In the theatre, Harold Pinter's play *Ashes to Ashes* opens. The rock musical *Rent* by Jonathon Larson opens the day after its creator dies suddenly. *This Wild Darkness*, American author Harold Brodkey's diary about his experience of AIDS, is published after his death. Novelist Doris Lessing brings out her *Love, Again*, Margaret Drabble publishes *The Witch of Exmoor* and Nigerian writer Ben Okri publishes his novel *Reading in the Dark*. In the United States, the top-grossing movies are *Independence Day* starring Bill Pullman, and Brian de Palma's *Mission Impossible* with Tom Cruise; also released are *101 Dalmatians* with Glenn Close, *Trainspotting* with Ewan MacGregor, *The Rock* with Sean Connery, and Jane Campion's *Portrait of a Lady*.

Births

Lourdes Madonna, daughter of singer Madonna.

Personalities born in 1996

Charitable in a practical way, individuals born in 1996 will use their business skills to improve the lot of the disadvantaged. They are likely to attract money and build up a secure base for themselves. They are intelligent, fast-thinking and -speaking, very much children of the new age, with the capacity to push through sensible changes successfully. Resourceful and self-sufficient, especially those born after 7 April with Saturn in Aries, they have stamina and determination, although they may also have a fear of failure. Those with Saturn in Pisces up to this date are worriers and slightly regretful individuals.

Lourdes Madonna
Born 14 October 1996, 4.01 pm Pacific Daylight Time, Los Angeles.
Chart: Sun, Mercury, Moon's North Node in Libra ◆ Moon in Scorpio ◆ Venus in Virgo ◆ Mars in Leo ◆ Saturn in Aries ◆ Jupiter, Neptune in Capricorn ◆ Uranus in Aquarius ◆ Pluto in Sagittarius

The daughter of the singer-actress Madonna, Lourdes Madonna has a charming, though secretive, Libra Sun—perhaps a hint of an unavailable father—which will make her difficult to know well. With aspects to creative, musical, though also vague Neptune, she may be difficult to pin down. Supremely sociable on the surface with hard-working, warm-hearted Venus in Virgo, she will go out of her way to make friends and family feel comforted. An emphasized Jupiter in Capricorn will attract a large circle of friends, who will always be supportive. Her diplomatic skills, tolerance and practical sense of vision will make her a natural teacher, even a political spokesperson for her own charitable and humanitarian causes, although it is likely that she will scatter her interests too widely when young. Mars in Leo makes her a stickler for perfection, as well as hard-working and keen to be of service, but noisy at times in team relationships.

Saturn in Aries suggests someone who has to grow up young and develop self-reliance early. In aspect to Saturn, she may be reserved about speaking too openly for fear of attracting criticism or being thought inarticulate. Her fear of failure will be stronger than normal. An intense Scorpio Moon squaring onto Mars suggests a fiery relationship with her mother, a formidable, rather possessive Leo. Lourdes will never show she is hurt, burying her feelings deeply out of sight. One comfort in childhood will come from books. With the Moon high on her chart, she is likely to settle in a home away from her place of birth and to enjoy travelling.

1997

A hopeful start to the year, with expansive Jupiter approaching inventive Uranus in Aquarius, pushes the general mood upwards. However, a particularly afflicted solar eclipse in September sees the shocking death of Princess Diana the day before the eclipse, the death of Mother Teresa two weeks later, and in Italy the earthquake that destroys 13th-century frescoes at the Basilica of St Francis of Assisi. This eclipse is one of a 19-year recurring cycle that occurred 13 days before the murder of the King and Crown Prince of Portugal in 1908, and five days before the murder of Earl Mountbatten in 1979; it was also around at the time of Princess Diana's birth in 1961 and that of Queen Elizabeth II in 1926, and in 1961 at the erection of the Berlin Wall and Dag Hammarskjöld's supposedly accidental death (see *Eclipses*, page 248).

215

Events

Princess Diana and Dodi al-Fayed are killed in a car crash in Paris; there is unprecedented mourning in Britain, with vigils being held and floral tributes laid at Kensington and Buckingham Palaces; pressure is put on the Royal Family to be more accessible. An earthquake in Assisi kills 11, injures 100, and damages the Basilica of St Francis and its frescoes. In Britain, the Labour Party wins a landslide victory; Tony Blair becomes prime minister. Mother Teresa dies, aged 87. The land speed record is broken at 766 miles per hour, breaking the sound barrier. Hong Kong, British since 1842, is handed over to the Chinese. Chinese leader Deng Xiaoping dies. In the IRA peace talks, a significant breakthrough is made. In the United States, British nanny Louise Woodward is found not guilty of the murder of a baby in her care, but an involuntary manslaughter charge still stands.

Science and technology

The world's first voice-recognition software is released; it can create written words on screen from continous speech. There are nearly 150 million Web pages on the Internet. The Hale-Bopp comet hurtles past Earth in spring.

Culture

In the world of popular music 'Candle In the Wind' becomes the biggest-selling single of all time after Elton John sings it at Princess Diana's funeral. The Spice Girls become a worldwide sensation, being the first group ever to have their first four singles go to No. 1 in the British charts. Other hits include Wham's *The Best of Wham*, and Bob Dylan's *Time Out of Mind*. On Broadway the musical *The Lion King*, produced by the Walt Disney Corporation, has its debut; and Irish dancer Michael Flatley opens in his own show *Lord of the Dance*, in competition with *Riverdance*, his earlier show. Charles Frazier publishes his novel *Cold Mountain*, and Philip Roth his novel *American Pastoral*. Poet Ted Hughes publishes *Tales from Ovid*, and English writer Graham Robb his biography of Victor Hugo. Top-grossing movie of the year is James Cameron's *Titanic* starring Leonardo di Caprio and Kate Winslet. Other film hits include Robin Williams in *Good Will Hunting*, Steven Spielberg's *Amistad*, Julia Roberts in *My Best Friend's Wedding* and Kenneth Branagh's *Hamlet*.

Personalities born in 1997

Fairly similar to those born in the previous year, they are self-reliant and quite tough. Saturn in Aries makes them opinionated, and Pluto makes them deep thinking. They hold strong views on religion, politics and education and want to convert everyone around them, although with Jupiter and Uranus in tolerant Aquarius they can be broadminded when it suits. They have a lively imagination and are confident about pushing their ideas. Those born with Jupiter in Capricorn before 22 January are resourceful about money, attract security, and are conventional and charitable. Uranus aspecting Pluto encourages a pioneering spirit and gives an interest in what lies beyond reality.

1998

Neptune starts the shift out of a 14-year stay in earthy Capricorn, where it uneasily attempted to bring idealism together with business practice. Now it moves into Aquarius for 13 years, joining Uranus already there and bringing that highly strung, psychologically challenging pairing to bear on a fast-moving world. Aquarius is connected with computers, the information revolution and the breakdown of global boundaries. Pluto continues through Sagittarius to bring its forceful presence to bear on religious differences and legal reforms. Self-disciplined Saturn, for the third year in competitive, aggressive Aries, is a tough, self-reliant influence—the resourceful get stronger. Jupiter is in tolerant, humanitarian Aquarius until 5 February, then moves into creative, kindly Pisces.

Events

Attempts are started to impeach US president Bill Clinton over the Monica Lewinsky sex scandal. The US government files lawsuits against Bill Gates' computer software company Microsoft for trying to monopolize the market. Corruption charges are brought in Pakistan against former prime minister Benazir Bhutto. US and British naval forces threaten to bomb Iraq if Saddam Hussein does not comply with weapons inspections. A bomb explodes outside an abortion clinic in the United States, killing one person. Bill Clinton presents a balanced budget, the first since 1969. Corruption scandals in Japanese financial institutions continue to mount, with the Central Bank being raided. Boris Yeltsin, the Russian president, dismisses all 29 of his ministers, forcing the state Duma to accede to his wishes. A peace agreement is reached in Northern Ireland. The Cambodian Khmer Rouge leader Pol Pot, who was responsible for nearly 2 million deaths, himself dies of a heart attack. In the United States, Theodore Kaczynski, the 'Unabomber', receives four life sentences for planting four bombs over 17 years. Nearly a quarter of a million Serbs living in Kosovo leave, while Albanians return to fight Serbian forces. The nuclear arms race in South Asia escalates as both India and Pakistan detonate nuclear weapons.

Science and technology

The World Medical Association calls for a ban on human cloning.

Culture

In the world of popular music Madonna releases her first album since 1994, *Ray of Light*. Singer Frank Sinatra, who made 1800 recordings in his long, successful career as a crooner, dies. In the world of literature Toni Morrison publishes her novel *Paradise* and John Irving *A Widow For One Year*. A first edition of Chaucer's *Canterbury Tales*, printed by William Caxton in 1476, is bought for £4.6 million by Sir Paul Getty. Among the year's most popular films are Steven Spielberg's *Saving Private Ryan*, *Primary Colors* with John Travolta, *The Horse Whisperer* with Robert Redford and *The Truman Show* with Jim Carrey.

Personalities born in 1998

A rather contradictory mix of the sympathetic and the rather determinedly self-contained, these individuals will work hard to create their own security, without much outside help. However, with Jupiter in tolerant Aquarius up to 5 February, or in kindly, creative Pisces thereafter, they will have a streak of charitable interest in making the lot of the disadvantaged easier. They will also be highly strung, and inclined to slightly irrational views. Exceptionally strong-minded, they will stick to their opinions fiercely, but will be interested in new ideas and high-tech ways of communicating, techniques that will revolutionize the workplace. Neptune in Aquarius between 29 January and 22 August, and after 28 November brings an idealism to humanitarian causes to those born then.

1999

The highly strung, disruptive Uranus–Neptune contact in Aquarius aspecting the February eclipse, then squared by restrictive Saturn in Taurus, sees the Serb ethnic cleansing of Kosovo blow up into the biggest European conflict since the Second World War. The full scale of the humanitarian disaster is seen on TV screens worldwide as the disorienting, undermining Saturn–Neptune square is exact in early April. The high-tension confusion continues through a difficult year, when the July and August eclipses pick up even more trenchant aspects from six planets. From July, Jupiter in Taurus is moving towards a Saturn–Jupiter conjunction in the year 2000 (last seen in 1940), making a combination of four outer planets in fixed signs across the solar eclipse, plus the Sun in Leo and Mars in Scorpio. The August eclipse is of the same cycle as held sway in 1945 around the Hiroshima nuclear bomb drop.

Events

NATO begins an air-bombing campaign over Belgrade to force Serb leader Slobodan Milosevic to stop the ethnic cleansing of Kosovo, but it merely intensifies his efforts, leading to one million refugees being forced across the borders. Milosevic surrenders in June, and NATO ground troops move in. Tensions mount as the Russians attempt to establish a separate sector. Bill Clinton escapes impeachment. King Hussein of Jordan dies. The EURO single currency is launched. The European Union Commission resigns *en masse* in defence against allegations of corruption against two of its members. Indian and Pakistani troops clash on the borders of Kashmir. Prince Edward, the Queen's fourth child, marries Sophie Rhys-Jones.

Science and technology

Monkeys, goats, pigs, giant pandas and elephants are being cloned, bringing the prospect of human cloning closer. The Hubble telescope captures dramatic images of the volatile Moon Io sweeping across the face of Jupiter. The Nobel Prize for Medicine goes to a researcher whose work on proteins could lead to new treatments for hereditary diseases.

Culture

Hit records include Boyzone's *By Request*, Abba's *Gold—Greatest Hits* and Robbie Williams's 'Millennium'. E. Annie Proulx, the American novelist, publishes her short stories *Heart Songs* to great acclaim. Pioneering feminist Germaine Greer produces *The Whole Woman* and novelist Jimmy Boyle publishes *The Hero of the Underworld*. Top-grossing movies include Terrence Malick's *The Thin Red Line*, *Shakespeare in Love* with Gwyneth Paltrow, *Elizabeth* with Cate Blanchett and Judi Dench, *Notting Hill* with Julia Roberts and Hugh Grant, *Entrapment* with Catherine Zeta Jones and Sean Connery, and George Lucas's *Star Wars*.

Births
Phoenix Chi Gulzar, daughter of Spice Girl 'Scary Spice'; Brooklyn Joseph Beckham, son of Spice Girl 'Posh Spice' and footballer David Beckham.

Personalities born in 1999
Highly charged, brightly inquiring, rather zany, and not always rational communicators, those born in 1999 have wild ideas which they cling to firmly. They are explorers of new realms in global cooperation, wanting to put forward idealistic humanitarian attitudes. With Pluto in Sagittarius, they are opinionated about politics, religion and education, wishing to convert others to their viewpoint. Those born with Saturn in Aries before 1 March are self-reliant and determined that everyone stand on their own two feet. Those born with Saturn in Taurus thereafter are careful with money, stubborn, creative and slightly paranoid. Jupiter in Pisces (up to 13 February) fosters sympathic temperaments; in Aries (13 Feb to 28 June, and after 23 October) it produces headstrong, dynamic types; and in Taurus (28 June to 23 October) it fosters an attraction to the good life.

Phoenix Chi Gulzar
Born 19 February 1999, 6.42 pm, London.
Chart: Sun, Mercury, Venus in Pisces ◆ Jupiter, Moon, Saturn in Aries ◆ Uranus, Neptune in Aquarius ◆ Mars in Scorpio ◆ Pluto in Sagittarius ◆ Ascendant in Virgo ◆ Moon's North Node in Leo

Brooklyn Joseph Beckham
Born 4 March 1999, 7.48 pm, London.
Chart: Sun in Pisces ◆ Mercury, Jupiter, Venus in Aries ◆ Saturn in Taurus ◆ Uranus, Neptune in Aquarius ◆ Pluto in Sagittarius ◆ Mars in Scorpio ◆ Moon, Ascendant in Libra ◆ Moon's North Node in Leo

Phoenix and Brooklyn are the first two babies produced by the singing sensation of the late 1990s, the Spice Girls, Phoenix being the daughter of 'Scary Spice' (Mel B), and Brooklyn the son of 'Posh Spice' (Victoria). Born only two weeks apart, both in the early evening, they have relatively similar charts. With outgoing, impulsive Jupiter in their relationship house, they are not going to be shy, retiring individuals, but are likely to share their parents' highly social whirl. They will attract romance, and marry confident, successful partners for love. Both are Pisces, the musical sign par excellence, with the New Age combination of rebellious Uranus and creative Neptune in high-tech Aquarius in the entertainment house of their chart. With determined Mars in resourceful Scorpio, they will be intensely ambitious to make money, although they will be erratic and rather too reckless at

219

points to make for an even course. The hard-working, rather professional placing of their Suns means that doing a good job will take precedence over flamboyant displays of ego. Both will be good at handling joint finances, and could even ultimately move in that direction.

Scary Spice's daughter with Jimmy Gulzar is the more secretive, keeping her fiery Aries Moon in check, and being wary of an overloaded emotional atmosphere at home. Her Virgo ascendant gives her a practical, caring image.

With a Libra Moon on the ascendant, Posh Spice's son with footballer David Beckham will be outgoing, diplomatic, and a calming presence for anyone he meets. His strongly placed Pluto in Sagittarius will make him an intense conversationalist, especially about spiritual issues or pet causes he considers important. Spoiled by his mother, he may tug against his father's control. He will opt for adventurous sports no matter what the opposition.

2000–2009

The expansive, though often contradictory, Jupiter–Saturn conjunction, a 20-year occurrence, starts the decade with high hopes, as it did in 1980 in Libra with the Prince and Princess of Wales's marriage, and in 1960 in Capricorn with Kennedy's presidency and the rise of the Beatles: a new 'messiah' usually carries the over-optimistic expectations of the collective. The Uranus–Neptune conjunction, although waning, speeds on the information revolution; aspecting the eclipses in 2000, however, it is likely to bring major political upheavals and world conflicts. The bleakly tough Saturn–Pluto opposition of 2001/2, usually a signifier of war, is a reasonably regular occurrence. Pluto stays in fanatical, self-righteous Sagittarius until 2008, fanning the flames of religious differences.

In 2003 Uranus starts the move into Pisces for seven years, a rather intuitive, mystical influence. There will be a revived enthusiasm for Eastern philosophies and the workings of the unconscious, new theories of the mind will be discussed, and the exploration of new realms will be promoted. Interest in computer technology will start to wane; doubts about genetic engineering, and about the extremes of medical interference in natural processes, will be voiced.

The Saturn–Neptune opposition of 2006 will be creative, although politically undermining. The approaching revolutionary Uranus–Pluto hard aspect, seen only every 30 years or so, will be felt from 2008 onwards. The last conjunction of this pairing occurred in Virgo through the tumultuous 1960s, the previous square in the years following 1932. This square starts with Pluto moving into Capricorn in 2008, starting a long, slow restructuring of political and business institutions that will alter the face of the capitalist economy. Pluto was last in Capricorn in 1774, when the American Declaration of Independence was signed, bringing a new form of democracy into existence and moving power away from the colonial masters. Uranus does not reach headstrong Aries until 2010, where it was last seen in the 1930s. The exact aspect will not happen until 2012, but is likely to include violent action as part of its effect. In 2011 spiritual Neptune will move into its own sign, Pisces, for 14 years, bringing religion back into mainstream culture.

2000

A tense, challenging year with four eclipses gearing up the mood, aspecting the inspired, enlightening but disruptive Neptune–Uranus conjunction, and squaring onto austere Saturn in Taurus in May. Predictions of economic cutbacks—always a Saturn–Uranus consequence—were fulfilled as the over-hyped tech stocks took a nose dive, wiping out many new start-up Internet companies. The Jupiter–Saturn conjunction in Taurus in May brought temporary elation, but disappointments loomed since most dreams were not backed by realistic expectations. Jupiter moving into communicative Gemini to oppose fanatical Pluto in Sagittarius in September/October boosted confidence but tended to strengthen those in positions of power.

Events

The much feared Y2K bug, forecast to cause a global technological meltdown, fails to materialize. The new century starts like a damp squib. In Britain the celebratory Millennium Dome turns out to be an embarrassing and costly failure. An escalation of the Middle East crisis occurs as the Camp David talks collapse. Bill Clinton's presidency, haunted by allegations of financial and sexual impropriety, comes to an end. George W. Bush beats Al Gore after an astonishingly protracted and acrimonious recount of votes. Zimbabwe slides into chaos as squatters violently occupy white farms and political killings increase. Explosions rock the British Embassy in Yemen and a US Navy destroyer in Aden. The Sydney Olympic Games go off successfully, though the Taliban complains as Afghan athletes are refused entry. Catherine Zeta Jones and Michael Douglas, Hollywood royalty, have a baby, then marry ostentatiously in New York. Madonna marries film-maker Guy Ritchie in Scotland amid great secrecy.

Culture

Stephen King is the first author to publish a novel, *The Plant*, as an e-book, available exclusively on the Internet. Heavy traffic crashes the site. Canadian novelist Margaret Atwood wins the Booker Prize with *The Blind Assassin*. J. K. Rowling's *Harry Potter* successes continue unabated. The film *Gladiator*, starring Russell Crowe, is a runaway success, as is the British movie *Billy Elliot*, about a boy ballet dancer.

Personalities

Highly strung individuals with the enlightening though stubborn Uranus–Neptune conjunction in their charts, they will be inventive though sometimes eccentric and rather contradictory. Not always cooperative, with Saturn either in square from Taurus or in trine from Gemini, they will walk their own road and not always feel obliged to do as they they would be done by. Those born before 14 February will be fiery, courageous, not always realistic but always upbeat. Those born before 9 August and after 15 October, with disciplined Saturn in materialistic Taurus, will be thrifty with money to the point of being tight, and will have a real desire to earn money from careers that are vocational. All will hold strong views on religion and politics.

221

2001

The hyperactive mood recedes slightly as the Uranus–Neptune contact separates, though with a Saturn–Pluto opposition approaching across mid-year and on, the mood is heavy. Saturn moves out of fixed Taurus in April into inquiring Gemini. With Pluto in fanatical Sagittarius across the zodiac, there is bound to be a clash of ideologies, political or religious. Saturn–Pluto creates an obsessive, tough, warlike mood. In exact aspect by August, it is squaring the Virgo Sun in early September when the plane attacks on the Twin Towers in New York and the Pentagon in the USA occur, triggering the US war on terrorism and the bombing raids on Afghanistan. The December Sagittarian eclipse is aspected by Saturn, Pluto and Mars in Pisces, creating a worrying world situation. Saturn aspecting Neptune helpfully brings a balance in charitable efforts. Jupiter moves through chatty Gemini into home-loving Cancer in July, close to the Cancer solar eclipse. Though this only serves to emphasize an over-expansive 3 South eclipse energy. The over-confident 'holy crusading' Jupiter opposition to Mars in early October marks the start of the US/UK war on terrorism.

Events

A major earthquake in Gujarat, Central India, on the exact line of the 1999 eclipse path, kills many thousands. An outbreak of foot-and-mouth disease in the UK, badly handled by the government, brings farming to its knees and effectively closes down the countryside. Trouble flares in Macedonia and the Middle East. Violent anti-globalization demonstrations disrupt G8 Summits in Italy and Sweden. A Nepalese Prince guns down several members of the Royal Family in their palace. Terrorist attacks on the World Trade Center, New York, and on the Pentagon in Washington leave 7000 dead. The US and the UK name Saudi exile Osama bin Laden and his terrorist network, based in Afghanistan, as the prime suspects, and declare war on global terrorism. Anthrax bacillus, hidden inside letters, kills several people in the USA working on Capitol Hill and in the media. The IRA agrees to start decommissioning arms. Trouble flares between Palestinian extremists and Israel. Actors Tom Cruise and Nicole Kidman divorce.

Culture

The British movie *Bridget Jones* launches to acclaim, and the first Harry Potter movie, *The Philosopher's Stone*, breaks box-office records. The Oscars are dominated by *Gladiator* and *Erin Brokovitch*, though Ang Lee's *Crouching Tiger, Hidden Dragon*, and *Traffic* and *Chocolat* also do well. Peter Carey wins the Booker Prize with *The True History of the Kelly Gang*.

Personalities

Strong-minded individuals with forceful opinions, those born before 12 July will be pushy, determined, successful and rather charitable. Sensible with money, keen on building security for themselves, they may also be rather erratic in their relationships, not always good at maintaining a peaceful, romantic mood. Those born after 20 April, with Saturn in Gemini in opposition to Pluto, will be immensely resourceful, with a great capacity for handling crises, though they will always feel themselves to be outsiders.

2002

Saturn in Gemini still opposing Pluto, and aspecting both the June and December eclipses, hints at another tough year, when absolute determination will be needed to resolve intractable political disputes and world conflicts. The eclipses themselves are in a difficult series, seen previously in 1966 and 1984. In the scientific arena, however, disciplined Saturn in sharp-thinking Gemini usefully aspecting inventive Uranus in Aquarius should produce breakthroughs. Jupiter moving through emotionally contented Cancer will shift into flamboyant, extravagant Leo in August, producing a festival of entertainment.

2003

Pioneering Uranus starts the seven-year move into mystical Pisces, bringing with it new art forms, a renewed interest in religion not circumscribed by the orthodox churches, and new psychological explorations of the inner mind; perhaps also explorations of as-yet untapped areas of the world or outer space. Saturn also moves its disciplined focus away from ideas as it heads out of Gemini into emotional Cancer, an uneasy three-year placing, although it does give some practical balance to Uranus's rather erratic attempt to find new meanings in life's philosophies. Jupiter puts on a colourful display in theatrical Leo until 28 August, when it turns its expansive attention to hard work and service.

2004

The outer planets are more settled, with Uranus in creative, mystical Pisces aspecting practical Saturn, bringing form to new religious, artistic or psychological ideas. Neptune continues in idealistic Aquarius attempting—not always realistically—to promote humanitarian causes. The approaching revolutionary, violent Uranus–Pluto square is still a few years away, although the effects spread out over a decade or so. Jupiter will move from workmanlike Virgo into fair-minded, sociable Libra in late September.

2005

The mood is much as the year before, with strongly argumentative Pluto producing heated, in-depth discussion, and Neptune pushing hard, but rather unrealistically, for humanitarian causes. Uranus in Pisces opens up new dimensions of thinking and creativity, while Saturn, having dampened emotional spontaneity for three years in Cancer, moves into Leo in July to exert discipline in financial dealings. Jupiter in sociable Libra has a concern for justice and better relationships; moving into Scorpio in late October it boosts financial ventures and sexual encounters.

2006

Saturn in Leo moving to oppose Neptune in Aquarius in August will produce concern, and a slightly panicky feeling of disorientation. This is a minor rerun of the 1999 aspect of this pair, when massive ethnic cleansing in Kosovo resulted in NATO forces bombing Belgrade, but without the jangled effect of Uranus, now moved out of Aquarius. The difficult September eclipse hints at separations and losses, and is afflicted by a violently disruptive combination of Pluto and Uranus. Saturn in Leo continues to hint at the need for restraint in speculation and investment, and will produce rather sombre movies or books. Jupiter stays in secretive Scorpio until late November when it moves happily into thoughtful Sagittarius.

2007

A betwixt-and-between year, with the waning Saturn–Neptune opposition still arousing worries through February, March and June. Although some years off, the approaching Uranus–Pluto square does give a hint of the violent upheaval it typically brings with it by aspecting both the March and September eclipses and creating an accident-prone phase. Pluto in Sagittarius is dogmatic about religious beliefs, and even in easy aspect to chilly Saturn in authoritarian Leo may give rise to a few sticky confrontations in August. Uranus continuing its erratic course through spiritual, dreamy Pisces will throw up interesting though eccentric ideas. In September, Saturn moves from Leo to occupy hard-working, health-oriented Virgo for three years. Jupiter moves from self-righteous Sagittarius into materialistic Capricorn in mid-December.

2008

This is the start of transforming Pluto's move into materialistic Capricorn for a period of 16 years, gradually altering the face of political and business structures. The initial effect of Pluto is always to dismantle the old before rebuilding, so it can mean difficulties in the early stages; Uranus approaching the disruptive, revolutionary square renders this almost inevitable, but it does not make its influence felt in any focused way until it moves into reckless Aries in two years' time. Expansive Jupiter stays in materialistic Capricorn for a year, bringing a financial boost.

2009

Pluto now firmly in Capricorn is forcing challenging debate about various new forms of government, based on the concepts developed during Pluto's stay for the past 14 years in Sagittarius on educational, legal and religious matters. It will not bring in peaceful changes, but the long-term result should be positive. The Uranian square will inevitably mean a bumpy ride for almost a decade, as rebels and revolutionaries insist on taking action. The old ways will be swept to one side, at times violently. Saturn stays in hard-working Virgo until late October when it moves into socially conscious Libra, but immediately comes into hard aspect with Pluto, always a tough call. Jupiter moves into tolerant, humanitarian Aquarius in January for a year.

THE BIRTH
OF NATIONS

5

Astro-profiles of 35 countries

Countries have symbolic moments of birth—coronations, revolutions or declarations of independence—so the planetary positions at that time provide an astrological chart that reflects national characteristics, specific talents and a pattern of history. During subsequent periods of expansion, turmoil, separation from colonial rule, or natural disasters, the astrological influences (transits) of that time reflect on the country's chart as they would on an individual's.

Finding the exact moment that defines a newly born country can be a problem. It is obvious when a new state is created, such as Israel in 1947, when at 4 pm on 14 May 1948 the prime minister David Ben Gurion proclaimed independence in Tel Aviv. The American Declaration of Independence on 4 July 1776, a profound event on which the notion of the American Dream is based, is easy to date, but controversy rages over the time of day it took place.

In countries with a history extending back through millennia, the moment of birth can be more complex. The United Kingdom has two working charts regularly used by astrologers. The coronation of William the Conqueror on Christmas Day 1066 is set for midday, although there is no historical record, so this time could be inaccurate. The chart used in this book is based on the Act of Union of Great Britain with Ireland which came into effect at midnight on 1 January 1801. The Brazil chart used here dates from the moment on 22 April 1500 when the Portuguese first set eyes on the country, which they then colonized; there is also an 1822 chart for Brazilian independence.

My rule of thumb is to test out the various charts to see which resonate more strongly with historical events and the coinciding astronomical movements. Usually one chart works better than others. However, the uncanny synchronicity of astrology and events often means that highly significant moments in a country's history occur either on the same day in the year, or with similar astrological configurations, despite being hundreds of years apart. The two UK charts, 1066 and 1801, both have Capricorn Suns less than a degree in difference. Similarly the two major turning points in South Africa's history, the setting up of the Union in 1910 and full independence from Britain in 1961, both occurred when the Sun was at nine degrees Gemini.

In addition, there is always the question of which country one is identifying with the chart. Is the real Iran best described by the beginning of the present parliamentary regime in 1906, or by the Ayatollah Khomeini's foundation of the Islamic Republic in 1979? In the turmoil, confusion and fast-moving events of the

Russian Revolution between 1917 and 1922, a variety of start dates are available. These questions and the complexities of changing history make mundane (social) astrology an endless fascination.

The birth of certain modern countries was induced to fit times that local astrologers had deemed as auspicious. Burmese astrologers chose 4.20 am on 4 January 1948 as the best time to celebrate independence, so the ceremonies took place before dawn in bright moonlight. The Khmer Republic of former Cambodia was similarly proclaimed in 1970 by General Lon Nol, who took astrological advice on all political matters. Both charts, interestingly, have Jupiter close to the horizon (ascendant), in theory a lucky influence. The subsequent histories of both countries would indicate, however, that other factors might have been given weightier consideration.

Ronald Reagan's inauguration as governor of California, thought to have been astrologically selected, was set for the unusual time of 16 minutes past midnight in 1967, creating a chart with lucky Jupiter on the midheaven (the career marker); and his presidency started in 1981 with an inauguration timed for a midheaven Sun, a glowing augury. With heavy health aspects, however, this chart might also have raised question marks about safer alternatives, given the assassination attempt and wounding that followed.

Fascinating similarities appear in the charts of connected countries. Both Chile and Argentina have a preponderance of mutable (highly strung, restless) planets stamped in major configurations across their charts. Spain, for so long their colonial master, has a more settled fixed chart, but the same key excitability is also reflected there.

Even at a simple Sun sign level, the astrology of countries works remarkably well. A materialistic, ambitious, authoritarian Capricorn Sun is a reasonable brief description of the United Kingdom, as well as Saudi Arabia. The United States is Cancerian, home-based, keen on family values, and eating-obsessed. Italy, home of opera, art, and not a nation keen on confrontation, is dreamy, creative Pisces. More aggressive Aries countries such as Bosnia-Herzegovina, Zimbabwe, the Ayatollah Khomeini's Iran and Scotland reflect the national identity. South Africa, for so long the archetypal split country, is Gemini, sign of the twins, as is the 1815 German Confederation chart, perhaps a testament to the splits that lay ahead— although the one used here, the 1871 German Empire chart, is Capricorn and equally apt. Singapore and Switzerland, both banking centres, are Leo, a sign astrologically connected to speculation, investment and wealth.

When major upheavals occur in a country's history the planetary transits show, often in detail, the nature and duration of the events. The period of the brutal Pinochet regime in Chile occurred when transiting, subversive Neptune was undermining the key element in the Chilean chart, lowering national morale and creating even more of a miasma of terror than before. Pinochet was ousted when explosive, freedom-loving Uranus joined Neptune to give impetus to pleas for a return to democracy. Egypt, Canada and Brazil all gained independence from their colonial masters when Saturn was moving above the descendant. In an individual chart this is the trigger for a separation from close relationships that have outlived their usefulness, and a step to maturity. When Britain experienced a series of accidents and disasters—the King's Cross fire, the Zeebrugge ferry sinking, the

Hungerford killings, major, high-profile child sexual-abuse cases—Pluto was aspecting the fixed grand square on the UK chart, which includes at one corner an afflicted Mars, a sign of misplaced aggression and skewed sexuality. When the economic recession of the 1990s was ongoing, hitting Britain and Saudi Arabia badly, the triple conjunction in Capricorn was crossing the Sun in the respective charts. The USSR fragmented in the late 1980s, as astrologer Liz Greene had predicted a decade earlier, when Pluto in Scorpio crossed the position of the Sun in the Russian chart. Equally when nations move through settled, peaceful times the chart will not be ruffled by major influences.

The 35 countries whose charts are interpreted in depth here are a mix of superpowers, emerging nations and significant hotspots of the recent past.

ARGENTINA

Moment of birth: 25 May 1810, 12 noon local time, Buenos Aires.
Effective independence for Argentina from the Spanish authorities took place when there was a turbulent contact between aggressive Mars and the Sun in Gemini, opposing a rather paranoid Saturn–Neptune conjunction squaring onto an edgily controlling, emotionally intense Pluto Moon in Pisces. The repressive government regime based on torture, murder and cruelty is signposted by this brutally perverse Mars–Saturn–Pluto triangle. This is the chart of a malcontent nation, with hair-trigger responses, living always on the brink of nervous collapse from overstrain, with almost a death-wish to destroy and tear down whatever fragile stability has been built up. When the Falklands invasion occurred in April 1982, revolutionary, headstrong Uranus was exactly aspecting the volatile, overloaded Pisces Moon. The pity is that there is a depth of artistic talent hidden here, as well as the capacity to introduce radically new ideas.

AUSTRALIA

Moment of birth: 1 January 1901, 1.25 pm, Melbourne.
A Sun–Saturn contact in Capricorn when Australia's independent constitution came into force, aspecting Mars in Virgo and the Moon in Taurus, points to an earthy national identity driven by low self-esteem. The bravado and shockingly direct outspokenness of the Mercury–Jupiter placing in Sagittarius disguises the uncertain confidence of a country, begun as a colonial outpost and peopled by convicts. The conventional traditionalism of Capricorn is here turned on its head into an inverse anti-snobbery, with contemptuous attacks on paternalistic British government. Dynamic, competitive, warlike Mars falls not surprisingly in the area of sport and entertainment. A hidden Venus–Uranus contact hints at a compulsive need to break sexual taboos, an inclination towards perversity, and a rather erratic approach to financial obligations.

BRAZIL

Moment of birth: 22 April 1500, 5.34 pm local time (sunset), Bahia, Brazil.
The moment the Portuguese arrived in Brazil is the symbolic timing for the foundation of modern-day Brazil, which reflects a more solidly based, less frenetic set of influences than exist in Chile or Argentina. The earthy Taurus Sun is close to serious, self-disciplined Saturn and sits across from very controlled Pluto in

Scorpio. There is a toughness here, an ability to withstand great pressures without budging or over-reacting—though Uranus in Aquarius in aspect to both does hint at a need for periodic revolutions and radical change. The counterbalance to what could be a depressive culture comes from the musical, creative Pisces Moon close to Jupiter in the chart area of entertainment, squaring onto sociable Venus in Gemini. That hints at a need for flamboyant display and a love of parties. Mars in Cancer is an emotionally volatile placing, given to dramatic outbursts of temper. When independence was proclaimed from the Portuguese in 1822, transiting Saturn was moving across the descendant, a typical influence for Brazil's new maturity (see *Canada* and *Egypt* below); crossing the Taurus Sun it signified a separation from the ruler father.

BURMA

Moment of birth: 4 January 1948, 4.20 am, Rangoon, Burma.
The moment of full independence for Burma, chosen as auspicious by astrologers, erected a chart with confident Jupiter close to the Sagittarian ascendant. The negative dogmatism of this placing is emphasized by the repressive Saturn–Pluto contact in Leo, hinting at conflicts in the country's belief systems. An aggressive Mars near the midheaven is a fitting reflection of the country's military rulership, which took power when brutal Pluto crossed Mars in 1962. The anti-government demonstrations of 1988 occurred when independent Uranus close to separating Saturn had crossed the ascendant, and both were opposing the uncooperative natal Uranus in Burma's chart. The masculine, materialistic Capricorn Sun is at odds with a strongly placed Moon Neptune contact (as in the India chart), pointing to the sacrifice of women. Aung San Suu Kyi, the imprisoned leader of the unofficial opposition, was awarded the Nobel Peace Prize when the Uranus–Neptune conjunction in Capricorn was aspecting both.

CAMBODIA

Moment of birth: 9 October 1970, 7 am, Phnom Penh, Cambodia.
The timing of the founding of the Khmer Republic was almost certainly set by astrologers. Like that of Burma, it was chosen so that Jupiter was on the ascendant, a theoretically lucky influence. The Scorpio ascendant with Jupiter, Venus and Neptune hints at considerable beauty, charm and natural resources. Like China, with whom its infamous Maoist leader Pol Pot had ideological links, it has a Libra Sun close to unpredictable Uranus, hidden—like the country for so much of its history—well out of sight. A tough Mars–Pluto contact in Virgo aspecting Saturn indicates a pattern of brutal, militaristic repression. When the Communist regime took over in 1975, marking the start of a four-year period of genocide—the 'killing fields' of the country's middle class and intellectuals— Pluto in Libra was opposing the Sun–Uranus contact, causing tremendous upheaval and destruction. When Vietnamese troops left in 1989, transiting Uranus and Neptune had finished aspecting the Mars–Pluto contact, and moving into Capricorn they had started freeing up the Libra Sun, as they moved into direct square. When Prince Siahanouk was made head of state in 1993, expansive Jupiter in Libra was starting to boost confidence as it came conjunct with the country's Sun and Uranus.

CANADA

Moment of birth: 1 July 1867, 12 midnight local time, Ottawa.

The Dominion of Canada's chart, with the Sun and unpredictable Uranus in patriotic Cancer opposite the midheaven, and a highly restless Gemini Moon, points to a country with contradictory needs for stability and constant change. A creative, personally ambitious nation, it can be moody, over-susceptible to insults, and rather prickly. A gung-ho, over-confident Jupiter in kindly Pisces opposite hard-working Mars in Virgo suggests high levels of confidence and—squaring onto Venus in Gemini—diplomatic skills and a superficial charm. But the rather depressive, over-conscientious, hidden Saturn in Scorpio opposing Pluto gives a hint of rigidity, an inability to compromise or open up to deeper levels of cooperation, especially in financial matters. Even the fiery Aries ascendant, which should present a clear-cut dynamic image, is masked by mystical Neptune. When Canada became fully independent in 1982, Saturn was just rising above the descendant in Libra, a maturing influence bringing heavier responsibilities; pioneering Uranus in Sagittarius was triggering the adventurous Mars–Jupiter opposition; and Jupiter was sweeping into a patch of beneficial change in Scorpio. Neptune opposing the Moon points to dissolving ties with the mother-influence.

CHILE

Moment of birth: 12 February 1818, 12 noon local time, Santiago, Chile.

Chilean independence occurred when a highly strung, disruptive Uranus–Neptune conjunction was opposing aggressive Mars squaring the bleakly tough Saturn and Pluto in Pisces, not dissimilar to the Argentinian chart. This suggests a malcontented country with a knee-jerk response to situations, and with strong urges to tear down what has been built up. Were it an individual person, this would suggest a tendency to mental breakdowns, every so often pushing past the point of endurance into complete collapse. There is a scattering of nervous energy, and a deep-rooted scepticism. There are hints of brutal perversity in these congregating planets. Undermining Neptune in Sagittarius was aspecting this grouping while Pinochet's regime (1973–88), internationally condemned for its record of torture, held power; only when Neptune and then Uranus had left Sagittarius was he ousted. The major Chilean earthquakes occurred in 1906, when Pluto in Gemini and Saturn in Pisces again aspected these key planets; and once more in 1965 when the even tougher Uranus–Pluto contact in Virgo opposed Saturn. It is a power-driven country with such overloaded anxiety that finding cooperative stability is difficult. If the energy can be stabilized there is a capacity for producing deep-thinkers and creative talent of an avant-garde kind.

CHINA

Moment of birth: 1 October 1949, 3.15 pm China Coast Time, Peking.

A delicate, diplomatic Libra Sun close to an indecisive Mercury and creative, spiritual Neptune suggests a China closer to the old aesthetic civilization of Ming porcelain and tea ceremonies—but this is fairly deeply buried below the surface. The central planets are all tucked away out of sight, which partly accounts for China's isolationist stance. More prominent in this chart is a shocking Aquarian Moon opposite a power-hungry, potentially dangerous and destructive Mars–Pluto conjunction in egocentric Leo. It carries a message about the ruthlessness—indeed, orgiastic delight in brutality—of Mao's Red Revolution and the Tiananmen Square massacre.

Uranus in aspect to the Aquarian Moon in March 1996 came precisely when China fired warning shots across the bows of Taiwan, trying to make a stand for greater independence. Given the placing of these planets in the chart, China will always blame others for its own intransigence and aggression, a tendency that can only heighten over the next few years.

Transiting Uranus made the first direct aspect to Mars on the China chart in 1999 as tensions with Taiwan mounted, and the NATO bombing of the Chinese Embassy in Belgrade caused national outrage, being interpreted not as an accident but as a direct act of sabotage. Anti-American feeling mounted over the handling of the Kosovan crisis, and a Sino-Russian coalition in opposition to the West was a real possibility. This aspect provokes fiery outbursts and explosive incidents, and would also be connected to the internal suppression of the Falung Dong religious sect.

CUBA

Moment of birth: 10 December 1898, 3.06 pm, Havana, Cuba.
Cuba, set free by Spain in 1898, has a hidden culture, and is highly strung and not always rational in its judgements. A Sagittarian Sun has its natural ebullience doubly buried, both by restrictive Saturn and by its secretive placing, leading to an isolationist stance. Born at the time of the fey Neptune–Pluto conjunction in Gemini—which is mystical, inventive but rather deceptive—opposing a jolting combination of Saturn and Uranus close to the Sun, this is a country of extreme contradictions. Great flamboyance, stemming from four planets in Sagittarius, makes sporadic appearances between times of repression and greyness—the colourful carnival and cigar culture sits uneasily juxtaposed with grey communism. However, with a well-placed Moon–Jupiter in Scorpio, Cuba takes its responsibilities towards the health and well-being of its workers very seriously. A chart with a concentrated mix of fixed and mutable planets suggests a high degree of nervous tension combined with great stubbornness, but little initiative to introduce beneficial long-term changes. The Bay of Pigs incident, which nearly triggered a US–USSR confrontation over Cuba's Soviet missile sites, occurred when Pluto in early Virgo was squaring Venus and Uranus in Sagittarius; this was a time of dramatic upheaval, leading into many years of high stress as Uranus joined Pluto in the mid-1960s to continue aspecting the major planets on the Cuban chart.

CZECHOSLOVAKIA

Moment of birth: 28 October 1918, 12 noon local time, Prague, Czechoslovakia.
A prominent Scorpio Sun was in evidence when Czechoslovakia's independence from two centuries of Austrian rule was established. With a powerful Pluto–Jupiter contact in patriotic Cancer also in aspect, this is a country that wants to fly its national flag with pride, and will push very hard to make its voice heard. But Mars, the planet of direct action, is badly placed out of sight, making assertion difficult. A deeply buried, rather paranoid collection of Neptune, Moon and Saturn in Leo also hints at an established pattern of feeling trapped and

paralyzed by forces beyond its control. The natural flamboyance of Leo peers out only occasionally, pushed underground by fears of too much visibility. Highly strung Uranus in opposition in Aquarius also hints at an erratic history with jolting shifts, attracting dictatorial situations. When Germany invaded in 1939, controlling Pluto in late Cancer was approaching aspect to the Sun, pushing freedom underfoot. In 1948 when the communist regime took over, undermining Neptune in Libra was aspecting the Jupiter–Pluto contact, making high hopes end in disappointment. The bleak Saturn–Pluto conjunction of those early years was repressive, depressive and immoveable. When the government resigned in November 1989 to wild acclaim, Jupiter was back in Cancer lifting national morale, and the transiting triple conjunction of Saturn, Uranus and Neptune in Capricorn was crossing the Czech chart's ascendant, meaning that a complete change of identity was inevitable.

DENMARK

Moment of birth: 5 June 1849, 12.15 pm, Copenhagen, Denmark.

A prominent Gemini Sun looked down on the signing of the constitution of modern democracy in Denmark, giving it a rather detached national identity, producing great thinkers and making it highly communicative but—with Neptune in Pisces squaring the Sun—not always assertive as a nation. A buried, though potent mix of Mars, Saturn, Pluto and Uranus in dynamic Aries suggests hidden undercurrents around sexual and financial matters that run exceptionally deep. It also fosters a feeling that the country has no control of world events, is not master of its own destiny. Truly volcanic below the surface, this is a nation that hides behind its tidy, rather fastidious Virgo ascendant, projecting an image at odds with the psychological reality. Universal suffrage was granted in 1908 when Uranus in Capricorn was opposing Neptune in Cancer and Saturn was entering Aries, all aspecting the rooted Aries planets in the Denmark chart and suggesting that this adult freedom was an unnerving experience. The non-aggression pact with Germany in 1939 was signed when the tough Pluto-in-Cancer square to Saturn, again in Aries, was also touching on Denmark's feeling of powerlessness. When it joined the EEC in 1973, transiting Pluto in early Libra was opposing the country's Saturn, and transiting Uranus in late Libra was in square aspect to the natal Uranus, hinting at a decision which brought real difficulty in its wake.

EGYPT

Moment of birth: 15 March 1922, 10 am, Cairo, Egypt.

Egyptian independence was declared when the Pisces Sun was in aspect to a rather flamboyantly explosive combination of Uranus in Pisces and Mars in Sagittarius. It marks out a national identity that upholds visions and can fight for holy causes, but maintains an erratic course with highs and crashing lows. A fair-minded grouping of Saturn, Jupiter and the Moon in Libra puts ideals before material advantage and provides a determination to find just compromises in international relations. When the British left Egypt in 1956, Saturn was moving towards the descendant, marking a time of maturity (see *Canada*, above) although with Mars close by a fiery parting of the ways was inevitable, with the Suez crisis flaring up immediately afterwards. President Nasser died in 1970 as Uranus in Libra exactly crossed the Moon's North Node, a point in destiny. The Yom Kippur war with Israel in 1973 occurred when Pluto in early Libra and Saturn in Cancer—a tough combination—were triggering the same important point in the Egypt chart, suggesting a fight for a decent settlement of the long-running dispute. When President Anwar Sadat was killed in 1981, the assassination-prone conjunction of Jupiter and Saturn in Libra was in place, aspecting the same points.

EIRE
Moment of birth: 24 April 1916, 12.25 pm, Dublin, Ireland.
The Easter Rising chart, which is symbolic of the determination for full independence, has an earthy Taurus Sun at the midheaven, fitting for the home of the livestock and horse-racing industry, and for a nation that expresses its sentiments in song. A communicative, impulsive Jupiter in Aries hints at the need to speak to an audience through literature, aspecting a hidden, dreamy Neptune in Cancer which promotes creative talents—although it can also suggest a tendency to drink or drug addiction through Neptune's need to escape the dull realities of everyday existence. The Irish poet W. B. Yeats's Nobel Prize was awarded in 1923 when Saturn in Libra was aspecting Neptune, giving tangible form to artistic talents. When Irish novelist and dramatist Samuel Beckett won his Nobel Prize in 1969, Jupiter in Libra was exactly aspecting Neptune again. The pivotal, explosive Mars–Uranus opposition sitting across the chart, the inheritance of the country's rebellious rise to independence, gives a fiery intolerance of interference in Irish home affairs. Eire's entry into the EEC, which proved a major financial boost, came in 1973 when Jupiter in Capricorn was heading to cross the rather down-trodden Moon, providing a feeling of comfort.

EUROPEAN ECONOMIC COMMUNITY (EEC)
Moment of birth: 1 January 1958, 12 midnight central European time, Brussels.
The EEC came into existence when a grand square of rather extravagant planets were in opposition and in square aspect to each other in fixed signs. Venus, a Taurus Moon, Neptune close to Jupiter and erratic Uranus, suggest a tendency to lavish expenditure and a deep-rooted resistance to change. The Moon's Node in resourceful, though possessive Scorpio in the financial chart area also hints at a reluctance to face up to limits on personal expenditure—someone else will always foot the bill. The materialistic, earthy Capricorn Sun opposite the midheaven is fitting for a organization that is largely agriculturally based. The hidden, controlling Pluto gives testament to the degree of power wielded behind the scenes, even on occasion subversively. The continuing fierce inter-community wrangling in debate is unsurprising with a resentful, irritable collection of Mars, Saturn and Mercury in hot-headed Sagittarius. When the Commissioners resigned *en masse* in the face of corruption allegations in March 1999, Uranus had just touched base that day exactly on the final point of the grand square, bringing to a climax a process of pressure for change, which had started four years earlier as Uranus made its initial contact. With undermining Neptune in place, the next decade does not augur well for financial robustness.

FRANCE

Moment of birth: 21 September 1792, 3.30 pm, Paris.

Present-day France was born out of revolution, so unsurprisingly it has a tumultuous chart pivoted on vengeful, ambitious Mars in Scorpio driven by a disruptive Uranus–Pluto opposition. Paradoxically a very fixed chart, it suggests a nation stubbornly aggressive, resistant to change and rather volatile. Essentially secretive, it does not bend easily to cooperative ventures, preferring—with Uranus in the area of foreign relations and partnerships—to strike an independent stance. Saturn, ruling communications, points to a respect for privacy in the face of an invasive press, and a reluctance to learn other foreign languages. The Saturn–Jupiter–Neptune opposition promotes charitable and creative enterprises, although it also reveals a deep fear of failure. The flamboyant Moon at the midheaven symbolizes rule by the people and a reverence for the feminine. A passionately intense Virgo Sun close to sociable Venus in Libra is undoubtedly at the root of the French reputation for sexy charm.

GERMANY

Moment of birth: 1 January 1871, 12 midnight local time, Berlin.

The effective start of the German Empire in 1871 occurred at a point when unpredictable Uranus and the Moon's North Node were close to the midheaven, suggesting a country whose direction would always be erratic and at times directionless, subject to great highs and crashing lows. Four planets in materialistic Capricorn, including the Sun and depressive, disciplined Saturn sitting opposite, point to a territorially proud nation for whom the fatherland, both feared and revered, is the key to self-esteem and identity. A deeply buried, controlling Pluto in Taurus close to the Taurus Moon represses the feminine, but resorts to underhand, perhaps occult methods of manipulation to gain power. Like the United Kingdom, Germany has a misleading, fair-minded Libra ascendant. The image is well polished, but it hides a belligerent Mars above the horizon and a deceptive Neptune opposing, hinting at lack of commitment to joint agreements. When the First World War started in 1914, expansive Jupiter and explosive Uranus in Aquarius were aspecting the key power planet Pluto in Taurus, arousing megalomaniac hopes; but the Saturn–Pluto conjunction heading into early Cancer opposing the Capricorn planets should have been a pointer to the brutal realities of a destructive war ahead. In 1918, Saturn in late Leo had been restraining Pluto for some time, and undermining Neptune was close to the Moon. Over the initial two-year euphoric start to the Second World War the massive Saturn–Uranus–Jupiter triple conjunction in Taurus was in place, crossing the German chart's Moon–Pluto conjunction.

INDIA

Moment of birth: 15 August 1947, 12 midnight, Delhi.

India did not achieve independence with Pakistan from the British at an auspicious time. The intensely heavy Saturn–Pluto conjunction, always an indicator of brutal times, misery for the masses, and a hard struggle, sits on top of Venus and the Sun in Leo, damping down a good deal of natural spontaneity. This is a country made for tough times, with massive internal communication problems, deep resistance to change, low self-esteem, and awesome fortitude. A highly subjective chart suggests

233

an inward-looking nation, rooted in the traditions of the masses and opposing the government. Confident Jupiter in the area of health and the civil service hints at the Indian skills in those professions. With no earth signs at all, there is in general, however, a lack of realism and little understanding of the virtue of structures, either political or industrial. A fiery, enterprising Mars–Uranus contact will promote wild, daring financial schemes but finding long-term security is difficult. In the troubled years of the Pakistan clashes in the mid-1960s just after the death of Nehru, India's first prime minister, unrealistic Neptune in Scorpio was undermining the nation's morale and affecting its sense of judgement. (Saturn was in the same place in Scorpio 20 years later when Indira Gandhi was assassinated in 1984.)

IRAN

Moment of birth: 1 April 1979, 3 pm, Tehran.
The Islamic Republic was proclaimed after the overthrow of the Shah of Iran by Ayatollah Khomeini in 1979 at a time of day when the energetic Aries Sun was in the chart area relating to religion. The nation's identity is thus formed around its belief system. Jupiter just above the horizon hints at an inner peace, although a deeply buried Mars–Mercury in Pisces points to an intensity of feeling, an aggressiveness where finances are concerned, a need to control sexuality, and a tendency to be involved in violent activities. When the Iran–Iraq war started in 1980 and the United States imposed trade sanctions over American hostages, Mars was then transiting out of hiding across the Iraq ascendant, creating a trigger point for confrontations. The position of Pluto accentuates an obsessive need to control communications, making official announcements self-righteous, and a lack of openness to negotiation.

IRAQ

Moment of birth: 23 August 1921, 6 am, Baghdad.
The new state of Iraq was set up in 1921 when the Sun, Mercury, Neptune and Mars were in Leo, a flamboyant, publicity-seeking combination. Noisy displays of theatrical rhetoric are to be expected, although paradoxically, since these planets are mainly hidden, there is much that goes on at a subversive level. Disruptive Uranus in the area of foreign relations further suggests an isolationist stance, with a wilful refusal to cooperate. The Aries Moon aspecting the Leo planets contributes to hot-headed, ill-prepared reckless actions. When, in 1958, the military coup occurred that set up the Republic of Iraq, Uranus then in Leo was crossing Mars, an explosive combination. At the invasion of Kuwait in August 1990, the powerful Leo solar eclipse aspected by a brutally ruthless Mars–Pluto connection fell in exactly the same astronomical position.

ISRAEL

Moment of birth: 14 May 1948, 4 pm, Tel Aviv.
Born in the midst of a brutally difficult period of the post-war years, and with a Mars–Saturn–Pluto conjunction close to its Leo Moon and squaring its Taurus Sun, Israel was never going to have an easy ride. There seem only two choices possible out of this chart—annihilate or be annihilated, be the victim or be the aggressor. A tremendous spirit of fortitude and determination, and huge resources

234

for periods of continuing crisis—Israel has all these in abundance. But whether she has the capacity for peace is questionable, or indeed a capacity for real transformation. Too many fixed planets, including Taurus, are always indicators of extreme resistance to change, like oak trees that blow down in a hurricane rather than bend. A new seven-year phase of unrest began in April 1996, as Uranus first opposed the four- degree Leo Moon on the chart and Israel launched an attack on Beirut in retaliation against Hezbollah terrorists.

ITALY

Moment of birth: 17 March 1861, 12 midnight Turin, Italy.
A highly creative meeting of the Sun, Neptune, Mercury and Venus were in musical, compassionate Pisces at the unification of Italy. High aspirations marked by a flamboyant, extravagant Jupiter in Leo promote wild courses of action without the practical capabilities to back them up. Essentially adaptable, rather restless, vague to the point of evasion about its national identity, Italy is a country with deep passions and no strong sense of direction. The Piscean paralysis accentuated by a Saturn opposition and a Capricorn Node suggest a lack of real masculine strength. An immensely powerful Mars–Pluto–Moon contact in Taurus makes the mother complex profound because of the intense Moon aspects; and the brutality of Mars–Pluto laid the foundations for the dictatorial Fascist movement. When Italy surrendered unconditionally in September 1943 and Mussolini fell from power, Pluto then in Leo was exactly in mathematical aspect pulling away the control and the power base. Uranus also at eight degrees Gemini had come full circle from 1861, landing on the chart point of Italy's wayward international relations.

JAPAN

Moment of birth: 11 February 1889, 12 noon, Tokyo.
The chart for modern Japan, with its detached, scientific Aquarius Sun prominently displayed, suggests a nation for whom a good reputation and an elevated rulership are vital to self-esteem. With Saturn in Leo sitting in opposition, a desperate will to succeed is guaranteed. Failure—the great fear—is not tolerated in this essentially paternalistic, Saturnine society, since it means annihilation of identity. This core aspect was being triggered by transiting Saturn and Uranus in late Taurus when Japan bombed Pearl Harbor in December 1941. Fortunate Jupiter in materialistic Capricorn falls in the area of business finances and international finance. The feminine signified by the Cancer Node is the unknown, a challenge too far. The mystical, creative, scandal-prone, disintegrating Neptune–Pluto conjunction emphasizes secret societies with an occult leaning, and subversive activities.

JORDAN

Moment of birth: 25 May 1946, 12 noon, Amman, Jordan.
A lively though restless Sun–Uranus contact in Gemini when Jordan's independence was declared could have indicated a country unable to settle and riven by dispute, but Jupiter and Neptune in Libra added a compassionate, visionary note. It is a nation driven by high ideals, with all of Gemini's flexibility to handle the constantly shifting maelstrom of Middle East politics. The sensitive

Pisces Moon governing foreign relations further emphasizes the softly softly approach to diplomacy. Not inherently strong or competitive, and with an inherent uncertainty of direction, when under King Hussein (a Scorpio) Jordan looked to smooth the rough edges. The brutally tough Mars–Pluto conjunction in Leo in the chart is deeply hidden, so behind-the-scenes plotting, manoeuvring, and keeping contact with dangerous allies was possible. Falling directly on this point in August 1990 when Iraq invaded Kuwait was a particularly malefic Leo solar eclipse aspected by Pluto and Mars. It aroused Jordan's deepest fears and led to Hussein's desperate negotiating stance. Disruptive Uranus was transiting opposite this same point when Hussein died after a long fight against cancer in February 1999, bringing to the surface massive grief and revealing the struggles for supremacy within the Royal Family, previously hidden from view.

LIBYA

Moment of birth: 24 December 1951, 12 midnight, Tripoli, Libya.
A strongly cardinal chart at independence in 1951 stamps Libya as an initiative-taker, a nation constantly seeking confrontational situations to whet its competitive appetite. A brutally perverse and explosive combination of Mars, Saturn, Neptune and Uranus, stoked up by the religious zeal of Jupiter in Aries, is a potent mix. Rashly impulsive actions are common in the name of a crusading cause. Libya has the capacity to destabilize but also to be a radical reformer for the good. The fourth-house Capricorn Sun, connected to roots and the land, suggests a country where home, agriculture and inner security are important. When Gaddafi staged his 1969 coup to declare a republic, revolutionary Uranus was squaring this Sun, causing sudden disruptions. When the United States bombed Tripoli in April 1986 in response to suspected Libyan terrorist activities, Neptune in Capricorn was undermining the holy-crusader Jupiter. The eight years following, marked by the triple conjunction in Capricorn, were the most devastating in Libya's history.

MONACO

Moment of birth: 9 May 1949, 12 noon, Monte Carlo.
A Sun–Mars–Venus conjunction in Taurus on the accession of Prince Rainier III hints at a country whose present identity is focused passionately on hedonism, entertainment and keeping up a charming exterior. The acquisition of wealth and hoarding of securities are key goals with the strong Taurean energy, as is a strong resistance to change. Heavier influences from Saturn and Pluto hint at an undercurrent of ruthlessness and contact with a darker agenda, maybe an attraction for dangerous liaisons. Obsessive secrecy about certain political or financial matters suggests a country that, despite its high-society image, is isolationist and an outsider in the European framework. The fair-minded, sociable Libra Moon close to delusional, subversive Neptune emphasizes a country that wishes to be seen as an ideal state, but much is illusion. When Princess Grace, a feisty Scorpio who held much of the dream in place, was killed in a car crash in September 1982, the transiting Saturn–Pluto conjunction then in Libra was aspecting the Moon, Neptune and the Moon's Node, an indicator of a brutal change in fortunes and public perception.

NEW ZEALAND

Moment of birth: 17 January 1853, 12 midnight, Wellington, New Zealand.

Another land-based, agriculturally oriented country, New Zealand became self-governing when an earthy Sun–Mars conjunction in Capricorn occurred opposite the midheaven. An essentially masculine, inward-looking culture, it prides itself on hard work and modest values. A lucky Jupiter well-placed in Sagittarius hints at an ease with money although—aspecting Neptune—not always at realistic levels of spending. A loaded sixth house, connected to health and service, points to an emphasis on these areas, with a good deal of control in evidence. This is a secretive nation, with a Scorpio ascendant putting up defensive barriers to outsiders. Saturn opposite can make the country appear rather off-putting, but it prides itself on its loyalty to long-time partners. A fire and earth chart, with only one water sign and no air, points to steam-rollering energy, with little interest in self-reflection or emotional sentimentality. The Saturn–Uranus conjunction in Taurus lends an impetus to inventive schemes that are practical and pioneering.

SAUDI ARABIA

Moment of birth: 15 January 1902, 3.45 am (dawn), Riyadh, Saudi Arabia.

The modern Saudi Empire in 1902 began when an expansive Jupiter–Saturn conjunction sat close to the Sun in Capricorn on the horizon (ascendant), a fitting description for an austere, male-dominated country with a talent for money-making. It indicates an erratic history of highs and lows; and also a contradictory national need for austerity as well as lavish indulgence. Venus and the Pisces Moon both in the chart's financial area doubly emphasize the extravagant spending that was obvious during high world oil prices. A sharply and aggressively outspoken Mars–Mercury contact, prominently placed, suggests a strong policy of reacting against interference and a refusal to compromise or have cultural customs criticized. The Moon's North Node close to the midheaven suggests a lack of long-term direction. Heavyweight Pluto falls in the chart area of speculation and enjoyment, close to oil-related Neptune. The critical moment for the Saudi economy came after the boom 1970s and early 1980s, when the transiting triple conjunction of Saturn, Uranus and Neptune, together in Capricorn from 1988, started to cross the key Capricorn planets in the Saudi chart.

SINGAPORE

Moment of birth: 9 August 1965, 4.15 pm, Singapore.

Full independence for Singapore came at the height of the tumultuous Uranus–Pluto conjunction in Virgo with Venus close by in this employment-oriented sign. This is a nation keen to revolutionize working practices, utilize the best of the new high-technology ruled by Uranus, and to improve education. Well-placed Jupiter in Gemini suggests a good national health and work record, though also a tendency to be too restless in trying everything at once. The disciplined Capricorn Moon on the ascendant also emphasizes the virtues of labour over indulgence. But the main driving force of the chart—the deeply buried Leo Sun in the chart area of joint finances—points to a strong interest and ability in banking and the handling of investments. Mars at the midheaven reinforces the image of a competitive country ambitious to succeed, though also fair-minded about agreements.

SOUTH AFRICA

Moment of birth: 31 May 1910, 12 noon, Pretoria.

Fittingly the Sun, close to Mercury, was in the split-personality sign of Gemini when the Union of South Africa came into being, and again when the republic was founded in 1961. The 1910 chart with Pluto at the midheaven suggests a nation ruled by a secretive, power-hungry government, where image belies the reality. A violent, explosive Uranus, Mars and Neptune opposition stamps a disruptive pattern on future lifestyle, laying the ground for terrorism and repression. These potentially destructive influences are channelled into a deeply buried Venus and Saturn in the area of international finances, pointing to an ability to hoard money, to handle reserves, even to dig up wealth. In the turbulent years of dismantling apartheid post-1990, the massive triple conjunction of Saturn, Uranus and Neptune in Capricorn—a once-every-700-year occurrence— was forcing through abrupt change and releasing democracy in an atmosphere of disorientation, anger and panic.

SPAIN

Moment of birth: 19 January 1479, 12 noon, Madrid, Spain.

A sociable, communicative Aquarian Sun, with three planets, including the Moon, in flamboyant Sagittarius, with an expansive Jupiter close to the sensuous Taurus ascendant, describe one part of the Spanish national identity. But a repressive, militaristic Mars–Saturn opposition squaring onto the Moon (echoed even more violently on the Argentinian and Chilean charts) tells the rest of the tale, of a heavier, darker streak in the national psyche. For three years from 1936, the transiting Neptune-in-Virgo opposition to Saturn in Pisces aspecting these planets, coincided with the brutal Spanish Civil War and the start of the Franco dictatorship. When Franco died in 1975, Saturn in Leo crossing the Moon's Node marked a point in destiny and, opposing the Aquarian Sun, a separation from the father, while Neptune in Sagittarius hinted at a panicky start to the new monarchy.

SWITZERLAND

Moment of birth: 1 August 1291, 11.25 am, Altdorf, Switzerland.

Five planets, including the Sun and enterprising Mars and Jupiter, fell in Leo, the sign ruling speculation and financial gain, when the Swiss Confederation formally began in 1291. The nation is less spectacularly flamboyant than this suggests because of hidden, power-hungry Pluto sitting across the zodiac in Aquarius. But all the Leo attributes of pride in reputation, obstinacy and love of money are there along with an obsessive Plutonic need for secrecy and control. When the scandal of the Holocaust gold illegally kept by Swiss banks emerged in 1997, transiting Pluto was then squaring Mars, dragging the underlying criminal behaviour out into the open against massive resistance. Saturn in Aries points to respect for the work ethic, a pride in self sufficiency and a lack of sympathy for the have-nots. This is mitigated slightly by a compassionate Moon–Neptune contact in fair-minded Libra. The Moon's Node in Leo at the midheaven suggests a lack of direction, or a reluctance on the part of the Swiss government to take a decisive leadership role in international affairs.

UNITED KINGDOM

Moment of birth: 1 January 1801, 12 midnight local time, London.

This chart is taken from the moment when Ireland joined Scotland, Wales and England to form the United Kingdom. It is dominated by an unusual grouping of planets in fixed signs in opposition and at square aspect to each other, known as a grand cross, indicating extreme stubbornness, a bull-headed, rather possessive approach to life and an inability to compromise or share with others. There is awesome stamina, courage and perseverance here, but a rigidity as well. Britons are deeply resistant to change, more intolerant than their soft-spoken Libra ascendant suggests, and given at times in their history to dictatorial behaviour.

The fourth-house Capricorn Sun, connected in an individual chart to home matters, here—in 'mundane' (countries') astrology—denotes that land and agriculture are vital to the nation's identity. Heritage, roots and family lineage are also valued. With social-climbing Capricorn as the national emblem, class was always going to be an issue. The work ethic is strong though impractical Neptune in the chart area of money suggests that financial mismanagement is more rife than Britons wish to admit.

The Moon in Cancer close to the midheaven, which here represents the government and the ruling classes, is apposite for a country so often led by mother figures (Queens Elizabeth I and II, Queen Victoria). Close by is Jupiter in Leo, which adores pomp, pageantry and historical drama.

In the UK's chart, the central grand cross, which denotes restriction and limitation, internal dissent and discord, hints at the need for a strong sense of purpose and compassion. It is in fixed signs, the most trying and testing cross to bear, describing a country with little emotional flexibility and harbouring a great deal of frustration and intolerance. Though dictatorial behaviour is the downside of this cross, there is also inner strength and the capacity to act as a stabilizing anchor for others. The UK's central fixed grand cross involves:

- Neptune in Scorpio in the second house (relating to money): idealistic, careless, sentimental, confused, in the chart area of personal finances, banking and the economy.
- Venus in Aquarius in the fifth house (relating to entertainment and financial speculation): pleasure-seeking, strong theatrical sense, extravagant speculation.
- Mars in Taurus in the eighth house (relating to international finances and sexual attitudes): strong desire for money and possessions, compulsion to control other people's money, deeply buried anger, resentment, vindictiveness, desire for revenge cloaked in secrecy, powerful sex drive though also deeply secretive; explosive when provoked.
- Mars aspected by Saturn, Neptune and Venus would suggest a skewed sexuality that has difficulty finding normal, healthy outlets. It is a sadistic culture at heart which has been sublimated into a strong military ethic.
- Saturn in Leo in the 11th house (relating to goverment institutions, the legislature, civil service, and long-term planning): compulsive drive for recognition and importance, dogmatic, professional interest in education, in financial or showbusiness management, responsible in friendship, loyal though stand-offish.

239

◆ Uranus on the ascendant and the Moon's North Node in the seventh house: preference to stand alone rather than fit into relationships which demand flexibility and compromise.

Like Russia, the United Kingdom experienced the years of Pluto in Scorpio (1983–95) as ones of turmoil, when old structures were torn down. Uranus and then Neptune moved into fixed Aquarius in the late 1990s rattling the foundations of British life and cracking the fabric of the constitution. These high-tension, jarring changes continue until 2003. Thereafter Neptune creates an undermining few years of low morale, lack of direction and financial panic.

THE UNITED NATIONS

Moment of birth: 24 October 1945, 4.45 pm, Washington DC.
The 50-nation agreement after the Second World War which became the United Nations was ratified at a time when a charitable, idealistic group of Neptune, Venus, Jupiter and Chiron (astrologically connected to healing) were together in socially conscious Libra in the chart area of medicine and service. Health has been one of the successes of the United Nations, which, with a Scorpio Sun, can be resourcefully determined, though a Pluto in Leo square to the Sun does put a paralyzing hold on the decision-making process. An awkward Mars–Saturn contact in Cancer also hints that the organization's base is riven by disagreement, at times resentment, and that military action interferes too much with its humanitarian aims. A restless Moon–Uranus in Gemini makes indecision or rapidly changing directives get in the way of maintaining a focused course.

UNITED STATES OF AMERICA

Moment of birth: 4 July 1776, 11 am local time, Philadelphia.
A strongly cardinal chart suggests a country that places high reliance on initiative, achievement and change. Four planets including the Sun in Cancer accentuate mothering, home and family-based values, and eating as a prime-time activity side by side with an obsession with being slim. It is definitely an oral, passive culture, with a greater desire to be liked than is obvious.

The initial friendliness and openness hides a deep need for self-protection and secrecy. The sugary sweetness of Venus–Jupiter—expressed in the phrase 'Have a nice day'—also belies the violent, self-assertive, uncooperative Mars–Uranus conjunction. Nothing is allowed to interfere with America's desires or opinions. Freedom of speech can arouse explosive feelings, and Mars–Uranus supplies the courage, though not always the sense, required to fight for democracy. Jupiter close to the Sun provides good luck and a self-confidence that constantly tries to expand everything it touches. Smallness is not an American ideal.

Pluto in Capricorn in opposition to the Cancer cluster of planets suggests that power is a major issue both within and outside the United States. This is a country that wishes to lead in business, finance and world government. Money is one of the driving forces in the US chart. An emphasized Saturn in square aspect to both Pluto and the Cancer Sun puts value on the results of slow, disciplined work. This mitigates the ruthlessness of Pluto and produces a concern for fairness and democratic justice. It has also resulted in a flourishing legal system. With such a prominent Pluto in the chart, the country goes through periodic states of internal crises trying to cleanse itself of past problems and eradicate old patterns of behaviour. Americans adore a challenge and will attempt to take over other countries' problems as a way of boosting their sense of national esteem.

There are no fire signs in the chart, which suggests a depressive underside to the buoyant good humour of American culture signalled by a midheaven Sun and Jupiter. At base Americans do not trust that good fortune will be there for them, so they have to work constantly to keep the ship afloat. Neptune on the ascendant is spiritual, sympathetic, creative and most connected to the movies, so as a nation the United States wants to appear helpful and artistic rather than power-driven.

The Moon in Aquarius is friendly and highly communicative, yet emotionally rather detached and slightly wary of too much intimacy. At times the obvious demand for free speech hides some highly clandestine activities. Pluto, intimately linked to the major planets, will go to almost any lengths to keep certain financial and government dealings deeply buried. Lack of fixed signs points to a lack of staying power. Great starters but not such good finishers, Americans have a highly developed capacity for change which helps them survive better than most through the rough patches.

USSR

Moment of birth: 7 November 1917, 10.52 pm Greenwich Mean Time, Leningrad.
The USSR was a deeply troubled nation, suspicious to the point of paranoia, outwardly belligerent, but essentially inward-looking. The chart is dominated by a powerfully grouping of planets, involving an almost psychotic combination of Uranus in Aquarius opposing a very hidden Neptune and Saturn in Leo squaring onto a power-hungry, secretive Sun and Mercury in Scorpio.

The Scorpio Sun situated at the lowest point of the chart indicates a nation tied to the land, with agriculture as its basic interest and industry. The common people were also the foundation on which it rested, though the hidden placing of Saturn, in the 12th house just above the horizon, suggests that executive power wass often wielded in secrecy in opposition to their wishes. The strong 12th house creates a fertile environment for subversive activity and underground societies, as well as a national tendency to alcoholism as an escape from reality. The atheist public image of communist Russia ran against the grain of an essentially mystical people who were deeply superstitious and drawn to occult beliefs.

Mother Russia is signified by the Leo Moon on the ascendant, a country that likes to suggest it is a protector of the common people. With Mars in Virgo, the work ethic and a rather dour belligerence are also heavily emphasized. Jupiter in Gemini in the 10th house, which identifies reputation, national prestige and the apparatchiks who wield power, highlights a ruling class who speak of fairness, justice and equality but whose arrogance is a weak spot. What was visible in Russia was rarely what is important, especially where the government was concerned. There always was and probably always will be a vast gulf between public image and private reality.

Confusion was endemic, along with constant anxiety and fear. This was a country that lived permanently on the edge—of chaos, of anger, of incompetence and of psychological breakdown. Communist dictatorship and even the feudal tsardom that preceded it may have been harsh, but they served, through brutality and deception, to hold together a nation that would otherwise have been in danger of sinking into psychic disintegration. The outward displays of anger on an international level were, likewise, often a symptom more of inner unease than any truly megalomaniac tendencies.

The years of Pluto in Scorpio (1983–95) were ones of breakdown, tearing down the past and destructuring, symbolically triggered as Pluto made its first major aspect to the interconnected grouping of planets that dominate the Russian chart, with the meltdown at Chernobyl in 1986. The avalanche of change continued into tragic chaos. Then, just as the USSR might have hoped for a settled period to rebuild on new foundations, Uranus entered Aquarius in 1986 for seven years, bringing jarring, jolting changes, with a recurrence of the 1917 revolutionary planetary positions in 2000.

ZIMBABWE

Moment of birth: 18 April 1980, 12 midnight, Harare, Zimbabwe.

The independence of Zimbabwe from its colonial past occurred when a fiery, intemperate Aries Sun was opposing controlling Pluto, and aspecting flamboyant, autocratic Mars in Leo close to the Moon's North Node—not a happy augury for a settled democracy, at least initially. The nation and the country's agricultural foundations are held down by Pluto's need for power with no argument. The maturity sought by Saturn in hard-working Virgo—emphasized but deeply buried—will be a long time arriving. Jupiter in early Virgo makes the healthy balance of ideals and material wealth difficult to find. The Mars–Uranus aspect is explosive, and erratic in direction; the Saturn–Neptune aspect is paranoid, given to a nervous scattering of energy, and a reluctance to learn the lessons of social obligations and sharing. There is a tremendous potential here for leadership ability internally and in the wider African context but perhaps only after major upheavals, perhaps two decades ahead.

ASTROCARTOGRAPHY

What happened where

6

Astrological geography is the most exciting development in astrology in recent years. Plotting the individual birth chart on a world map throws up truly fascinating insights. Essentially it calculates on which longitude and latitude individual planets in the birth chart work most effectively, or are heightened in their influence. Developed single-handedly by the late Jim Lewis, a San Francisco astrologer, it has opened the door to a whole new field of information. Birth charts for individuals, countries or organizations can be illuminated with this extra dimension, pinpointing where they will operate at maximum strength in career, love or danger zones.

HOLIDAY GUIDE: RELAXATION ZONES

Astrocartography can be a helpful holiday guide in choosing the specific zones of the world where an individual will have the best chance of relaxing. My own Sun, Jupiter and Chiron (the planet of healing) on the I. C. (at home) lines run right through California, which is why some years ago I chose Big Sur as a retreat—a real life-saver in times of stress.

CAREER GUIDE: ACHIEVEMENT ZONES

Career success lines indicate where ambitions will be achieved. Sean Connery, born in Edinburgh, Scotland, has his Jupiter (luck)–Pluto (extremely) midheaven (career) lines through Los Angeles, and his Neptune (film)–Sun (identity) midheaven line through New York. Other Hollywood stars share similar markers. It is possible to earn money or achieve success from places marked by astrocartography yet never go there. One City trader with his high-flying career lines (Venus–Pluto on the midheaven) through Tokyo traded with considerable success on the Nikkei although he never left the City of London. A major Scottish fish exporter and trawler-fleet owner has his success lines running up through the Atlantic Ocean.

MARS: WARRIOR ZONES

Mars lines tend to indicate where you will be aggressive, accident-prone or irritable; for most individuals this gives a hint of which countries or regions should be avoided or approached with care. For political leaders, these are the lines on which they go to war. Uncannily every American president in recent times who volunteered or was pulled into military activity did so on a world zone through

243

which one of their four Mars lines ran. For Roosevelt it was Pearl Harbor; for Harry Truman, Japan and Korea; for Kennedy, Lyndon Johnson and Ford, it was Vietnam; for Jimmy Carter, Iran. Margaret Thatcher's Mars on the midheaven (the key Mars line) runs straight through the tiny Falkland Islands, where Britain declared war after the Argentinian invasion in 1982. Even more bizarrely the UK 1801 birth chart (see page 239) plotted on a world map also has its Mars midheaven line exactly on the longitude for the Falklands—Margaret Thatcher matched the national mood. Both Bill Clinton and Al Gore have Mars lines through Russia.

VENUS: LOVE ZONES

On a happier note the Venus lines indicate where love matches are likely to occur. Yoko Ono, born in Japan, has her Venus midheaven line straight through Liverpool, where Beatle John Lennon was born, with whom she shared a high-profile marriage until his tragic death in 1980. Jackie Onassis had one of her four Venus lines through Greece, where she lived with her second husband, Greek shipping magnate Aristotle Onassis. Queen Elizabeth II also has her Venus ascendant (a diplomatic match) line through Greece, the birthplace of her husband Prince Philip. Princess Diana had her Venus on the I. C. (indulgent home) line through Egypt, the country of origin of Dodi al-Fayed, whom she was allegedly planning to marry before she was tragically killed in the Paris car crash in 1997.

In the case of love zones, the birthplace of the partner appears more significant than the meeting place. One friend of mine has an American husband whom she met and lived with in Europe, though her Venus line is through Detroit, his birthplace.

PLUTO: DANGER ZONES

Even astrologers are in awe of the fact that John Kennedy had his Pluto midheaven line, calculated from his birth chart, straight through the middle of Dallas, Texas, where he was assassinated in 1963. This was always going to be a threatening zone for him. Pluto signifies power, death and rebirth, destruction and re-creation.

Obviously not everyone dies on their Pluto midheaven lines, since regular world travellers will cross theirs several times a year. Some individuals are born with Pluto on their midheaven and continue a productive lifetime in that place, often gaining an influential reputation for themselves. Kennedy's birth chart has an unaspected and therefore uncontrolled Pluto, meaning it will act like a loose cannon, either exerting too much power or being on the receiving end of it.

Other factors have to come into play—dangerous, accident-prone transits, for instance—before these trigger lines become truly life-threatening. I crossed my own Pluto midheaven line two years ago in the Eastern Mediterranean on a working holiday, having discussed with other professional astrologers in advance the pros and cons of going. No major adverse transits to my chart were running, though there were minor ones. The massacre at Luxor in Egypt occurred only two days after I visited the historical site—a near miss! And I had a serious nose-bleed, requiring hospital treatment. One astrologer whose Pluto I. C. line runs through Tasmania in Australia was on a visit there several years ago when a gunman ran amok, killing several people. He was nowhere near the scene but his awareness of death was heightened because of his proximity. Christina Onassis had her Pluto I. C. line through South America on line with Buenos Aires, where she died of a pulmonary embolism in 1988. Diana, Princess of Wales had cross aspects to every one of her four Pluto lines on the same latitude as France, with the Pluto ascendant/Sun I. C. crossing on the Paris meridian. When she died she was in a dangerous, accident-prone three years with Pluto squaring her natal Mars–Pluto conjunction in the chart area of travel and foreign countries, with a major eclipse aspect one day after her death, so the additional factors were looming large.

Yet Pluto is also about influence and transformation. Princess Anne has her Sun (identity)–Pluto (influence) midheaven (career) line through Africa, where she does gruelling work, travelling in dangerous areas for her charitable efforts for the Save the Children Fund.

ASTROCARTOGRAPHY CHARTS

SEAN CONNERY

Born 25 August 1930, 6.05 pm Greenwich Mean Time, Edinburgh, Scotland.
Coming from fairly inauspicious beginnings in Edinburgh, Sean Connery has restrictive Saturn on the horizon when he is born, giving him a defensive air, rather doubtful of the motives of those he first meets. When his chart is relocated to Los Angeles, Jupiter and Pluto sit on the midheaven, signifying great success, acclaim and influence. Venus—charming, diplomatic and popular—is now on the ascendant. Born with a hidden Virgo Sun in his chart close to creative, dreamy Neptune, he can be exceptionally secretive. But if his chart is relocated to New York and the American eastern seaboard, he now has Neptune, astrologically connected to the movie business, beside his Sun midheaven (key success). This line also runs down through the Bahamas, where he has a permanent home. For many years his retreat was in southern Spain, where his Chiron (healing) on the I. C. (home) line runs, continuing down through Morocco, where his second wife Micheline was born. One of his four Venus lines runs through Australia, the home of his first wife, Diane Cilento, though this line is close to Uranus on the midheaven, suggesting that sudden career shifts would make a long-lasting relationship difficult to maintain.

DIANA, PRINCESS OF WALES

Born 1 July 1961, 7.45 pm Greenwich Mean Time, Sandringham, England.
Diana's creative Cancerian Sun came into its own through middle America as it shone brightly at her midheaven there. A glittering public career would have been guaranteed. Her Jupiter (easy) on the I. C. (home) line runs through New York and down to the Bahamas, both places where she was happy to relax and feel accepted. Her Venus (love, affection, indulgence) on the I. C. (home) line, and the Jupiter ascendant (confidence-bringer) line both run through Egypt, the home of Dodi al-Fayed. Her Sun I. C. line (spiritual home) runs through India where she frequently visited Mother Teresa, and which was also the home of one close friend, an Indian heart doctor, after her separation from Prince Charles. Her Neptune (sacrifice, pity for the suffering) midheaven line runs through Africa, as does her Jupiter ascendant, giving her confidence to raise her land-mine campaign to international notice. Her other Jupiter midheaven and Neptune descendant lines, with much the same meaning, run through the Far East, Cambodia, Laos and Vietnam, suggesting

she had much to do in future in this mine-strewn area before her life was cut short. She had Pluto cross lines ('parans') through Paris, northern France, and significantly through the Mediterranean, the scene of sailing holidays a few weeks before her death, hinting that this was not a safe area for her. Jupiter in the midheaven crossing her Venus ascendant also in the Mediterranean zone perhaps distracted her, suggesting as it does glittering acclaim, a glitzy lifestyle and a good deal of lavish indulgence.

JOHN F. KENNEDY

Born 29 May 1917, 3 pm Eastern Standard Time, Brookline, Massachusetts.
Mars on the ascendant—always a bullish aspect—in Kennedy's relocated chart runs just to the right of Vietnam, with Jupiter and Mercury ascendant lines close by, suggesting high hopes and extravagant promises. What might have been a hint of the eventual outcome, and of America's humiliation, was his Neptune I. C. and Saturn I. C. lines in the area, pointing to extreme concern, paranoid worry, sacrifice and limitation. His earlier stand-off over Cuba to force the withdrawal of Soviet missile bases there in the Bay of Pigs crisis was successful perhaps because of the Jupiter (success) midheaven and Uranus (inspiration, pioneer spirit) descendant cross-line on the latitude of Cuba: this was a lucky, audacious gamble that came off. Kennedy's Pluto midheaven line running straight through Dallas, where he was assassinated in 1963, is an unnervingly accurate reflection of a meeting with the death-dealing world, which is one of Pluto's faces. This fate is something he could perhaps have avoided if he had handled more carefully the power given him by the American people.

UNITED KINGDOM

Born 1 January 1801, 12 midnight local time, London England.
Key fascinations here are the Jupiter midheaven line, suggesting success, though also over-reaching ambition, which runs from South Africa northwards through the old British colonial Rhodesia, Tanganyika, Sudan and Egypt, and up to Belgrade, Poland and onwards. In the 19th-century scramble for Africa, Britain aimed to take territory from 'Cape to Cairo' on exactly this line; in the 20th it went to war over issues concerned with this longitude further north in Serbia (in the First World War) and the invasion of Poland (in the Second World War). In 1999 Britain again took a leading part, with the Americans, in sending NATO to war for the first time in Kosovo, exactly on this line. The aggressive Mars on the descendant line in the UK chart also tracks across Africa, through almost every war zone involving British troops from Cape Town up through Mafeking—scene of the sieges in the Boer War—and directly through Khartoum in the Sudan, where the British commander, General Gordon, died and his garrison had to be relieved in 1885. It then moves north, crossing Egypt just south of Suez—site of the 1956 Canal crisis—then across into Kuwait to Iraq, scene of the military operation known as Desert Storm in 1991. Saturn and Neptune lines also crossing in Iraq hint that outright success may fail because of a lack of nerve. The other UK Mars midheaven line runs through the Falkland Islands, scene of the 1982 Argentinian conflict.

THE MYSTERY OF
THE ECLIPSE

Crisis or opportunity?

7

Feared by primitive man as bringers of plague and pestilence, and seen as a sign of the gods' anger, eclipses of the Sun and Moon are regular six-monthly occurrences. The solar and lunar eclipse always fall two weeks apart. At an individual level, eclipses are seen nowadays by astrologers as opportunities for growth and development, challenging but not doom-laden. They do, however, appear to coincide with significant outer events, sometimes with uncanny precision. This may not be so surprising, since we know there is evidence in nature of a tangible response to the atmosphere during eclipses. Monkeys become nervous and wake up during them, even when they are hidden by clouds. Mistletoe sap rises significantly. My own impression from working in a mental hospital was that psychological disturbances became heightened: the intake in the acute admission wards always went up in the days around eclipses.

Eclipses are thought to have an influence over the following six months or so, although their effects are usually more obvious in the month immediately surrounding them. Astrologers regard eclipses as wild cards, not always consistent in their effect, although there are additional factors to be taken into account which may act as a trigger. One factor is the particular cycle itself. As the early Chaldeans noted, eclipses occur in the same sequence every 18 years 11 days, or 6585.32 days, which is known as a Saros cycle. These cycles are given Saros numbers, and similar events do occur when a Saros cycle repeats.

Strong aspects from major outer planets to the eclipses also intensify the effects. Saddam Hussein gathered his troops on the Kuwaiti border in July 1990 three days before the solar eclipse in Cancer on 22 July, opposed by the huge triple conjunction of Saturn, Uranus and Neptune in Capricorn (see *Multiple Conjunctions*, page 25). The lunar eclipse two weeks later on 6 August in Leo, aspected by a threatening Mars–Pluto opposition, saw the United Nations impose sanctions and US troops moving in. The next solar eclipse on 15 January 1991 in Capricorn was aspected again by the massively powerful triple conjunction, and one day later Operation Desert Storm launched against the Iraqis.

The unstable Uranus-in-Capricorn opposition to Neptune in Cancer was in key aspect to eclipses in those signs during 1906 to 1908, when there were a series of particularly devastating earthquakes and natural and man-made disasters around the globe. In 1906 a colliery disaster in France killed 1800 miners within three weeks of the eclipse, and 1000 died as quakes struck San Francisco. Six months later, close to the next eclipse, Chile was partially destroyed by earthquakes, and

247

a Hong Kong typhoon killed 10,000. The following year, on the day of the solar eclipse itself with Uranus–Neptune exact, 800 died in an earthquake in Jamaica. Further disasters followed, with the bubonic plague in India and a major famine in Russia killing millions. The pattern repeated in 1909, the final year of the exact Uranus–Neptune opposition, with the eclipses falling in the same signs. The king and crown prince of Portugal were assassinated, and on the December Capricorn eclipse, an earthquake in Sicily killed 200,000 (see *1906–1909*, pages 66–74).

America faced its worst disaster since Pearl Harbor when the suicide plane attacks brought down the World Trade Center Twin Towers in New York on 11 September 2001. The solar eclipse preceding was in Cancer, the US's national chart Sun sign, a hint of a major crisis approaching.

THE SAROS CYCLE

Each of the 18 cycles of eclipses in this odd 18-year repetition has a slightly different effect, some of them more obviously represented in outer events than others. Some have particular relevance for certain nations, such as Britain and the United States.

In Britain, the 18 North cycle has particular relevance for the Royal Family, as does the 11 North. American history resonates strongly to eclipses falling in key areas, represented by two separate sets of Saros cycles, both returning in the same sequence every 18 years approximately. Significant events that strongly affect the American psyche appear to fall between 15 South and 16 North; these include the Pearl Harbor bombing, the death of Elvis Presley, the Oklahoma bomb and the O. J. Simpson trial. Also coinciding with key events in 20th-century American history are 1 North eclipses, around which the bombing of Hiroshima and J. F. Kennedy's assassination took place, as well as the deaths of both of Kennedy's sons.

18 NORTH

Diana, Princess of Wales died on 31 August 1997, one day before the solar eclipse in this cycle, which is usually interpreted as illness or accident-prone and given to obsessive worry. There was an unprecedented outpouring of grief in Britain and around the world. An estimated 2 billion people watched her funeral on television on 7 September, and it took the United Kingdom a month to get back to normality. Pluto in Sagittarius was squaring the eclipse.

Uncannily the solar eclipse of this cycle 18 years previously fell on 22 August 1979, just five days before Earl Mountbatten, the Queen's uncle, was killed along with three others by an IRA bomb while holidaying in Ireland. That same eclipse, squared by disruptive Uranus in Scorpio, also saw the Fastnet Yacht Race disaster (14 August 1979), in which 17 people died when a hurricane struck. Coincidentally, on 7 September 1979, Hurricane David killed 1100 in the Dominican Republic.

Rolling back one in this series to 1961, the August solar eclipse was the closest to the birth of Lady Diana Spencer (in July), and fell two days before East Germany sealed off the border with West Germany, closing the Brandenburg Gate, and building started on the Berlin Wall. In the following month Dag Hammarskjöld, UN Secretary-General was killed in a plane crash in the Congo. In October a volcanic eruption on the island of Tristan da Cunha forced the inhabitants to leave. This Leo eclipse was close to explosive Uranus in Leo and Neptune in Scorpio.

Back to 1943 the 18 North solar eclipse in August fell as the tide of the Second World War was turning, with the Allies invading Italy and Mussolini surrendering. Six months later in February 1944, with the 18 North lunar eclipse in place, the Germans launched the heaviest air raids on London since 1941; the Queen and her sister Princess Margaret stayed in London for the course of the war, as the Queen Mother felt this would help keep national morale high.

Back another 18 years, two of the most influential women in Britain's history, and world figures in their own right, were born. Margaret Thatcher's birth in October 1925 fell within the influence of the 18 North solar eclipse, and Queen Elizabeth II's, in April 1926, within the influence of the 18 North lunar eclipse. Both eclipses were aspected by a rather paranoid square from Saturn and Neptune.

Within two weeks of the 18 North lunar eclipse in 1908, aspected by the unstable Uranus–Neptune opposition, another two members of European royalty met sudden ends when King Carlos I of Portugal and the Crown Prince were murdered in Lisbon.

11 NORTH

Queen Victoria, Britain's longest-reigning monarch, died in 1901 under the same 11 North eclipse cycle as occurred over the period of the abdication in 1937 of Edward VIII, her great-grandson, who gave up the throne to marry Wallis Simpson. Eighteen years later in 1955 the great British statesman and prime minister Winston Churchill finally resigned because of ill health in the months following the same eclipse. There were hugely significant events over the next two occurrences as well. In 1973 Britain joined the European Community three days before the solar eclipse. On the next cycle Margaret Thatcher, Britain's first woman prime minister and the century's longest-serving, resigned seven weeks before the next 11 North solar eclipse, which occurred in January 1991, 12 days before the Allies launched Operation Desert Storm to recapture Kuwait from Saddam Hussein's Iraqi forces. One month later an IRA bomb exploded outside No. 10 Downing Street while a Cabinet meeting was in progress.

4 NORTH

The worst maritime disaster of all time occurred only two days before the April solar eclipse in the 4 North series; this was when the British luxury liner *Titanic* hit an iceberg and sank, with insufficient lifeboats, in the icy waters of the North Atlantic, with the loss of 1500 of its 2340 passengers. Six months later, the lunar eclipse in this series occurred only six days before another sinking when the British B2 submarine sank with the loss of 14 lives after colliding with a German liner. On the next cycle in 1930, the solar eclipse saw the signing of a treaty in London by the five great powers to limit the size and number of warships and submarines held. The lunar eclipse in the autumn of 1930 coincided with another disaster as the British airship R101 crashed and exploded in France, killing 44, only two days before. Similarly the 4 North lunar eclipse 18 years on in 1948 occurred three days before a KLM plane crashed in Scotland, killing 34.

In 1966 the maritime theme continued, with British prime minister Harold Wilson holding an unsuccessful meeting with Rhodesian breakaway leader Ian Smith on board HMS *Tiger* to try to settle the dispute in the aftermath of the lunar eclipse. More shockingly, eight days before the lunar eclipse, a mine slag slip at Aberfan in Wales killed 116 children. Also in 1966, the infamous Moors Murder case in London, when Ian Brady and Myra Hindley were tried and convicted for the torture and murder of several children, finished in the month of the 4 North solar eclipse. In the most recent cycle in 1984, the solar eclipse fell four days before the British barque *Marques* sank off Bermuda in the Tall Ships Race with the loss of 19 people; and six weeks after London policewoman, Yvonne Fletcher, was shot in the Libyan Embassy seige. The 4 North lunar eclipse fell in early November that year, just weeks after the IRA bomb intended for Margaret Thatcher exploded in Brighton during the Conservative Party Conference.

16 NORTH/15 SOUTH

On 7 December 1941, the Japanese made a surprise attack on the US Naval base at Pearl Harbor, destroying eight battleships and 300 aircraft, bringing the US into World War II. The 16 North solar eclipse, falling 10 weeks before, had peaked in its trajectory across the heavens exactly above Pearl Harbor.

Eighteen years on in 1959, a return of these 16 North eclipses saw the Cuban government expropriating US-owned sugar mills and plantations. Then in 1977, the death of 'the King'—Elvis Presley—occurred in August two months before the 16 North solar eclipse and four months after the 15 South eclipse, which is traditionally interpreted as bringing collective grief and loss. The United States returned the canal zone to Panama four weeks later.

In 1995 a bomb blew up the federal building in Oklahoma City on 19 April, killing 166 people. The 15 South solar eclipse fell 10 days later on 29 April. Marlon Brando's 25-year-old daughter, Cheyenne, committed suicide on 16 April.

Across the intervening months as the cycle moved into 16 North, the trial of O. J. Simpson for the murder of his wife, Nicole Brown, in 1994, riveted and shocked the American public, with live television coverage around the world. After months of conflicting evidence and accusations of police racist bias, he was found not guilty three weeks before the 16 North solar eclipse.

1 NORTH

The world's first atomic bomb was dropped by American forces on Hiroshima on 6 August 1945, four weeks after the 1 North solar eclipse with an exact conjunction of Saturn squaring onto Neptune. It killed 130,000 people and led to the Japanese surrender.

On the next cycle of this eclipse 18 years on, John and Jackie Kennedy's premature baby son, Patrick Kennedy, died on 9 August, two weeks after the solar eclipse in 1963. Martin Luther King was delivering his rousing civil rights speech in Washington to 200,000 African-Americans campaigning for black civil rights four weeks after the solar eclipse. Three months later President John F. Kennedy was shot in Dallas. The same cycle repeating in 1981 saw US forces shoot down two Libyan planes, and the US air traffic control strike. Then in July 1999, with tragic and eerie synchronicity, J. F. Kennedy's son John was killed in a plane crash three weeks before the 1 North solar eclipse.

In previous 1 North eclipses, Charles Lindbergh made the first solo, non-stop transatlantic flight, from New York to Paris, in 33 hours, in 1927; and in 1909 a major earthquake destroyed Acapulco, two weeks after the eclipse. The next eclipse in this series occurred in August 1999, in the midst of the Balkans Kosovar crisis, with NATO forces, at war for the first time since 1945, trying to halt the Serbian ethnic cleansing and genocide of Albanians.

6 NORTH

The other eclipses that coincide with fated moments for the United States occur on the 6 North cycle, which oversaw the *Challenger* Space Shuttle disaster, the death of Martin Luther King and the kidnapping of the Lindbergh baby. These eclipses are interpreted as focusing on issues around father or authority figures.

The deaths of the seven crew members of the US space shuttle *Challenger*, which exploded shortly after take-off on 28 January 1986, shocked a watching American TV public. The 6 North solar eclipse fell nine weeks later, in the month that saw US servicemen bombed by terrorists in Berlin and the US bombing Libya in retaliation for its suspected involvement.

The previous 6 North solar eclipse on 28 March 1968 fell one week before Martin Luther King was assassinated in Memphis, Tennessee, leading to riots and looting in major cities in protest. King, inspired by Mahatma Gandhi's ideas on non-violence and passive resistance, was an inspired orator, best known for his unforgettable 'I have a dream' speech to 200,000 African-Americans demonstrating in Washington in 1963 (see *Uranus–Pluto*, page 33, and *1963* and *1968*, pages 166 and 173). His convicted white assassin, James Earl Ray, was sentenced to 99 years' imprisonment. Two months later Senator Robert Kennedy was shot in Los Angeles.

In 1950 a US aircraft was shot down by the Soviets. Back in 1932, the tragic Lindbergh baby kidnapping that created widespread public anguish happened six days before the 6 North solar eclipse on 7 March. World-famous aviator Charles Lindbergh's 20-month-old son was kidnapped for ransom, sparking off one of the biggest man-hunts in American history, with 100,000 police involved. The President promised to move heaven and earth to find the kidnappers; even gangster Al Capone offered a $10,000 reward. But the baby was found dead on 12 May.

On the previous cycle in 1914, US troops bombarded Veracruz in Mexico to prevent German munitions being shipped in, seizing it within three days of the 6 North solar eclipse; they withdrew six months later, 10 days after the 6 North lunar eclipse.

WORLD EVENTS AND OTHER CYCLES

Two days before the 1 North eclipse of 31 July 1981 Lady Diana Spencer married Prince Charles in Westminster Abbey, watched by a television audience of 700 million people around the world. This cycle, not generally seen as a luck-bringer, is interpreted as putting a great deal of pressure on personal relationships. Speaking of it in *The Eagle and the Lark*, Australian astrologer Bernadette Brady remarks, 'The individual would be wise not to make any hasty decisions since information is distorted and possibly false.' Tiredness or health problems are also associated with it.

Prince William, Diana and Charles's eldest son and heir to the throne in succession to his father, was born on the day of the solar eclipse in June 1982. This cycle, called 2 Old North, is due to end in 2036, hinting that he may be the last monarch in the present dynasty and will outlive his royal position. This series is challenging in effect, dealing with separations or the ending of a union, although the long-term outcome is hopeful (see *Nelson Mandela* below). In June 1982 the Argentinians surrendered defeated after the Falklands War, and in the few weeks following Israel invaded the Lebanon, and the Hyde Park IRA bomb in London killed guardsmen and horses. The Queen's bedroom was also broken into by an intruder, who sat on her bed for a chat! This cycle is repeated in July 2000.

On the day of the 6 South lunar eclipse on 24 April 1986, seen as manic and forceful, a major accident at the Chernobyl nuclear power station near Kiev in the USSR sent out nuclear fall-out greater than 1000 Hiroshima bombs. A radioactive cloud drifted into the global atmosphere, threatening health, contaminating land and causing widespread alarm.

Nelson Mandela, former president of South Africa, has a curious affinity with eclipses. He was sentenced to life imprisonment in 1964 on the day of the Gemini solar eclipse in the 2 Old North series (which also oversaw the birth of Prince William), hinting at separations and challenges but with an ultimately hopeful outcome. His release from prison 26 years later came two days after the Leo lunar eclipse in the 10 North series, which was also in place in the weeks before his birth in July 1918. Its core meaning is linked to communications, frustrations, inhibitions and the need to move quietly. He became president of South Africa on the day of a Taurus solar eclipse in 1994 in the 14 South cycle, generally thought to be successful after a long period of hard work. Bernadette Brady writes: 'During this eclipse period individuals should push for the acceptance of their ideas. It can bring the long-awaited breakthrough.'

In the weeks following this 14 South solar eclipse in 1994, the Channel Tunnel was opened after eight years of work and billions of pounds spent; Aleksandr Solzhenitsyn returned home to Russia after a 20-year exile in the United States; Tony Blair took the Labour Party to victory in the British elections, the party's first win in 18 years; Yasser Arafat went into the Gaza Strip, his first visit to his homeland in Palestine in 27 years; and the IRA announced a ceasefire after 25 years of bombing.

THE CENTURY AHEAD

What the stars have in store for us

8

Prophecies of the future tend in two directions: one towards apocalyptic endings, when the Universe as we know it ceases to exist; the other towards a golden age, thought to have once existed, and which will return when all injustices are removed. The likelihood is that neither will occur.

Nostradamus, the great French seer whose elliptical quatrains have excited so much interest over 500 years, thought that astrology alone was not sufficient to make major predictions. He used a combination of astrological and clairvoyant vision to make his sweeping predictions. Most famously he predicted a major cataclysm for July 1999, when the Leo eclipses beside the Sun, Mercury and Venus were aspected by an extraordinary group of fixed planets—Uranus and Neptune in Aquarius, Jupiter and Saturn in Taurus, Mars in Scorpio. But even he thought that life continued thereafter.

What is clear, when reviewing the astrology of the 100 years ahead, is that the period should be less stressful than some other centuries. The highly strung Uranus–Neptune pairing, spanning the new millennium until 2002, is the last of the outer conjunctions for more than 100 years. Uranus, Neptune and Pluto will not come together again in any combination in the lifetime of the next three generations. The 20th century saw three such pairings—of mystical, dissolving Neptune–Pluto in 1900, disruptive Uranus–Pluto in the mid-1960s and highly strung Uranus–Neptune in the early 1990s.

Neither are there the massively powerful triple conjunctions such as tipped the fifth century into the Dark Ages, fertilized the glorious Renaissance of the 14th century, or fragmented the USSR in the final decade of the 20th century. (See *Multiple Conjunctions*, page 22.)

THE OUTERMOST PLANETS

JUPITER

During the first century after the new millennium, there will be three Jupiterian triple conjunctions, milder in their effect than the conjunctions just mentioned.

- **Jupiter–Saturn–Pluto in Capricorn in 2020**. This will repeat some of the effect of those planets coming together in 1981 (in Libra), when the Prince of Wales was married and assassination attempts were made on Ronald Reagan and the Pope. There was also martial law in Poland, riots in Britain and a

253

show trial of the 'Gang of Four' in China for treason, in the aftermath of the bloody Cultural Revolution. Previously, in 1881, these planets together coincided with the election of President James Garfield in the United States, and his assassination four months later. Saturn–Pluto is always tough, but Jupiter brings hope of improvement, or softens the brutal effect. The year 2020 will be especially memorable, since the eclipses in January and June will be aspected by the triple conjunction, heightening its effect.

- **Jupiter–Saturn–Neptune in Gemini in 2060**. Not seen since 1524 (then in Pisces), this will mark a time of high ideals, when the underdogs of society claim their rights. Women will come to the fore. Last time around it coincided with widespread peasants' revolts in Europe.
- **Jupiter–Saturn–Uranus in Capricorn/Aquarius in 2079**. A repeat of the 1940/42 triple conjunction in Taurus, this is not likely to be as warlike in its influence as the previous occasion, since it falls in less power-hungry signs and the Pluto square is absent. New constitutions will be put in place, and new national boundaries may also be established. An economic upsurge is likely.

PLUTO

Pluto will move slowly through five signs.

- **In Sagittarius until 2008**. Intense fundamentalist religious disputes will continue, but intellectual discussions will also be promoted. Profound experiences will convert many to new belief systems, or a revised outlook on life.
- **In Capricorn from 2008 until 2024**. Old political and economic structures will slowly be overturned, some even reduced to rubble. The Uranus square from Aries from 2010 until 2018 will make this placing violently revolutionary at times. The phoenix will arise from the ashes as it did last time around in 1776 when America declared independence and set a new form of democracy on its way.
- **In Aquarius from 2024 until 2044**. Powerful reforming social movements will get under way, with an emphasis on tolerance and friendship rather than hierarchical government. Last time around this placing coincided with the French Revolution in 1792, based on the ideals of 'Liberty, Equality and Fraternity'. Helpful aspects from Neptune in Aries, and Uranus in Gemini until 2035 will favour mystical ideas, an understanding of other realities, and advances in science.
- **In Pisces from 2044 until 2067**. This will bring creative and spiritual ideas to the fore.
- **In Aries from 2067 until 2096**. This will be an explosively energetic period, a time of action, exploration and courage. Last time Pluto was in Aries (1823–52) it coincided with the golden age of the American frontiersmen—heroic though violent—who opened up the West, as well as European revolutionaries.

NEPTUNE

- **In Aquarius until 2012**. This period will be marked by the rise of humanitarianism as an ideal, though theory and practice may not always match.

- **In Pisces from 2012 until 2026**. In this creative sign, Neptune will promote a highly spiritual phase, when there is a lack of will to cope with the violent confrontations brought by the Uranus–Pluto square (emphasized until 2018).
- **In Aries from 2026 until 2038**. Moving uneasily into this sign, it will make direct action difficult, perhaps bringing pacifist, 'flower power' movements to the fore. The square from Uranus in Cancer through the 2030s will be highly strung and inclined to eccentric, irrational cult beliefs. Enlightenment will be the goal.
- **In Taurus from 2038 until 2067**. Here, Neptune is idealistic and not realistic about economics. Money will be wasted and recessions likely.
- **In Cancer from 2067 until 2080**. As in 1900–1914, the dream will be of paradise homes, idyllic families and peace.
- **In Leo from 2080**. Roaring inflation may bring temporary excitement.

KEY DECADES

The decades to note include the 2010s, with revolutionary ferment. Pluto in Capricorn will pick up a dramatic square to disruptive Uranus in aggressive Aries from 2011 onwards, running towards a peak of activity in 2014 and 2015. Governments will abruptly fall. In less stable democracies there will be bloody coups. Global capitalism will be in turmoil. In 2019 the bleak, war-mongering Saturn–Pluto conjunction makes its first appearance since 1981 (previously 1914), but is softened by Jupiter. There may be a major upsurge of powerful business and economic activity, though outbursts of dictatorial greed are also likely. The 2020s coast along thereafter; as do the 2030s, though with rather jangled, disaster-prone Uranus–Neptune squares (see *1906–1908*, pages 66–71) there could be catastrophes out of the normal order. The trickiest decade will be the 2040s, with Uranus in fixed Leo still squaring Neptune now in Taurus, and opposing Pluto in Aquarius, with, in 2042, Saturn in Scorpio. This will almost certainly bring major catastrophic earthquakes, as well as rebellions and intransigence in political disputes. Pluto in Aquarius, squaring onto Neptune in Taurus, with Saturn and Uranus involved in complex aspect, was around for the Vesuvius eruption in AD 79 when Pompeii was buried.

Intriguingly these same Uranus, Neptune and Pluto aspects are around in 3797, when Nostradamus predicted the world would end.

THE NEW CENTURY WORLDWIDE

THE UK, USA, RUSSIA AND CHINA

Britain started shedding its imperial past through the turbulent Uranus–Pluto 1960s, as former colonies gained independence. The years from 1984 onwards have seen a slow, painful reassessment of its world role and inner constitutional structure, with the fixed grand square in the 1801 chart being pressured by Pluto (1984 to 1995), then jolted by Uranus (1996 to 2003) and finally undermined by Neptune (1998 to 2012). Major changes in the form of government are in focus in 2001–2002, with jarring transitions into the European Union, the destruction of the 1000-year-old hereditary House of Lords, and further

255

fragmentation of Scotland and Wales. Neptune brings its dissolving action to bear from 2003, with no productive financial patch for almost a decade thereafter, and national morale low. Then Pluto's entry into Capricorn in 2008 and Uranus's into Aries in 2010 herald a rebellious few years of disruption and upheaval, especially in the area of agriculture; there will be mass protests at home, and fraught international relations with possible conflict involving Europe, the Middle East and Japan, the year 2013 being a crunch point. Sweeping changes in the monarchy are inevitable between 2015 and 2018. Neptune in Pisces from 2012 to 2026 will bring an epidemic of illnesses; these are not cataclysmic but are difficult to shift.

Repressive government or a dictatorial British leader may emerge around 2020 to reassert authority, starting with high hopes but bringing disappointing results. The 2020s and 2030s should be relatively calm, with the 2040s looking like the most difficult decade of the next century, especially through 2041 and 2042.

Russia's quarter century of major turmoil and transformation, which started in the mid-1980s, runs through a repeat of the 1917 revolutionary influences over the changing millennium, then slides into a disintegrating finish in the few years after 2002 with low national morale. The broad sweep of the 21st century should mercifully give Russia a chance to recover some semblance of normality, at least at an internal level, for about three decades, until the stressful 2040s. However, Russia will be drawn inevitably into the global aggravation of the mid-2010s, and involved in angry clashes with the United States, the United Nations and China around 2014 or 2015. The 2040s will bring about another complete reorganization of the country, which again will have to suffer a decade of confusion and chaos before a fragile stability is reconstructed.

The pressures on the United States are less than those on the United Kingdom or Russia over the next decade, with fewer fixed signs in its chart. Nevertheless Uranus crossing the Aquarian Moon in 2001 and 2002 brought an emotionally volatile mood, with outbursts of high feeling. Pluto picking up Mars in 2004 and 2005 will bring significant, violent international confrontations. Relations with Israel, Egypt and Japan look highly unsettled, with resistance to American foreign policy from France and Germany. With the Neptune square at the same time, there may be an internal earthquake or natural disasters on a larger scale than usual to contend with. Only by the end of the decade from 2008 onwards, with Pluto in Capricorn starting to oppose the American Sun, Venus and Mercury in Cancer, will any really major challenge be made to national prestige and government from a grass-roots level. The turbulent 2010s will be marked by Middle Eastern flare-ups and major disagreements with both Russia and China, and there will be considerable political challenges to the established power structures from 2012 onwards. The years 2014 and 2015 are stressful as corruption is uncovered and outworn ideas are dismantled. The year 2020 is a key one for the United States as it enters an entirely new phase of its history, almost as significant as that inaugurated by the Declaration of Independence itself.

The sleeping dragon of China, having been awakened to angry rumbles through 1999 and 2000, should settle back into a more peaceful decade with economic pressures looming large until 2002. Neptune undermining Mars inevitably brings a panicky sense of failure, and an inability to act decisively causes a temporary paralysis of will until 2006. With Pluto also aspected, there may be major earthquakes or unprecedented natural or nuclear disasters. China will lurch back into dynamic gear, explosively at times, from 2008 onwards, noticeably after 2012. Relations with India, Japan, the USSR, the United Nations and even Australasia will then be under immense strain. The year 2040 will produce a leader to inspire the hope of a new great Chinese civilization, and 2080 is the time when China will flourish as never before.

THE EU, UN AND NATO

The European Union has cleared the major hurdle from 1998 through to January 2000, with jolting Uranus disclosing major dissent within the ranks which could have collapsed the Union altogether. The resignation of Commission members *en masse* in the face of corruption allegations fell on the day in 1999 that Uranus moved to 15 degrees, exactly triggering its indulgently stubborn T-square. It has a couple of years' respite before lurching towards the upheaval of Uranus opposing Pluto from April 2003 for two years, which may drag more corruption and behind-the-scenes power play into the open. During this difficult period, when even the viability of the organization will be questioned, change will be determinedly fought every inch of the way; the UK especially will be at loggerheads with France, and undermining Neptune will lower confidence. The next major period when there will be outright revolt among members is 2012 to 2015. If the European Union survives, then 2020 will see an entirely new basis under construction, with rigorous controls in place.

Between 2002 and 2006 there will be a complete revision of the United Nations' philosophy and *raison d'être*, as Pluto in argumentative Sagittarius opposes the controlling Moon–Pluto conjunction in Gemini. Debates will be long, bitter and threatening at points, souring any hopes of international cooperation. But there will be a general airing of grievances that can only strengthen its long-term outlook. The really crucial test will be as Uranus in Aries and Pluto in Capricorn, in aspect from 2012, overstretch its resources considerably, with serial global hotspots to monitor. The years 2011 and 2012 will be disorienting and panicky, but 2016 is the conflagration year, with aggravation running through until 2022. This is when the United Nations will meet its moment of truth, one unlikely to be matched for decades thereafter.

With Uranus opposing its midheaven Pluto, undermining its power base, and putting its actions under scrutiny, NATO eases its way towards a positive change in 2002 and 2003 after the extreme pressure it was under through the escalating Balkans crisis of 1999. Uranus moving into Pisces in 2003 for several years will, however, shake up its identity, making compromise solutions difficult to find. The year 2005 is jarring, with intransigent attitudes making contradictory decisions all too likely. Reckless initiatives will come to be regretted. From midway through the 2010s, NATO will be drawn into conflict again, though without much heart and questionable success. Morale will be low, indecision rife.

EIRE, CANADA, DENMARK AND SWITZERLAND

The expansive but unpredictable Jupiter–Saturn conjunction over the millennium on the Eire Sun and midheaven could prove a turning point in the country's rapid expansion since joining the European Union. Extravagantly high hopes, perhaps with a new charismatic leader, could be heady but prove disappointing. Uranus is an unsettling energy around European/Irish affairs for a few years, accompanied by Neptune's rather eroding influence, especially on finances, until 2008. Given too much too easily, Eire is now having to face reality, with cutbacks and failed ventures increasingly obvious. Eire's relationship with the European Union will undergo a troubling few years, with a complete overhaul of priorities and expectations until after 2007. The Anglo-Irish cooperative pact will hit a disillusioning patch as well in 2004, with a major effort needed to keep it on track. There will be moments of great elation and of total despair running towards 2009, with angry clashes and possible outbreaks of violence between 2010 and 2013.

Canada's confidently positive approach will get a major lift from 2004 onwards, after a couple of dampening years when minor financial setbacks cause a temporary slow down. High spirits and rather dramatic displays of national chutzpah will keep Canada on the world stage as a cheerleader through troubled times. Neptune will aspect both Saturn and Pluto through 2005 and 2006, causing some concern, but the buoyant mood will cover over much of the underlying jitters. Thereafter another minor blip as Pluto opposes the Moon in 2007 will see an upsurge of emotional feeling and a determination to cleanse the past. The early years of the 2010s may see several changes of government, with a constantly shifting political scene.

Denmark is moving through an upsurge of national confidence with a determination to be a significant force and voice on the international scene. The first decade of the 21st century will be relatively plain sailing, though a sense of false happiness around 2006 may prove delusory and could be financially costly. The troubled 2010s seem especially stressful for Denmark, with involvement either in global conflict or in trying to suppress unrest at home. There will be a major upheaval in the country's financial insititutions, and it will be difficult to maintain stability almost until 2020.

With Uranus triggering several years of jolting disclosures, Switzerland's relatively stable history is given a severe a shaking, from 1998 until 2003. Neptune follows hot on its heels right through the first decade, undermining what were thought to be solid structures and a firm reputation. The old foundations no longer feel solid. There will be financial repercussions as Switzerland's reputation for integrity is questioned. The 2010s will be a decade of recouping and reorganizing, less agitated than for some other countries.

JAPAN, INDIA, PAKISTAN AND SINGAPORE

Japan's progress towards restoring national morale after the economic disasters of the late 1990s will be a slow and awkward process, with jolting Uranus crossing its Aquarian Sun and raising nervous tension until 2002, and squaring Neptune until 2003, which will cause panic. Hidden secrets will emerge as Uranus opposes Pluto until 2005, shaking a national morale highly dependent on pride. Financial corruption up to government level, and exposure of further mystical, delusional cult beliefs, will show a new image to the international community which will not please. Saturn, then Uranus opposing Neptune and Pluto through these years also hints at the possibility of earthquakes and natural or perhaps man-made ecological disasters. Japan's relationship with its neighbours in Australia, New Zealand and China will be strained until Pluto leaves Sagittarius in 2008. Thereafter Japan has to cope with several years of Neptune's influence—never a good business prospect—until 2012.

The unsettling years of the end of the 20th century have left India and Pakistan gasping for a breathing space to regroup. Uranus opposing the Leo Sun has opened new windows of opportunity, though at considerable cost in terms of instability and constant change. Luckily Pluto will put a firm hand of beneficial control on the affairs of both countries through 2004 and 2005. Neptune slowly wending its way in aspect across five Leo planets until 2009 may be easier for inherently spiritual countries to handle since it emphasizes the intangible rather than the material, but there will be a loss of direction. Pluto opposing Uranus in 2006 and 2007 will see the old ways cleared out and a complete new beginning, though there will be violent clashes along the way to 2008 and beyond. Pluto squaring Neptune in 2012 is disaster-prone, bringing either man-made or natural catastrophes.

Singapore's economic success and financial talent will come under increasing strain from late 2000 onwards for several years, as it grapples with and resists forced change. Pluto squaring Saturn in 2001 and 2002 will bring cutbacks, but not for long as Singapore's immense resilience will help it pull through to an even more glorious success in the years around 2006. The mid-2010s will be angrily competitive, perhaps because of the troubled global situation, with a crisis of confidence in 2016. Extreme endurance will be required if Singapore is to force its way through to better times, but in 2021 it will arise shining bright to move into easier times.

GERMANY, FRANCE AND ITALY

Germany's need to appear in control will be shaken by Uranus, as it rattles a few financial or sexual skeletons out of the closet through to 2002. There will be a major clearing-out of old corruption and an economic blip, but thereafter there should be a general regrouping of national strength. The relationship with France is under strain in 2004, perhaps because of German's bullish demands, with the European Union partnership causing major headaches until 2007. Neptune is undermining Pluto until then, which suggests an underlying malaise in the economy which is slow to shift. Pluto squaring Mars and then crossing Saturn from 2008 will be stressful—violently so at times—as the old Germany is forced to abandon unworkable ambitions. Old political and business structures will be forcibly brought down. The revolutionary 2010s will see Germany either in turmoil or causing it. Relations with the United Kingdom, United States and France will be explosively aggravated.

France meets the new millennium and the early years of the 21st century in a mid-life crisis, rebelliously uncooperative and reacting aggressively to interference in the hope of propping up flagging national morale. Born out of a revolution, France was pitched back into dramatic times until Uranus cleared Mars in 2002, partly perhaps because of increasing disagreements within the European Union, especially with the United Kingdom and Germany. The Franco-American interface, which is never friendly at the best of times, hits an all-time low in 2005. In 2007 and 2008, as Pluto heads to square the late Virgo Sun—which always indicates a time of reconstruction under pressure, with some loss—Neptune also starts to undermine confidence, causing a directionless patch until 2010. France may be less affected than some countries by the 2010s, and will emerge in 2020 implacably determined to be in control. With the triple conjunction of Jupiter–Saturn–Pluto on the ascendant of the French chart, this will be a major new beginning.

Like France, Italy will go through a crisis-ridden three years from 2006, with Neptune creating a ripple of panic about failure, and Pluto squaring both the Pisces Sun and dreamy Neptune, always a hugely disorienting experience. Italy's strength is in not determination but adaptability, so the changing governments may find themselves at the mercy of circumstances outside their control. Unable to make a firm stand, or find the will for decisive action, they may crumble under pressure. However, there is likely to be an artistic revival— an outpouring of creative talent—to compensate.

ISRAEL AND THE MIDDLE EAST

Israel's very fixed chart with a Taurus Sun and four Leo planets, including the Moon, Mars, Pluto and Saturn, has been in the same extraordinarily stressful patch as other fixed countries like Russia and the United Kingdom since the middle of the 1980s. Uranus continues to jolt and jar itself through to an edgy, rather disruptive close in 2003, but by then Neptune, with its slow, dissolving action, makes determined action difficult, if not impossible, for the years up to 2011. The Israeli chart seems less disrupted through the troubled 2010s, even with a Middle Eastern flare-up inevitable. Relations with most of the neighbours, bar Jordan, are aggravated, but Israel would not seem to be the centre of the conflict.

The Mars, Saturn, Neptune and Moon congregation in Libra in the Libyan chart would seem most likely to attract the major revolutionary disruption from the Uranus–Pluto square of 2012 onwards, with violence flaring inside and outside the borders. Egypt appears also to be centre of violent arguments, with difficult relationships all round with Israel, Iraq, Jordan, Saudi Arabia and the United Nations. There will be a major set-to with the United States in 2007 and 2008, which will end up in a determined break in diplomatic relations.

Iraq is facing its next major upset in 2005 and 2006, with Pluto squaring Saturn and Jupiter close together in Virgo, resulting in highly unstable reactions. With Neptune at the same time opposing Mars, signalling a panicky sense of failure, a paralysis of will might be expected—or the opposite, as a theatrical gesture is made to divert attention from the disintegrating internal situation. But relations with the wider international community and neighbouring states do not look fraught until the mid 2010s.

Iran, like Libya, has a key cardinal T-square of powerfully determined Pluto, Jupiter and the Aries Sun, triggered by the influences in the years following

2012. There will be a strangely uncertain period between 2003 and 2006, with a disaster-prone three years when flare-ups are possible as Pluto squares Mars, always a brutally determined combination. Relations with the United States and United Kingdom, as well as neighbouring countries, will be highly volatile.

With Neptune approaching Mars in 2003, Saudi Arabia has not yet regained its former power or resources—indeed, it feels more undermined. Pluto crossing Uranus in the same period suggests a major internal shake-up, with a radical overhaul of direction and strategy, though it will not be a smooth transition. Pluto's long, slow haul through Capricorn from 2008 onwards, crossing the core planets in the Saudi chart and culminating in 2020 with the triple conjunction, will be the key point of revival, with a new leadership exerting authoritarian control over the new phase.

EASTERN EUROPE

The key Balkan chart for Bosnia-Herzegovina set for 1992 shows little sign of settling down. Indeed, revolutionary Uranus squaring Pluto, then crossing the aggressively independent Mars in Aquarius (which brooks no interference), will make the years up to 2003 an obstacle course of violence and brutality. In 2004 Neptune starts to undermine the seemingly unstoppable drive for revenge and annihilation. No initiatives seem to work well for a few years. It is an exceedingly unhappy, misery-ridden time until Neptune moves into Pisces in 2012. Reconstruction or destruction will start again from 2012 as Uranus and Pluto activate the excitable Aries Sun tied into an irrational Uranus–Neptune conjunction. The churning cauldron of Balkan history will boil again for a few years before subsiding for a longer stretch of peace in 2020.

As the European country geographically closest to the Balkans, Greece is in a state of considerable agitation until well after 2003, with a time of undermining morale as Neptune crosses the Sun during 2004 and 2005 and opposes Saturn, which is prone to excessive concern. By 2006, as the stressful influences lessen, Greece will begin to recoup, with the years thereafter being more straightforward.

Many of the Eastern bloc countries such as Czechoslovakia, Poland and Hungary share similar charts, since key moments of their symbolic or actual independence dates were around the same periods in 1918 or 1989. Like Russia, they are returning to their revolutionary beginnings as Uranus completes its 84-year cycle in 2001, so they will be struggling to find a balance between freedom and social order, democracy and economic strength. Attuned to an erratic history of repressive government in between periods of independence, they will see-saw and come close again to dictatorial rule at points. Pluto crossing Mars around 2004 and 2005 heralds intensely frustrating, angry times. The effect may be marginally delayed for Poland, with 2008 being the trigger point. But nothing will force them to backtrack, as the 2010s, with revolutionary Uranus and Pluto starting to activate the powerful Jupiter–Pluto conjunctions, will clearly show.

SOUTHERN AFRICA

South Africa, now set on the road of democracy, is revising its strategy in the post-Mandela era. The Jupiter–Saturn conjunction crossing its Gemini Sun could bring an expansive mood, and the hope that a new leader will inaugurate a golden age. But utter realism will be required if disappointment is to be avoided. Neptune aspecting the Sun in 2002 and 2003 suggests that compassion rather than escalating violence is needed, with a bleak Saturn–Pluto square in 2003 forcing a pause to rethink. Jolting changes in 2005 and 2006 with Uranus squaring the Sun could bring much-needed relief from high tension, with open debate. More power in the hands of the people is a necessity around this time, with old elements being rooted out. A relatively stress-free few years follow on, with 2016 being the next key trigger point for problems. Violence will flare until 2021, with the danger of a coup. There may also be trouble from across the border in Zimbabwe, where the situation looks highly unstable at times. Relations between the two countries look panicky and tense in 2001 and 2002, stretching tolerance to breaking point. Firm handling on both sides will be needed in 2006.

Uranus will cause a crisis of confidence in 2002 as it bounces in opposition to the flamboyant Leo Mars in the Zimbabwe chart. A theatrical display of machismo or bravado may result. But the tough three years begin in 2004 when Pluto starts to square Saturn and cross Neptune. Financially at a loss, without a long-term strategy or the will to take decisive action, the country could slide into famine or further into bankruptcy. The apathy or disintegration may run on, with only one major jolt in 2009, until 2020 when a revolution, *coup d'état* or overthrow of whichever government is in control is inevitable.

For Zambia, the millennium started on an upsurge of giddy hopes and wild enthusiasm, which will be hard to back up with solid results, but the good faith is there in triplicate. The turbulent 2010s will be less of a problem for Zambia than for Zimbabwe, though there is a tricky patch to negotiate in 2002 and 2003 as Uranus causes a rather disruptive swing, with moments of great elation, some violence and rapid financial adjustments. The years 2007 to 2010 are low in energy, with morale at a low ebb and health problems to the fore. From 2012 for a few years there will be a relatively docile time.

SOUTH AMERICA

Both Chile and Argentina—former Spanish colonies with liberation charts from 1810 and 1818—are affected by similar pressures as Pluto progresses through Sagittarius until 2008. The South American economic crisis hit Argentina earlier as Pluto started dismantling old securities from 1997 onwards, with panic not lifting until, by 2004, there is a general clearing out. The highly strung, fragile stability of the country will not stand the strain easily, fearing disintegration at points. The old controls will be removed, and there will be an urge to tear down anything that is a reminder of the past. But there is a real chance to emerge with tremendous creative potential for the future, though political and economic reforms will be violently opposed at every step of the way. The 2010s may be a quieter time, rather undermining at points, but not beset by the revolutions that are affecting the rest of the world.

Chile will take longer to construct a new base, with 2003 to 2006 being its moment of truth. Earthquakes similar to that of 1906 may recur as Pluto again triggers the deeply buried Neptune–Uranus conjunction. Financial repercussions are also unavoidable as the country faces an internal meltdown.

There may be mass revolts, even a *coup d'état*, as Chile's unstable democracy struggles to weather its first major storm since the late 1980s. Only by the time Neptune has cleared the Aquarian Sun in 2009 will the result be clear.

With a steadier Taurus chart, Brazil will still face the 21st century with unsure aims. Neptune will cause widespread worry as it aspects Saturn in 2002 and 2003, and then the Sun in 2004. At the same time disruptive Uranus is attempting to clear the ground for a new phase, though chaos may result as the old power structures no longer hold the reins of control. There could be outright violence between 2006 to 2009 as Pluto triggers the country's excitably aggressive Mars–Uranus opposition. Then Brazil should be set for a more solidly based peace.

Cuba, facing a long, slow haul as Pluto crosses its Sun–Saturn conjunction in Sagittarius, may be mourning the loss of a father figure in the next few years. The autocratic government of Fidel Castro, with high principles of helping the poor but always contradictory in its approach, is undergoing a major transformation until 2005. Heavy pressures as Pluto crosses Saturn in 2001 and 2002 will bring economic hardship and fears of failure with Neptune opposing Mars. Pluto's final aspect to Neptune in 2005 will bring widespread confusion and chaos, perhaps natural disasters to add to poverty. The years thereafter will roll along less eventfully.

NEW ZEALAND, AUSTRALIA, BURMA AND TIBET

Entering the new millennium on an expansive note, New Zealand is capitalizing on a lucky patch, and should go from strength to strength economically with only a temporary dip along the way. Relations with geographical neighbours China, Japan and Russia will prove stressful at points, especially around 2005 to 2007. After 2012 a jolting few years may upset New Zealand's agriculture and the property market as Pluto crosses the Capricorn Sun–Mars conjunction in the country's chart, with Uranus either posing health problems or encouraging public-service disputes. A major change in direction is likely as the country emerges into the 2020s with a tougher national mood and more resilience.

Australia may bump through economic upheavals into the 21st century more uncomfortably than New Zealand, but an amazing resurgence of confidence will emerge by 2006. Over-enthusiasm and inflationary plans will bite the dust as Pluto opposes Neptune at the same time (until 2007), with some danger of natural disasters, either nuclear, meteorological or in the form of earthquakes. But Australian bravado will ride high. After 2010 a tough few years may dent national esteeem, as Pluto crosses Saturn and forces changes against strong resistance. As 2020 approaches, the triple conjunction of Jupiter–Saturn–Pluto will sit on the midheaven, an indicator of firm direction, new hope bringing the old pioneering spirit back to the fore.

Burma's military dictatorship, rattled across the turn of the millennium by Uranus opposing the brutally tough Saturn–Pluto conjunction (until 2001), will see another and more major revolt in 2005 as Pluto opposing Uranus sweeps away a good deal that is uncooperative, and as Neptune, following behind in the same year, starts to undermine repressive control. By 2013, Pluto will force an economic turn-round, beginning with a period of severe shortage, with internal revolutions and high-profile deaths as the revolutionary Uranus–Pluto square aspects the country's Moon Neptune, a marker for the sacrifice of women.

Tibet's 50-year struggle against Chinese invaders will flare up in 2002 and 2003 with emotional protests and a determination to break away from control, though the major period where the battle for supremacy will be fought is in the years 2007 and 2008. A two-year tug-of-war will ensue, with an uncertain outcome, though China's weakness and paralysis of will through the years around then may be a boost to Tibet's hopes. Neptune will continue to erode China's tight grip on Tibet in the years to 2012. Through the turbulent years thereafter there may be United Nations or even NATO involvement in trying to find a humane resolution.

INDEX